THERESA MAY

First published in 2018
by Eyewear Publishing Ltd
Suite 333, 19-21 Crawford Street
London, W1H 1PJ
United Kingdom

Graphic design by Edwin Smet
Author photograph by Tim Jackson
Cover photograph by Getty Images
Printed in England by TJ International Ltd, Padstow, Cornwall

Publishers note in British contemporary usage it is more and more standard
to capitalise titles as little as possible – hence prime minister, home secretary,
president... unless these titles are directly used in the naming of a person, or
instead of the person – so, Prime Minister Cameron, or President Obama...
or the President or the PM... but not always – and many of the articles and
quotations here still follow the older rules. One is tempted to silently amend
them, except when this would falsify the actual published texts. Therefore,
the chaos that reigns gently in this text's use of capitalisation is no more than a
mirror of the slight unruliness of naming that still occurs in a British society torn
between deference to majesty, and lèse majesté.

Set in Bembo 12,5 / 17 pt
ISBN 978-1-911335-28-3

WWW.EYEWEARPUBLISHING.COM

CHRISTOPHER JACKSON

THERESA MAY

POWER, CHAOS AND CHANCE

A POLITICAL HISTORY
OF MODERN BRITAIN

 EYEWEAR PUBLISHING

To Jade, with all my love,
and to Beau who helped me type
the last word of this manuscript
three days before his second birthday

PROLOGUE

I have felt myself compelled by the unusual nature of recent events to consider the relationship between power and chance. What follows is not a straightforward biography of the woman who emerged from the hectic summer of 2016 as the prime minister of the United Kingdom. It is a measure of the sheer improbability of 2016 that when Theresa May assumed the premiership, there were no books about her whatsoever. Everyone was caught thrillingly off guard. The biography in the nature of, say, Charles Moore's magisterial volumes on Margaret Thatcher or Robert Caro's books on Lyndon Johnson, is currently stymied by the sheer busyness of the protagonist. As I write, May is making history – or on the receiving end of it – every day: she toils in a circus of memes and soundbites, tweeted at and railed against, mocked and analysed.

Instead, this is a study which could equally be applied to the French revolution or to the life of Alexander the Great. To live through recent times has been to find the powerful of the age – Cameron, May, Trump, Putin – seep into the domestic space to an unusual extent. The 2016 vote to Leave – whether one viewed it as an esoteric liberation, or an unlooked-for disaster – was the swerving in of politics. Many who weren't especially political beforehand found they had to be political now – and the politically conscious went about addled by the enormity of it all. The battle lines were drawn. The question of power, and who wields it, had become a more urgent question than previously: there had been a lurch – perhaps even an unravelling of the liberal settlement. One began to think about how power works, what would be possible for the new prime minister, and to what extent the world really can change according to an electorate's collective protest.

Our best route to understanding can be to survey the road we've come. We can take our pick of famous names: Alexander the Great, Caesar, Napoleon – those figures so much more apparently interesting than anyone in the upper echelons of today's Conservative Party – and be sure that each would have understood the summer of 2016 all too well. Perhaps it is not too much to say that the year had an epochal feel, and shared certain characteristics with 1917, 1789 or 49BC: there was the same chance of an opening and the seizing of it; the identical whiff of change and the question of how to exploit it; and the opportunity for those suitably placed to assert themselves against a turbulent reality. Throughout these pages, we shall be witness to an ancient force operative in the modern world. For all her weaknesses and her much elaborated-upon flaws, Theresa May is a reminder of the tremendous urge some plainly have towards the assertion of themselves.

There is comedy to be found here, of course. In Mervyn Peake's *Titus Groan* (1946), before the ill-fated baptism of Titus, Doctor Prunesquallor has the following exchange with the marginalised Lady Clarice and Lady Cora, sisters of the Countess Groan. Prunesquallor asks the pair what they want from life:

'It's power we want,' Lady Clarice repeated. 'We'd like to have that.'

'Yes, it's what we want,' echoed Cora, 'lots of power. Then we could make people do things,' said the voice.

'But Gertrude has all the power,' came the echo, 'which we ought to have but which we haven't got.' [1]

May became Gertrude with all the power which others didn't have. She could make people do things.

And yet in spite of that, there is the sense that a certain fragility and even powerlessness also pertains to this prime minister. May came to prominence at a time when the world, already raucous with the Internet, became louder still. We were suddenly conscious – even as we submitted to her rule – that power might be located not just in 10 Downing Street but elsewhere: in news stations, in banks and law firms, in Twitter and Facebook, and even (the referendum was a democratic exercise after all) in ourselves. That is why I have felt the need sometimes to depart from a too-linear description of her life, into the complexity of the country which greeted her. What follows is partly intended to convey to the reader the quiddity of May in the typical biographical fashion: we shall meet in Parts I and II a woman kindly but somewhat austere; a fashionista who has her Spartan side; a person quintessentially English in her loves but who spent the early part of 2016, however nominally, as a supporter of the Remain campaign in the referendum.

But there has been a sense throughout her premiership of someone caught up in, and responding to, the mood of the nation – and swept up also in the exhausting involutions of Brexit.

Multi-layered complexity is the fundamental fact in politics of our times – perhaps it is simply the ground note of the age. It is as if we have gone beyond postmodernism now into an entanglement which the mind cannot quite assimilate, and so we long to escape from it. It is the basis of this book that modern reality needs to be faced down, even if that process might sometimes seem to tire us. The intricate nature of post-Brexit reality is not something which I have felt able to spare myself – or the reader. The result is a book which escalates in complexity, and at times will seem almost to devour its subject. In Part III, we shall see May grapple with the office of home secretary; in Part IV we shall dive into the history of Europe and Conservative thought; in Part V, we shall encounter the issues that May was charged with handling as prime minister; in Part VI, I shall attempt some thoughts about the larger meaning of May's politics – and of politics itself.

It is my belief that this is the only way to render a subject like May: just as the Renaissance artists knew that the objects surrounding their subjects and the landscape beyond mattered as much as flesh-tint or figure, I have needed to show the roil and press of the society May so precariously governs, and the detail of the problems seething in her experienced brain. We do not know what the Mona Lisa was smiling about, but after completing this book the reader will know why Theresa May is occasionally shown to be frowning.

Yet in these pages, too, I hope there is joy: the sense of the thrill of the game of politics, and the possibility perhaps that if we can indeed move closer to unpicking the knots of modern life, then we might be able to build a viable future – even, as climate scientists tell us, so apparently late in the day. At times, this biography is a secret memoir, and one which I would never have had the drive to write had I not become a father. I have wanted to think about a politics different to what we've had these past years: one better capable of fronting the chaotic nature of things – and to attempt to imagine a civilisation better suited to the wife and son to which it is dedicated.

But given the urgency of the times on both the national and planetary scales, does a figure like Theresa May, apparently ill-suited to the enormity of the moment, even warrant our sympathy? There are those who think not: the strain in the prime minister-voter relationship, caused by the remoteness of government in an era of rising population, can sometimes make us queasy about the very fact of power, and alert to the failings of those who wield it. But it is possible to imagine another viewpoint. In John Updike's *Rabbit Angstrom* novels (1960-2000), the eponymous hero is always piously supportive of whoever happens to be president. It was an attitude shared by his creator: Updike himself could never join in the rage aimed at Lyndon Johnson over Vietnam – and later, George W. Bush over Iraq.

Leaders are presented as vulnerable souls saddled with impossible tasks. In Updike's play *Buchanan Dying* (1974), the protagonist says: 'To be President of the United States, sir, is to act as advocate for a blind, venomous, and ungrateful client; still, one must make the best of the case, for the purposes of Providence.'[2] One can imagine Theresa May on her bad days – and there have been plenty of those – agreeing with that.

Perhaps it's bad manners to the universe to wallow too much in pessimism. In another context, Updike wrote: 'Confusion is just a local view of things working out in general'[3]. At times, one has felt that May, though sometimes deservedly criticised, has at least made a virtue of patience and muddling through – of trusting to a certain buoyancy which life appears to contain. It has never felt in the May era as though we can fall back on the Carlyle view of history where heroes like Marlowe's 'mighty Tamburlaine' [4] bestride the stage. Instead, the May administration has seemed a reminder that by a hero we mean someone rare: Abraham Lincoln was preceded by James Buchanan, and succeeded by Andrew Johnson.

One might also add that in a curious way the May era – which we are about to see beginning now – was a time when one felt especially conscious of nature. This was not just because its fragility was so much in the discourse; it was because whenever human beings struggle with leadership something must rush in to enliven the gap. The reader shall discover that these processes – mysterious, and in their way wonderful – are what this book is about as much as its protagonist: the forces which hold the world together even as we seem intent on pulling it apart.

CJ, London, September 2018

PART ONE

THE THERESA MAY MOMENT

1 – THERESA MAY'S LEADERSHIP ANNOUNCEMENT

It was 30th June 2016. A week had elapsed since the surprise of the referendum result. In millions of homes the nation was coming to terms with the strangeness of it all. Politics – that business conducted remotely behind the high railings of Westminster, and in the close whispers of beige conference rooms – had done a rare thing: it had brought about a shift in one's sense of self.

Those who had voted to Leave, felt a sense of renewal about the national project – the wind of the majority at their backs. If one had voted to Remain, one was, quite suddenly, strangely cut-off from a former sense of belonging to country. This was now itself revealed to have been illusory, a spectral imagining of no use now in these new times. Between these two points, where euphoria and rage were the dominant emotions, there was the full range of ambivalence and indifference which always comprises the mind-life of a nation: those who could shrug and say it didn't matter; those who took comfort in their understanding that all would pass and the world return to its known equilibrium; those who had voted to Leave without quite expecting victory, and now had to raise an eyebrow at what they had done; and those who had elected to Remain but who in the wake of the result, proclaiming themselves democrats to the core, accepted that what's-done-is-done, while opting privately to disown any negative ramifications the decision might accrue in the future.

Among this last group was Theresa May, arguably the Cabinet minister in Cameron's government with the least pizzazz about her. But she was preparing to do something which very few people get to do: she was about to come before us with real plausibility as a would-be prime minister.

THE TENOR OF THE ANNOUNCEMENT

To most people she was as familiar as someone they'd met once or twice, but can't quite place. It is only in moments like this – in May's case, as she made her announcement in an unnamed room in Whitehall – that people begin to assess the temper of the person who may come to rule over them (and in May's case did). True, those who follow politics – or those with the state of the police force or immigration particularly on their minds – had already formed preliminary views of the then home secretary. But home secretaries are not prime ministers. They are viewed differently, as an agent of the prime minister. Power isn't fully concentrated in them; to the extent that they are not prime minister a perceptible whiff of failure, of powerlessness, pertains to them. That's why so much changes when the prime ministership is up for grabs and senior politicians jostle for position. In any case, all that the seasoned observer knew about May would now have to be reassessed in light of this new claim May was making, finally voiced aloud: the wish to be prime minister.

Millions of different relationships between May and individuals within the nation were at that moment forged. These would keep intact the great principle of variety: no two responses would be the same, although one can guess at broad camps. Many would hold off worrying about her until some later time; and some, sceptical about politics, or busy with their own woes and triumphs, were already aspiring to ignore her for the long term. But there was no escaping it. The country was already forming patterns around the fact that Theresa May wanted to lead the nation, that plenty of her colleagues had endorsed her to do so: reluctantly or otherwise, a consensus was emerging that May's was a valid proposition. A reciprocal relationship of a new kind had been sought; the nation's most powerful party had conspired in her seeking it; and the nation, incrementally and variably, and even in cases when there was a genuine attempt not to think about her, was already accommodating a leader-subject relationship. This is how power works: a bestowal from above, and then a seeping down and spreading. The success of the leader will be determined by what kind of information travels within that first power dissemination. Is the leader good or bad? Is she likeable or surprisingly irritating?

Does she wish to do good things? If so, what are her chances of actually doing them given what we know about her?

Over the next months, as the success of May's gambit took hold, the country would need to pause and consider certain matters. These might seem trivial but they would ultimately contribute to the minutiae of the nation's experience: whether to pronounce her name *Ther-ay-sa* or *The-reez-a*; whether to like her clothes, or form a positive opinion about her husband, her marriage, the quiddity of her manner. These sit alongside the democratic duty: whether to consider her 'trustworthy' or 'competent' should a pollster ask the question; and whether to vote for her should an election come around. At the moment of announcing her leadership, there was an interesting gulf between her relative unknownness at that time, and the celebrity she would soon acquire, although her essential reticence, and her general unsuccess, would always make her feel less 'famous' than some of her predecessors, Cameron and Blair. Despite this, a few months later, if someone in the United Kingdom were to be injured and an ambulance man or passing Samaritan wish to gauge their mental acuity they might ask: 'Who is the prime minister of this country?' The answer – tripping off the lips of the coherent – would be this woman who arrived so innocuously into the routine of the nation.

Theresa May couldn't have been more polite or circumspect about the bluntness of the intrusion. Facing down the hungry earnestness of the cameras, she said with gentle insistence:

> I have invited you here today to announce my candidacy to become the Leader of the Conservative Party – and Prime Minister of the United Kingdom.[5]

This was self-assertion couched in the language of invitation. The cordiality of it all masked the egoistic implications: *I am auditioning to be the most important person of the 65 million or so in this country.*

As May explained her reasons for taking this drastic step in her personal affairs, viewers made their assessments. Here was a woman ambitious, but also shy. Perhaps until now she had been happy to be sidelined: the onset of the May prime ministership was difficult to divorce from this sense of sudden reveal. She had an additionally familiar look to anyone who happens to inhabit a Conservative constituency. The modern Conservative MP is sanctioned by a world almost too bound up in cliché to be plausible. It is the world of fêtes and cricket-matches, of supermarket openings, and raffles attended by the medallioned local mayor. May stood in the metropolis on that day as an embodiment of a certain kind of England – an England earthier, less privilege-laden, than the one from which David Cameron had hailed. For some, the prime ministership of May might seem like the elevation of a local humdrumness, but this would be to underestimate her. It was the culmination of much work. She was on the threshold of leadership, because she had been ratified by her Maidenhead constituents who, over a period of nearly 20 years, had re-elected her services as an MP. With David Cameron – at this moment, rapidly morphing into her predecessor – one saw his ascendancy, perhaps a little unfairly, through an Etonian lens.

And it was Cameron who May mentioned straightaway in her usual business-like way:

I want to start by paying tribute to the Prime Minister.[6]

The Cameron years receded as May delivered her terse, clipped appraisal. We were immediately inhabiting a world less jocular.

It was possible to make another observation, which had nothing to do with luck. May was relaxed; one felt witness to a kind of relief. The future prime minister had this in common with one of her predecessors, Gordon Brown: she arrived before us with a demonstrable experience for the task. In Brown's case this did not turn out well; his ten years as chancellor made him look weary as prime minister. In the case of Theresa May, it might be that we end up lamenting her lack of heroism, and we may lament her policy directions: she was even then in her glory set to fail. But we shall never be able to say that she came to us unready. Qualified, too busy for a long announcement, and eminently feasible: like this, Theresa May come before us wanting to be prime minister.

The notion of her began accumulating in millions of minds. The fact of her power began to be established.

But the words she spoke were forgettable: it was a primarily visual experience.

2 – THERESA MAY'S 'IMAGE'

How did May look as she delivered those unmemorable remarks? Some in the press made mention of the tartan jacket she wore, and deemed it a reference to the ongoing importance in a potential May administration of the union with Scotland (Chapter 27). This is a familiar form of analysis which May – shortly to become the country's second female prime minister – has always endured: the sense that her clothes must mean something. But there were other observations to be made. When she speaks, May gives an impression of frailty: the delicate features can look as though they might fragment with nervous panic; the hunched shoulders make us wonder whether in person she might be slight; the voice is never quite in control as if its owner would dearly love to be elsewhere. Some have questioned whether her Type II Diabetes diagnosis will leave her with sufficient energy for the job. In truth, one never doubts this: she is too determined, too much able to take care of herself, for us to worry about her.

Even so, her gaze would not be quite so adamant, one suspects, if she hadn't had to combat certain adversities.

And it is this – the pure fact of her standing there, and commanding that audience – which is one of the properties of a politician.

THE PROJECTION OF POWER

The modern world is the apotheosis of image-consciousness.

We are overwhelmed by snappy renditions of the surfaces of things, the projection of selves and the outlines of an idea – life as a succession of visual claims. On Facebook, we command each day our own personal galleries; we whizz and dart across time and space, by turns furtive and eager to assert ourselves. The Internet is both cinema and gallery: any *Google* search promises you images of what you were interested in – the solving appearance of a thing is just a click away. In this climate, one's look becomes as important as one's substance: the manner of a thing can outweigh its true meaning. This can seem to create the need for deception, except that human beings have always been looking, which is to say we are practised at twigging when something isn't right. Our times exhibit a craving for authenticity – from Obama's obvious goodness, to Sanders' true rage, and Corbyn's apparent dignity. May doesn't fit this pattern: it is partly this which makes her an unsuccessful wielder of power. Some of this is endemic in contemporary visual language: for instance, in her leadership announcement, May stood before rows of impressive-looking books, implying a mastery of literature, a common trope of the knowledgeable leader. But leaders have always sought to project an ideal image. Every portrait or photograph is a small career opportunity – a chance to plant yourself in the minds of those you rule, as you might wish to be remembered. A poster is a rally in the making.

And there are sculptures which have produced submission in subjects. If we wish to understand the May moment it will be instructive to go back in history. Consider, for instance, Fig. 1. It is to be compared with this description by Suetonius of the great Emperor:

Fig 1. Augustus Caesar. Augustus may have looked like this, but not, I think, towards the end of his life. Nevertheless, this was the image of eternal youth and vigour that was promoted right up until his death.[7]

He had clear, bright eyes... His teeth were wide apart, small, and ill-kept; his hair was slightly curly and inclining to golden; his eyebrows met. His ears were of moderate size, and his nose projected a little at the top and then bent ever so slightly inward.[8]

The Suetonius description shows us the minutiae of a face of consequence: we can imagine those 'clear, bright eyes', and those 'ears of moderate size' listening to what we might be saying. The meeting eyebrows, and the unique trajectory of the nose cap off a portrait of idiosyncrasies. If we didn't have Suetonius' description of Augustus we might be more inclined to swallow the propaganda of his godlike heroism. By contrast May is drastically visible. She cannot follow the path of Alexander the Great who in a thousand coins and sculptures had promulgated the bland look of idealised power (Fig. 2).

Fig 2. Alexander the Great – another idealistic rendition of a human face.[9]

Does the television era sever the modern leader like May from this history of deception? Theresa May's predecessor David Cameron also revelled in image. Just after assuming the leadership of the Conservative Party, Cameron flew to Svalbard in Norway and was photographed there – admittedly to some derision – hugging a husky. It was an attempt to rebrand his party as eco-friendly: in spite of a patchy record on the environment, he was never convincingly pegged as a climate denier.

Meanwhile, in Figure 3, we see a relaxed prime minister, watching a Chelsea football match with an assortment of leaders and officials from the quaint pre-Trump era. Cameron's sleeves seem rolled up for the photographer's benefit.

Fig 3. Leaders at the G8 summit watch the overtime shootout of the Chelsea vs. Bayern Munich Champions League final in May 2012.[10]

The May announcement was of a piece with this. May is less remote than Augustus or Alexander were to their contemporaries: we see her not through the sculptor's imaginative eye:

she is given to us by the camera's severe scrutiny. To be able to look is an opportunity for knowledge if we look rightly. It can escort us to the junction where art criticism and political analysis fuse.

IF WE LOOK AT MAY, WHAT DO WE SEE?

At the time May announced her campaign for the leadership, the best-known image of her was on her Wikipedia page (Fig. 4). This was subsequently replaced by her official Downing Street photo.

May wears the same tartan attire that she wore for her announcement. It is, at first, an essentially inscrutable face, hoarding more than it gives. May is not quite the Ice Queen of Nick Clegg's description: it isn't possible to say it is entirely without kindness. One suspects she is a reluctant sitter, as if apologetic about the extent of her ambition. The knowledge that she is well-known enough to be photographed, sits alongside a certain self-deprecation. The smile is a concession – the kind that wants to get this over with, and return to work. The photo commemorates a brief hiatus from a busy schedule: one imagines it to have been one of the less enjoyable parts of a workaholic's day. The tension might also be attributable to the Home Office portfolio in government which May held for longer than any politician for some 50 years. Time away from her desk is time when crime statistics might be rising, or some awful new plot unfolding. It is a primarily workmanlike face, more conscious of duty than success.

Figure 5 is also instructive. It shows May before a featureless backdrop giving a talk – gesturing, weighing, explaining. May

Fig 4. Theresa May, 2015.[11]

came before us as some-
one whom we are used to
seeing apparently in pos-
session of a strong view-
point – someone who
can pose as the answer to
problems. Her plausibility
as prime minister derives
from the fact that she has
been doing this with most
people hardly noticing for
a long period of time. The
audition process for prime
minister is a remarkably
anonymous one. May comes before us as the embodiment of
certain experiences: of meetings held, decisions taken, desks
arrived at. To be prime minister, one must be in the position

Fig 5. May speaking at the Girl Summit.[12]

Fig 6. May opening a church fete in 2007.[13]

to be prime minister. May conducted that process with a re-straint at odds with rivals such as Boris Johnson or Michael Gove: when the crucial moment came, people were less tired of her, her flaws were not so known, and her plausibility could be swiftly established.

May left her ambition implied: she was less ambitious-seeming, although presumably no less ambitious.

There is another image of Theresa May we might wonder about, one more outdoorsy – the May of her Maidenhead constituency, as in Figure 6. This shows May out and about – not a creature of the office, but a street-canvasser. John F. Kennedy once said that every mother in America wants their son to become president; they just don't want them to become politicians first. This image reminds us that May has done the dull work, humbling herself repeatedly before the people of Maidenhead. The road to Downing Street is paved with supermarket openings and unexpected microphone feedback.

Finally, in Fig. 7 is another May we ought to know. This is how she looked around David Cameron. May tilts her head quizzically towards her boss. Her deference appears guarded, even insincere. I am interested in the unimpressed glance, and the awkwardly pivoting leg. It is an image of someone paying her dues. We see two prime ministers – one soon to ascend, one already there – and a natural tension arises: there are not enough jobs available to meet the ambitions that are always surfacing in the hearts of human beings.

The image is another measure of how remote our democracy has become from us. Do May and Cameron like each other? We do not know. We think we know that Cameron and Osborne like each other, because we have been told as much a thousand times. But really when we consider our politicians together we never know for sure what we are being let in on. We glimpse rumoured alliances – the suspicion of affinity, and the rumour of strain. We look, as if craning necks towards some remote plinth, as these people play out their appointed dramas, and in so doing,

Fig 7. Prime Minister David Cameron is met by May on his first visit to the Home Office.[14]

alter our own lives for private reasons we do not know. Often too, as we shall see in Part V, they do so in ways we don't have time to fathom, or are simply unable to comprehend.

This image of May alongside Cameron is also apt because it is only thanks to Cameron's fast-unravelled premiership that May attained the position she found herself in.

Like this Theresa May impressed her way into our lives: bursting out of our screens – sudden, familiar, and a member of a recognisable elite.

3 – AGAINST SOCIABILITY: MAY AND DAVID CAMERON

All politicians stand in relation to others. The course of events, the product of both logic and chance, will every now and then bequeath a new administration to the British people. We talk at such moments of 'the transfer of power' as if power were a constant. But power is not a constant: a similar opportunity is transferred – in this instance, the prime ministership, but each possessor of it has different abilities, and priorities, and in any case meets a distinct set of circumstances.

The interdependency of predecessors with successors, and incumbents with rivals can be seen also in our own time. For instance, John Major would make no sense in a vacuum. He could only have risen to be prime minister in precisely the circumstances that he did rise, as Margaret Thatcher's successor. And Major begat Blair who begat Brown who begat Cameron. Like this our prime ministers come to us, a procession of difference, where each new occupant expresses – or is meant to express – some new mood in the country, and therefore a novel range of possibilities and hopes. The new arrival, as May was in 2016, is an implicit rebuke to what has gone before. Obviously, this is not new. To return to US politics, Ronald Reagan's sunniness can still look like a necessary antidote to Jimmy Carter's earnestness. Donald Trump might represent weariness in some quarters with the highbrow Obama presidency. He embodies a certain lurking silliness in the American consciousness.

As a result of this, some process of self-definition needs to be carried out. Of course, it's possible to take that assertion too far. Gordon Brown went to significant lengths to show he wasn't Tony Blair. On his first meeting with President George W. Bush, he frowned sadly at the pranksterish president's decision to greet him on the airport runway in a buggy. In this instance, snubbing a major ally was seen as a too-elaborate way of emphasising that Brown was himself and not some other prime minister. To return then to May's leadership announcement, it appeared necessary to May, in her position as David Cameron's possible successor, to tout her seriousness. In fact, she went further, and even attempted to make a virtue of her unsociability – and even to some extent her own uninterestingness.

> I don't gossip about people over lunch. I don't go drinking in parliament's bars. I don't often wear my heart on my sleeve. I just get on with the job in front of me.[15]

May came before us as one of our least clubbable politicians. Her ascension threatened to inaugurate the heyday of some new teetotalism. Suddenly, as the May premiership hoved into view, we were less Cameron-like, and more May-esque. Further, these claims of sobriety and dogged competence also contrasted with the personalities of certain colourful contemporaries: Michael Gove, who, claiming never to want power, nevertheless sought and failed to seize it; and Boris Johnson, who chose not to seek it, having demonstrably structured his life up until that moment around the expectation that he would.

DAVID CAMERON, HIS FALL

'All political careers... end in failure,' wrote Enoch Powell. We are not in a position to say that David Cameron bucked this trend. At the time of her announcement, Theresa May stood in relation not so much to David Cameron, but to the failure of David Cameron. May continued in her 30th June announcement:

> It's easy to forget how far the Conservative Party and our country have come since David Cameron was first elected leader in 2005. Thanks to David we were elected into government for the first time in 18 years, we won a majority in the House of Commons for the first time in 23 years...[16]

Cameron's main accomplishment, in other words, was a modest amount (the 2015 majority was exceedingly slim) of electoral success. May went on to defend the Cameron record, particularly on the economy, but it was too soon to think of him in fond terms. Indeed, perhaps it shall never be possible to think of May's predecessor in terms of these accomplishments, editing out the question of Europe altogether. The Cameron part of the statement was little more than a moment's rote praise, which drew attention to the boiler plate nature of May's language.

Cameron had pleased no one while also failing to remain above the fray. May was compelled to praise a failure. Transitions are cathartic: after disaster, any novelty is a kind of hope. But there was also a conspiracy of silence at work here, deriving from the fractious state of the country. In Britain today, power is always swapped amid the utterance of platitudes. The very uninterestingness of May's speech might be taken as instructive. Politics has become the unsaid: the imagery and vocabulary of high politics bore little relation to the real emotion residing in the country.

David Cameron's CV speaks of facility and good luck: Eton, Oxford, Conservative Head Office, Carlton. He became opposition leader very shortly after entering parliament. Even when he became prime minister, he seemed to wear that mantle lightly, as an inherited right. Over time, power became a microscope on his flaws, as it always does. Cosmopolitan, international, he was never a natural creature of his party. This in turn led him to underestimate a radicalism which had made its way onto the back benches of his party, sometimes to reside around the Cabinet table. When it came to the referendum over the EU, he exhibited a tendency to gamble – not because he was inherently reckless, but because he found it psychologically convenient to put the matter to rest. Cameron is the sort of man who will always seek an easy life. If such a person goes into politics he will discover the borders of his gifts – but he is unlikely to be too much fazed by the discovery since it won't impinge on his ease. True, there is evidence of a darker side: affability could cede to arrogance. Indeed, on that strange morning of 24th June 2016, when the results for the EU referendum came in, he explained his decision to resign by asking his advisors rhetorically: 'Why should I do the hard shit?'[17] One can appreciate his difficulty in enacting a vote which had not turned out as he had wished, but it suggests a deficit in dutifulness. It is hard to imagine May uttering a sentence like that.

The differences between May and her predecessor do not end there. Cameron was known for his relative lack of interest in detail; May is noted for her passion for it. Put in the same position as Cameron on 24th June 2016, her pragmatic side would have taken up the challenge, as she did in similar circumstances after the snap election results came in. The May premiership existed within the shocking psychology of Cameron's fall; it was natural for her to present herself as the antidote to all things Cameron. It is therefore not surprising to find that May stands not just against sociability, but also against laziness, and even likeability, since these were properties associated, fairly or unfairly, with the Cameron administration. In her leadership announcement, May showed herself duty-bound by the niceties of political discourse to be respectful about her predecessor, but the statement is full of the tension of these unsaid things.

For the Remain voter, David Cameron created a tragic situation without being interesting enough to have a tragic flaw. The ooze of his personality appears unequal to the scale of the difficulties he unleashed. Outsized self-confidence after years of plausible muddling-through proved eventually unfounded. Power which had been worn lightly should after all have been worn more carefully, and its ramifications examined more closely. He left the country in a mess, but one whose origins weren't even necessary. For the Leave voter, he seems weak, and an irrelevant purveyor of a watered-down Toryism, which borders on Blairism. Cameron left the stage with the audience bamboozled: what was the play really about? If it had been about power, then it ended with powerlessness. If it had been

about competence, then it culminated incompetently. Cameron's political life unravelled without satisfactory dramatic
development – to an unsatisfactory character must be added
an unexceptional plot. His wins seem too small and inevitable to justify such long occupancy of 10 Downing Street. He
made a decision based on a referendum which nobody except
the smallest men were clamouring for. It is as if the hero in a
Greek play suddenly switched tack not after communion with
the gods but according to some chance overheard remark by
the chorus.

All this gave May the opportunity to write a more interesting play. Certainly there was at the time of her announcement
an appetite for a new page in English history. In fact, there
is some evidence that May realised the nature of that opportunity. Here, for instance, is the opening of a May profile in
the *Spectator* by Harry Cole entitled 'The Big Beast in Kitten
Heels':

> 'She doesn't rate Cameron any more. She did, but not any more,' con-
> fides a friend of the Home Secretary. 'There was a time early on when
> she would want to please David, but slowly she has seen just how
> incompetent that operation is. How the PM will say he will do one
> thing, only to be drawn in another direction. She's given up on him.'[18]

Perhaps this is too dramatic: they worked together and would
no doubt have continued to do so had the referendum not been
lost and had Cameron not resigned. But the country turned to
a woman greatly unlike its former leader. May is neither jocular nor cavalier – she believes in roots, hard work, self-sacrifice.

And yet there would come a time when May would be in David Cameron's position. It is even possible that she shall play the outgoing prime minister role opposite Michael Gove or Boris Johnson. These two were also inextricably linked to the moment of her rise, and May contrasted herself effectively with them at the necessary moment.

4 - AGAINST CLEVERNESS:
THERESA MAY AND MICHAEL GOVE

Fig 8. Michael Gove in his natural habitat at the think-tank Policy Exchange.[19]

The room in which May made her leadership announcement also deserves mention. The announcement took place in a foreign policy think-tank on Whitehall – the Royal United Services Institute. A week later on *Sky News,* Kenneth Clarke, the former Chancellor of the Exchequer, would be caught on camera saying that May knows little about international affairs. But one doubts her choice of venue represented an attempt to give the impression of having educated herself on a weak policy area: more likely, it was simply a short walk away from the Home Office. One imagines May did not wish to stray too far from her desk – even for an announcement of this importance. But a few hours after May's speech, Boris Johnson, the presumed favourite for the leadership, would announce that he would not stand for the position in a hotel near St James's Park. History will note that Johnson went on to be a particularly difficult foreign secretary to May, but perhaps it will be difficult for people years from now to know how inevitable his prime ministership seemed until the day of May's announcement. It's true that there was something undeniably genteel about his stumble that day and May's concomitant rise, lent it by the aesthetics of London's most expensive rooms. In the Conservative Party, you win or lose with maximum politeness. Emotions must never be seen to run too high. One can almost forget that all the manoeuvres are not meant to be an end in themselves, and that the resulting victor will be able to dictate whether missiles fall in Syria, or whether children growing up today shall continue to enjoy a free health service.

And how shall the figure of Michael Gove be remembered? He shall never be considered an uninteresting minister, but he shall probably never do something so memorable as what he did that day – had in fact done a moment before May began speaking. This came when he withdrew his support for Boris Johnson and instead announced that he would be seeking the prime ministership himself. This was the unexpected culmination of years of self-deprecating remarks on this score which now needed to be pored over again in order to revisit their insincerity.

The principal result was that it created a sense during May's announcement that everything was falling into place for her. As May began her speech, there was a perceptible frisson of excitement in the air which one hadn't usually associated with her. Her announcement was more exciting than it would otherwise have been; it partook of the drama of the day. What would later come to seem lack of inspiration looked like calmness at a time when the need for a steady hand was paramount.

It was another useful distinction for her to make.

UPON GOVE

Michael Gove is one of those men we sometimes find in politics who gives the appearance of knowing about everything, except human nature. His brilliance is widely attested, but even those who admire his facility admit to finding it tiring. People as clever as Gove always have a high opinion of cleverness – not necessarily because they are pleased to be clever, but because cleverness is exhausting to sustain, and what they are really admiring is their own energy. Until that momentous summer of 2016, Gove had been able to temper these talents with sporadic shows of humility, difficult to distinguish from a kind of keening. For instance, the justice secretary, former education secretary and (under May) future environment secretary often repeated the claim that he didn't have what it took to be prime minister: his humility appears to have consisted of a loud proclamation of his own faults, intended to attract incredulous rebuke, or else to pre-empt criticisms from the mouths of others. These vivid displays of humility may be preferable to the inability to understand its need at all, but they are still a function of pride. His was a coquettish ambition which reveals itself to the owner of it at the last moment, when it has long been transparent to others. Gove's career was a drawing-room flirtation with the highest office. Alongside

Gove, Theresa May appears to have exhibited nothing more complicated than greater self-knowledge about the fact of her ambition. She played a steadier hand, not perhaps because she was inherently better at playing politics, but because she had bothered to look at her cards.

Gove's career is strewn with voluble precocity. The ability to talk marked him out, but his career raises questions about what politics ultimately is. Gove spent time during the referendum down at the Chancellor George Osborne's house in Dorneywood, playing chess with his old friend. The gesture was a gallant one, intended to show that everyone would come together after the vote in post-match friendship. But it may also be taken as evidence of his lack of human understanding. Gove seems a man continually afflicted with bogus certainty. His career often shows him confidently legislating at people as if they were pawns, and then coming up against the fact that they are people. The principle revelation about his time at the Department of Education was that teachers might also have ideas about how to teach. His time as justice secretary was far more successful, and shows, in his scrapping of Chris Grayling's justice-prohibiting court fee, and in his restoring books to prisoners, that Gove was capable of great good when the right kind of zeal was upon him. But zeal was always upon him, which meant he could sometimes rush very quickly in a surprising direction. Such people are unable to do things in moderation – the brain is always whirring at the self-same pace. Theresa May has been accused of coldness by some – but as we shall find in Part III, she knows that each problem that comes across her desk is primarily a human problem, and also that solving it might not always be a race.

Everyone testifies to Gove's initial charm. But in the long run morality is not his first concern – intellectual valour is more important. We know from Nick Clegg's *Politics: Between the Extremes* how quickly Gove's initial charm can cede to bitchiness when circumstances become heated. Gove comes at problems armed not with questions but with answers. His is the essentially stagnant precocity that makes up its mind on all questions some time in teenagerhood, and may never be inclined to revisit anything. It was characteristic that within 24 hours of deciding to run as leader, he was ready to stand before the electorate with a 5,000-word speech explaining why. In this, he resembles Ted Cruz in America: the zealot who will make the situation fit around his zeal and not the other way around.

Another aspect of Gove contrasts with May. The possessor of his kind of intelligence will often experience calamitous breakdowns in friendship. In firing Gove, May would state that colleagues were worried about loyalty (it is one of the more appealing things about Gove that he learned his lesson on this occasion, and duly returned to the front benches). By contrast, although May has few friends in politics, they are all close ones: her former joint chiefs of staff Nick Timothy and Fiona Hill spring to mind, as does her former first minister Damian Green. Even so, at the crucial moment, May benefitted from the comparison with Gove. May is among the least verbose of politicians. Abrupt, even taciturn, her energies are not devoted to explaining her actions, but to actions themselves. Gove could do a thing in five minutes and then take fifty to tell you why he'd done it, whereas Nick Clegg told David Laws that May has 'no small talk whatsoever – none'.[20]

There could hardly be a greater contrast between May's lack of interest in self-justification, and Gove's epic volubility, with his 'emotional need to gossip,'[21] as Boris Johnson's chief advisor put it. This would not be a clever-clogs administration. It aspired to greater seriousness than mere brilliance.

A SPAT OVER SCHOOLS

Given these contrasts, it isn't surprising to learn that May and Gove had clashed in the past.

The story is worth telling primarily because it tells us something of May. It came during what became known as the Trojan Horse Affair. It is our first window into May's *modus operandi*.

The affair began in 7th March 2014 when media outlets picked up a leaked letter in which certain Islamists boasted about the existence of Operation Trojan Horse. The boast claimed that radical Islamists had successfully managed to push an Islamic agenda into Birmingham and Bradford schools, among other places. The apparent plan was to jettison Christian prayer, sex education and mixed education. It was an attempt to take advantage of the fact that the relatively new academies (introduced by Blair and continued by Cameron) are able to pursue independent curricula.

The news, if it could be proven to be true, struck at the heart of then Education Secretary Gove's idea of free schools – schools run by interested parties at the community level free from local authority interference. But it also called into question the extent to which the then home secretary Theresa May was tackling radicalism. A back-and-forth ensued. Inevitably, everything escalated into complexity. Sir Michael Wilshaw, the Chief Inspector of Schools and head of Ofsted, leapt into action, and began investigating various schools. By 9th June 2014, he was in a position to state that there was an 'organised campaign to target certain schools', and added that some governors had attempted to 'impose and promote a narrow faith-based ideology' in secular schools.[22] The 'row' had soon reached the Cabinet table. It is difficult to be sure precisely how things went, but by 4th June 2014 May, feeling embattled, had let it be known that the matter was not her fault in a published letter:

> The allegations relating to schools in Birmingham raise serious questions about the quality of school governance and oversight arrangements... Is it true that Birmingham City Council was warned about these allegations in 2008? Is it true that the Department for Education was warned in 2010? If so, why did nobody act?[23]

If this plaintive and emotional letter was designed to bait Gove, then it succeeded. Soon 'people close to' Gove were briefing against the Home Office and accused with maximum cliché the then Head of Security and Counter-Terrorism Charles Farr of failing to 'drain the swamp' of extremism in Britain. May retaliated by publishing correspondence intended to show Gove's recalcitrance on the issue.

Cameron was forced to intervene. This led to the firing of May's special adviser, Fiona Cunningham (later Fiona Hill), and Gove was forced into making an apology.[24] It is difficult at this distance to discover the ins and outs of it all, although Fiona Hill's later firing after the snap election, and all the whispers about her harsh style of dealing with people, would make one suspect her involvement, even if we didn't also know that Hill was in a relationship with Farr. Perhaps the thing became personal more quickly than it should have, and May failed to control the ratcheting up of unusual emotion.

It is noteworthy that of the two ministerial protagonists in the Trojan Horse Affair, May and Gove, it was May who kept quiet and avoided having to abase herself with public apology. And it was also May who kept her job (Gove would shortly afterwards be moved to the Chief Whip's Office, a notable demotion). And May got her own way in another respect: as we have seen, she would later reinstate Hill, although only to have to let her go a second time. Where Gove rants, May machinates. Where he falls on his sword, May takes a step back and keeps reasonably calm. One doesn't observe this in order to absolve May entirely – no one comes out of this affair well – only to point out the difference. Gove once stated that what was needed was not a cool head, but 'a heart burning with a desire for change'. The Trojan Horse Affair illustrates that the proverbial burning heart can become a comet that dramatically flames out. David Laws has quoted Nick Clegg as saying that Gove is a 'bit of a Maoist'. Most of us if we had to choose between instability and stability at the very top would choose the latter.

If May had a lucky predecessor in Cameron, she also had a fortunate rival in Gove. And her good fortune didn't end there.

5 - AGAINST CLOWNING: MAY AND BORIS JOHNSON

Fig 9. Alexander Boris de Pfeffel Johnson, former guest host of
Have I Got News For You (and Foreign Secretary).[25]

If 2016 was an unpredictable year, then Boris Johnson is an emblem of that unpredictability. For most of 2016, Johnson did a plausible impression of a prime minister-in-waiting. For a brief period after he declined to run against Theresa May, he reverted to a former identity – a well-paid journalist and biographer of William Shakespeare who happened also to have a safe seat in the House of Commons. Then a few weeks later, he executed the quickest of resurrections to become foreign secretary, as we shall see in Chapter 24.

For now, it is enough to note that Johnson was another figure who May successfully outmanoeuvred.

The presence of Boris Johnson on the national scene throughout 2016 served to remind that May is something Boris is not: serious.

BORIS JOHNSON, THE COMEDIAN IN POLITICS

The prospect of Johnson as prime minister was always an ambivalent one. On the one hand Johnson possesses a vocabulary, a sense of humour and a breadth of reference that has been lacking at the top of our national politics for a generation. Dennis Healey was more cultured, Harold Macmillan better read, and the Johnson wit is nothing when compared to his hero Winston Churchill's. But he was, for a while – particularly as London mayor – an undeniable breath of fresh air in British politics. Johnson deserves credit for eschewing soundbite in an age which is largely enslaved by it. He is an essentially romantic figure in an unromantic age. It is still not impossible to think that in an age where Donald Trump can be president, Johnson can yet detoxify himself sufficiently to become prime minister.

But there is a lot to say in the opposite direction. Johnson was an attractive prospect when he was harmless. Perhaps he had, in fact, never been as harmless as he seemed. He had played a significant role in shifting the national debate on Europe in the 1980s, with a spate of comedic columns in the *Daily Telegraph*, lampooning the EU with a note of vacuous jingoism which his hero, too much concerned with international relations, would never have stooped to: where Churchill would mock de Gaulle, Johnson mocks the French. In these, he didn't always show the responsibility a writer should. This, for instance, is from an article about a trip made by Tony Blair to the Congo, and was always indefensible:

> What a relief it must be for Blair to get out of England. It is said that the Queen has come to love the Commonwealth, partly because it supplies her with regular cheering crowds of flag-waving piccaninnies.[26]

In the piece, he also referred to the 'watermelon smiles' of Africans. But Johnson's trajectory was permitted by the British electorate so long as it could be written off as a joke: surely, he would never occupy a position of real consequence.

All that changed during the European referendum. We began to see the strategy behind the jokes and the mussed-up hair. The clown had jested his way into a position of power. The suspicion crystallised: Johnson really was intent on bringing the comic mode of being into politics, where it hasn't traditionally belonged. The career of Boris Johnson ultimately meets this objection: if one is primarily funny, one should urgently seek out work as a comedian.

Johnson would never take this path. His dishevelled appearance belied an appetite for power that had first been in evidence to a classroom of young Etonians when Johnson had been asked by a teacher what he would like to be when he grew up, and he had replied that he wished to be king of the world. But if the ambition to be prime minister is to be presented as an argument against him, then history as we know it would need to be cancelled. Even so, on the EU, Johnson had got himself into a muddle. His bedfellows in the referendum may have surprised even him: he had found himself among the wrong people – or perhaps he had accidentally exposed the sort of people he rightly belonged with. Ambition is often Gordian. Until that moment, he had seemed more comfortable in the international world of opportunity and money: he was a neoliberal with a Tory sense of humour about 'abroad'. But even his jokes about other cultures were a pose coming from someone who had grown up in America and who speaks French. On the eve of the referendum he had written two speeches – one pro-Remain and one pro-Leave. This was portrayed in some sections of the press as an essentially Machiavellian act in and of itself. A likelier explanation, and perhaps as serious a criticism, is that it shows a man who hasn't really thought through the meaning of a war which he has suddenly committed to generalling on one side or the other.

Once Gove had parted ways from Johnson, it was clear that it had been all for nothing. As May rose to speak, the world was becoming more serious: a certain Johnsonness was seeping out of the picture, and Johnson's own announcement speech had to submit to a hasty rewrite. In this, delivered hours after May's, Johnson quoted Brutus' speech from *Julius Caesar*:

> This is not a time to quail, it is not a crisis, nor should we see it as an excuse for wobbling or self-doubt. But as a moment for hope and ambition for Britain. *A time not to fight against the tide of history but to take that tide at the flood and sail on to fortune.*[27]

Johnson had read his Shakespeare, but in Shakespeare the clown cannot be king. If Theresa May has read the classics, then she has done so quietly without fanfare. May reminds us that politics ought to be a pursuit with a purpose.

A quip about Thucydides is no atonement for not having read your brief. But if Johnson has taught us that it is possible for devastating ambition to lurk within the apparently harmless parameters of a jest, then it must also be said that we shall come to hanker for humour in time. May is among the least quotable politicians of her generation; and her generation is the least quotable of all generations. In June 2016, the nation didn't coalesce around the Johnsonian wit. Pithy asides would be of little use when it came to negotiations with the European Union.

This then was another aspect of the May luck: the people opposing her were the sort of people she could beat, at that precise moment. And the competition still feels narrow. Theresa May can sometimes seem like an emblem of the fact that the best people no longer go into politics.

6 – THE POTENTIAL OF THE ADMINISTRATION

UnCameronlike, unGovelike, and unJohnsonlike: yes, all these. But the May administration at its outset was also an implicit rebuke to George Osborne and all his works.

As we proceed through this book, we shall find May clashing with Osborne: sometimes, their clash can seem to stand for the greater rift that became apparent in the country in midsummer 2016. The acrimony that existed between them can seem an embodiment of two irreconcilable aspects of the Cameron administration, which have not yet been squared by her own administration. Under David Cameron, May was charged with keeping net migration figures down. Osborne's job as chancellor was to bring in business to the country, which inclined him to champion free movement of workers, and to pursue goals commensurate with the neoliberal settlement of international trade. These arguments would be bequeathed to their successors, Amber Rudd and Philip Hammond, although with both having been Remainers there was perhaps greater synergy between them than there had been between May, temperamentally a Leaver, and Osborne, the arch-Remainer. Between May and Osborne one suspects a clash of personalities – and if Osborne's subsequent editorship of the *Evening Standard* with its fiercely anti-May headlines is anything to go by, antipathy on the ex-chancellor's side. May was hardly sentimental in turn. She fired Osborne when she did assume the leadership.

But there was serious policy disagreement between the pair too. This can also be seen in her attitude to Chinese and other potentially 'bad' investment into the UK economy, as we shall see in Part V.

FOR BETTER OR WORSE, A GOVERNMENT

May had expected her announcement to be the first in a months-long campaign. Instead, it was a sort of accidental victory speech.

And as soon as the announcement had finished, the May government had acquired its key and tempo: it would be formed around her personality. One notes how few opportunities prime ministers have to set a mood for their administrations. For May, her next opportunity would be on the steps of 10 Downing Street after having seen the Queen. But by then she would be telling us what we already knew: this government would be deliberate, decisive, and unshowy.

Administrations are bulwarks against chance. It is one's government – competent or shambolic, dull or inspirational – which the prime minister has as a chief weapon against the multiple unlooked-for contingencies of politics: all would depend on her and her team. But of course, governments are never wholly effective – they cannot entirely master events: chance keeps seeping in. At its core, May's administration had a sobriety which was promising, particularly given the chaotic times out of which it had arisen, but it would need every last piece of competence it could muster to deliver on the enormous task of leaving the European Union. One could be reasonably sure that it would not be cavalier with decision-making or liable to gamble, as Cameron had been – but to an unusual degree there was no room even for the well-meant bad decision. In the same spirit, it would eschew cronyism, and anything that might smack of breezy self-confidence, but the government had to be watertight in order to keep together a party riven down the middle with its perennial split over the European question.

It was to be forensic and careful, and dominated by what May calls 'my method'. Here is Jason Cowley explaining it in the *New Statesman*:

> She weighs and balances the evidence and consults with her closest advisers before acting. She considers it wise to make haste slowly and, I was told, allows the 'logic of the situation' to dictate her actions. She chooses the outcome she wants and works backwards from there.[28]

This pre-snap election description verges on the hagiographical, and almost suggests that we are lucky to be listening in on a master at work. But it is how she evidently sees herself. May does not spout Goveian rhetoric. The May era was to be a time of straightforward accomplishment, and quiet progress.

Administrations, then, are rather like Jane Austen characters: we get a sense of them before we get any detailed description. May is, of course, not to be understood primarily in terms of associations. It is to show how a public figure morphs slowly into a household name – into a leader. Leader and public enter into a symbiotic relationship, whereby the leader responds to what she thinks the electorate wants, and the electorate accommodates that response: it is a kind of dance, out of which shall emerge the next condition of the nation.

But its success shall be entirely down to what power structures are in place: how efficiently the government is run; whether loyalty is engendered for the new leader around the Cabinet table, in the party and in the country; and how efficiently an optimum standard of governance can be reached before events begin to come at that government. The apparatus of power must be built swiftly and surely: the character of the leader must be maximised into the leadership role in the creation of authority and direction. The beneficiary of chance, May now needed to begin to fend chaos off – after a fashion, to wrest control from the forces that had landed her with power.

She stood before us then with latent possibilities, and intent on that particular administration. Gradually, over time, the possibility of the administration ceded to the administration itself. Her Conservative MPs selected her ahead of the hardcore Brexit candidate Andrea Leadsom (whom we shall meet again in Chapter 22). The number of MPs who backed her was too much for Leadsom to feel able to fight the election among the 300,000 or so Conservative Party members in the wider ballot. This was a leadership election won among colleagues.

After a brief period of defiance, a botched interview and other questionable claims about her CV, Leadsom withdrew. At which point, upon the obliging resignation of Cameron, Theresa May became prime minister. Interest in May reached a critical point. The arrival of a new prime minister sends us eventually from Twitter to Wikipedia. Only once May had cleared these predominantly party-based hurdles, did we feel able to head back into the dark backward abysm of time and try and find out more about her.

At that point the nation had permission to wonder with some earnestness: Who is Theresa May?

PART TWO

MAY'S PRE-HISTORY

7 - A BRIEF DISCOURSE ON OBFUSCATION

Before we look at her past, let us note, but attempt not to get bogged down in, a certain duality: May is vastly known, and vastly unknown. This difficulty is inviolable, and intentionally so.

May has now achieved a fame only prime ministers and a handful of major achievers in science and the arts attain – the kind that shall reliably echo. Her place in history is also guaranteed by her six years as home secretary, one of the four great offices of state, a period which she handled with her usual dogged determination, and without frills.

Surveying the record, it is a relief to note that our democracy at least functions to this extent: it is impossible to get where May has got without leaving numerous traces on the public record. Parliament has scrutinised what she has been up to, and she has had to oblige. Journalists have asked her for interviews and she hasn't been able to say no to every last one of them. The biographer is able to sift voluminous amounts of information: her voting record, her speeches, one-on-ones, appearances before committees, forewords to white papers, statements in response to the publication of white papers, town hall Q&As about the statement in response to the white paper, and so forth. We can see how each bill she proposed morphed during the parliamentary process to become what it became, and then, finally, how successful any given bill was at addressing what it was intending to fix. It is the ledger of a skilled, but essentially workmanlike parliamentarian. It also amounts to an impressive record of hard work.

But it can also seem as if the life of Theresa May is a vast and perhaps upsettingly successful attempt to fend off future biographers. The enigma of May stems in part from the mechanisms of modern power: May's voting record, for instance, is part testament to her loyalty to the Cameron government, and before that, the future prime minister showed herself loyal to a succession of unsuccessful leaders of the opposition in the shape of William Hague, Iain Duncan Smith and Michael Howard, all of whom espoused agendas different to Cameron. She has been rewarded for her loyalty to these also-rans with promotion. While in theory we have a record of all that May has thought, stretching back to her entry into parliament in 1997 on every major issue of the day from health to education, to ID cards and Iraq, it isn't in fact clear that this is what we do have. One is never quite sure how often she bit her tongue at the behest of the whips' entreaties, or how often she cast half-hearted votes.

How proud was she to stand in the 'aye' lobby on the day of the Iraq vote? How often had she been secretly ashamed to vote for the latest George Osborne budget? To be sure, the rebellious instinct occasionally came through. One such flash of contrarianism was her brief opposition to the Blair administration's 2004 increase of university tuition fees from £1125 per year to up to £3000 per year. But if this was the real May, it was a rare glimpse and she may not have particularly enjoyed breaking cover: under Cameron she would vote in favour of a much larger increase to fees. Has Theresa May known her mind, but deliberately kept it from us? Or is she lighter than that, unburdened, opportunistic?

And how intentional is all this slenderness of information? Again, we are confronted by our essential exclusion from the process which governs us. We do not know, because we cannot know, this person.

AN APPEARANCE ON THE ANDREW MARR SHOW

With May, a thinnish loyalty is compounded by extreme carefulness of utterance. May speaks the language of modern power, which is to say she is very expert at appearing to speak while saying little. It is not that she is a bad communicator, it is that she deliberately obfuscates. This capacity to emit words which might be taken as authoritative, but which in fact convey no real information is a crucial skill in the modern politician. Here, for instance, is May interviewed on *The Andrew Marr Show* in September 2016, her premiership in full swing, three months after the announcement with which we began.

> Marr: Prime Minister, your first statement to the country outside Downing Street [see Chapter 23], you talked a lot about your – burning injustices in the country, you mentioned women being badly paid, black people not being treated properly by the justice system, and so on and so on. Are you going to be the kind of Prime Minister who uses the power of the state to correct these injustices?
>
> May: Well, I want to see a country that works for everyone, Andrew, and that's what's going to be the driving force of my government. And

that's looking at a society that works for everyone, an economy that works for everyone.[29]

In time speech patterns like this would cause her to be dubbed the Maybot. One can see why: in this instance, the answer given bears almost no relation to the question. Although some have tried to make a virtue of this, speech like this cannot be other than anti-democratic: it is a door closed, and blinds drawn. Here, Marr pressed the point, but May continued to obfuscate. In this interview alone, all the folly of her 2017 snap election campaign can be discovered in miniature: it is as vivid an indicator as any to how drastically she had failed to make good on the potential described in Part I. Leaders are always given the benefit of the doubt; so was May. But here one sees her speaking a language unlikely to turn that potential into anything of account. It is language which vacates the space where powerful utterance should be.

Can one make allowances? The dramatic dip in political discourse is an offshoot of fear – fear of upsetting one's own party, fear of making a 'gaffe', and above it all, fear of not being re-elected. But it is a fear which, if given way to, only makes the feared loss of popularity more likely to come about. The Marr interview (and indeed any interview May has given) might be compared with this excerpt from a 1915 interview with Winston Churchill conducted with *The New York Herald* at the height of World War One:

'For the first time in her history, Great Britain can say, 'The seas are free.' In the days when France was at war with us, no single victory, however important, brought us a security comparable with that which we enjoy today. Even after Trafalgar we knew nothing like it... The action of a navy is necessarily slow,' Mr Churchill continued. 'The pressure which it exercises upon an adversary is unintermittent. It may be compared to the inexorable grip of winter, which nothing can for long resist.'[30]

To read this is to mourn what we have lost: politicians sufficiently confident to think aloud, to roam in language, and try opinion on for size as a function of freedom. This language is essentially egalitarian because it is informative: metaphors are democratic. Churchill's use of language makes one feel one knows him: we near him as he speaks. With Theresa May, every word puts distance between her and us. To these difficulties must be added the deliberately slender biography. With Winston Churchill, or even with a contemporary politician like Barack Obama, we know their stories because they have told them to us. May has told us so few stories about herself, and the ones she has told – one thinks of her naughtily running through that field of wheat – link to no overarching narrative. This is frustrating since who she is will have a bearing on the kind of prime minister she will become – and therefore on the direction of the nation.

But since she has refused to tell us her story, we must recreate it. Perhaps this lack of information has caused some to overstate the strait-lacedness of May. All human beings are founded in quirk. May cannot hope to avoid the telling eccentricity: she has her quiddity.

8 - THERESA MAY'S EARLY LIFE

Theresa Mary May – her married name sounds like the beginning of a nursery rhyme – was born Theresa Brasier in 1956.

May belongs to the generation who remembers the rundownness of the British economy in the 1970s. The chief political fact of the lives of everyone born around May's time would be the premiership of Margaret Thatcher. As a conservative born at that time, May received certain assumptions, which her career generally espouses: that it is levelling and efficient to privatise state-owned assets; a distaste for unions due to a natural distaste for disruption in general and Scargillism in particular; that Britain can still 'punch above its weight' on the international stage, especially if it stays close to America; that the European Union is lucky to have us; and that the 'crown jewel' of the UK economy is its financial services sector. This is not to say that all these assumptions are necessarily false, or indeed that Theresa May must be assumed to subscribe to all of them, but these things, together with a Gladstonian Christianity based around 'hard work' and a love of monarchy, would comprise the intellectual climate of her adult political life. It might explain for instance why her contempt for Labour leader Jeremy Corbyn is laced with schoolmarmish exasperation. Conservatives like May have been disagreeing with socialists like Corbyn for nearly half a century. They not only disagree with him, but are tired of the argument.

May is bound up in that historical moment; sometimes one

senses her bumping up against the limits it bequeathed, but the Thatcher premiership did give to May's generation a sense of belonging, synonymous with being in the right. May's generation was relieved to discover that the country had a post-war role other than terminal economic decline. Alan Hollinghurst's *The Line of Beauty* is a portrait of a society which, while unjust towards homosexuals and shallow in its money-worship, is nevertheless reinfused with an undeniable vitality. May and her contemporaries have not only seen this dark carnival come to pass, but they have also seen Thatcherism ratified by subsequent governments, even – to a large extent – by Labour ones. The condition of the Thatcherite is to have been right twice: the Thatcher view was endorsed three times by the electorate, and then subsequently vindicated by Tony Blair's New Labour Party.

Over time, some socio-cultural Thatcherite assumptions such as the party's position on same-sex marriage have been challenged, and the nimbler among May's generation – May among them – came to appropriate the Blairite language of inclusiveness without altering their underlying economic notions. But at the same time, some within the Conservative Party began to think differently, and hanker after a restoration of the nation state – a life perhaps just as mercantile, but with a certain quasi-mystical Britishness at its core.

What is most noticeable about May's early life is how much it answers to this other idea of England, distinct from associations of international free trade and a Cameronian cosmopolitan approach. She would, in theory, at least be well-placed to understand the wish to give voice to this new England.

A RELIGIOUS CHILDHOOD

There is a redolence of the past about May, which is difficult to distinguish from a religious upbringing. It is the essential timelessness of an austerely spiritual outlook on life. Puritanism crops up throughout history whenever people have sought modes of life not wholly defined by the acquisition of money. Prayer cannot expect to alter at the pace of commerce.

If the awakening of some deeper community bonds is indeed to be her mission, then May had an apt upbringing. Her father, Hubert Brasier, was an Anglican clergyman, well-known and well-liked in the seaside town of Eastbourne (Fig. 11) where she was raised. The town's most famous political association would not appeal to May: Karl Marx and Friedrich Engels spent much time here, and Engels arranged to have his ashes scattered off the pier after his death. All top-level UK politicians eventually become Londoners, but perhaps it is

Fig 10. Eastbourne, where Theresa May spent her first years.[31]

worth remembering that May, who can seem so much a creature of Whitehall, is also a girl of the seaside. Perhaps there is also apt imagery here: May, the future prime minister of a Britain outside the European Union, began her life beside the channel, that symbol of division between us and the continent. Her baby years were spent next to the very fact – the separateness of the island from the continent – which would be the chief contributor in her acquisition of power.

At the outset, then, May was exposed to an England somewhat reminiscent of Larkin's great poem 'To the Sea', full of 'the miniature gaiety of seasides'. We know that later in life she would listen to cricket on the radio, a fact redolent of another Larkinesque detail in that poem: 'ears to transistors, that sound tame enough/under the sky'.[32]

Even so, one wouldn't want to make too much of this. Early in life May's father moved to Oxfordshire, whereupon May became what she would to some extent remain: a creature of the shires. It was certainly a sheltered upbringing, one of minimal rebellion (those fields of wheat again). About May's England, the worst that could be said is that it is too austerely proud to be itself, and not some other less blessed country. It is an England of cricket and automatic Conservative Party membership, of dutiful (and far from ecstatic) attendance of the Sunday church service, and a welter of other duties which should sound too clicheic to be real: making a cake for the village fête, handing out leaflets at local elections and general elections, and even the propagation of certain character traits – modesty, propriety, hard work, thrift, all bound up in the assertion-by-example of an Anglican morality. Such traits, admirable in themselves, each have their flipsides: modesty might shade into blandness; propriety can easily turn judgmental and reduce the nation's portion of inspiration and vitality; glorying in the importance of hard work can sometimes lead to the scapegoating of the poor as 'lazy'; thrift can lead to ungenerosity; and membership of the Church of England – a national church, after all – can also tilt into a genteel xenophobia toward the Other, whether that be other branches of the Christian faith, or adherents of other religions.

May's career is a tale of clinging with surprising tenacity to this view of life. True, she has made her compromises – but she has taken care to make them quietly.

But her father was not political. May would later tell Andrew Marr that he had seen his role as parish clergyman as an inclusive one, and had made an active effort to conceal any political leanings from his flock. On the one hand, May's upbringing reminds one of a side of England that can be satirised – as it was by Craig Brown in the aftermath of the Brexit vote: 'Break out the spam, Mabel, we've done it!'[33] But, on the other hand, such an idea of England can also give rise to an admirable sense of duty, and we find this in Theresa May's heritage. Her grandfather Tom was in the army and fought in India during World War One, dying in Wandsworth in 1951.[34] She never met him, but nevertheless referred to him in her announcement speech:

I know some politicians seek high office because they're driven by ideological fervour. I know others seek it for reasons of ambition or glory. My reasons are much simpler: I grew up the daughter of a local vicar and the granddaughter of a Regimental Sergeant Major, public service has been a part of who I am for as long as I can remember.[35]

Politicians are skilled at joining up the dots retrospectively – and indeed particularly at the moment they are announcing that they intend to be your prime minister. May has presented herself as the Sussex girl who learned valuable lessons in her girlhood. The suggestion is of a life of quiet attainment, where the office of prime minister has come her way only as the accidental offshoot of an all-consuming sense of duty.

MAY'S RELIGION

You don't get to be 60, as May is at time of writing, without experiencing some sadnesses. May's came all at once. Hubert Brasier died in a car crash in 1980, her mother the following year from multiple sclerosis. From her scarce utterances, one gets a sense that her father was particularly influential. An image exists of May as a girl, sat between her mother and father on a sofa in her sparsely furnished childhood home. Her father, wearing his collar, smirks slightly. He is one of those people who is too tall ever to be comfortable in sofas, and has to fold his body at an awkward angle as if in a deckchair (in just this way his daughter would pose for the first photograph of her Cabinet). Her mother sits primly with her hands around her knees, with the light falling along a face which, like May's in Chapter Two, doesn't look as though it enjoys having its photo taken. But this in turn makes one look for Hubert's hands, and one sees, with a little shock, how tenderly he is holding Theresa's. One has a sense, down the years, of simple domestic love.

There is the possibility that the tragedy reinforced his memory, and redoubled her faith. There is the grief whose scale leads by an obscure process not to a rejection of the world, but to reconciliation with it. One suspects that May has experienced the sombre kind of personal growth – perhaps the profoundest kind – that devastating loss can bring.

Whatever the truth of that, there is little doubt that May is serious about her religious faith. She still attends church regularly on Sundays, as much as her now busy schedule permits. May stated in her frank *Desert Island Discs* interview with Kirsty Young – at time of writing, still the best resource we have on May – that the church is 'part of me' and that it 'frames my thinking and approach'.[36] Of course, many a politician has said the same sorts of things without them seeming very plausible. But one wonders what 'framing of approach' May might mean. Is God actively consulted George W. Bush-style? Or is her faith an integrated fact more quietly at work, and not the kind of deity one ought actively petition for enlightenment? But May is inscrutable here too. The best that one can do is return to this idea of duty – of faith and works as one and the same thing. Theresa May might agree with James 2:2: 'What does it profit, my brethren, if someone says he has faith but does not have works?'

Pragmatism at its worst is a lack of any belief; at its best, it is the eclectic refusal of dogma. There is the suggestion that the May family was not strictly Anglican in the decision to send Theresa to St Juliana's Convent School for Girls, a Catholic school. There is a whiff of what CS Lewis called 'mere Christianity'. This might be defined as the belief that the disputes of the Reformation ought to be laid to one side in favour of an espousal of what is held in common between branches of the faith. If we accept this view, then May's faith is broad as well as deep.

There are other indicators of this depth. Her final choice on *Desert Island Discs* was her favourite hymn, 'When I survey the wondrous cross'. Asked by Young to account for this choice, May stated it would make her feel part of a congregation in her island solitude. Here are the words:

> When I survey the wondrous cross
> On which the Prince of glory died,
> My richest gain I count but loss,
> And pour contempt on all my pride.[37]

Only someone who has long been part of a congregation would bother to imagine herself into the loneliness she might feel if denied involvement in one. And any politician attempting to simulate religious faith would hardly be able to come up with something so plausible. In the same programme she also recalls singing this hymn together with her father, alone in the vicarage:

> Therefore we, before him bending,
> This great Sacrament revere;
> Types and shadows have their ending,
> For the newer rite is here;
> Faith, our outward sense befriending,
> Makes our inward vision clear.[38]

The words are a translation from Thomas Aquinas – not somebody one normally associates with Theresa May, but here they are, inextricably linked. The image of father and daughter singing this hymn around the kitchen-table is austere and moving. That Theresa Brasier did not rebel against such an upbringing, as many girls with the 1960s raging around them did, is perhaps one of the chief facts about her. She was conformist in an age when liberation was fashionable. We cannot plumb the depths of this, except to speculate that one possible reason a child will not rebel against an imposed regime is because kindly parents have been doing the imposing. If that is so, then that makes an already sad sequel sadder still.

There were to be not one but two sad postscripts to her early life. The first tragedy came with horrible suddenness, the second was unpleasantly drawn out.

On October 12th 1981, Hubert Brasier was driving his Morris Marina on his way to deliver evensong. He edged out onto the central reservation and was killed by an oncoming Land Rover.[39]

Later that year, Theresa's mother died from multiple sclerosis. This illness is habitually misreported in the media. It is a disease which, as May states in her *Desert Island Discs*, regularly plateaus only to give way to unforeseen developments. Those who suffer from the disease, and those who care for them, typically learn to be pragmatic: it has a way of teaching one to be grateful for the moment that one has, and not the moment one might be travelling towards. It asks one to be – and I mention this because they are phrases often used about May both by herself and by others – pragmatic and to 'get on with it'. Whether this trait of quiet doggedness was caused by her mother's condition, or whether it was accentuated by it, there is no way to know. In a poem 'Campaign' published just after the catastrophic general election in 2017, the poet laureate Carol Ann Duffy would write of her rhetoric as an 'empty vicarage'. I am not sure if that's fair: it is just that it is quietly peopled. Many seem to note fragility in May, and detect the girl in her. Not everyone finds it in themselves to be sympathetic about this. Her failure to be sufficiently 'strong and stable' in the 2017 election would earn much mockery. But it is also possible to glimpse in May a vulnerability which may be traceable to this time: she is among the grieving who has never quite grasped their grief, and there is the suspicion that she has chosen instead the unexamined life. Lack of self-knowledge is a flaw the world tends to punish severely. We ultimately cannot stand to see someone not themselves, and will use the ballot-box, if necessary, to communicate that to them.

But this is to rush forward again in time. There was also good news around that time: before the dual tragedy had happened, Theresa Brasier had become Theresa May.

9 – THE WAY TO PARLIAMENT

Maggie and Dennis. John and Norma. Tony and Cherie. Gordon and Sarah. David and Samantha. Hoisted romances which we all observe, and feel we must consider. Or if we don't consider them, we need to choose not to consider them – because there they are, before our eyes, part of our national imagery.

And now: Theresa and Philip.

At first glance, May's decision to read geography at St Hugh's College, Oxford seems an unexpected one. Knowing her upbringing one expects her to study theology; knowing her eventual career one prepares oneself for PPE. But, at this time, Lord Patten – a former Home Office minister under Thatcher, and Secretary of State for Education under Major – taught political geography at the university, and there is the possibility that his presence may have sparked her decision to go down this route. On the other hand, one wouldn't want to make too much of Patten's presence. With May, there is no mentor in the mould of, say, Derry Irvine to Tony Blair, but instead the occasional suspicion of affinity here and there: to Patten perhaps, to Nick Timothy and Fiona Hill, and to Damian Green. This is not to say May is an original without need of guidance. More likely, there is simply less razzmatazz about her influences. It's possible that to tout one's mentors too loudly is an impropriety to May, who would equate it with immodesty. More likely, her parents were of such importance to her that she needed no additional guidance, and has retained faithfulness to their joint memory since their deaths.

Although one expects to write of Oxford as May's escape, there is something too rooted and familial about her for one to feel justified in doing so. It is as if she were born an adult, so serious and committed as to never particularly be tempted by rebellion. One instead wonders whether this period was a logical development in a far-sighted plan. Immediately we get the first hints of a decorous ambition. It doesn't flare out with the energy of wild showmanship that one glimpses in, for example, future Prime Minister Blair's unexpected attempt to be a rock star, as the front man of *The Ugly Rumours*. Nor is there anything to match the implications of that famous Bullingdon photograph, where David Cameron already has the entitlement of someone who might one day seek power. May's early ambitions instead have a barely stated, even breathed quality. A contemporary of hers, the future Lady Hood, was quoted in a piece in the *Daily Telegraph*: 'I remember her [May] saying, 'One day I will lead the [Conservative] Party'[40]. That sentence needs to be read without the second set of square brackets, in order to get a flavour of how invested May already is in her early 20s in the Tory movement. It is worth noting for instance how the party in question is presumed to be conservative: you can be reasonably sure that no one within earshot of the remark will ever have voted Labour. This overheard utterance links up with the words May would later speak on the steps of 10 Downing Street after visiting the Queen to accept the offer to form a new administration. On that day, she would explain to the nation that her party's full name was the Conservative and Unionist Party. It was a lesson delivered from a perch of long-standing membership.

For someone so solitary-seeming, May exhibits a surprising need to belong to things. Of course, in her stated commitment to social justice since she became prime minister, she has been remarkably quick to redefine what her party stands for. As with her involvement with the church, one wonders whether the belonging matters more than the precise nature of the organisation to which she has chosen to belong. It is the flipside of her solitariness: Theresa May is not so solitary as she might be. She has chosen, after all, the life of the fray – one of noise.

THE MAN AT THE OXFORD UNIVERSITY CONSERVATIVE ASSOCIATION DISCO

One thing that no prime minister avoids: collisions with the famous.

At Oxford, May was introduced to her husband Philip May by Benazir Bhutto. The occasion was an Oxford University Conservative Association disco. As prime minister of Pakistan, Bhutto would later embark on a broadly Thatcherite agenda in the mid-90s, before her assassination at the hands of an Al-Qaeda member in 2007 – by that time Theresa would have held a wealth of shadow cabinet positions. May exhibits a trait one usually finds in prime ministers – namely, the early decision to move in circles likely to help her to become prime minister at some later date. Like this – congenial, relaxed around the famous – Philip May enters the story, and almost immediately embarks on another decades-long disappearing act. With Philip, the biographer again runs into a conspiracy of silence: if

Fig. 11 Benazir Bhutto, who introduced Theresa May to her husband Philip.[41]

one thought one knew little about Theresa, one shortly discovers one has met someone even more elusive.

Of course, there are a few things we do know. Philip May grew up in Liverpool, the son of a shoe wholesaler and a French teacher. After this, the biography thins.

But within Philip, there is an intriguing surge, then fizzle, of ambition. It was he, and not his future wife, who became speaker of the Oxford Union. But afterwards there appears to have been a pact that Theresa would pursue politics, while Philip would settle into a seemingly comfortable life in the City where his strength is reported to be his affability. Today, walking down Downing Street, smiling out from behind round spectacles trustingly, he suggests the sort of person who simplifies life by liking other people, and finds himself liked in return. There are already those who argue that he has made too much money, and that he will serve as an emblem – as in their way the Camerons did – of inequality. But there is little that is showy about the Mays, especially when compared with the Camerons and the Blairs: if this is wealth, then it is of the genteel, even shabby kind.

There is a story, now almost a semi-comic myth, about how one day at the Oxford Union May was asked to speak against the motion: 'Sex is good... but success is better'. One can picture even at this remove the slightly bogus hilarity of it all. It is hard to imagine May not wincing as she was forced into the minor embarrassment of having to argue the point: what one generation might find amusing or even titillating, a later generation will smile on. Still, it isn't necessarily a small point that May derives from this quaint generation: it is another aspect of a certain innocence that nevertheless doesn't preclude the will to power. We might even go further and wonder whether there is something incorruptible about May.

A few small points need to be made about our heroine's career between Oxford and her entry into parliament in 1997, and one big one. The big one is a leitmotif of this book: we don't know much about it. The small ones are that she worked from 1977-1983 – giddy years that overlap with Margaret Thatcher's rise to power – at the Bank of England. She has as much experience in finance as her brief rival for the prime ministership Andrea Leadsom. But Leadsom's chief pitch before her dramatic withdrawal on 11th July 2016 after the motherhood scandal (see Chapter Twenty-Three) was her experience in high finance. This proved in the end to be embellished; let us briefly note that May has taken care to cultivate a CV that can need no embellishment. Another point: May subsequently took on a position at the Bank of England from 1985 to 1997 as a financial consultant and senior advisor in International Affairs at the Association for Payment Clearing Services. One is reminded again of that 2016 *Sky News* blooper just before May became leader, when the former chancellor Kenneth Clarke was caught saying that May knew nothing about foreign affairs: here we see the international dimension, albeit in the financial context. It might be seen as another warning not to underestimate the breadth of May's experience. There is no Gap Year in May's CV, no downtime or concession to relaxation. It might be said that she took to steadily increasing the likelihood of her eventually becoming prime minister until probability collided with reality.

All this is heartening when one considers that she comes before us at a time of considerable crisis where every last piece of knowledge will be of cardinal importance.

On the other hand, it can sometimes seem that this very doggedness and commitment to work has allowed some to claim that she has 'no personality.'

UPON CHARISMA IN MODERN POLITICS

However, even there, a caveat needs to be introduced. It may be that charisma is the most overvalued quality in modern prime ministers. A brief skim through the Chilcot Report into the Iraq invasion can tell you all you need to know about the possible pitfalls of having it – or being deemed to have it. Everybody knows how Tony Blair, who took an obscure pride in conducting the prime ministership with theatricality, found great difficulty in seeing past his own 'flair' to the real ramifications of his actions. Cameron, in his decision to offer the European referendum, was guilty of a comparable flaw. But if we wanted a measure of the rottenness of our politics and the way in which it is reported, we must remind ourselves that neither Blair nor Cameron, those proponents of soundbites and cliché, could possibly be called charismatic by any wider measure. In politics, Obama is charismatic; Churchill was certainly charismatic; it is a fair bet that Julius Caesar was too. In terms of the word's wider application, Peter Ustinov was charismatic; Charles Dickens was charismatic; if we were to travel back in time, we would likely be struck by the charisma of Christopher Marlowe. Blair and Cameron do not appear to qualify by any of these barometers: to call them charismatic is to risk the word losing its meaning. Even if we take 'charismatic' to mean a figure who inspires devotion to others we can see from the ends of Blair and Cameron, both cheerfully stabbed in the back by colleagues, that neither qualifies on that score either.

Our contemporary politics appears to inhabit a world where even stated virtue is null: we are continually witnessing a catastrophic misuse of language. A politician spouting cliché can be called 'good on detail'; a person talking nonsense can be referred to as a 'straight shooter' and someone drunk or rude is 'clubbable' and a thousand similar word-crimes which, taken in aggregate, create a surreal reality.

How much will Theresa May change this? In her early appearances at Prime Minister's Questions, one was reminded again of how haltingly words arrive, as if language were essentially unloved by her. On the other hand, there is a sobriety about May that might make one focus more on the substance of what she says than on how she says it. In any case the probable clichés about her – that she is a 'strong woman' who takes 'tough decisions' – may have been used up during the Thatcher years. Besides, cliché is a luxury of superfluous times. When things are in flux – as they have been ever since the EU referendum – there is no time to waste on convolution, and people tend to speak more straightforwardly.

However, this business of 'charisma' is a different question to the issue of whether a person has any interests outside politics. Christopher Hitchens once said that politics should only take up 30 per cent of a person's life. We, the electorate, easily bored by the ins and outs of many policy areas, naturally wish to know what that other 70 per cent might look like, if a given politician like Theresa May hadn't made that 30 per cent something more like 99. It is an interesting paradox that the 'charismatic' politician – like Blair or Cameron – can usually be demonstrated to have fewer real interests than the allegedly duller person like May or Major. Major, the mocked straight man, went off to the cricket after losing in 1997. Cameron, the flamboyant showman, was back in the Commons for the Trident vote a week after losing power. Though he has now left the House of Commons altogether, it is difficult to say what it is that he loves. It might be that in the UK at least we have it all the wrong way round: the really devoted politicians are the Blairs and Camerons, whereas it is the Majors who really experience the variety of life beyond the chamber.

As we shall see in the next chapter, Theresa May is in the Major and not the Cameron-Blair mould in that respect.

10 – AN INTERLUDE ABOUT GEOFFREY BOYCOTT

Theresa May's hero is the legendary Yorkshire and England cricketer Geoffrey Boycott.

One writes that sentence with a certain trepidation. To do justice to May, one must immediately move to point out the kind of sentence which it is not. It isn't, for instance, the May equivalent of a statement like *Gordon Brown is a fan of The Arctic Monkeys*, as indeed he did claim to be, though never very convincingly. There was a weak-mindedness about the Iron Chancellor, a tendency to dither, which sometimes caused him to listen to the rank absurdities of focus groups. And it is certainly not akin to David Cameron's claims to support Aston Villa, which backfired on him when in an unguarded moment he accidentally claimed to be a supporter of West Ham. It is perhaps not too extravagant to suggest that slips like this percolated in the country around the time of the referendum, and even contributed in untold ways to the outcome. In July 2016, if the chants at Euro 2016 of 'We're voting Brexit!' are to be taken at face value, real football fans booted out a *faux* one. May's love of cricket is pleasingly different: it is a genuine interest that resurfaces time again in reports regarding her. If someone from May's past, lobbied by a journalist for a quote about her, wants to remind us that she is more light-hearted than we think, they might say, as someone did in a recent article in *The Guardian*: 'She would make jokes – a lot of them were cricketing jokes, to be fair.' Our real loves are casual like this, because they are entrenched. They come to witnesses as incidences in the whole.

Of course, May's interest in cricket is also predictable. It might mark her out again as both a product of, and advocate for, the idea of England which we have already glanced off a couple of times. It is also another expression of her love for her father. Here is an excerpt from an interview in the *Daily Telegraph*:

> She was brought up listening to Test matches on the wireless with her father. Her pin-up was – I kid you not – one Geoffrey Boycott. 'I have been a Geoff Boycott fan all my life,' she admits, laughing. 'It was just that he kind of solidly got on with what he was doing.' Theresa to a Tee.[42]

May, then, is partly a creature of that kindly world of Brian Johnston and Jonathan Agnew – of happy, almost sleepy ruminations, and cake sent into the commentators by listeners – a world where if you like cricket, you are assumed to be among friends. It is a measure of the power of the office that this fact, which might be taken almost as a matter of indifference in a home secretary, is not a small point in a prime minister. A cricket fan is always essentially an innocent – in thrall to the sound of leather and willow. May has been known to remark to friends that she is shocked by the sort of things that come across her desk at the Home Office. Her love of cricket

Fig. 12. Geoffrey Boycott, May's hero.[43]

is a means out of that world of imminent terrorist plots and (in her view) troublesome immigration figures into a world of ghostly figures moving along mowed green – the polite rain-like applause as the ball careers towards the ropes, and the fielder flails to scoop it back – three runs not four.

Cricket is an element of continuity in her life, running through her relationship with her father and husband, and, becoming in the end, in her fandom of Geoffrey Boycott, a metaphor for her political career.

Why Geoffrey Boycott? For those unaware, Boycott is one of England's leading run-scorers in Test Match cricket with 8114 runs to his name. Slow, not at all showy, he is just as famous now for his outspoken frankness as a commentator (and slightly UKIP-ish views) as for his cricket career. During his time on the field Boycott made a virtue of doggedness, although the deliberateness of his play would sometimes cause exasperation among teammates. The legendary all-rounder Ian Botham (who also emerged as a Leaver in 2016) would on one occasion deliberately run him out to speed up play. Boycott is also an Englishman of a kind ultimately becoming rarer in these mobile times: one inseparable from the county, York-shire, from which he hails. For the great cricket writer John Arlott, the word for Boycott was 'lonely'; around the Camer-on Cabinet table, Theresa May is known to have cut a similarly apart figure.

Drip-fed information as we are, we are left to make certain inferences about all this that we wouldn't feel inclined to make if we knew more. For instance, we are free to draw the con-clusion that May is a fan of Boycott because he, like her, is a success. But it is also natural to speculate as to whether Boycott – that famously patient player, and dogged accumulator of runs – is some sort of cricketing equivalent of a certain former home secretary. One wonders whether the comparison is a tri-fle too obvious to be true. And yet one would feel differently if May expressed her admiration for a swashbuckling batsman – a flamboyant chancer like Virender Sehwag or Adam Gilchrist. Then we might feel that Theresa May is an essentially expan-sive and imaginative person who is able to appreciate qualities that she herself doesn't possess. The Boycott pick seems to cor-don off this possibility.

And yet in the realm of cooking, we do indeed find this other Theresa May. Here she plumps – again this comes from her invaluable *Desert Island Discs* interview – not for the Geof-frey Boycott of chefs, Delia Smith, with her careful ingredi-ents measurements and severe instructions as to how things ought to be done – but for that Gary Sobers of the kitchen, Jamie Oliver, with his cheerful abundance of ingredients, and inherent 'flair'. The simple narrative about May proves not to be true, or at least proves instead to be one of many narratives.

This second 'Jamie Oliver' May is the same May who likes the musical *Jersey Boys* and is tolerant of Abba. It is the same woman who is happy to laugh at the wryness of Jane Austen (her *Desert Island Discs* choice of book was *Pride and Prejudice*).

It is the dash of yellow on the skirt she wore on the day she became prime minister.

11 - A DAY IN WESTMINSTER IN 1997

All the while that May was working in these finance jobs, her life was advancing along a dual track. She was holding down this difficult work while also pursuing her political career as a local councillor for Durnsford ward in Merton. During this time, May won a reputation as a careful and diligent councillor, well-known for returning the phone calls of constituents assiduously. Here is Tory Councillor David Williams reminiscing about those days:

> She [May] was also a very good ward councillor. We used to make fun of her for a voicemail message she left for her ward constituents. She would say, 'Your call is very important to me, please leave me a message and I will try and get back to you'. It's common nowadays but back then it wasn't. We all thought it was a bit over the top. But she truly meant it, and it showed how much her constituents meant to her.[44]

'A bit over the top' – thus does a person of prime ministerial energy seem at the comparatively somnolent local level. The impression is of her having too much energy to be contained in anything but the national arena.

Interestingly, there were others alongside her who would also rise to Cabinet level – most notably Chris Grayling, eventually to prove a disastrous justice secretary as well as, later on, May's campaign manager and, subsequently, transport secretary – and Maria Miller, a future Secretary of State for Culture, Media and Sport and Minister for Women and Equalities, who would fall foul of the expenses scandal in 2014. In 2016, there was some cursory talk of this 'Wimbledon set' having replaced Cameron's 'Notting Hill set', and indeed it is worth emphasising that May is the first prime minister since John Major to have immersed herself to such an extent in local politics. But she was looking for more: inevitably, May began hunting around for a seat. She was the failed Conservative candidate in the 1992 General Election for the seat of North West Durham. In this contest, she came up against the future leader of the Liberal Democrats, Tim Farron. In May's first appearance at Prime Minister's Questions, Farron would attempt a wistful recollection of their time together in the north of England, asking the new leader to pause and wonder a little that two future party leaders should once have campaigned against each other in such unheralded fashion:

> May I, genuinely, warmly welcome the Prime Minister to her position? She has come a long way since we were on the hustings together in North West Durham, and she is no doubt reflecting on the fact that she is receiving more support in the Chamber than either of us received in Consett working men's club.[45]

It was a genuine attempt to reminisce, but either the Prime Minister doesn't like to do so in general, or she didn't want to think about that particular defeat at a moment of triumph. In response, May was prepared to acknowledge the shared memory, but not without slapping Farron down at the end of her remarks:

I am very happy to remember the days that the hon. Gentleman and I spent campaigning in North West Durham at the time of a general election. Little did the voters of North West Durham know that the two unsuccessful candidates in that election would become leaders of two of the country's political parties, although I would point out to the hon. Gentleman that my party is a little bit bigger than his.

May also contested an unsuccessful bi-election in 1994 in Barking. But by 1997 – an inauspicious year for Conservatives with the John Major administration about to be swept away by the high tide of Blairism – May was selected to fight the new seat of Maidenhead, formed out of parts of the constituencies of Windsor and Wokingham. In the selection process, she came up against a certain David William Donald Cameron, but was selected ahead of him on account of her greater experience of local government – another instance of May's dedication paying dividends. This was a reasonably safe seat, although eight years later it would look somewhat less so, when May would be threatened with the Liberal Democrats' much vaunted though largely unsuccessful 'decapitation strategy' in the 2005 general election. In that year, as in the two elections since, she has steadily increased her majority, culminating in a 65.8 per cent win in 2015.

At time of writing she occupies the fourth safest seat in the country.

UPON THE MAIDEN SPEECHES OF PRIME MINISTERS

Theresa May's maiden speech in the House of Commons was delivered to little fanfare on July 2nd 1997. It is worth looking at in detail since it gives one the sense of an unguarded May – something, one suspects, more like the real one. It is true that there is a 20 years' gap between her ascension to the prime ministership and this address. But something in the nature of the speech – its self-assurance, and sometimes hectoring tones – confers on it a certain grim timelessness. This may derive from its subject matter of education, a topic which May is especially passionate about – often, if her early period as prime minister is anything to go by, to her own detriment. The early months of Theresa May's premiership saw her revert to a somewhat antiquated argument over grammar schools, but to read her maiden speech is to wonder whether she ever left the topic: it's an argument that seems always to be ticking around her brain. In 1997, the immediate context was the debate surrounding the Blair government's swift abolition of the Assisted Places Scheme for independent schools.

Its awkward humour suggests nervousness on the part of our protagonist. For instance, in the following passage May details her arrival in Parliament:

> My own confusion was great when I was in the Members Lobby and the hon. Member for Dundee, West (Mr Ross) rushed up to me, himself in a state of some confusion, and encouraged me to put my name on the list for the ballot for private Members' Bills. He was astounded when I looked at him and said, 'Why?' Obviously, he had mistaken me for one of the ladies on the other side.

It is all suggestive of the unease of the first-timer. Even over-heard in Hansard like this, it reminds us that May is a less nat-ural performer than some of her predecessors. Whereas Blair and Cameron sometimes seemed to be in the job partly, even primarily, for the theatre of it, May has had to overcome an in-herent shyness. One never quite believed Tony Blair's claim in his last PMQs that he had never stopped fearing the House of Commons: Blair's were the nerves of the natural speaker who knows that with the right will, anxiety shall be mastered, and turn into the required performance.

By contrast, Theresa May really does get nervous. Even by mid-2017, when she was well-established in the position, there was still that slight strangulation in the throat – the sense that words will not always be there for her when she needs them. This of course turned out literally to be the case in her 2017 conference speech, when a sore throat caused her great diffi-culties with her delivery. By all accounts, this nervousness is there in person too. Here are Liberal Democrat David Laws' first impressions on meeting her:

> I first met her in 2010. I was sitting in my Treasury office, overlooking St James's Park, me in one armchair and the Home Secretary in the other, with no officials present. She looked nervous.[46]

Nervous at the despatch-box, then, and perhaps generally a lit-tle on edge. If so, then it is worth noting that her nerves have been faced down, if not mastered, in a thousand different and demanding situations for 20 years or so. This might be taken as another yardstick of her determination.

In maiden speeches, MPs are expected to describe the geography of their constituency. It is interesting to note how this task can bring out something of the personality of an MP. For instance, here is Blair describing his Sedgwick constituency:

> Sedgefield town itself is at the crux of the constituency. It contains some new industry, the important hospital of Winterton and also has its prosperous residential parts. Travelling south from Sedgefield, one enters a different world altogether. One can tell that it is different because it is the place where the Social Democratic party ceases telling the people that it represents the Labour party of Attlee and Gaitskell and begins saying that it represents the Tory party of Butler and Macmillan.[47]

One notes the desire to make of the world a drama – a stage on which a man might play a part. We can glimpse the whole Blair administration: the wish to rush into a jurisdiction, and assert oneself, to take up the 'good side' in some dormant struggle – here, Sedgefield might almost be Iraq. By contrast, here is Cameron describing Witney with the boyish enthusiasm and perhaps somewhat superficial zest which would end up characterising his administration:

> It is a privilege and an honour to represent the constituency of Witney and the people of west Oxfordshire. Witney is a seat rich in history and blessed with some of England's most stunning towns, villages, buildings and countryside.[48]

The mind wanders beyond politics into a general sense of well-being. There is no detail here, only good cheer and a boundless faith: here is the mind that offered the European referendum to the British people according to the quasi-Wodehousian hope that things in the end tend to turn out well for David Cameron.

In the maiden speech of Theresa May, we get something more meticulous. The opening of her speech in fact reads like an undergraduate paper written by the geography student that she is:

> The advantages for businesses in the area are many. Not only is it a pleasant and attractive place in which to live and work, but there is a high-quality labour force on which to draw. Maidenhead also has the advantage of proximity to the motorway network, to London and, of course, Heathrow. Those are advantages for business, although it must be said that they also create some problems for local people – night flights into Heathrow, noise from the A404(M), the need for another bridge across the River Thames, the threat of motorway service stations and the threat of development.

One notes that both Blair and May have an interest in the natural layout of things whereas Cameron – light on detail – illustrates no such interest. However, Blair's sense of space is infused with drama – and his role in that drama. One sees that the problem for Blair wasn't that he didn't note the geography of places, but that the psychology he saw in them was primarily his own. May is also interested in the way a landscape flows and fits together but the 'I' doing the describing is not so much hyperactively observant as authoritatively aloof.

> It also includes some lovely tracts of Berkshire countryside, including what I would describe as some of the prettiest and most delightful villages in the country.

'I would describe' – a mere turn of phrase, you might say, but as always with May there is this slight sense of remove, of an individual that will not always necessarily impose herself. It is the May who would not want government to intrude too much in people's lives. There's also this:

> Although not much has been written about Maidenhead, it is a town steeped in history. I was reminded of that yesterday morning as I watched the mayor unveil a plaque in the town centre to commemorate the site of the 13th-century chapel that was the predecessor of the current borough church of St Andrew and St Mary Magdalene.

'I was reminded of'. Ruminative and noticing – reluctant to be involved. I wonder whether Ken Clarke's observation that May has no interest in foreign affairs might be in some way traceable to this slight detachment. May strikes one as forensic by nature as opposed to visionary. She delves deeply into what comes into her purview, but isn't especially interested in creating new landscapes for herself unbidden. She turns with the slow gaze of the hawk but does not career with the Blairite eagerness of an ambitious puppy. All of which is enough to make one wonder what sort of a foreign policy prime minister May will end up as. One thinks of her as instinctively isolationist in some respects, and yet over the years she has cast many a vote in favour of military invasion – in Iraq, Syria and Libya.

In any case, now we have a geographer as prime minister. Blair's is the speech of someone who wants to be prime minister right away; May's is the speech of someone who will be prime minister in her own time. Cameron's seems to say: 'I will be prime minister if you want me to be – probably you will – but it hardly matters to me one way or the other.'

Of the three, Blair is the least happy just to be an MP.

MAY ON EDUCATION IN 1997

At the time of writing, there is much discussion surrounding May's approach to education: we shall look at her attempts to expand the grammar school system in Chapter Twenty-Nine. May initially made social justice a ground note of her administration. If this doesn't mean a better education for the poor, then it isn't quite clear that it can mean anything at all.

As we have glanced off, upon entering government Blair's immediate aim was to get rid of the Assisted Places Scheme, which had been an early education reform of Margaret Thatcher's first administration. It had been originally intended to help talented poorer children into independent schools, provided they scored within the top 10-15 per cent in the entrance examination. For the Blair government, the policy was elitist since that top 10-15 per cent tended not to be filled by the high achieving poor. It was noted that the scheme turfed up very few children from disadvantaged groups such as the children of manual workers, or those from black and Asian families. Instead, places tended to go to children with parents in the services industries, with the children of teachers scoring particularly well. Many an education reformer has had to accept in the end the Darwinian instincts of parents. At the time of Blair's rise to power, schools were, by common consent, underfunded. There was the fear that funding ploughed into the 10-15 per cent created a dearth in funding for those who failed the test. By the end of the Blair years, funding per pupil would increase by 48 per cent in real terms - or £1,450 more per year per child.[49] The emphasis under New Labour was funding across the board, and not the creation of schemes designed to lift a few children into a better life. The Blairite was more worried about what happened to you if you failed the test.

What is the Conservative able to say in opposition to this? The question is particularly worth asking since May is still saying now what she was saying in 1997.

In her maiden speech, May was adamant: 'I totally refute the concept that underpins the Bill – that, if everybody cannot have it, nobody should have it.' The Tory mantra on education is that standards should be high. It is rare to hear an advocate of grammar schools or policies like the Assisted Places Scheme talking for long without invoking the god 'opportunity'. May also emerges here as a staunch opponent of reducing class sizes as the best way to improve teaching:

When I was the chairman of a local education authority, we had many interesting debates about the impact of class size on the quality of education. My concern about the Bill and the way in which it will operate is not only that it will abolish the Assisted Places Scheme, but that the assumption behind it is that the prime determinant of the quality of education for our children is the size of class in which they are taught. It is not: the prime determinant of education quality is the quality of teaching, and that is a function of the quality of teachers and the way in which they teach.

This would be a detour into a dead debate if the debate weren't still ongoing, with Labour continuing to pledge a reduction in class sizes, and the Tories equally keen to emphasise the importance of good teaching. The tone of the speech – as well as its proscriptions – reminds us again what a partisan creature May can be. In time, the Blair government would abolish the Assisted Places Scheme, but it would also do things that were anathema to the left. For instance, Blair's academies, as set up in the 1998 Education Act, would be permitted to select pupils based on ability. May would have known when she delivered her maiden address that education secretary David Blunkett had already decided to keep open the 164 grammar schools that existed at the time. He would also later demonstrate his willingness to wrest failing schools from local authority control, and hand them to private companies[50]. May's maiden speech shows her tendency to think in binary terms: one must either state that one thinks good teaching matters, or one must say that class sizes matters. It is a case of picking one side of the argument and doubling-down on the consequences. And yet it is reasonably obvious to anyone who has sat in classrooms – which is more or less all of us – that both matter, and that it is not hard to imagine a more edifying debate about how to establish an effective relationship between the two.

One final point about that day in Westminster when nobody could have expected that they were listening to the first Hansard-recorded utterances of a future prime minister: it concerns the ending to May's speech:

> The Bill will not improve academic excellence or the quality of education in our classrooms. It will take away opportunities from a large number of children, who would benefit from a quality of education that they would not receive without the assisted places scheme. Furthermore, it will reduce parental choice. The Government are saying to parents, 'You don't know best – we do.'[51]

May likes to end her speeches and contributions at the despatch-box with a verbal thump like this. One thinks of her rejoinder to Jeremy Corbyn at her first PMQs: 'Remind him of anyone?' It is an aspect of her that plays specifically to her party – it is again May as the tribal animal. It has the demerit of being off-putting and bullying if you're not on her team, or an undecided voter.

Even so, one wouldn't want to be harsh. It was her first speech, and a time not for revolutionary thinking but cautious careerism. If this was the case, then her subsequent career shows that it worked.

12 - IN THE SHADOW CABINET

May's maiden speech would have alerted her superiors to the fact that in a probably safe seat, an ambitious team player had arrived on the Westminster scene. Theresa May would be quickly promoted; in fact, she was shuffled around various shadow departments with almost alarming speed. One is never sure when one looks at Theresa May's parliamentary career before her ascension to the Home Office in 2010 quite what to feel – or what May herself would have felt about it all. Did leaders feel she was unremarkable but competent enough – a useful person to shift from role to role? Did they imagine how high her star would rise? And did May herself feel shunted about, or flattered to be so useful in such a variety of contexts?

Here then is a list of the various shadow cabinet positions she held from her arrival in parliament until her promotion to the position of home secretary at the start of the Cameron-Clegg coalition of 2010:

Shadow Spokesman for Schools, Disabled People and Women (1998-June 1999). Shadow Secretary of State for Work and Pensions (January 2009). Shadow Education and Employment Secretary (1999-2001). Shadow Transport Secretary (2001). Chairman of the Conservative Party (July 2002). Privy Council member (2003). Shadow Secretary of State for Culture, Media and Sport (June 2004). Shadow Leader of the House of Commons (December 2005).

The topic of her maiden speech may have paid some dividends. In retrospect it might almost be seen as a job pitch, as she took on those significant roles under William Hague, first in schools, and then at education. Other roles at the ministries of transport, and at culture, might reassure us that when she comes to make big decisions about things like whether to proceed with HS2 or what to do about the BBC, that she can be expected to know about such issues in more detail than someone who hasn't held those positions. It is also worth noting the major areas where she has had little experience. Her time at the Bank of England might make one disinclined to say she knows nothing at all about finance, but she has steered clear at all times of the Treasury. Kenneth Clarke's verdict about her experience in foreign affairs, though we have been minded to treat it with a little caution, should also be mentioned again here.

Her years in opposition also provide very little in the way of experience in health, and in environmental matters – except if we count conversations she would have been privy to around the Cabinet table. It is interesting to note that in what seemed a largely confident reshuffle upon assuming the prime ministership, May made two decisions which seemed like possible blunders at the time and which might still be considered misguided: firstly, in keeping Jeremy Hunt on as Secretary of State for Health, and secondly in abolishing the Department for Climate Change and appointing the far right-winger and champion of deregulation Andrea Leadsom to the post of Secretary for the Environment.

The move to Shadow Leader of the House of Commons in 2005 was widely seen as a demotion. On the other hand, there are worse things for a future prime minister than to have spent time working in close concert with the whip's office, and with MPs. We can fast-forward 10 years or so from that appointment and recall the huge numbers of MPs who stood behind her when she was elected Leader of the Conservative Party and wonder how much of her support was due to her immersion in the parliamentary party around this time. Without such overwhelming support among MPs, there would have been less call for Leadsom to quit. Prime ministers are fortunate like this – or perhaps since there always has to be a prime minister, great good fortune will ripple back retrospectively through the apparently mundane shufflings of a shadow cabinet to confer an accidental benediction on the backstory of a chosen individual like May.

The impression is that leaders wanted her on the pitch, but were not quite sure where to put her, or in what capacity.

Her role as party chairman also deserves to be considered. It was in this capacity that she made her famous 'nasty party' speech to the 2002 Conservative Party conference. This speech, her most famous moment until the dizzying events of 2016, although not quite the stirring piece of rhetoric it is sometimes billed as, brought a phrase into our political discourse. The famous passage reads:

> There's a lot we need to do in this party of ours. Our base is too narrow and so, occasionally, are our sympathies. You know what some people call us – the nasty party.

I know that's unfair. You know that's unfair but it's the people out there we need to convince – and we can only do that by avoiding behaviour and attitudes that play into the hands of our opponents. No more glib moralising, no more hypocritical finger-wagging.

We need to reach out to all areas of our society.

I want us to be the party that represents the whole of Britain and not merely some mythical place called 'Middle England', but the truth is that as our country has become more diverse, our party has remained the same.[52]

It is a classic wounds-licking speech of a Party in opposition, and is laced with self-pity – 'I know that's unfair. You know that's unfair'.

But it is worth noticing that May had diagnosed the problem for the Conservatives before David Cameron was even in parliament, although with her austere manner, one suspects that she could never have 'modernised' the party so effectively as he did. Read today, every word of the 'nasty party' speech reflects back with startling clarity those wilderness years of electoral misery. It was an impossible time for the Conservatives: as one reads May's words, one wonders what point there was to belonging to the Conservative Party at all. We have already seen how Blair extended selection into the academies system. Blair had also claimed that he was 'intensely relaxed' about wealth creation, in addition to expressing open-mindedness about privatisation of the NHS, and instigating a Thatcherite foreign policy of projecting British strength in troubled jurisdictions. May's speech is not so much one of moral defeat, but electoral perplexity.

There are some interesting moments. For instance, in this passage we are made to realise how rapidly an apparently impregnable position for the centre-left was lost by a single decision:

> Just over a year ago, on the 11th of September, terrorists killed over 3000 people in New York - many Britons among them. George Bush and Tony Blair deserve the gratitude of everyone for standing up to the forces of evil.

> And they deserve our thanks as well for the action they are taking to disarm Saddam Hussein.[53]

There were many who felt roughly the same at the time, who have subsequently reversed their position upon learning about the fallibility of the Blair administration's intelligence. But as a hat trick of votes in favour of intervention in Iraq, Syria and Libya shows, May hasn't altered her position on foreign policy since this speech in light of later events.

So this was the high-water mark of Blairism. Pre-Iraq, Conservatives had no means of arguing against the Blair government. A few years later, just before leaving office, Blair would tell a meeting of his parliamentary party that if they played their cards right, New Labour could be the main force in British politics for a hundred years. But for the decision to invade Iraq he might have been right, and anyone who doubts this ought to read May's speech. May flounders throughout.

She states that the NHS is falling apart, but she must have known that an unprecedented round of funding had been embarked upon. She states that schools were crumbling, but we have already seen spending per pupil rising dramatically under the Blair government. The only critique that could be made against Blair was from the left, and that was the one the Conservatives were unable to make. There is some evidence that May learned her lesson: her branding of the Conservative Party as a force for social justice is the exact mirror image of the Blair project, intended to rob oxygen from Labour under Jeremy Corbyn in the same way Blair had once done to her party. Blair would have to wait until after his premiership, and the advent of Jeremy Corbyn, for a comprehensive front-bench critique of his policies. From the likes of May, he was only ever likely to get this frustrated indignation.

As a personal rebranding exercise May's speech must be counted a success. It was also successful in starting the lengthy process of detoxifying her party. But as an intellectual critique it cannot rise above a moan.

TOWARDS WHITEHALL

Theresa May's time at Shadow Secretary of State for Work and Pensions is interesting in that she shadowed Yvette Cooper MP – the wife of former Shadow Chancellor Ed Balls, and herself an unsuccessful leadership candidate against Jeremy Corbyn in 2015. Cooper would subsequently write an article outlining her understanding of May. This commemorates a rivalry between the two which began in the dying days of the Brown administration, with May as part of Cameron's expectant opposition. It was carried over to the Coalition government, when Cooper moved to shadow May when our heroine became home secretary. The piece displays the nuanced comprehension of a long-standing opponent:

> I respect her style – it is steady and serious. She is authoritative in parliament – superficial attacks on her bounce off. When the Tory establishment call her 'a bloody difficult woman' she rightly wears it as a badge of pride. But the flip side is that she is not fleet of foot when crises build, she digs in her heels.[54]

But May's time at Work and Pensions would be brief. A General Election was upon the country, and nobody expected Gordon Brown, tired and irascible, to do much better than lose to David Cameron. May could have expected to enter government, but it seems unlikely that she would have been promoted to the position of home secretary upon the formation of the eventual Coalition government in concert with the Liberal Democrats, if she hadn't acquitted herself well in the expenses scandal which hit Westminster not long before the election.

It began – as the juiciest scandals do – with a scoop, this one landed by *The Daily Telegraph*, which revealed a widespread misuse of taxpayers' money among elected members. The most eye-catching claims revealed the pettiness of greed. Labour MP Harry Cohen was ordered to pay back £933.38 after spending £150 on a vase, £324 on a bedside cabinet and buying four beds in four years.[55] Lembit Opik of the Liberal Democrats billed taxpayers for the £40 summons for his non-payment of council tax, and £2,499 for a new plasma TV screen.[56] Home Secretary Jacqui Smith had claimed expenses which contained pay-per-view pornographic films watched by her husband. It suggested a rotten polity: around 230 MPs had 'flipped' their second homes, changing the designation in order to maximise their expenses. But there were many MPs who weren't culpable – Vince Cable, Gordon Brown and David Cameron among them. Another was Theresa May. May was duly sent out by the Conservatives to explain to the nation what had happened. We shouldn't deem it a small point that May, during a period when it was usual to make an easy gain, refused to do so. Of course, it might also be said that with her husband making plenty in finance there was less temptation for her. However, there is something in May's character – whether we call it aversion to risk, propriety, morality, caution or canniness – that one senses would never put herself in the position of having to defend herself when it isn't necessary.

Was it this which made Cameron take the unexpected decision to move her to one of the four great offices of state in 2010? It will not have hurt. In the meanwhile, New Labour had unravelled with startling speed. A ludicrously strong electoral position had been surrendered because of lingering resentment over a single foreign policy decision: Iraq. The ensuing Brown government had found itself immediately on the receiving end of the global financial crisis. The words 'Northern Rock' swirled around his premiership, and the world began to understand that deregulation of the financial sector, thrilling though it had been, had had secret consequences. Margaret Thatcher – who Brown invited to Downing Street in a seeming bid to draw a favourable parallel between two tough leaders, the Iron Chancellor and the Iron Lady – had once said that her greatest achievement was Blair himself. She had bequeathed a consensus even to her adversaries. Blair passed the mantle onto Cameron but not to the leaders who would succeed him in his own party. In retrospect, the combination of the financial crisis and Iraq was enough to make New Labour pause and wonder whether it really wanted to be New Labour after all. Under Ed Miliband it decided, with a strong shove by the trade unions, that it probably didn't; under Jeremy Corbyn, it announced that it certainly didn't.

Two more things had changed by the time Theresa May had become home secretary. In the first place, Cameron had gone a long way towards completing the modernisation of the Tory Party, which we have seen May beginning in her 'nasty party' speech. In Chapter Two, we saw him take his trip to the North Pole to hug a husky. Cameron also wondered aloud about whether people ought to be more open-minded about the clothing decisions of young people, and was swiftly ridiculed by a Labour press release as having put forward a 'hug-a-hoodie' agenda: the label stuck. But Cameron deserves praise for moving his party in the direction of a more tolerant outlook. At the time of his departure, he was rightly able to claim credit for having seen through the introduction of gay marriage, although he had needed Labour votes to get the legislation through.

A second development competed with this project of modernisation. The Eurozone crisis, which escalated in the weeks before the 2010 General Election, would alter the debate about economics in the UK for the foreseeable future. In the lead-up to the 2010 General Election, it began to emerge that the Greek economy, which had seemed to boom viably for most of the 2000s on the back of a series of EU-funded infrastructure projects, was in serious trouble, experiencing both declining revenues and soaring debt. It was essentially a balance of payments of crisis. In effect, the capital inflows, which had seemed like such a good thing, were a problem, and had led to significant overvaluation. Investors in time became worried about the debt their investment was creating and began to pull that investment: this led to difficulty in the country making debt repayments.[57] Tied to a foreign currency, the economy could not reset. Grexit was a buzz word long before Brexit was. It looked as though the country, unless it received generous terms from countries whose principal goal appeared to be to teach it a lesson, would either need to toil under the imposition of German austerity, or leave the Euro. Some commentators still wish that the Keynesian approach to economic difficulty had been on the table. But it never was. What Paul Krugman would call German morality play economics had already won the day. The results would not prove good:

> In contrast [with the American stimulus approach], the ECB decided to raise interest rates – a contractionary policy – in 2011. The result: While the US economy started to heal, the Eurozone tipped into a double-dip recession. Things got so bad, particularly in Greece, that it looked like the entire Eurozone system could collapse.[58]

David Cameron, Nick Clegg and George Osborne were all complicit in this approach. We shall look at the effects of all this on Theresa May's tenure at the Home Office in Part III. Nor would the European Union's handling of the Greek crisis help the Remain side of the argument when it came to the 2016 referendum: some would vote against the status quo on the grounds that the European project was already unravelling in any case. Of course, there would be irony there. By the time of the Brexit vote, that rationale for a Leave vote would be taken by those who argued for the same austerity policies to be applied to the UK that had already caused stagnation in the European Union. The Greek crisis was seized upon by Brown's opponents to discredit any kind of stimulus approach to a contracting economy.

The General Election results when they came in were disappointing for Cameron and for the Conservatives. They provided a further novelty: the necessity of the Conservatives and Liberal Democrats to form a Coalition government. It was Benjamin Disraeli who once said that England does not love coalitions. In the event of it, Britain found it didn't particularly mind. Still less did David Cameron mind it. We will never know how different things might have gone for Cameron had he governed for a second term alongside the Liberal Democrats, but in his first term, finding himself out of sync with his party on certain issues, it was always helpful for him to have someone to turn to – or hide behind – when the far right made its inevitable demands on him.

We can be sure that May would have never been able to present herself as a moderate unifying force in any other scenario than the very specific one offered in the summer of 2016.

And she wouldn't have been able to run credibly for the prime ministership if she hadn't functioned as home secretary from May 2010 until the time of the referendum.

PART THREE

HOME SECRETARY

13 - THE OFFICE OF HOME SECRETARY

Theresa May walked into 2 Marsham Street as only the second woman to hold the office of home secretary (the first had been Jacqui Smith whose expenses we have just seen providing embarrassment in the previous chapter), and only the fourth to hold one of the great offices of state, after Smith, Margaret Thatcher, and Margaret Becket, who had briefly held the foreign office brief under New Labour. Even if May had not risen to be prime minister, her six-year period as home secretary would have made her easily the second most powerful woman in the nation's recent political history.

Even so, the job of home secretary, while a very powerful post, is also not necessarily a sought after one: there are those who have been appointed to it and ended up roundly cursing their luck. It is a highly visible department but it is always up against insuperable difficulty – in Marsham Street, failure is the norm. Occupants can sometimes appear to lurch from one joyless shambles to another. In seeing how May fared in this position, we must enter a murky world of passport queues; shadowy police operations reminiscent of an unglamorous version of *Spooks*; morally queasy phone-tapping; sticky extradition controversies; stubborn immigration statistics; volatile crime numbers; complex police organisation; the ever-present possibility of imminent terrorist attack; and the misery of modern slavery. This is the inclement nature of the job May held for six years. It is drab but intermittently sensational weather, an overcast afternoon in Surrey, with occasional thunderstorms.

This brings us looping back again to May's leadership announcement. In that speech, May did something more than recall her time as home secretary: her time in the job was her pitch. Here is the relevant passage from her speech:

> ... These are all burning injustices and as I did with the misuse of stop and search, and deaths in police custody, and modern slavery, I am determined to fight against them. You can judge me by my record. As Home Secretary I was told I couldn't take on the Police Federation, but I did. I was told I couldn't cut police spending without crime going up, but crime is lower than ever. I was told I shouldn't start asking questions about police corruption, but everywhere I've seen it, from Stephen Lawrence to Hillsborough, I've exposed it. I was told I couldn't stop Gary McKinnon's extradition, but I stood up to the American government and I stopped it. I was told I couldn't deport Abu Qatada, but I flew to Jordan and negotiated the deal that got him out of Britain for good.[59]

These claims must be dug into: what May did or didn't do as home secretary will therefore be examined in the next chapters.

Most are agreed that there was one important thing she didn't do as home secretary: she didn't screw it up too badly. It has almost become a cliché to observe, after having pointed out that Theresa May is a very long-serving home secretary, that the office has been the graveyard of many a political career. This is only half-true. It has also often been a stepping-stone to the highest office.

GHOSTS OF HOME SECRETARIES PAST

Former occupants of the office of home secretary who later went on to be prime minister include Lord North, Robert Peel – who changed the job out of all recognition by founding the Peelers, known to us now as the police – and H.H. Asquith. But it was Winston Churchill's tenure as home secretary that provides the best example of the pitfalls and possibilities of the job. I hope the reader will not mind the digression: I have found that there is no way to gauge May's performance in her role without examining what others were able to do with it.

Two brief stories regarding Churchill shall give us a flavour of the role May eventually came to hold. Almost as soon as Churchill took up the position, he became embroiled in the Rhondda Coalminers' Strike. The origins of the strike centred on the opening of a new coal seam at Ely Pit at Penygraig. After an initial period of work, the company who owned the pit – the Naval Colliery Company – began to complain that the miners were working slower than usual. The miners retorted that the new seams were more stubborn than their predecessors. The matter escalated swiftly: the owners posted a lock-out notice, and the miners responded by going on strike. Strike-breakers were called in; the miners picketed the site. Within a few days, windows were broken in the town.

The Chief Constable of Glamorgan, although he had 1,400 police at his disposal, nevertheless panicked and called the General Officer commanding Southern Command. So 400 troops – army and cavalry – were dispatched. According to his biographer, Martin Gilbert, Churchill only found out that the troops had been dispatched at eleven o'clock the following morning. Churchill decided the matter had better be handled by the police after all, but once rioters spread into the village of Tonypandy, Churchill allowed one squadron of cavalry to stay. When Churchill offered the strikers an interview with the senior government arbitrator, *The Times* thundered that if loss of life should occur as a result of the strikes, 'the responsibility will lie with the Home Secretary'. As Theresa May would attest, he was not the last home secretary to hear an indignant threat like that.

Later in the House of Commons, Kier Hardie spoke of the impropriety of having sent troops into the area at all. Churchill is still loathed in parts of Wales today. The story reminds us that whenever something bad happens in the country, it is usually the home secretary's job to deal with, if it is not the prime minister's.

But if home secretaries run the risk of being loathed, they also run the risk of being ridiculed. Another incident from Churchill's tenure is of interest. During a burglary in 1911, three anarchists, Fritz Svaars, 'Joseph', and a Conradian anarchist called 'Peter the Painter' had shot and killed three policemen and then been traced to a house in Sidney Street. A siege had ensued. Churchill, never one to remove himself from danger when there was a chance to see crisis up close, took himself down to the East End to see for himself. The house in which the wanted men were holed up began to burn down. When the fire brigade arrived, Churchill ordered them not to put out the fire. He later explained to Prime Minister Asquith: 'I thought it better to let the house burn down rather than spend good British lives in rescuing those ferocious rascals'.[60]

Interestingly, an image surfaced (Fig. 13) of Churchill observing the siege which provoked a mixture of amusement – wasn't this, after all, typical Winston? – and synthetic outrage. For instance, Arthur Balfour thundered in the House of Commons: 'I understand what the photographer was doing, but what was the right honourable gentleman doing?' For us, it is a useful image – it shows precisely what today's home secretary can never be: a person in the line of fire, close to the front lines of the security struggles of the day. These scrapes, combined with the headache of needing to deal with the question of whether to reprieve criminals in the days of capital punishment – a system Churchill loathed – caused Churchill to remark to the House of Commons in 1948: 'I found it very distressing nearly forty years ago to be at the Home Office. There is no post that I have occupied in Government which I

THE HOME SECRETARY AT SIDNEY STREET.

Fig 13. One of Theresa May's predecessors Winston Churchill, getting very near the action at the Siege of Sidney Street in January 1911.[62]

was more glad to leave.'[61] Coming from someone who by that stage in his career had occupied almost every post, this was saying something.

The last person before May to make it to the premiership after holding the position of home secretary – James Callaghan – would agree with Churchill's verdict on the role.

Callaghan spent much of his time embroiled in increasing difficulties in Northern Ireland – problems which today might fall to the Northern Ireland secretary, or the prime minister. But immigration was also a contentious issue during his tenure. He pushed through the Commonwealth Immigrants Act 1968 in just three days. This legislation amended a previous act – passed by the Macmillan administration in 1962 – restricting the rights of Commonwealth citizens to enter the UK. Hugh Gaitskell, the Labour party's then leader, had called it 'cruel and brutal anti-colour legislation'. This did not deter Callaghan: in passing his legislation, he included explicitly racial provisions, aimed at addressing a perceived influx of Kenyan Asians into Britain. Every so often there is a very bad day in the House of Commons, and this was one of them. In addition to crises, the home secretary is also lumbered with this most contentious of political issues.

May's New Labour predecessors provide a useful catalogue of all that can go wrong as home secretary.

Alan Johnson got into difficulty after it emerged that MI5 had known about the alleged torture suffered by UK citizen Binyam Mohamed in Guantanamo Bay. Johnson made it as far as the 2010 General Election without resigning but a record of survival in the post was not the norm in the Blair years: Jacqui Smith was sacked after the expenses scandal, but before that lapse had been in difficulty over her refusal to downgrade ecstasy from a Class A drug, and over the government's much disliked Identity Cards Scheme. Before Smith, John Reed had declared the Home Office 'not fit for purpose', an accusation that has always dogged it, although he was the first person to hold the position to say so quite so explicitly. Reed would go on to be lumbered with a variety of problems from the prisons' overcrowding crisis in Birmingham, as well as a worrying array of terror plots. Reed's predecessor, Charles Clarke, had been shown the door when on 25 April 2006 it was found that 1,023 foreign prisoners had been freed without being considered for deportation: this included 41 burglars, 20 drug importers, 54 convicted of assault and 27 of indecent assault. Before Clarke, David Blunkett had stoked controversy by calling civil libertarianism 'airy fairy'.

The misery that can come to those who hold the office is various. But there is another side to the job. Churchill's final view of his time at the Home Office is in stark contrast to his initial excitement. Violet Asquith noted that he was full of 'excitement and exhilaration' upon being given the job. Churchill showed that great good can be done in the office which we are about to see Theresa May occupy. For instance, Churchill embarked on an ambitious round of prison reforms, reducing solitary confinement to one month for first offenders and to three months for repeat offenders. He also created a distinction between criminal and political prisoners – these were of benefit to the numerous suffragettes imprisoned at that time.

Further, he took the first steps towards opening prison libraries, and spent a remarkable amount of time immersing himself
in individual cases with a view to creating a culture of more
clement sentencing.

Fig. 14. The great reformer Roy Jenkins,
arguably the most successful of May's predecessors as Home Secretary.[63]

This spirit of liberalism
reached its height during
the tenure of Roy Jenkins.
Jenkins – perhaps
May's greatest predeces-
sor in this role – famously
replaced the board in the
Home Office on which
condemned prisoners were
listed with a drinks cabinet
– a spirit of bibulous good cheer which it is hard not to smile
about. Jenkins abolished theatre censorship: this had the effect
of releasing a group of naked hippies onto the London stage
in the shape of the musical *Hair*. There are plenty of plays we
wouldn't have today in the absence of that decision. Jenkins
refused to allow birching for prisoners, supported the legal-
isation of abortion, and also backed the decriminalisation of
homosexuality. It was as if a frown of judgemental disapproval
had been lifted off the face of the nation because of one man's
– one home secretary's – spirit of tolerance.

In the age of the EU referendum, one cannot resist observing that Jenkins made a very important speech as home secretary in 1966:

> I do not regard it [integration] as meaning the loss, by immigrants, of their own national characteristics and culture. I do not think that we need in this country a 'melting pot', which will turn everybody out in a common mould, as one of a series of carbon copies of someone's misplaced vision of the stereotyped Englishman . . . I define integration, therefore, not as a flattening process of assimilation but as equal opportunity, accompanied by cultural diversity, in an atmosphere of mutual tolerance.[64]

One wonders how different the 2016 EU referendum would have been had we had a home secretary like Jenkins around to argue that position with such eloquence. I raise these examples to show that May was not a home secretary like Churchill or Jenkins. She never exhibited the wide-rangingness of Jenkins' approach, or the imaginative energy of Churchill's. Jenkins and Churchill did not so much occupy the office as wield it – they saw in it the possibilities of a broadly imaginative idealism.

On the other hand, May was never as cruel or thoughtless as Callaghan, and she did (as we shall see particularly in Chapter 17) some good.

As we have seen, May is the forensic politician who sticks to her brief. To examine Jenkins' career is to wonder what kind of prime minister he would have made. Again, power is elastic – in that each office, while in some sense the same office, contains a changeable amount of power which precisely tracks the ability, energy, imagination, and other traits of the holder of that office at a particular time. In one sense, Margaret Thatcher held the same amount of power as, say, Anthony Eden: both were prime ministers. But in another sense, by being herself, she held more power, since she was able to do more with it at that particular point in time. It is the difference between potential and actual power. Likewise, May held the same office as Jenkins or Churchill, but she filled that post with less vitality than either. But she also occupied her position with a certain canniness which most of her New Labour predecessors lacked. Power isn't homogeneous in another respect: it opens up onto morality. It can be a force for good or its opposite. Where is Theresa May on that spectrum?

14 - MAY AND THE POLICE

The first thing one usually hears said of May's time as home secretary is that 'she took on the police'.

May is still known as 'Cruella' in the force, with just enough self-pity on the part of the police for it to qualify as amusing. Taking into account Stephen Lawrence, Hillsborough and the abuses of their 'stop and search' powers, the police can often seem like a bully extravagantly nursing a minor scar. On the other hand, one wouldn't want to skim over the inconvenience that the May cuts have undoubtedly caused those who have dedicated their lives to the task of keeping us safe.

This tense relationship began – as so often in the Cameron-Clegg government – against the backdrop of government cuts. In the aftermath of the 2008 crash, George Osborne had argued that the best remedy for a collapsing economy was to cut the deficit. The deficit – the gap between government expenditure and its income – had risen as a result of the recession.

The last New Labour years were a time of declining taxable income, and rising unemployment benefits. In 2010, upon assuming the chancellorship, Osborne had set up the Office for Budget Responsibility and commissioned a government-wide spending review. To tackle the deficit had become a government mantra. It was often prefaced by the notion that there was no alternative but to do this dramatically – when there was indeed an alternative, which was to address the deficit without so much alacrity. It has been noted that around this time the terms 'budget deficit' (a snapshot of the national finances in any given year) and the notion of the 'national debt' (everything the government has to repay) became more or less interchangeable in the mouths of many politicians and commentators, contributing to an atmosphere of confusion in the public discourse. Ryan Bourne, head of economic research at the Centre for Policy Studies, and co-author of a study on this issue called 'A Distorted Debate' – was critical of certain metaphors peddled by Osborne and Cameron, falsely equating household expenditure with government expenditure:

> The Government has often said that it wants to pay the nation's credit card off. But if it wants to use that analogy correctly, it should be saying that it wants to reduce the amount that is added to the credit card debt each year – that is, reduce new borrowing.[65]

Confusion at the linguistic level will always lead to confusion at the policy level since policy must always be expressed in language.

Throughout the early years of the Coalition, it became usual to assert that the government was trying to reduce the national debt, when the reduction of the deficit was the government's real ambition. There were mitigating circumstances if one was confused. Osborne himself had told the 2011 Conservative Party conference: 'We should never take our eyes off the prize: a British economy freed from its debts'[66]. But the Coalition in fact planned to increase the national debt by £600 billion over the parliament. True, it wished to reduce national debt *as a portion of GDP*, but this is a different thing – and anyway the eradication of all debt is not necessarily desirable:

the British government has been in debt for three centuries, not to anyone's particular concern, and the US government has enjoyed a time of undoubted ascendancy despite being in debt since 1835.[67] According to M.I.T.'s Ricardo Caballero, the debt of stable, reliable governments – and there is no government more stable than the British government – provides 'safe assets' that are of assistance to investors mindful of managing risk, facilitate transactions, and avoid what Paul Krugman calls 'a destructive scramble for cash'.[68] It is true that the private sector can create safe assets too, but if the 2008-9 crash taught us anything it is that a sure thing in the private sector is never really a sure thing, and that any healthy economy should have activity revolving around the stability of a democratic government.

It is hard not to feel therefore that as Theresa May took her seat at the Cabinet table that she was surrounded by, and perhaps contributed to, an atmosphere of ignorance and confusion. We might also fast-forward to the vote to leave the European Union and wonder to what extent a general sense of unease surrounding a false economic discourse contributed to the wish to deliver the likes of Osborne a surprising decision.

Nevertheless, Osborneomics – and by association the home secretaryship of Theresa May – would proceed according to the following faith: fiscal probity would segue via a necessary period of pain into confidence. This would mean increased investment, trickle-down expenditure and growth. If economics is the study of human behaviour in relation to money, then we can note a possible difficulty with this: people in pain don't usually feel tremendously confident. The country's deficit problem was frequently exaggerated. It had even been argued that Gordon Brown's overspending under Labour had triggered a financial crisis which everybody knew to be essentially global in nature.

The electorate in 2010 was presented by Cameron and Clegg with an apparent economic orthodoxy. Those in favour of a more moderate approach ran for the hills: 2010 was an impossible time to be a Keynesian economist in the UK because it made you sound like a Brownite, which by that time, after 13 years of New Labour, no one particularly wished to be. What did May make of it all? There is plenty of evidence that she agreed with the Osborne approach, not least in her continued involvement in a government that espoused it. There is also evidence that she still concurs. In her first appearance at Prime Ministers' Questions she would speak in Osborne-like terms, saying to Jeremy Corbyn: 'He talks about austerity, but actually it is about not saddling our children and grandchildren with significant debts in the years to come'.[69] But, again, debt has been bequeathed from one generation to another for centuries in one way or another: it is a norm.

All of which makes one feel we must admit at least the possibility that neither Osborne nor Cameron – and probably not May – particularly understands the public finances.

Like this, pursuant to an exaggeration, and amid a confusion which she may have shared and therefore contributed to herself, May's tenure as home secretary began.

CUTS AND RESTRUCTURINGS

From Theresa May's perspective there was no way to be home secretary at that time and not cut spending in her department: when she took office, every government minister was asked to cut their department's budget, except those in the 'ring-fenced' departments Health and International Development. With rising annual costs of 4 per cent, it is still argued that the NHS needed more investment than a nominal protection from spending cuts, as we shall see in Chapter 28. But across government, every minister was asking themselves the same question: not 'Should I cut?', but 'What to cut?' As is normal with things like this, large structural changes would be made to co-exist with small readjustments. At May's Home Office, the civil service had no choice but to fall in line. BBC Home Affairs correspondent Danny Shaw was droll: 'There could be no clearer sign of budget-tightening at the Home Office than the sight of its most senior civil servant, Permanent Secretary Sir David Normington, travelling standard class to the Acpo conference with Policing Minister Nick Herbert.'[70] We can see that a certain amount of cutting in government budgets is sometimes salutary if it asks people to sit in a similar train seat for much less money. On the other hand, no one could have argued that these straitened circumstances were solving the financial crisis.

Theresa May did not have to look long at her department to come back with the obvious answer of where to cut: the police. Whereupon, like many a politician before her, she adamantly pledged the improbable, telling the annual conference of the Association of Chief Police Officers in Manchester in June 2010 that she was 'determined front-line availability should increase even as budgets contract.'[71] As is often the case, the world began to surmise that the difficult had not become any less so simply because a senior politician had said that it would be done. Over the next years, the police budget was cut by 4 per cent a year. By 2015, according to the Police Federation 17,000 jobs were lost as a result, a figure projected to rise over time to 22,000 jobs. But how problematic have these cuts been? One thing in favour of the government that wishes to cut is the way in which the human imagination cannot compute the precise effect of such numbers: a statistic never calibrates for you precisely in what ways communities have been affected, or precisely how inconvenienced the police have been. The Cameron government would sometimes look fleet-footed precisely because with cuts affecting so many areas, it was hard to know where to bestow one's attention.

But it must be said that, apart from a 27 per cent spike in violent crime reported by the Office for National Statistics in January 2016 not long before May's rise to the premiership, the country has not been noticeably less safe. Instead, statistics released in 2014 showed that crime had fallen by 10 per cent, with the Crime Survey for England and Wales showing a 13 per cent fall in violence, household theft down 19 per cent and vandalism down by 8 per cent, although more concerning reports of a London with a crime rate worse than New York's would emerge over the next years[72]. Crime Prevention Minister Norman Baker was triumphant: 'England and Wales are safer than they have been for decades with crime now at its lowest level since the survey began in 1981.'[73] Even the 27 per cent figure might be explained away: the increase in violent crime was particularly evident in the South-East and London, and so might have been due to increased immigration, although one would certainly want better evidence than we have been given so far to lay the blame here. Others point to a cut in detective numbers, caused by their relocation onto historic sex abuse cases. Of course, it might also be that there is some delay in the effect of cuts being reflected in the figures, and that we are only now seeing an increase in crime related to those cuts. But for the time being, May is able to argue that her cuts were made with reasonable smartness.[74] She would in fact attribute the improvements to red tape savings and the scrapping of targets:

> The striking thing is we were able to deliver these changes not despite spending cuts but because of them – by focusing our minds and forcing us to look critically at how we deliver services.[75]

The police have not been pleased, expressing their dismay that short-term cost-cutting measures are being confused with reform. May, in her 2015 speech to the Police Federation, referred to the chair of the organisation Steve White as 'the boy who cried wolf' in relation to the cuts. White would retort at the following year's conference: 'If I sound like the boy who cried wolf, well the word on the street is that there have been verified sightings of the wolf.'[76]

The Cameron government managed to make these cuts while also retaining to some extent its reputation for compassion. This was partly because of the presence of the Liberal

Democrats within the Coalition. But this was also the era of the Big Society, where the hope was voiced that the effect of the cuts would be mopped up by an outbreak of charitable works among citizens. These would-be armies of volunteers never quite roamed the streets: human nature is perhaps too static to cooperate with the top-down whims of governments. The idea fizzled out over time, although the bank Big Society Capital was set up, and still functions today. Even so, at the outset of the Coalition, everything was seen through a Big Society lens. May was not immune to this. Her eventual consultation paper on the police would be called 'Reconnecting police and the people' and was essentially a blueprint for local citizens to become more involved in their neighbourhoods' policing. Here is May in the foreword:

> The mission of the police which was established by Sir Robert Peel as preventing crime and disorder has not fundamentally changed... But over time the model for policing initiated by Peel has slowly been eroded. His revolutionary model for policing in London was so successful, Parliament legislated for similar bodies across the country but subject to local accountability by people who knew the locality and what was wanted... Over time however the role of central Government grew. As the number of police forces fell, police authorities took on bigger areas. They have since become remote and invisible, without the capability and the mandate to insist on the priorities of local people.[77]

Part-nostalgic history lesson, part-pragmatic Conservative blueprint, this shows the May method. One also notes her regret about the way in which society hardens over time into government. Couched in May's austere language, this is really a Cameroonian document, emitting a sense that all manner of thing would be well even if the government opts out of people's lives, and therefore very distinct from the woman who would one day stand in front of 10 Downing Street, having just become prime minister, to announce that she wished to help the 'just about managing'.

For May, the police had become a remote entity – as she put it, 'disconnected from the communities they serve'. And, indeed, local police are not characters in communities to the extent that they once were: historically, the British have taken the comic view of their law enforcers, and few now know a Dogberry, Inspector Japp, or Wodehousian bobby adding colour to local life. What did the home secretary propose to do about it? Her principal innovation was to scrap police local authorities and to invest power instead in a new role in society – the democratically-elected police commissioner. After two police commissioner elections, we are not in a position to call this a success. It certainly hasn't unleashed the local interest in policing that May seems to have expected. Turnout in November 2012 – the first PCC elections to be held – was a miserable 15 per cent. The turnout rose to the mid-twenties for 2016. There have been complaints that the government has done little to promote their own elections, and two of May's predecessors Alan Johnson and Charles Clarke have called for the elections to be scrapped pointing to this 'derisory public mandate'.[78] Policing had in theory been wrested from local authorities into the hands of the people, but if the people were pleased about it, they celebrated to an unusual extent with abstention in these elections.[79]

There was further reorganisation. May also scrapped an innovation of the Blair Administration, the Serious Organised Crime Agency (SOCA), and replaced it with a National Crime Agency. Blair explains his inspiration for SOCA in his memoirs:

> Often the dealers and pimps would carry around thousands of pounds on them, or drive fancy cars. It was of course impossible to prove these amounts of money were the proceeds of crime, but allowing them to do this had two deleterious consequences. First and obviously, they could conduct their affairs more easily. Second... it gave them a cachet and status in the neighbourhood.[80]

The department had been set up to try and combat this state of affairs which he felt was improperly dealt with by existing law. And yet its remit – 'to combat organised crime, Class A drugs, illegal arms dealing, human trafficking, computer and hi-tech crimes, money laundering, extortion, kidnapping, and murder' – bore more than a passing resemblance to the remit of its predecessor the National Crime Squad. The accusation is that this was reorganisation for the sake of it. SOCA would now be absorbed into May's National Crime Agency – sometimes referred to as Britain's FBI – which has a remit, according to its website to 'tackle serious and organised crime, strengthen our borders, fight fraud and cyber-crime, and protect children and young people from sexual abuse and exploitation'.[81] May experienced some difficulty in defending the restructuring on *The Andrew Marr Show*:

AM:... SOCA, the new body SOCA, what was wrong with the old system that you need to bring in a new body?

TM: Well the National Crime Agency will have within it what was SOCA but it will have a number of what are called 'commands'. It's going to focus on a number of different areas. It's going to have an economic crime command for the first time.[82]

One notes that money laundering had already been within the remit of SOCA, which makes the economic crime command seem a bogus first.

So was this to restructure at great expense over a quibble? For some, May was also following a pattern of concession to the securitariat – the intelligence and police chiefs – which had begun in the Blair years: some commentators lament this environment of nationalised crime-busting. In an article for the *Guardian*, Simon Jenkins escorts us back to what he considers a more sensible era:

Thatcher's home secretary, Willie Whitelaw, told a story of how his police and security chiefs would troop into his office for an annual chat. They always said the same thing. They needed more power, more weapons, more phone taps, more surveillance, more powers of detention, more general curbs on the freedom of British subjects in the name of national security. Whitelaw would roar with laughter and shout: 'Well done, chaps.' The chaps would smile and reply: 'It's always worth a try, chief.' Whitelaw would order a round of drinks and send them packing.

That stopped under Blair.[83]

The conservative mind – and May is an example of this – sometimes exhibits a tendency to consider the police as emblems of the state and therefore to be battled: hence her evident pride in having 'taken them on'. But very often the dislike of the state does not always extend to herself as minister. By early 2016, May was preparing plans to handover terrorist operations from the Met to the National Crime Agency – and the NCA would report directly to the home secretary. It is difficult to square this increased centralisation with her wish for the people to be more connected with the police.

STEPHEN LAWRENCE AND HILLSBOROUGH

Is there any justice in May's critical attitude towards the police?

Unfortunately, it is possible to point to instances in the lead-up to and during the Coalition years, where the police have acted in a way which has caused many people, and not just Theresa May, some concern. It amounts to a dark pattern in our public life.

The murder of Stephen Lawrence was carried out by five or six white youths in Eltham in south-east London on 22nd April 1993. It is a measure of how sluggishly and ineptly the investigation moved – as well as of the slow progress of all government enquiries – that this remote event would land on May's desk. The murder laid bare prejudices within the police: an enquiry led by Sir William Macpherson had concluded in 1999 after an investigation into the murder that the force was 'institutionally racist': a racist murder had been compounded by racist policing. Years later Peter Francis, a former undercover police officer, would report that his superiors had asked him to find 'dirt' on members of the Lawrence family shortly after the murder. Even today it is difficult to say what is more shocking – the incompetence of the original investigation where police appeared not to know the law, or this cavalier approach to a family's right to privacy and to their grief. May was blunt, calling the Francis revelations 'profoundly shocking and disturbing'.[84] The enormity of that verdict was one no home secretary could ignore. Certainly, it has remained with May. Years later, on the steps of Downing Street, having just accepted the offer to form a new administration, she would state: 'If you're black, you're treated more harshly by the criminal justice system than if you're white.'[85] It was impossible not to think of Lawrence when she said this.

The Hillsborough disaster dated from even further back. It happened during the 1989-90 FA Cup semi-final between Liverpool and Sheffield Wednesday. A crush ensued in two central pens in the Leppings Lane stand. It was the tragic consequence of a moment of misjudgement after chief superintendent David Duckenfield ordered the opening of a gate, leading to what would turn out to be a deadly influx of supporters. This was an isolated mistake, but it is now understood that the number of fatalities was especially high – 96 dead and 766 injured – because the police's system of crowd control was also faulty. The ensuing investigation again illustrated widespread corruption in the police. The Lord Taylor report would later call the police 'evasive witnesses'. He went on:

> It is a matter of regret that at the hearing, and in their submissions, the South Yorkshire Police were not prepared to concede they were

in any respect at fault in what occurred... [T]he police case was to blame the fans for being late and drunk, and to blame the Club for failing to monitor the pens... Such an unrealistic approach gives cause for anxiety as to whether lessons have been learnt. It would have been more seemly and encouraging for the future if responsibility had been faced.[86]

The sequel to this incompetence was an attempt to smear football fans – unfortunate slurs on the characters of the dead and injured.

Worse was to come. The subsequent Hillsborough Independent Panel uncovered the full extent of the cover-up with the majority of the blame placed on the police.

May would be stern with the Police Federation in 2016:

I do not believe there can be anyone in this hall who does not recognise the enormity of those verdicts, nor can there be anyone in policing who does not now understand the need to face up to the past and right the wrongs that continue to jeopardise the work of police officers today.[87]

For May, these were not isolated instances but evidence of a rotten organisation. She has also expressed concern about police misuse of 'stop and search' powers on the streets. These powers, according to the findings of an inspection by Her Majesty's Inspectorate of Constabulary, in about 1 in 4 cases are still not conducted according to reasonable grounds. When one considers that around a quarter of a million of these stops are made per year, there remains the likelihood that there are over 60,000 instances a year – or if you prefer, around 5,000 a month – when people are on the receiving end of upsetting encounters with the police. It is primarily a racial problem – you are seven times more likely to be stopped by police if you are from a minority ethnic background. May introduced reforms to the Police and Criminal Evidence Act Code of Practice A to refine their use. It may be that we haven't heard the last on this – May pledged on their introduction that if the abuses didn't cease then she would return with primary legislation to face the problem. In early 2016, the police regulator reported that the police hadn't been persuaded to change their ways.[88]

Other incidents complete the grim picture. One was the death of Ian Tomlinson, a street vendor who died after being struck by police officer Simon Harwood during the 2009 G-20 summit protests. Another, much less serious, was 'Plebgate', where minister Andrew Mitchell was unfairly dismissed from his post as Government Chief Whip for calling police 'plebs' during an altercation in Downing Street: a libel court would ultimately decide against Mitchell, but seven officers were accused of misconduct in relation to the matter. One reason one tends to think of Theresa May as a sound home secretary is that she was successfully opposing an institution which was notably on the defensive – and on the defensive because of their own failings. One also suspects her feelings towards the police won't have been mitigated by the police vindictiveness surrounding the dismissal of Damian Green in late 2017.

Even so, an irony must also be noted: a recent YouGov survey from 2016 showed that 71 per cent of the public trust the police, while only 15 per cent trust politicians. These findings can create an atmosphere of unreality about the famous dressing-down that May gave to the Police Federation in 2014. If the YouGov poll is anything to go by, it might very easily, one suspects, have been delivered the other way around from the police to the politicians.

In this instance, May entered to smatterings of polite applause, but exited in an atmosphere of stunned silence. Here she is in full flow:

> The Federation was created by an Act of Parliament and it can be reformed by an Act of Parliament. If you do not change of your own accord, we will impose change on you.[89]

It was a theatrical moment but not without substance. May put forward 36 recommendations which the force adopted immediately after the speech. The reforms included an end to the automatic right of the federation to enrol police officers as members – henceforth the emphasis would be on the freedom of officers to choose. The payment of fees to the federation would also be optional. May demanded to see federation accounts – in 2016, backed by the righteousness of the *Daily Mail*, she would suggest that the federation was still using subscription fees to fund holiday homes, and threaten this time to cut public funding altogether. One suspects that her move to Downing Street was met with mixed reactions by the force. On the one hand, at least she had gone – on the other, she was now more powerful than ever.

Was May right to 'take on the police'? Few would deny that the Stephen Lawrence case, and the Hillsborough disaster – although historic snapshots of the police – do show a culture that needed amending. No home secretary could have completely absolved the police when faced with these revelations, although one suspects the Blair government – witness for example, Blair's defence of the police with regards to the shooting of John Charles de Menezes – would have been less combative than May. It might also be said that her police cuts, when set against, for example, the Lansley-Hunt reforms at health seem wise, particularly if violent crime statistics do not continue to rise in the next years.

But in another area May had far more difficulty. Furthermore, her failure to manage it would arguably contribute to the country's decision to leave the EU in 2016.

This area was immigration.

15 – MAY AND IMMIGRATION

In the summer of 2013, if you happened to be walking through any one of the London boroughs of Ealing, Brent, Hounslow, Redbridge, Barking or Dagenham, you might find yourself looking, somewhat unexpectedly, at a strange van. If you looked a little harder, you might wonder whether you were looking at something stranger still: a bigoted van. A billboard on its side read: 'In the UK illegally? Go home or face arrest.'

Thus did the debacle of the Go Home vans begin. Not that it was really as ongoing as all that: Theresa May's Home Office would soon disown it as a mere pilot scheme.

But it would have been worth looking a little closer at the side of that van. In the upper right of the billboard the claim was written: '106 arrests last year in the area★'. That asterisk, initially mysterious, turned out to be a footnote. Zoe Williams explained: 'The asterisk is there to indicate that this is a made-up figure, relating to no particular area, and no particular week.'[90] Put another way, May's department had gone to considerable expense to state something in apparently unequivocal terms, only to offer the caveat that the statement didn't mean anything. At £10,000 – the cost of the stunt – this must be among the more expensive walk-backs in history, especially from a government that had committed itself to tackling waste. Perhaps the damage to the well-being of shoppers was minimal: it's unlikely that many did really stop and examine these vans, since the Home Office would later concede that there had only been two of them across all six boroughs.

One is left to imagine these two passive-aggressive van routes wending through the poorest parts of London. If it were any other minister we might wonder whether she was even aware of what was happening. But this is Theresa May, who gets only five hours sleep a night, and is meant to be in control of her brief. One excuse she is never in a position to give is that her back was turned: because her back is never turned. To rob her of the traits of thoroughness and decisiveness is to rob her of a large portion of the qualities she's meant to have.

What was the intention of the scheme? It seems unlikely that anyone can have seriously expected them to reduce immigration levels. Was it an attempt to give the impression of Home Office activity on a key Cameron pledge to reduce net migration into the tens of thousands? Perhaps the motivation was electoral – to peel away some UKIP voters in advance of the 2014 European Parliament elections.

It is the sort of *Thick of It* folly that often happens in government: without it, Armando Iannucci would need a new career. A hare-brained idea sprouts, no one puts the brakes on it, and then within 24 hours the home secretary finds herself on the *Today* programme defending a policy that she wishes hadn't gone ahead. One could enlarge upon the absurdity of it. It would have taken a highly sensitive illegal immigrant to return to their country of origin pursuant to a footnoted threat on the side of a van. But none of this quite explains why the story ran so long. It was not just the silliness of it all: it was because there had been a glimpse of something that May had long claimed to stand in opposition to – nastiness. The unfortunate impression can sometimes be that May doesn't mind a bit of nastiness from time to time – provided immigrants are on the receiving end of it.

Of course, one shouldn't overdo this. It is fair to point out that the Go Home vans stand out in May's time at the Home Office as a rare mess. Even so, it is instructive to know how her errors look. A May mistake often has the feel of having been embarked upon for reasons of political expediency. The Go Home vans saga is reminiscent of the decision to appoint Boris Johnson foreign secretary: in that instance, the Brexit camp was appeased for the time being, but at the future cost to the British people of Johnson representing them overseas. Each stems from a desire to move the pieces on an important issue while really doing little – we shall note in Chapter 24 that Johnson was moved to a great office of state, even as that office was sliced in three. May's moves can be clever in narrow political terms, but less admirable in moral terms – and moral failing, one expects, will eventually rebound on her politically anyhow. The episode of the Go Home vans enabled her to seem tough on immigration for a small price tag, but it is hard to paint it as an overall win for her.

May's centralising instincts were also in evidence. Rita Chadha, from the Migrant and Refugee Forum of East London, was quoted as saying in relation to the Go Home vans scheme:

> None of the boroughs knew anything about it. No local council had been consulted. Even the police knew nothing about it.[91]

This might be mere thoughtlessness, but there is just a slight redolence of the imposition of the poll tax under Margaret Thatcher about it: a tendency towards the roughshod but quixotic decision. It is not hard to imagine some future Theresa May, cocooned in power, one day doubling down on some misguided notion of this nature – although post snap election she will likely never have sufficient power to do the stupid things a large majority can sometimes enable you to do. And stubbornness will lead to the unnecessary alienation of those who should have been on her side. In relation to the Go Home vans episode, Vince Cable said, 'It was stupid and offensive, and I think it is very unlikely that it will continue.'[92] It didn't continue, but a dangerous tendency had been exhibited.

THE LABOUR INHERITANCE

What does Theresa May think about immigration?

The immigration story of the Cameron administration is one of frustration and failure to reverse the large increases of net migration during the Blair era. Blair had been obsessed during his first term in government from 1997-2001 about the asylum system that he would later recall, in execrable prose, as having been 'broken, incapable and adrift in a sea of storms'[93].

But when it came to 2004, and the expansion of the European Union to include the so-called A8 countries – the Czech Republic, Estonia, Hungary, Latvia, Lithuania, Poland, Slovakia and Slovenia – the Blair government didn't take a hard line. These countries constituted what Donald Rumsfeld called New Europe – this phrase might be deemed a cheerful salutation to those countries who, unlike EU stalwarts such as France and Germany, were more inclined to support the 2003 invasion of Iraq. From Blair's perspective, there might have been specific diplomatic benefits to be garnered from a lenient approach. The main reason why immigration in the UK increased so dramatically as a result of the accession of the A8 countries, was not – as is often written – that the Blair government had taken its eye off the ball and produced no decent report about the possible effects of A8 accession. In fact, a voluminous report, so badly written as to be virtually impregnable, had been produced by a group of leading economists on behalf of the Home Office entitled 'The impact of EU enlargement on migration flows'. The trouble was more prosaic – it was that no one had read it.

Specifically, nobody seems to have given proper attention to page 57, which points out that if Germany chose to impose 'transition controls' on migrant workers, then a significant portion – around a third – would migrate instead to the UK. Britain, Ireland and Sweden didn't impose these controls.[94] When Germany did, it created a spike of migrants towards those other three. The Office for National Statistic estimates that between 2004 and 2012, the net inflow of migrants from the new members was 423,000: the real figure is probably higher and we won't know a more precise figure until the 2011 census is properly analysed.[95] Events had overtaken the Blair government. But there was a significant strain within the administration that didn't mind the increase anyway. Research led by Performance and Innovation Unit deputy director Jonathan Portes – work praised by Blair himself – had argued in favour of the economic benefits of migration. The Blair government, in seeing so much influx to the country, had got roughly what it wanted. The report had announced its conclusions in the foreword:

> The evidence indicates that, whilst migrants constitute a very diverse set of people, with different characteristics, contributing in different ways to the UK economy and society, overall migration has the potential to deliver significant economic benefits.[96]

This view – level-headed and couched in the language of reason – would not survive the increased migration of the Blair years. By 2010, with the rise of UKIP, it had become one of the most important issues for voters – after perhaps the state of the economy. By 2015 and certainly by the time of the 2016 referendum, it would become arguably the main issue, though partly because it had become interwoven in the minds of many with the economic welfare of the nation.

In its 2010 manifesto, the Conservative Party had pledged an annual limit on the number of non-EU economic migrants to the UK, with access only for those who bring 'most value to the British economy'.[97] Over time it emerged that the government would cut net migration into the tens of thousands per year. May had been lumbered with an impossible task. It is true that in 2012 she managed to push the number beneath 200,000 for the first time in around a decade. But her record would in general be one of failure, as net migration spiked in the last years in the Coalition, reaching 333,000 for 2015.[98] The inexorable rise of a figure that both the Conservative Party and

UKIP wanted to keep as low as possible is the other consistent theme, along with the Osborne cuts, to all that May attempted at the Home Office.

Typically, we never quite know what our protagonist feels about this failure to lower the migration figures. Does she mind it all that much? Does she seriously intend to fix it? This opens up onto more general questions: is May's failure to 'tackle' immigration attributable to any incompetence on her part? Or is the system, in a world of porous borders and linked-up technology, simply impossible to fix? This author suspects that May has tried hard, and with reasonable competence, to remedy a situation which does gnaw at the Nick Timothy in her. But she is in the position of someone standing on a beach and raising a hand to try and prevent the onset of a tidal wave. In the time after Brexit, it seemed possible that the country might discover that though 17 million people had expressed their willingness to be posted alongside her on that beach, a tidal wave would remain a tidal wave – and globalisation still globalisation. In this regard May might need to accept the limits of her office. Even so, by the time May became prime minister, her inscrutability on this issue was becoming another frustration: by 2018, the future of the country continues to depend on whether May wishes to fight for a new arrangement regarding borders in preference to complete access to the single market – or whether she shall plump for access to the single market, with perhaps only cosmetic alteration to border policy.

In the Phase One agreement signed in December 2017, May conceded the right of EU citizens residing in the UK on the date of EU withdrawal to retain their family reunification rights, and offered a 'transparent, smooth and streamlined' approach for applicants. To the Leaver, this looks somewhat like capitulation: it begs the question what the vote was for if there is to be such affinity between life post-EU and life during our membership of it. The Remainer might be permitted to wonder whether the principal result of the rupture will be to have one's passport change, like a ruddy man choking, from burgundy to blue.

THE TRADITIONAL LURCH FROM CRISIS TO CRISIS OF A HOME SECRETARY OF THE UNITED KINGDOM

In 2011, a 'crisis' arose out of a decision that looks odd against the backdrop I have just described: it was May's decision to relax – briefly – the UK's borders. This was intended as a short-term measure: May had ordered the scaling back of passport controls on people entering from the European Union during the summer travel season. The supposed champion of tough border controls became for a few months the advocate of the European holiday-maker. When the relaxation of the checks on these travellers emerged, there was an immediate outcry about a possible breach of security. The memories of September 11th and the London July bombers continue to frame the discourse: one of the terrorist's chief legacies is tortuous queues.

May had already established a reputation for control freakery: if that was the case before this event, the tendency will have been exacerbated by it. Her initial defence was that the relaxation was a pilot scheme – a defence also used, as we have seen, during the Go Home vans saga. She ended up claiming that UK Border Force officials, and in particular UK Border Force boss Brodie Clark, had gone beyond their remits and darkly suggested that he must take responsibility for 'unauthorised actions'.[99] Here, she was outflanked by Yvette Cooper who jubilantly produced a memo that appeared to contradict May's position. Reading the allegedly offensive memo in full one comes into an understanding of how whipped-up many of our contemporary 'crises' are. Not to fully absolve May from attempting to blame the matter on Clark, but the supposedly scandalous document instead reads like a record of reasonable good sense.

> On HMI authority (or CIO authority outside HMI operational hours) you can:
>
> 1. Stop opening chips on EU passports
> 2. Stop swiping children's passports on EU if they are in a school group or clearly travelling with family
> 3. Stop routinely asking questions of visa holders. In other words, once you have established the passenger is the rightful holder of a genuine document which contains a visa which confers leave to enter you should allow them to proceed, subject of course to a WI check.
>
> In all instances, however, if you feel there is a specific risk, you may continue to perform these discontinued checks *at discretion*.[100]

This then is the domain of the home secretary. It is an essentially prosaic reality, distinct from the Farageish world of shady alarm and the grim England-ruining spectre of the Other. Instead we discover a world of memoranda into which grammatical infelicity is permitted to enter; the entrenched jargon of process (WI, HMI); and again, the snaking airport queue, always at its longest when you're at your tiredest. All this bears no relation to the UKIP soundbites with which the far right have sometimes aimed to lend a dark glamour to the essentially lonely act of settling in the UK. Immigration often works like this: like most fears, it isn't scary up close, when you take its measure.

May experienced another episode of this nature in the shape of the 2014 passport crisis. It is another opportunity to reflect on the essential misery of the job of home secretary: one is in charge of a range of dull procedures where there is no glory in their going right, but great blame attached to their going wrong. Here's how it happened. In the summer of 2014, the passport services saw what Cameron and May would later present as an unforeseen spike in passport applications. Passport offices were ill-equipped to handle the numbers. The figures were alarming: 34,635 people faced delays in the issuing of passports. Ex-Labour ministers lamented a falling-off in once-high standards: there is a sense that cuts to the passport office budget may have caused difficulty in providing the sort of flexibility it required. May was charged with fixing it all. What ensued is another example of May's reluctance to take ownership of a problem. Her claim that the high numbers of applications had been unforeseeable proved to be false. It had indeed been foreseen – and, a little embarrassingly, foreseen in public in a foreword of a 2013 report expressly written for her to read. This was by Paul Pugh, Interim Chief Executive of the Identity and Passport Services. Here is the relevant passage:

> We continued to transfer responsibility for processing passport applications from British nationals overseas, in partnership with the Foreign and Commonwealth Office. In December 2012 we received our first applications directly from our customers overseas. This process will be complete in 2014 when IPS will be providing passport services for approximately 350,000 additional customers worldwide annually.[101]

It isn't clear whether May simply did not read it or whether she had read it and decided to tackle it at a later time. Either way, her initial reaction was to enter a period of denial. One wondered sometimes when reading the record of her time as home secretary how she would fare as prime minister should things go wrong in the full glare of publicity. Either she would be able to hide more effectively, and put up ministers to shield her from blame, or perhaps there shall come a day when there is no-one to blame, and she would need to cultivate a different response to criticism.

Eventually, May kicked into gear. She moved backroom staff to the frontlines. Meg Hillier, a former passport minister, wondered in the *Guardian* if front room staff could ever be effective now that backroom staff were being asked to vacate their posts.[102] May also instituted an extension by a year on existing passport applications, which critics saw as kicking the can down the road. But the storm passed, and May survived – as thus far she has always done. It is a leitmotif of this book that her survival instinct is not the least of her qualities.

But she always does so without offering a memorable statement of principle about what she really feels about the issue at stake – in this case, immigration. It is often left to others to report back what her real feelings are. Here for instance is Steve Hilton, David Cameron's director of strategy at the outset of the Coalition, who was charged with trying to get an entrepreneur's visa past May:

> After the normal Whitehall processes had failed, I was deputed to speak to her. It was a bruising encounter. Theresa made a simple argument very directly: the prime minister had given her a clear target, to bring net annual immigration below 100,000. She would not countenance anything that jeopardised that.[103]

But again everything shades into inscrutability. Is May here opposing the move because she does believe in lower immigration numbers? Or is she doing so because Hilton is encroaching on her brief? Once more, we do not know.

THE AIRED HUNCHES OF THERESA MAY

Which brings us to one of May's arguable low points – her speech to the Conservative Party conference in 2015.

This was May's big anti-immigration speech and, coming just after Cameron's surprise 2015 election victory, was made in the knowledge that a referendum on the UK's European membership was just around the corner. One isn't sure how much her heart was in it – in this case, one rather hopes it wasn't. In this passage she plays to the right wing of her party:

> Because when immigration is too high, when the pace of change is too fast, it's impossible to build a cohesive society. It's difficult for schools and hospitals and core infrastructure like housing and transport to cope. And we know that for people in low-paid jobs, wages are forced down even further while some people are forced out of work altogether.[104]

The objection to this is that it flies in the face of the evidence – and again evidence May was meant to have seen. In a paper written by the Department of Business Innovation and Skills – which is, in fact, under the umbrella of her own department – entitled 'Impacts of migration on UK native employment: An analytical review of the evidence', the opposite conclusion had been reached expressly for the home secretary's benefit:

> Since 2008 the performance of the UK economy has been weaker whilst net migration has remained relatively high, and during 2009 and 2010, labour market outcomes deteriorated for both UK natives and migrants. However, employment levels for UK nationals have been rising more than those of foreign nationals over the period 2012/13.[105]

This makes it clear that the weak performance of the economy was related to the global recession and not migration. Furthermore, the rising employment levels at the time May is discussing call into question her other conclusions. May is making a case that she either knows, or should know, to be false. It is true that the report presents some *obiter dicta* in the opposite direction: that 'there is evidence of some labour market displacement, particularly by non-EU migrants in recent years when the economy was in recession.' But taken in its entirety, the report obviously intends to make the opposite case, and on far greater authority than the hunches aired by May in the one speech of the year when a large number of people were likely to be listening to her.

The report is also adamant that in times of economic strength – as the Cameron administration claimed the economy to be – the labour market tends to adapt more easily to influx. May is selling a false prospectus in two respects. Firstly, she is saying that immigration is apparently disastrous for the employment prospects of UK nationals, which it isn't. Secondly, if it did have any small negative impact then it wouldn't be having it at the time of giving the speech because of the much-touted strength of the economy. James Kirkup parroted the speech in the *Daily Telegraph*:

> If you haven't seen reports of it, allow me to summarise: 'Immigrants are stealing your job, making you poorer and ruining your country. Never mind the facts, just feel angry at foreigners. And make me Conservative leader.'[106]

This might be flippant, but Kirkup is surely right that this was a leadership speech, one with a post-truth politics air about it. It doesn't necessarily read any better because her leadership run ultimately proved successful. In fact, it is difficult to think of a comparably small-minded speech by any of her predecessors.

This then is Theresa May on immigration: essentially inscrutable as to her core beliefs but determined to occasionally throw some crowd-pleasing remarks to the right of her party, and to the UKIP voter. She knows what such voters like to hear: 46.1 per cent of her Maidenhead constituents would vote to leave the EU in 2016. And yet there is that other May who, in her own words, 'gets on with the job', and is too sensible to, for instance, deny people their summer holiday because of a prevailing debate about net migration. This is May the technocrat: it is a more appealing side simply because it is more suited to her predominantly workmanlike nature. May isn't a thinker; she is someone happy to immerse herself in the running of systems. It is as if she doesn't relish the wider implications of her brief; she simply likes to have a brief.

How damaging will this eventually prove in a prime minister? On the one hand, one wouldn't wish to overpraise the notion of the 'imaginative' politician. In his memoirs, when Tony Blair philosophises he is more banal than he realises. When, in his biography, he talks about restructuring the Home Office, he is interesting because after ten years of running the country he knew a good deal about that department – it didn't matter that he had never read Foucault. If one is imaginative, one should write a novel, not run a government department. But during his premiership when he was at his most creative, he could sometimes produce – through the sheer energy of imagination – disasters such as Iraq that would have been beyond the capacity of his more prosaic predecessors to invent.

And yet there is no doubt that the powerful must select priorities and find novel ways to solve problems: Churchill would be the most effective example of this restless approach to power. Never still, never happier than when a scheme was afoot – he could spin out a solution from scratch. May is emphatically not this kind of politician. And yet she has arguably been fortunate in the historic moment in which she is asked to play such a prominent role: her initial task is clear – to leave the European Union while keeping the UK intact. What one worries about is the things that she might be able to avoid doing from an *electoral* standpoint but which she actually does need to do *morally* – climate change is the most pressing example here. One cannot imagine Blair or Churchill ever leaving that alone, but one can easily imagine May doing so, unless it became politically impossible for her not to do so.

Another is foreign policy where there is no blueprint for prime ministers to follow, and which she seems to have little flair for. Interestingly, there was more than you'd expect in her time at the Home Office to make educated guesses about how she would handle that side of her brief.

16 – MAY AND EXTRADITION

The life of a home secretary is of course doggedly domestic. We have also seen that its principal character is prosaic: it is a life of memoranda wielded at border officials; the recitation of immigration statistics, or the hearing of them recited in accusation at oneself; and it can involve much time fretting helplessly about the murder rate. Blair used to say that the Home Office brief was the hardest job in government because it is the only one where your clientele is actively trying to oppose you: murderers and terrorists do not attend meetings. It brings us, as perhaps no other office does, close to something else: the tedium of power which, for so many, is a persuasive enough reason not to seek it. There is also a Le Carré-esque sense of closeness, almost claustrophobia, about the role of home secretary – of being stuck in a room with a set of intractable problems with little more than a view of what Tennyson, no fan of London architecture, called the 'long, unlovely street' for company:

> While far away
> The noise of life begins again,
> And ghastly thro' the drizzling rain
> On the bald street breaks the blank day.[107]

The job has a run-down and miserable feel that stems, one sometimes suspects, from its sheer Britishness, and the way it opens up onto a certain redolence of national decline.

But in the age of globalisation, even the home secretary can find the international situation insinuating itself into their life. The student of May's time at the Home Office can still find, strewn along that busy course, early hints of the future prime minister's capacity for foreign affairs.

THE GARY MCKINNON AFFAIR

According to the American authorities, if at some time between February 2001 and March 2002, you felt the patriotic fervour stirring within and the consequent necessity of joining up to the United States Military, then you might have gone onto the website www.defense.gov and found yourself faced, not with any information about what to do next, but instead an unexpected accusation: 'Your security is crap'.

Also according to the US authorities, if around the same time you were awaiting the supplies of munitions in the Atlantic as a member of the US fleet, you might find that your delivery never came. And at some point during that period, it is alleged that an employee somewhere in the vast military complex of the US, turned on his or her computer to find the following critique of their country's foreign policy segueing into a portentous announcement:

> US foreign policy is akin to Government-sponsored terrorism these days... It was not a mistake that there was a huge security stand down on September 11 last year... I am SOLO. I will continue to disrupt at the highest levels.[108]

Finally, it is also the case that if you were an auditor for the US Military some time after this period you might happen – perhaps with a hooked eyebrow – on an unusual outgoing in the accounts of that august organisation: $700,000 spent on researching the disruption activities of one Gary McKinnon.

Several facts about McKinnon would cause his file to land on the desk of Home Secretary Theresa May. The first is that he is Scottish and therefore under her jurisdiction. Another is that he has – we now know – Asperger's Syndrome.

McKinnon believes in UFOs – or at least his claim is that his hack was an attempt to search for evidence of them. For the US government, the case has always been a relatively simple matter of breach of security, and the consequent wish to punish the perpetrator for his gumption. In the UK, it became a case about mental health, and therefore a cause célèbre for well-known people like novelist Nick Hornby and actress Emma Noble, both of whom have children with autism. This knowledge of McKinnon's autism was in the future. Instead, things began as you would expect them to begin when someone has hacked into the computer system of the world's only superpower. McKinnon's computer was seized after a police interview in 2002. By November 2002, a grand jury in the Eastern District of Virginia had entered seven counts of computer-related crime against him. But at that point in time, McKinnon had something in his favour: this all occurred before the US-UK Extradition Treaty of 2003 had been agreed and its associated act pushed through Parliament. This meant that McKinnon could not be extradited. McKinnon therefore entered an administrative limbo.

During this time, he began to fear – the Americans would say, irrationally so – that he would end up in Guantanamo Bay. In fact, the Americans ended up explicitly saying that McKinnon would not serve in any supermax facility. The affair nudges us back pre-Trump and pre-Obama to Bush's gung-ho and occasionally harsh America: public opinion about its treatment of prisoners would be an important aspect of the case against McKinnon's extradition.

The extradition treaty came into force in 2007 and remains controversial. It is characterised by its opponents as imbalanced – that it is easier for the US to extradite UK citizens than for the UK to extradite US counterparts. It has also been seen as a Blairite lapdog arrangement – the UK as loyal junior partner, an extradition equivalent of those embarrassing meets at Camp David where Blair looked happy to be there, and Bush presumptuous about an ally he seems in retrospect lucky to have had. The nub of the matter is that the US requires 'reasonable suspicion' to extradite in accordance with the Fourth Amendment to the Constitution; the UK requires 'probable cause' – which is considered by some to be a higher standard of proof. In 2012, reviewing the whole matter of extradition, the Home Affairs Select Committee sought to show that the position was too nuanced to merit outrage:

> ... there is a body of respectable legal opinion which suggests that there is little or no distinction in practice between the 'probable cause' and 'reasonable suspicion' tests. Nevertheless, the imbalance in the wording of the Treaty, which sets a test for extradition from the US but not from the UK, has created the widespread impression of unfairness

within the public consciousness and, at a more practical level, gives US citizens the right to a hearing to establish 'probable cause' that is denied to UK citizens.[109]

On the face of it, this is slightly less than clinching: if a treaty is a thing made up of words then the imbalanced wording of a treaty is an imbalanced treaty. Sloppiness of drafting had caused a headache. But perhaps hardliner opponents of the treaty were asking for an impossible world. At the centre of it all is the fact that different countries have different laws, and that it is reasonable for treaties to fit around those. Baroness Scotland of Asthal had told the House of Lords in the debate around the 2003 Act: 'Complete reciprocity has never been a feature of our extradition arrangements.'[110]

It was a call for realpolitik. For now, these controversies were in the future. The celebrities hadn't yet queued up, and Nick Clegg – who would be another voice ranged against the existing extradition laws – had not yet become deputy prime minister. When the act rubber-stamping the treaty came into effect in 2007, McKinnon became subject to bail conditions, and was forced to sign in each day at the police station. He was also confined to his home each night.

A man with a proclaimed love of science fiction had become embroiled in the wrong kind of narrative: he had become a legal drama.

By 2008, McKinnon's lawyers were telling the House of Lords that they could block the extradition if there had been abuse of process, and the House of Lords were disagreeing. The case boomeranged back from the European Court of Human Rights to undergo judicial review. McKinnon's lawyers continued to argue that May's predecessor as Home Secretary, Alan Johnson, had overlooked medical evidence that McKinnon would take his own life in the event of his extradition. The *Daily Mail* under Paul Dacre, concerned to irritate the Brown administration, continued its campaign on McKinnon's behalf, and was for once on the side of the vulnerable: even a stopped clock tells the right time twice a day.

Like this the case continued, fought as much in newspaper columns as in the courts. McKinnon undoubtedly benefited from the tigerish advocacy of his mother, Janis Sharp. Feisty and street-fighting, one suspects that if everyone had a mother like her, our extradition system would fall apart. Her advocacy contributed to the popularity of the cause: whereas for Johnson, a simplistic outrage had arisen out of a complex case. By 2010, the case had passed to May. Her decision whether to extradite would have to be made under Article 3 of the European Convention of Human Rights. This is meant to have a high bar. As home secretary, Johnson's instinct had been to comply with the Americans. He explained his criticism of May's approach in an article for the *Daily Telegraph*:

> ... she deported a man with practically the same conditions very recently. It's also my understanding that, as recently as July, she wrote to the US authorities stating that there were no legal or medical grounds on which she could stop McKinnon's extradition. She also set out the ramifications for national security if she lowered the Article 3 bar.[III]

Nevertheless, May decided not to extradite. For some, it was a humane gesture. For others, it seemed she had bowed to populist pressure. Here she is explaining her decision to the House of Commons on 16th October 2012:

> After careful consideration of all of the relevant material, I have concluded that Mr McKinnon's extradition would give rise to such a high risk of him ending his life that a decision to extradite would be incompatible with Mr McKinnon's human rights.[112]

Sharp was understandably jubilant: 'Thank you Theresa May from the bottom of my heart – I always knew you had the strength and courage to do the right thing.'[113] Years later, William Hague – Foreign Secretary at this time – would tell the story of US officials complaining to him, and append his own response: 'This was a decision made by the Home Secretary after considering all the facts... Mrs May is known in government for going into things thoroughly... but she is not known for changing her mind once she has made a decision. When she's decided something, my advice is to accept that's the end of it.'[114]

In some quarters, the decision is now seen as a sign of strength, and has even been interpreted as a signal that May will be a prime minister who 'stands up to the Americans' (this has not always been the case, if one thinks of that image of her holding hands with Donald Trump at the White House). It used to be said of Margaret Thatcher that she would turn up at the White House and tell Ronald Reagan what she thought – and then tell him what he thought. Some people will always like this: the plucky Brit standing up for good old-fashioned common sense. But the episode might just as easily be seen as giving in to populist sentiment. For critics such as Alan Johnson, the law is one thing for May when nobody is looking, and quite another when celebrities are queuing up. Beneath the steely May image, there is this wish to be liked – a wish, to refer back to her most famous speech, not to be *seen to be* nasty. As we have glimpsed in the episode of the Go Home vans, this is a different thing than not being nasty.

ABU QATADA

The other high-profile extradition case that May faced during her time as home secretary – and which she also mentioned in her announcement speech with which we began this book – was that of Abu Qatada.

This is a man many more times dangerous than McKinnon. The hacker is essentially passive-aggressive, confined to his room. Qatada has always been out on the streets – an old-fashioned agitator. He was born on the West Bank at a time when Jordan had occupied that territory: his life gets rapidly less innocent from that point onwards. A stint in Pakistan may or may not have seen him forge ties with the fledgling Al-Qaeda organisation: he denies it but years later, in the aftermath of 9/11, a poem in praise of Osama bin Laden, attributed to Qatada, was widely circulated. Qatada is that highly 21st century animal, the terrorist-poet: he is able to endorse the mass killing of Westerners while also retaining a sense of himself as an intellectual. But if we wish to read Abu Qatada's poetry, we are likely to be disappointed. It has apparently experienced the fate described here by Robyn Creswell and Bernard Haykel in the *New Yorker*:

> Isis, Al Qaeda, and other Islamist movements produce a huge amount of verse. The vast majority of it circulates online, in a clandestine network of social-media accounts, mirror sites, and proxies, which appear and disappear with bewildering speed, thanks to surveillance and hacking.[115]

But a representative poem by Osama bin Laden himself might be quoted as an example of the genre Qatada is working in:

> Father, I have travelled a long time among
> deserts and cities.
> It has been a long journey, Father,
> among valleys and mountains,
> So long that I have forgotten my tribe, my
> cousins, even humankind.[116]

Fig. 15 Abu Qatada[117]

Qatada can sometimes seem like this — someone who has 'forgotten... humankind'.

Qatada was expelled from Kuwait after the First Gulf War. He claims afterwards to have been tortured in Jordan. By June 1994, he had been granted asylum in the UK on the strength of false documents and granted leave to remain in June 1998. Around this time, he allegedly plotted to carry out terror attacks in Jordan, including a foiled plot against an American school in Amman. He is also alleged to have targeted Israeli and American tourists and western diplomats. The welcome he had received at the hands of Her Majesty's Government did nothing to soften his views: his is the kind of rage which does not recognise hospitality. By 1999, he had delivered a rancid sermon outside the Finsbury Park Mosque recommending that Americans 'should be attacked, wherever they were'. Qatada continued to refuse to make allowances for his hosts: he claimed there was no distinction between Americans, English and Jews — which of course, at the basic human level there isn't, except that Qatada was here espousing blanket murder. Reliably anti-Semitic, he reserves a special place of loathing for the Jewish people. In 1995, he had already issued a fatwa against lapsed Muslims and their families. Thus does an angry man declare war on the entire world: his is the morbid and essentially adolescent tale of the unappeasable self. The September 11th attacks in 2001 were a high point for Qatada. It was not just a thrilling act of war, but also a triumph perpetrated by a protégée: Muhammad Atta, one of the attackers, had been a devotee of Qatada's sermons.

It is a record of crime posing as scholarly respectability.

By 2002, the law had begun to catch up with Qatada. The one-time glory of his notoriety may have come to seem of ambiguous value. October 2002 found him in Belmarsh prison under a sentence he would become used to over the next years: threat of deportation. A hint of the bully's cowardice surfaces around this time. Qatada has often let it be known that deportation means to him fear of torture in Jordan. 2005 saw Qatada placed under control order under the new Prevention of Terrorism Act. In 2009, the law lords overturned a previous decision by the Court of Appeal which had stated that a return to Jordan would have breached Qatada's rights to a fair trial under Article 6 of the European Convention on Human Rights. On that occasion Lord Hoffmann had declared: 'There is in my opinion no authority for a rule that... the risk of the use of evidence obtained by torture necessarily amounts to a flagrant denial of justice.'[118] This appeared to align the House of Lords with the Cheney-Rumsfeld view on torture, and flies in the face of much research on the topic. It also contradicted the position the House of Lords had earlier taken on the matter in *A v Secretary of State for the Home Department (No 2)*. It was a depressing instance of fickleness in our highest courts on a point that ought not to be up for debate in the era of water-boarding. One suspects the judges were swayed by the unpleasantness of the personality at the centre of the trial: a case of playing the man and not the ball. It was unsurprisingly overturned by the European Court of Human Rights, providing the unpleasant spectacle of Qatada being awarded £2,500 as reimbursement for the whole ordeal.

This decision was handed down on 17th January 2012, by which time our heroine was in position as home secretary.

Meanwhile, other issues had surfaced. Qatada's continued stay in the UK was costly, as London Mayor Boris Johnson explained in a good article for the *Daily Telegraph*:

> He has never contributed to the UK economy, never paid a penny of tax; and yet he has cost at least £500,000 in benefits and other payments, and the bill is set to soar. In tough economic times, Abu Qatada represents a completely mad and unnecessary expense for the police – and a throwback to an era of public-sector waste.[119]

In 2013, the Court of Appeal had agreed with Qatada's lawyers that it would be wrong for the cleric to face extradition to a jurisdiction where there was a realistic chance of evidence being used against him that had been obtained under torture. May would later state that the appeal had been spurious and rail against the European Court of Human Rights as well. (Interestingly, we have just seen her hiding behind Article 3 of the convention in order not to extradite McKinnon). However, May found a solution to the problem by negotiating a treaty with Jordan, in which the Jordanians provided assurances that evidence obtained under torture would not be used against him. This successful deportation has a sequel: when he returned to Jordan, Qatada was cleared of the 1998 bombings campaign and was last heard of in 2014 offering a lukewarm critique of Isis whereby he denounced the radical movement's treatment of fellow Muslims, while roundly endorsing its treatment of westerners. Despite May's intervention, Qatada is still somewhere unknown, dreaming of murder, or poetry, or both.

Did all this mean that May would always be tough or smart on terrorism? One thinks of her response to the Westminster attacks ('Enough is enough'): she would become comfortable in the language of outrage. And a Britain without Qatada would be a happier place. The episode showed May to be capable of decisive decision-making and imaginative solutions when the goal before her was clear.

THE EUROPEAN ARREST WARRANT

We have seen how one aspect of the Qatada case was the contention surrounding the overturning of the 2009 House of Lords decision by the higher European Court of Human Rights. But we have also seen May shielded by the Human Rights Act in relation to the Gary McKinnon decision. Asked to pick which case really illustrates May's attitude to the Strasbourg court, it isn't difficult to plump for the first. May has long let it be known that she would like to see the Human Rights Act scrapped. Here is a much-criticised passage from her speech to the Conservative Party conference in 2011:

> We all know the stories about the Human Rights Act... about the illegal immigrant who cannot be deported because, and I am not making this up, he had a pet cat.[120]

This was May again in tribal mode. One notes the strain in that 'I am not making this up'. When May strays beyond her natural seriousness into humour she must fall back on exaggeration: this can never be funny because by definition it cannot be based on the truth where comedy is to be found. More important-ly, her information turned out to be false. The Judicial Office looked into the matter and returned with the claim that she had misrepresented the case. Ken Clarke, ever blunt, called the claim 'childish'.

However, May arrived at a more nuanced position when it came to the decision on whether to opt in on the European Arrest Warrant.

This warrant is operative across all European member states: once it is issued it requires the relevant state to arrest and detain the individual in question. It is considered by most peo-ple to be a useful tool of enforcement in an era of international crime. One person who doesn't think so is Jacob Rees-Mogg, whom Theresa May would clash with on this occasion. Speak-ing at a Bruges Group event, Rees-Mogg had called the Euro-pean Arrest Warrant 'an important stepping stone towards a single European criminal law',[121] and claimed to see in it an in-fringement on ancient rights. He raised the possibility that UK nationals were under threat from scenarios whereby 'a corrupt policeman in a distant country with a foreign language insists you're arrested and there's no protection'.[122] We have seen from our chapter on the police that the corrupt policeman is perhaps just as likely to be found in the UK as the foreign territories Rees-Mogg refers to. But Fair Trials International also argues that the system can lead to injustice: warrants have sometimes been issued years after the alleged crime, and there have been instances of police brutality in relation to the warrant also.

At any rate, in holding these strong opinions, and being a man famously meticulous about parliamentary process, Rees-Mogg was not likely to be happy about giving them up without a debate and a vote. This made it a source of outrage for him when May tried to bypass parliament over the issue.

The context to all this was the Treaty of Lisbon, signed on behalf of the UK by Gordon Brown in December 2007. Pursuant to this, member states would need to decide whether or not to opt in or out of over 130 criminal justice measures. May opted out of them in their entirety, which was the only way to opt back in to 35 of them – most notably the European Arrest Warrant. Initially, it was indicated that MPs would get a chance to vote specifically on the warrant – in the event of it, Speaker John Bercow revealed that MPs would have the opportunity to vote on only 11 of the measures, and not the warrant. May's mistake here, by her own admission on *Desert Island Discs* a few weeks later, was to misjudge the mood of the chamber. The suspicion remains that there was such contention surrounding the warrant that the only way to avoid a rebellion on the issue was to eschew a vote. One by one, Conservative MPs lambasted a surprised May. It was 'a travesty of our parliamentary proceedings' (Bill Cash); it 'seemed sly' (Sir Richard Shephard); it was 'the way of tyranny' (Rees-Mogg).[123] In the end David Cameron himself had to rush back from the Lord Mayor's Banquet to stave off a rebellion to have the vote delayed.

It was not the most edifying spectacle in terms of parliamentary process. But in the capitals of Europe, EU leaders had taken note that May, though capable of being furious about pet cats and so forth when the cameras were on her, was more pragmatic when immersed in the detail of a given problem. When she became prime minister in 2016, there were some who found consolation in the episode of the European Arrest Warrant: when it came down to it, she could incline towards cooperation, and good sense.

It is a trait we have already noted: her idealism is usually trumped in the end by an acceptance of how the world is. But May rarely reaches these compromises without first having let the world know how unpalatable they are to her: one sometimes thinks she could play her cards a little closer to her chest. She will let it be known that she would very much like to do something radical – and then proceeds to do the expected.

This makes her moments of idealism all the more marked. The ideals of a pragmatist are likely to be deeply cherished by their possessor since they fought their way up against the natural grain of being. This is the case for May particularly with the issue of modern slavery.

17 - MAY'S MODERN SLAVERY ACT

Most of us like to think of the word 'slavery' as going hand in hand with the word 'abolition'. If you go to the parliamentary archive, you can see a copy of the Abolition of the Slave Trade Act (1807). Then if you walk a half mile down Whitehall to the National Portrait Gallery, you can come face to face with T.E Lawrence's magnificent portrait of William Wilberforce (Fig. 16) who fought that legislation into being.

With our observations about May's 'image' in Chapter Two in mind, here is a politician somewhat at odds with our understanding of the contemporary MP. It is the face of a man who hasn't lived to advance his career, but to advance a cause. It is an image of power subordinated in a human being to morality – of power satisfactorily utilised. Wilberforce is shown by Lawrence towards the end of his life. He has aged well, we think, because he has aged along a vector of kind acts, but he also looks wistful. It is not the face of a man who has succeeded, but of a man tired of defeat: the portrait reminds us that toil is humbling, and that success often doesn't feel like success at all, but instead like exhaustion.

Fig. 16 William Wilberforce painted by T.E Lawrence in 1828.[124]

One reason for this might be that the Slave Trade Act, which he had put forward some 20 years before this portrait was painted, hadn't led to the abolition of slavery – only the abolition of *trade* in slaves. In fact, the 1807 Act was just the first victory in a campaign that would last for a quarter of a century, and which would culminate in the Abolition of Slavery Act in 1833, which had its third reading in the House of Commons three days before Wilberforce's death. The day it was passed was one of Parliament's very good days.

But it still might be argued that the act was optimistically named because slavery continues in a variety of guises in the UK today. To enter into this topic is to confront the persistence of the human desire to exploit vulnerability. If Wilberforce were alive today he would still have cause to be melancholy. It is possible to look at the advances made in the last few hundred years and conclude that the great humanitarian causes are past. Unfortunately, it isn't the case, and it is to Theresa May's great credit that she has found one and sought to redress it. We are in the realm of the spotless intention, and our only question will therefore be the efficacy of what has been presented to parliament.

It is worth doing so with a particular thought in mind. In respect of most of what we have seen so far, May can be seen carrying out policies within a framework set by Prime Minister David Cameron. It was Cameron not May who decreed that immigration be reduced into the tens of thousands; and it was George Osborne who demanded that the Home Office budget be cut by 20 per cent. What we have seen so far has not been without initiative – how and where May slashed spending in her department told us much about her. But on the issue of slavery we are presented with a case study as to how May handles the business of primary legislation. Here, then, is the Modern Slavery Act, sponsored by her and one of her ministers Lord Bates – it is hers.

THE EVIL OF MODERN SLAVERY

It didn't happen immediately. In 2014, four years into her tenure, May's department instituted the Modern Slavery Strategy, which built on previous research conducted by May's National Crime Agency into this problem. Its findings were alarming: there are between 10,000 and 13,000 potential victims of modern slavery in the UK.[125] This work, conducted by Chief Scientific Adviser Professor Bernard Silberman culminates in this estimate which he himself labelled a 'dark figure'. It is a suggestive phrase: this is a dark world, one into which those who hold the power do not want the government to travel at all. Silberman's report lifted the veil on numerous lives of hitherto concealed misery – those condemned to work in a range of industries against their will, not just in the sex industry in London, but also in a condition of silent woe across a startling range of industries. The following summary on the globalslaveryindex.org is a door into a distressing variety of drudgery, frustration, injustice and shame:

> ... labour exploitation amounting to modern slavery has been found across multiple sectors, including, but not limited to, factories, agricultural and construction sections, car washes, nail

bars, restaurants and bars, the tarmac and paving industry, and the maritime sector. Some victims have been identified in the scrap metal and recycling industry, chicken catching, selling DVDs, cleaning, nannies and taxi drivers. These cases are incredibly diverse, impacting men, women and children.[126]

If this were a disease, we'd be calling it a pandemic. One must think not just of the misery of the individual life as it must be lived, but also of the wasted potential – the would-be artist or composer or entrepreneur or athlete, full of latent ability, condemned to spend their term on this planet as someone else's property.

Unfortunately the problem doesn't stop there: according to a report by the Human Trafficking Foundation entitled 'Life Beyond the Safe House', those who do manage to make themselves known to the authorities haven't been appropriately handled by the state. The *Guardian* summed up the ways in which the system often fails people when they are at their most vulnerable:

> Some were placed in inappropriate housing – for example women who had previously been forced into prostitution were placed in mixed-sex accommodation – after leaving safe houses. Others found themselves placed in areas where they had previously been exploited and were at risk of isolation, trauma and depression.

While it is true that it impacts both sexes, it is also a problem that predominantly affects women. The UK National Referral Mechanism in 2014 found that there had been 2,340 potential victims of trafficking from 96 countries of origin, of whom 61 per cent were female and 29 per cent were children.[127] One doesn't need to be a feminist to be alarmed by this, but one senses that as a feminist May feels the urgency of the problem keenly. Likewise, one doesn't need to be a Christian or anything other than a compassionate human being to wish this state of affairs corrected; but here we also see May's activist Christianity in action.

So to the Modern Slavery Act. In introducing the bill in its third reading, May delivered a passionate description of the problem the legislation is intended to tackle. It is worth quoting in full since it shows a righteous indignation at odds with her cold image:

> The injustice and suffering experienced by victims of modern slavery is often difficult to comprehend: young girls raped, beaten and passed from abuser to abuser so that they can be sexually exploited for profit; vulnerable men tricked into long hours of hard labour before being locked away in cold sheds or run-down caravans; people made to work in fields, in factories and on fishing vessels; women forced into prostitution; children forced into a life of crime; and domestic workers imprisoned and made to work all hours of the day and night for little or no pay. Those are the harsh realities of modern day slavery, and those are the crimes taking place not in the distant past, but in towns, cities and villages in Britain today.[128]

This shows the passion May is capable of exhibiting. It is surely an attractive trait in anyone, and a needed trait in a prime minister.

THE CONTENTS OF THE LEGISLATION

What did May's Modern Slavery Act do?

A point of emphasis needs to be made. It was to a large extent a bill which tightened law enforcement. This might sound obvious, but it was a misstep for those on the Labour benches – Yvette Cooper among them – who had wanted a bill focused on victims, and the provision of reform for the life beyond the safe house which we have just seen failing many. Even so, it would have been odd to focus on the government handling of victims' recuperation without doing anything to address the offence itself. In this respect, the bill consolidated all offences of trafficking and created new offences. Section 62 of the 2003 Sexual Offences Act had to submit to a rewrite: grooming – or in the words of the original act 'committing an offence with intent to commit a sexual offence' – would now include any offence of exploitation, not only sexual exploitation offences. At the same time, trafficking offences from that act were moved across to this one, and for the first time the legislature of the United Kingdom made a distinction between domestic servitude and trafficking. Like this, parliament slowly grapples with chaotic external reality, and the nuances of evil. Meanwhile the maximum sentence for slavery and human trafficking was increased from 14 years to life imprisonment to few people's lamentation. Slavery and Trafficking Prevention Orders and Slavery and Trafficking Risk Orders were also introduced to restrict the activity of individuals where they pose a risk of causing harm. No-one was in any doubt that in this instance the law needed strengthening, and May deserves credit for strengthening it.

Nevertheless, as we have glimpsed, May's Modern Slavery Act has attracted particular, but nonetheless important, criticisms. There is evidence that a chance for a more imaginative bill was missed. For instance, Labour MP Sarah Champion would speak with passion throughout the committee stages of the bill about the need for the legislation to incorporate language enabling local authorities to assess whether they were dealing with a child or not — this would have been the first time that an offence of child exploitation would have been recognised in law. When it came to the third reading of the bill, which had no such provision in it, Champion asked May in the House of Commons why her ideas hadn't been included. She received the following reply:

> ... we looked at the issue of child exploitation and took a lot of advice on it. The worry was that if it were referenced in the Bill in the way suggested, that could lead to certain actions and activities falling within the description of child exploitation that were never intended to be part of the Bill. In short, I am afraid that the law of unintended consequences would have kicked in and a disbenefit would have resulted from having that aspect in the Bill.[129]

This reply would prove unsatisfactory. A year later, by which time May had become prime minister, it had become clear that of the 982 children spotted as victims of modern slavery since the act, 60 per cent had gone missing. In many cases the presumption is that they had returned to their traffickers. Champion was unequivocal: 'The new Prime Minister should be ashamed that she hasn't acted on the protection for children in the Modern Slavery Act.'[130] The non-inclusion of the child exploitation provision shows the sometimes depressing workings of British democracy: a point is put with democratic passion at committee, rebutted by lawyers behind closed doors, dispatched by a minister in the House of Commons, and then railed against in a newspaper article. Perhaps Champion spoke too much in anger: reading the debates right through, one doesn't feel as though May should feel shame. It might merely be that she should look at the facts and propose amendments to the act.

Meanwhile, child slavery has continued. The independent commissioner created by the Act Kevin Hyland would later express concerns that offences to minors committed under the Act were not being investigated properly: 'The real concern that I have is that in 2015 we had 986 cases involving minors, yet the official figures show that there's only 928 actual crime recorded incidents. So that means... potentially the cases involving minors are not being investigated properly.'[131]

Meanwhile Yvette Cooper would write a year or so later in the *Guardian* article I have quoted in a previous part of this book:

> Rightly, her Modern Slavery Act promised a crackdown on people smugglers. Wrongly, it left out protection for domestic workers from slavery.

Anthony Steen, chair of the Human Trafficking Foundation, seconded this, describing the bill as 'a lost opportunity', adding: 'We have majored on the wrong thing. It is positive in the sense that it is an entirely new initiative, but is it going to do anything?'[132] However, while Steen's worries were fair, they were ultimately taken into account, and the legislation became more victim-oriented: the final draft of the Act includes a statutory defence for victims compelled to commit crimes, court powers to order perpetrators to pay reparations to victims, provision of advocates to support child victims, and statutory guidance on victim identification and victim services.[133] It has undergone refinement over time and is indicative of a flexibility not usually attributed to May. By 2015, the government had also launched a new helpline for victims.[134] All this arguably makes Cooper's characterisation a year later in that article somewhat unjust: it feels like points-scoring as opposed to a fair assessment.

Nevertheless, Safeandsoundgroup.org identifies another possible shortcoming with the Act. Clause 2, which covers human trafficking, requires evidence of *intention* to exploit when moving a child between locations. This is a high standard of proof. It might be perfectly possible to have evidence of movement, but not the intention to exploit, which will in some cases make prosecution fiendishly difficult. The Report of the Modern Slavery Bill Evidence Review observes that in many cases the police will have to settle for a lesser offence.[135] At its worst, then, the Modern Slavery Act might be taken as a too offences-oriented Act where the offences themselves aren't even satisfactorily drafted.

The first year under the Act provided mixed results. A 2016 review conducted by barrister Caroline Haughey found that 289 offences were prosecuted under the new legislation, which included a 40 per cent rise in the number of victims referred.[136] That was progress of a kind, but Haughey also pointed to the following difficulties:

> There is a lack of consistency in how law enforcement and criminal justice agencies deal with the victims and perpetrators of modern slavery. We need better training, better intelligence and a more structured approach to identifying, investigating, prosecuting and preventing slavery, including learning from what works and what does not.[137]

May – by that point PM – responded with an additional £33.5 million and a new taskforce. This money will be aimed particularly at people-trafficking trade in countries such as Nigeria. By 2017, 2,255 modern slavery offences were reported in England and Wales, a 159 per cent increase on the previous year.[138]

We are faced therefore with a landmark measure that doesn't entirely work: the two traits are interlinked – it is the UK's first stab at a very complex problem and will doubtless be tweaked over time. In the final reading of the bill the Labour MP Frank Field put aside partisanship and congratulated May:

> Fifteen months ago there was no talk of this Bill, and tonight there are a few scratchy comments about whether it could be an even better world-class Bill.[139]

Haughey seconded this around the time of the publication of her review, calling the act a 'benchmark to which other jurisdictions aspire'.[140]

These happier verdicts provide us with some needed perspective. All in all, the day this Act was passed was one of those happy days in the House of Commons, where a good thing is done by those who wish to nudge the world in the direction of justice. Wilberforce would have approved.

In fact, reading the back-and-forth of the debates, one is in a completely different world to the bogus partisan arguments I noted in Chapter 11 in relation to education, and as far as can be from the atmosphere of the EU referendum campaign which we shall shortly enter.

18 –THE 'SNOOPERS' CHARTER'

Interestingly there was one major thing which May didn't tout in her announcement speech: she would have been doing herself few favours if she had. It was the Draft Investigatory Powers Bill, better known as the Snoopers' Charter.

It has been said that we are living in the age of Edward Snowden. Before a man of Snowden's gumption, mere politicians must simply adapt. Theresa May has not been able to avoid this. But, then again, the age of Snowden would have been impossible had we not already been living in the age of NSA and GCHQ – and by association, a world of home secretaries. Around 20 minutes north-east of Gloucester you will find, rearing up before you as a huge architectural fact, GCHQ, or Government Communication Headquarters. It is cathedral country, but the great disc in the earth reminds you what we spend our money building nowadays – not on the spiritual architecture that would please Hubert Brasier, but on utilitarian buildings on the vast scale necessary for the work of world leaders like his daughter.

Fig. 17 GCHQ[141]

As we shall see, May's work as home secretary has contributed to the likelihood of this building becoming one day bigger still.

THE UNHAPPY FIGHT FOR AN UNPOPULAR BILL

May's eventual legislation had an earlier abortive incarnation. It was the Draft Communications Data Bill. This didn't pass because it was too contentious. But its subsequent incarnation the Draft Investigatory Powers Bill would receive royal assent at the end of 2016. The first version of the bill was opposed during the Coalition by Nick Clegg and would have been killed altogether but for Cameron's unexpected majority in 2015. It might be said, therefore, that May's bill is one of the few tangible legislative results of that Cameron victory which looked so consequential at the time.

The politics surrounding the initial bill were headachey for all concerned. The Coalition enjoyed some areas of agreement on security policy – most notably on rolling back Blair's unpopular ID cards scheme, which both the Conservatives and the Liberal Democrats saw as indicative of a too fussy state. But on the collection of data, there was disagreement not just between the coalition partners, but within the Conservative Party. Cameron and May favoured giving MI5 as much power as they felt they needed, but Kenneth Clarke, then in the roaming position of Minister without Portfolio, had told Nick Clegg:

> I advise you not to take too many briefings with MI5 and MI6. They always try and frighten you to death and get you to agree to something that soon looks like a police state. We have to get the balance right.[142]

The evidence suggests that Theresa May took too many such briefings. One gets the impression from reading Laws' account that May would not have been that concerned to 'get the balance right' had it not been for objections from his side.

It was a measure bound to expose divisions within the Coalition. Nick Clegg had sympathy for targeted surveillance, but what May would eventually propose was too much an infraction on civil liberties ever to be palatable to the wider Liberal Democrat party membership. The collection of data in the modern age runs up against a problem previous generations did not face: intercepted letters cannot be reproduced with the same ease as intercepted e-mails, so the possibilities for misuse of collected data is that much greater. Clegg would have been in trouble with the left of his party if he had assented whole-heartedly. Over time he decided that he was running too many risks if he proceeded at all. Theresa May was asked to go away and think about her legislation. When she came back, the proposed changes were too small for Clegg. This led to an unpleasant sequel:

> The reaction from the Home Office was immediate and unpleasant: briefings to newspapers that 'Clegg is the friend of paedophiles and terrorists'.[143]

It was not an approach calculated to appease Clegg; even Cameron was sympathetic with the Liberal Democrat leader. One would ideally wish to balance the Laws account with the Home Office view, or at least a view from the Tory side, but most of the Conservatives involved are still in government, and few have written memoirs: the Liberal Democrats, ousted in 2015, mostly have. In the meanwhile, we can note that, with May, nastiness is usually snide. She never breaks cover when she's at her worst. It is the wisdom of the serpent, which has enabled her to seem innocent as a lamb. The inner workings of the Coalition are also on view – Cameron, Clegg and Laws were united by a cosmopolitan blokeiness, which May could never partake in. The matter also became heated quickly because, for May, it was potentially a resignation issue. Her predecessor Alan Johnson, increasingly a thorn in her side, had stated that if, as home secretary, May was unable to produce legislation to protect UK citizens, then she couldn't expect to remain in position. Government ministers, and especially home secretaries, are fighting for their careers every day.

Once Clegg had withdrawn his support in April 2013, the Bill foundered. The politics hadn't helped, but then data collection is an issue which, one feels, particularly after the Snowden revelations, no government feels entirely comfortable with. Nobody wants a terrorist attack that could have been prevented; and no government wants to be *seen* to be promoting anything resembling a police state. Pre-Snowden governments had reached a compromise behind closed doors: to quietly assemble such an apparatus. Post-Snowden, that accommodation became impossible. The chief question now is what it should have been all along: how much private data is the government permitted to collect from its citizens? Under this first attempt at the legislation, phone providers and Internet companies would have been required to hold information of internet activity in relation to private citizens for a year. This is sometimes known as 'bulk harvesting'. A review commissioned by President Obama called 'Liberty and Security in a Changing World' had been clear on this point:

We recommend that Congress should end such storage [bulk telephony metadata] and transition to a system in which such metadata is held privately for the government to query when necessary for national security purposes. In our view, the current storage by the government of bulk meta-data creates potential risks to public trust, personal privacy, and civil liberty.[144]

This was an American report but it was an authoritative attempt to address a problem identical to the one May was seeking to fix. Other objections were raised. For instance, there were doubts that the systems installed in Internet service providers were powerful enough to handle such large amounts of data. By January 2015, David Cameron had opened a further debate about encryption, asking rhetorically: 'In our country, do we want to allow a means of communication between people which we cannot read?'[145] The answer, to those who had thought about the matter, is a resounding 'yes' since the same encryption codes which unfortunately protect terrorists, also protect people's credit card details, online communications, banking and many other things from being read.

One has a sense of this being a new debate that politicians are struggling to comprehend. They have not yet found the language with which to address the problem. May would have to try again.

SECOND ATTEMPT

How much difference is there between the first Coalition era bill, and the second version – The Draft Investigatory Powers Bill – placed before Parliament in the spring of 2016, and passed towards its end?

May went – once again – on *The Andrew Marr Show* to explain:

> Well it is quite different from the Draft Communications Data Bill in a number of ways. It doesn't have some of the more contentious powers that were in that bill. So, for example, we won't be requiring communication service providers from the UK to store third party data, we won't be making the same requirements in relation to data retention on overseas CSPs [Communications Service Providers]. And crucially… we will not be giving powers to go through people's browsing history.[146]

These were presented as substantive alterations. But those who had seen the first measures as a Snoopers' Charter, were not about to abandon the label this time around.

What do the shifts mean in practice? Later in that Marr interview, May would lay to rest the encryption debate: 'Encryption will not be banned within the bill'. Secondly, those Internet service provider systems which we saw as overburdened under the legislation as it had first been proposed, would now have no requirement to collect third party data from overseas. Third party data – data purchased by a marketer from an outside source – is generally considered less accurate, and therefore less intrusive, than first party data, which is data directly collected by the company behind pages with which Internet users interact. Thirdly, and more importantly, the Home Secretary claimed that there was a fundamental change in this version of the legislation to the *nature* of the data collection. May had initially hoped to secure the authorities the power to look at the actual page on a website a user had visited; now they would only be able to look at what website was being looked at. It is the cyber equivalent of having access to a phone bill, but not being able to listen to the call.

But there is a caveat to this. These powers, characterised as non-intrusive in debate surrounding the measures, can be expanded under May's bill after the issuance of a warrant. The question then becomes: 'What are the oversight arrangements for the issuing of warrants?' This has traditionally been an important part of the job of the home secretary, but some have wondered whether a busy minister in the most challenging department of government – getting by on five hours sleep a night, we might recall – really has time to give the appropriate level of attention to each case. May herself had called it: 'a responsibility that [...] perhaps occupies more of my time as Home Secretary than anything else'[147]. May received three sets of independent advice on this, and came up with a compromise, telling Parliament:

> So, as now, the Secretary of State will need to be satisfied that an activity is necessary and proportionate before a warrant can be issued. But in future, the warrant will not come into force until it has been formally approved by a judge.

> This will place a 'double lock' on the authorisation of our most intrusive investigatory powers. Democratic accountability, through the Secretary of State, to ensure our intelligence agencies operate in the interests of the citizens of this country, and the public reassurance of independent, judicial authorisation.[148]

This was initially accepted by shadow home secretary, Andy Burnham, as a reasonable approach. However, after consultation with Lord Falconer, the shadow justice secretary, he changed his position:

> On closer inspection of the wording of the bill, it would seem that it does not deliver the strong safeguard that you appeared to be accepting. The current wording of the draft bill requires the judge to review the 'process' undertaken by the home secretary in the same way applied to a judicial review.[149]

Burnham soon realised that this was not the same as the collaborative approach of formal approval May had seemed to be announcing.

Meanwhile, seven judicial commissioners would be given power of veto over intercept warrants. This was also contentious. For Simon Jenkins, it placed too much burden on the independent judiciary. According to his view, the average judge is someone all too thrilled to be enacting a real-life *Spooks*, and likely to be in thrall to the shadowy world of espionage. This feels like caricature: anyone who has ever sat through a judicial review in the Royal Courts of Justice knows that the place has a dusty sobriety that can neuter even the headiness of being reminded of the existence of MI5. On the other hand, there is genuine concern still about the escalation of the state, and, in particular, whether it is needed at this time. Much depends on an interpretation of the times we live in. Is this peacetime or is this war? The peculiar nature of the modern threat, characterised by the rise of lone terrorist cells, creates difficulties of interpretation. The atrocities are perpetrated by those of an unprecedentedly nihilistic bent, but casualties have been few in number. We do not face the kind of state threat that quite justifies wartime measures. But we do not live in unblemished peace. The champion of civil liberties can seem cavalier about safety; the advocate of greater powers for the police can easily seem alarmist.

At one end of the spectrum, Bella Shankey of Liberty stated:

> This bill would create a detailed profile on each of us which could be made available to hundreds of organisations to speculatively trawl and analyse. It will all but end online privacy, put our personal security at risk and swamp law enforcement with swathes of useless information.[150]

At the other spectrum of the argument, we have May:

> The threat is clear. In the past twelve months alone six significant terrorist plots have been disrupted here in the UK, as well as a number of further plots overseas.

> The frequency and cost of cyber attacks is increasing, with 90 per cent of large organisations suffering an information security breach last year.

> And the Child Exploitation and Online Protection Command estimate that there are 50,000 people in this country downloading indecent images of children.[151]

Of course, in making the argument May has one advantage: she sees the details of the plots; the likes of Shankey, and indeed everyone else, do not.

The debate will always split between those who do not quite see their daily visits to news websites and their e-mail as any great space of liberty that needs defending, and those who know their Orwell, and can easily imagine that it might. Supporters of the Shankey position could also point to the relatively slim likelihood of succumbing to a terrorist attack: since September 11th 2001, until the passage of this act, 57 people have died from terrorist attacks in the UK – 56 from the 2005 July bombings, and Lee Rigby of the Royal Regiment of Fusiliers. But those who would wish to support the May position can point to numerous foiled attacks – from the Glasgow International Airport attack in 2007 to the Leytonstone tube station attack in 2015 – not to mention, of course, the attacks in Westminster and Manchester in the lead-up to the 2017 General Election. It is indeed, as Kenneth Clarke observed to Nick Clegg, a question of balance – never a very satisfying conclusion, but in this instance, probably the right one.

To observe this issue unfold under a Conservative government, is to find oneself missing the Coalition. However exasperating it was at the time for the main players, it is an example of fruitful interplay between two camps, and can show our democracy engaged in a helpful back and forth. When powerful people like May are irritated by the inability to get something done, there is always the possibility that their worst instincts are being frustrated.

BREAKING FOR THE REFERENDUM

The revisited 'Snoopers' Charter' was in fact the last piece of major government business before the break for the referendum. Cameron's expectation would have been to return to parliament after a successful victory for the Remain camp, tidy his legacy with his Life Chances scheme, and then depart as a prime minister who had served a decent while, without experiencing electoral defeat like Major, and without being booted out by his own party like Thatcher or Blair.

The choice is in your hands. But my recommendation is clear.

I believe that Britain will be safer, stronger and better off by remaining in a reformed European Union.[152]

In the next section we shall see how that worked out for him, and how the country aligned itself. What followed was to be like that scene in Jane Austen's *Persuasion*, when Louisa suffers her concussion, and the lives of all the characters are changed. Except that this would occur on the national scale.

Meanwhile, in Westminster, something else might have been noticed. While everyone else manoeuvred, Home Secretary Theresa May did very little. As the months unfolded, it would be seen that everyone who tried to manoeuvre for the prime ministership – Osborne, Johnson, Leadsom, Gove – made the wrong moves. It was in retrospect not a time for hyperactivity: the right move – to do nothing – perfectly matched the instincts of our heroine. She could not have known as people went off on the campaign trail how quickly she would become prime minister. But then the country was about to enter the realm of the unprecedented.

To understand why and how, and to what extent, we need to understand a little more about Europe.

PART FOUR

ASCENSION TO POWER

19 – THE EUROPEAN UNION UP TO THATCHER

To consider the ascension of Theresa May to prime minister is to be presented with an infinite chain of causation: all prime ministers depend on the courses their predecessors took. It is possible to imagine butterfly effects – those that did happen, and those, which we might label negative butterfly effects, which didn't. In May's case, if Blair hadn't sided with the Americans over Iraq, or if Cameron had decided not to pursue the referendum, those decisions would also have rippled through history to become some other set of events, which might well have meant any number of things, including Theresa May not being prime minister. As Boris Johnson knows to his cost, the prospect of power can recede just when the hand that expects to feel the metal of the crown is reaching out – an optimistic grasping can become a flailing about in pure air.

Theresa May's premiership may have happened without the EU referendum. She was ideally well-positioned to at least make a play for the leadership regardless of how the Cameron premiership had ended. If she managed to survive the hypothetical years after a Remain win in the referendum unscathed – in the Home Office, always a big 'if' – then she would almost certainly have been facing an untarnished George Osborne, a less loathed Boris Johnson, and any number of others who might have positioned themselves in the meanwhile. The premiership Theresa May did attain isn't possible to separate from the unusual circumstances of the EU referendum. Her ascension feels like a fittingly unexpected conclusion to an improbable set of events. Her premiership is what Dante might have called – though he used the phrase in another context – an 'accident of substance'.

Europe is traditionally a dangerous leitmotif for any Tory prime minister. Indifference to Europe, hatred of Europe, exhaustion with Europe: these are all national realities – realities which in June-July 2016 mixed in a particular way to suit the ambitions of Theresa May.

Another factor which we shall find percolating around the time of the EU referendum – and perhaps the largest – was ignorance about Europe. The second most googled question in the UK in the days after the vote was 'What is the EU?'

OUT OF THE EMBERS OF WAR

During the referendum campaign, David Cameron went to the British Museum to make a speech on the UK's strength and security in Europe. In this he made a claim that would earn him derision from the Leave camp – namely, that Britain's membership of the European Union was crucial to ongoing peace.

> Can we be so sure that peace and stability on our continent are assured beyond any shadow of doubt? Is that a risk worth taking? I would never be so rash as to make that assumption.[153]

In the ramped-up atmosphere of the campaign, this could easily be made to look like alarmism. In the ensuing back-and-forth, it was notable how arguments about national destiny quickly become a chance to quote and claim Winston Churchill. Boris Johnson, his biographer, was minded to think Churchill would have voted to Leave. In fact, he went further and equated the EU with the great man's chief adversary: 'Napoleon, Hitler, various people tried this out, and it ends tragically. The EU is an attempt to do this by different methods.'[154] The methods were indeed different – so different, many felt, as to be not worth the comparison.

Cameron meanwhile was emphasising the risk:

> As I sit around that table with 27 other prime ministers and presidents, we remember that it is pretty extraordinary that countries are working together to solve disputes and problems. We should listen to the voices that say Europe had a violent history, we've managed to avoid that and so why put at risk the things that achieve that?[155]

Cameron wasn't overstating his case at all. The Second World War really did happen and the EU really did come into being as a direct response to it. The ensuing 70 years appear an object lesson in the notion that when the financial interests of nations intertwine, war between them becomes immediately less likely. In pointing out that the EU had been designed to prevent a recurrence of cataclysm, Cameron was only being responsible.

And it *was* Winston Churchill who, in the wilderness period after he was ousted from Downing Street by losing to Clement Attlee in the 1945 General Election, travelled to Zurich to make a famous speech about international affairs. He did more than any other politician to articulate the idea of what would become the European Union. He was unequivocal. After observing that much of Europe had just emerged from a new Dark Ages, he stated the remedy:

> What is this sovereign remedy? It is to re-create the European Family, or as much of it as we can, and provide it with a structure under which it can dwell in peace, in safety and in freedom. We must build a kind of United States of Europe.[156]

A Brexiter might retort that Churchill considered Europe 'the fountain of Christian faith and Christian ethics'. His Zurich speech did not envisage, the argument runs, anything like the sort of monstrous European Union, potentially incorporating Turkey, and teeming with ISIS, which we find looming today. In fact, Churchill had in another context had this to say on the topic of Turkish-UK relations in a 1943 letter to the President of Turkey İsmet İnönü:

> There is a long story of the friendly relations between Great Britain and Turkey. Across it is a terrible slash of the last war, when German intrigues and British and Turkish mistakes led to our being on opposite sides. We fought as brave and honourable opponents. But those days are done, and we and our American Allies are prepared to make vigorous exertions in order that we shall all be together... to move forward into a world arrangement in which peaceful peoples will have a right to be let alone and in which all peoples will have a chance to help one another.[157]

It is worth remembering what the European Union in its infancy was designed to avoid. It was loss of life on an epic scale: the young men who never came home, the families and marriages torn apart, the rank absurdity and the vile cruelty of it all. It is the world described by David Jones and Wilfred Owen, the subject-matter of *Catch-22* and *Slaughterhouse Five* – and none of it could have been invented by David Cameron. The European Union was, in its essence, an attempt to say: never again. Henry Fielding had joked in *Tom Jones* that all human disagreement should be expended in fist fights: if you cannot kill your foe, the original cause of the fight drains away. The EU went further. It was a way of saying: voices raised, perhaps, but never again bombs, tanks and guns.

Fig. 18 Robert Schuman[158]

We must add that on that score it has worked: nothing like the world wars has happened since. Of course, one is free to claim that the era of European peace from 1945 until the present day is a mere coincidence that has nothing to do with the EU. But it is certainly suggestive that at the same time as a supranational organisation came into being designed to alleviate the tension that always flows out of the relentless promotion of narrow national interest, that tension was indeed alleviated.

In the event of it, Churchill did not during his second period in office lead Britain into the European Coal and Steel Community. But the tone he had set outlived him. Meanwhile, the first structures of what would become the EU had come into existence. The Council of Europe was established in 1949 as a result of the Treaty of London. Right from the beginning, in the preamble to that document, we can begin to gauge the idealistic nature of the times:

> The Governments of the Kingdom of Belgium, the Kingdom of Denmark, the French Republic, the Irish Republic, the Italian Republic, the Grand Duchy of Luxembourg, the Kingdom of the Netherlands, the Kingdom of Norway, the Kingdom of Sweden and the United Kingdom of Great Britain and Northern Ireland,
>
> Convinced that the pursuit of peace based upon justice and international co-operation is vital for the preservation of human society and civilisation...

It is hard not to enjoy the emphasis of the word 'convinced': Europe was a serious response to a serious time. Article 1 of the Treaty would go on to state:

> This aim shall be pursued through the organs of the Council by discussion of questions of common concern and by agreements and common action in economic, social, cultural, scientific, legal and ad-

ministrative matters and in the maintenance and further realisation of human rights and fundamental freedoms. [159]

There are few who would quibble with that goal – but to leap in mind from the signing of the Treaty of London to the present time, we can see how easily good intentions can miscarry. We might also note a certain symmetry: the city in which the project was born, was the same in which much of the 2016 referendum drama took place.

Another significant voice emerged at this time in the shape of French foreign minister Robert Schuman. In Strasbourg in May 1950, Schuman issued what became known as the Schuman Declaration. One of the founding documents of the European project, it went beyond the idea of mere discussion that we see in Article 1 of the Treaty of London. It envisaged a relationship far more self-conscious and intertwined:

> The European spirit signifies being conscious of belonging to a cultural family and to have a willingness to serve that community in the spirit of total mutuality, without any hidden motives of hegemony or the selfish exploitation of others. The 19th century saw feudal ideas being opposed and, with the rise of a national spirit, nationalities asserting themselves. Our century, that has witnessed the catastrophes resulting in the unending clash of nationalities and nationalisms, must attempt and succeed in reconciling nations in a supranational association.[160]

Schuman's was a wide-ranging and eclectic mind: he was able to cite Dante, Aquinas and Kant as influences upon his pan-European ideas. Boris Johnson would try and draw a distinction during the 2016 campaign between cultural Europe, which he claimed to be a fan of, and political Europe, which he was campaigning vigorously against. But for Schuman, and his advisors Bernard Clappier and Jean Monnet, political and economic union would be based precisely on that cultural affinity which Johnson would later seek to separate out.

To this day, the date of the Schuman declaration is meant to be the reason we celebrate Europe Day on 9th May. The notion of a Europe Day will be news to many. Some prefer to celebrate the date on 5th May, and the Ukrainians celebrate it on the third Saturday of every May. But of course, many of us don't celebrate it at all, because we haven't heard that we are meant to be doing so. An idea that originated among high-minded statesmen has never quite filtered down to the level of true feeling among citizens. In retrospect we can see that once Churchill left the scene, Europe was denied a poet-statesman who could articulate Europeanness to Europe in a convincing and meaningful way. There is a world of difference between Churchill's Zurich speech, and Cameron's announcement before calling the referendum: 'I do not love Brussels'. As the story of the European project progresses, one even begins to wonder how much human beings really like peace; eventually it makes some people antsy. It is as if by evolving in nomadic life, and in warfare, too much sedateness eventually riles us, until we are inspired to shake things up with a touch of danger.

The decision to leave the European Union might be understood as the unloosing of a widespread nervous energy.

BEYOND THE SCHUMAN DECLARATION

Schuman's declaration was prophetic. Coal and steel – the resources necessary for modern warfare – would shortly be under the supervision of a supranational body. For the first time, diverse national interests would need to be referred back to an umpire. This arrangement was formally established at The Treaty of Paris in 1951 between France, Italy, Belgium, the Netherlands, and Luxembourg, and West Germany.

This treaty also gave birth to the High Authority and the Common Assembly. These fledgling structures would morph in time into entities unloved in practice even by many who supported them in theory. The High Authority would become the European Commission, and the Common Assembly would become the European Parliament.

The European Commission is the legislature. It is independent of national governments and charged with 'upholding the interests of the EU as a whole'[161]. It upholds these interests by drafting proposals for new European laws. These it then presents to the European Parliament, which, at present, has 785 members from all 27 (soon to be 26) EU member countries – evidence of a growth unimaginable in the 1950s.Parliament then votes on those laws and, along with the Council – consisting of government ministers from each country – produces a budget. But at the time of the signing of the Treaty of Paris, all this complexity was latent within an unimaginable future. Whether we deem the eventual European Union a reasonably logical fulfilment of its initial ideals, or whether we see it as a tragic deviation from them, it is hard to argue that the feeling behind the project was misguided. However, we can see that for the European project to be attempted at all, there would always have been – at some point – contentious overlap between the 'interests of the EU as a whole' and respective national interests. A French farmer might want something different from a London financier – or rather they might both want the same thing – money – but that might not always be as forthcoming as each would wish. As the project advanced, its inherent difficulty was revealed.

As a result of the Treaty of Rome (1957), the steel community would become the European Economic Community. Once again there was a restatement of a core principle in the preamble. The community would be expanded in order to 'preserve peace and liberty and to lay the foundations of an ever closer union among the peoples of Europe'.[162]

Those words 'ever closer union' would evoke for some on the British right a dangerous possibility: the dilution of national character. It was also at this point that the 'four freedoms' came into being as a basis for what the Treaty also referred to as 'continuous and balanced expansion': free movement of persons, services, goods and capital. The language of harmony sat alongside what some would deem the vocabulary of encroachment: 'continuous', 'ever closer'. To the sensitively patriotic, these were not glorious developments, but a spectre to fret about.

Equally, it helps us to understand that when years later Nigel Farage or Michael Gove – or Theresa May – talk of removing these freedoms, they are challenging what to many is a noble and essential principle. It might be added that they are doing so having joined the project tardily – like someone who arrives late at a party and demands a change of music.

BRITAIN V. CHARLES DE GAULLE

An immense set of circumstances had been set in motion, which could only tend in time towards messiness. The original project had been embarked upon high-mindedly, but in an *ad hoc* fashion. These haphazard structures could survive plausibly so long as there was a prevailing high-mindedness among nations. But what if the personalities in the upper echelons of European politics were to change?

The world was about to find out in the shape of Charles de Gaulle.

Over time, the UK began to realise it could not stay out of the European Union and expect to remain competitive. The hard fact was that Europe had proven itself economically successful. Farming boomed throughout the 1960s on the back of the Common Agricultural Policy; the removal of customs duties successfully increased trade. Harold Macmillan decided to apply to join, but he hadn't reckoned on de Gaulle, who humiliated the British prime minister by theatrically exercising his veto in full view of the press. It was one of those rare moments in high politics when nicety goes out of the window, and we get a glimpse of a nationalistic passion where we had expected to find statesmanlike pragmatism. De Gaulle had feared that the UK was still too much a partner of the US ever to participate fully. It might be said that the 2016 vote to Leave has proven him right. On the other hand, fifty years of cooperation before that time might equally be said to have proven him wrong. De Gaulle's difficult attitude would outlive him. Seriousness had been jettisoned for pettiness, and it is at moments like those that people start to remember their nationality – to nobody's benefit when the intention is to create a supranational order. Resentment of the French entered the UK bloodstream: as of June 24th 2016, it might almost be said that this longstanding gripe became national policy.

It took de Gaulle's departure, after he lost a domestic referendum on decentralisation of government powers, to pave the way for Ted Heath. Heath would take Britain into Europe – at that time known as the EEC (European Economic Community). He was supported in the endeavour at the time by Margaret Thatcher – an irony history would later note, given her later Euroscepticism. Signing up for membership was a moment of great emotion for Heath who rose to the occasion with some stirring language:

> We recognise it as a great decision, a turning point in our history, and we take it in all seriousness. In saying that we wish to join the EEC, we mean that we desire to become full, whole-hearted and active members of the European Community in its widest sense and to go forward with you in the building of a new Europe.[163]

But Heath was also a cranky personality – again, the idiosyncrasies of a national leader would alter the character of an idealistic project. Here is Charles Moore reviewing Philip Ziegler's biography of Heath:

> Heath's style, when arguing his case for his great cause of Europe, or for anything else, was not, in fact, to argue at all. As Ziegler points out, he had no gift for exposition, because he was utterly uninterested in what others thought. This is why people felt cheated, and still do to

this day, about the terms on which Heath took Britain into the EEC. He never took the British people into his confidence.[164]

This is, in fact, arguable. The subsequent victory for the Remain side in the subsequent 1975 referendum shows that the British people didn't feel particularly alienated from his position at that time. Moore may be foisting a later Euroscepticism onto an earlier Heath. But it cannot be denied that to observe the back-and-forth between the British and French in the 1960s and 70s is to observe something very different to the statesmanship of Churchill and Schuman. The European project was mutating according to whichever personalities happened to come along: it had lost its character of peaceful consensus.

In the UK, a referendum was deemed necessary. In calling for one, Harold Wilson displayed a wisdom which David Cameron would later lack: he decided to remain above the fray during the campaign and announced that he would enact whatever outcome the British people delivered. The result was a resounding win for that day's Remain camp, with over 67 per cent of the vote. Another significant difference between 1975 and the way things played out in 2016 was the role of the press. In 2016, David Cameron found most of the tabloids, at the behest of press mogul Rupert Murdoch, ranged against him. Instead, the newspapers were roundly pro EEC-membership in Wilson's day, with only the *Spectator* and the *Daily Worker* arguing for out. In 1975 it was Tony Benn, a prominent Leave campaigner, who was pilloried by the vast majority of journalists. By 2016, Boris Johnson – an equivalent thorn in Cameron's side – would be championed by the likes of the *Sun*, the *Daily Mail* and the *Daily Telegraph*. In retrospect the resounding result in 1975 may have galvanised Cameron to authorise his own fateful referendum years later.

Interestingly, the campaign generated identical passions – passions that would sleep for forty years before being awoken by Cameron in 2016. For instance, the arguments between the Europhile Roy Jenkins – still at this time Home Secretary – and Benn, the Secretary of State for Industry, had a ferocity which anyone who lived through 2016 will recognise. Here is Jenkins:

> I'm afraid I find it increasingly difficult to take Mr Benn seriously as an economic minister. The technique is just to think of a number and double it, and if challenged you just react by thinking up some new claim.[165]

This might almost be George Osborne talking to Boris Johnson. This is the way that history proceeds, neither by repetition nor by novelty, but according to variations upon known themes. The issue of Britain's relationship with Europe plainly has a kind of eternal quality, capable of pulling similarly on the heartstrings of generations. But Jenkins' demonisation of Benn may have had a price. In his diaries, Benn records the speech he gave to Cabinet in March 18th 1975:

> We have confused the real issue of parliamentary democracy, for already there has been a fundamental change. The power of electors

over their law-makers has gone, the power of MPs over Ministers has gone, the role of Ministers has changed. The real case for entry has never been spelled out, which is that there should be a fully federal Europe in which we become a province. It hasn't been spelled out because people would never accept it. We are at the moment on a federal escalator, moving as we talk, going towards a federal objective we do not wish to reach.[166]

This is Benn, of the far left, sounding rather a lot like late period Margaret Thatcher, or any period Nigel Farage. By 2016, Benn's arguments had won the day – not so much with his own side, but with the Conservatives. Reading the debates of that time, one finds it surprising that in 2016 Labour leader Jeremy Corbyn campaigned to remain in the European Union at all: all his natural friends in the party from Benn to Barbara Castle and Michael Foot have always been opposed to European Union membership. But another oddity at that time was the pro-Europe passion of the then Leader of the Opposition Margaret Thatcher:

Everyone should turn out in this referendum and vote yes, so that the question is over once and for all, we are really in Europe, and ready to go ahead.[167]

One day she would become famous for saying 'No, No, No', thumping her hand on the despatch-box in a rage that we shall see her bequeathing to her progeny in the party. But this was a more innocent time: on the day before the 1975 referendum she wore a jumper with all the flags of European nations on it.

But people didn't know her then. They didn't know for instance, that in British politics, once Margaret Thatcher enters the fray, for better or for worse, everything changes.

20 - THE CONSERVATIVES AND EUROPE

From this point onward, the tale of the UK and Europe must be told primarily in relation to the Conservative Party. Although it had been Tony Benn who had most loudly opposed British membership of the EEC during the 1975 referendum, it was the Tories who ended up fetishizing the issue, almost always to their own electoral disadvantage. The question arises as to whether the party would ever lose power at all were it not for Europe. It will be impossible to understand the Theresa May premiership without getting a sense of the tensions seething beneath. Benn's passion was within reason. He could talk about other things. Once Euroscepticism became a cause for the right, that ceased to be the case. Europe would become an obsession, and this was to some extent the doing of Margaret Thatcher.

Thatcher would bequeath Cameron a party enraged about the issue. He had announced his intention to avoid it in his first party conference: 'While parents worried about childcare, getting the kids to school, balancing work and family life, we were banging on about Europe'[168]. As we shall see, it didn't make any difference for Cameron that he had stated his desire to avoid the topic: it would come to define him in any case.

Theresa May, defined by it from the outset, and owing the fact of her premiership to its existence, cannot possibly avoid it.

THE EVOLUTION OF MARGARET THATCHER

Margaret Thatcher held more views on Europe than most. Certainly, she changed her mind more than any modern prime minister – other than perhaps Churchill who was so fiercely energetic and rampantly quotable, that he is a separate case study, representing all life.

Part of the reason for this is that Thatcher could only with regret take up any middle position: she was either fiercely for things or aggressively against them. If she was pro-Europe, then she would wear a jumper saying so; if against, she would slam her fist on the despatch-box, and not mind if her anger split her own party. And yet there was a timeline to all this – a series of points she had to navigate, which look in retrospect like nuanced development, but which to live through may have been a kind of lurching. On the face of it, Thatcher's initial stance in favour looks impossible to square with her eventual opposition. But once you start to investigate her time in office, reasons emerge for so dramatic an evolution.

In the first place, Thatcher was relatively ignorant about European matters around the time of the 1975 referendum: over her time in office, the more she found out about the European project the less she liked it. At the referendum campaign launch on 16th April 1975, by which time Thatcher had already successfully challenged Heath, Thatcher had said with Heath in attendance: 'Naturally, it's with some temerity that the pupil speaks before the master'.[169] This bout of modesty would pass, as her brief was mastered. This had a concomitant effect: once Thatcher moved from opposition to leadership following her election victory in 1979, she was charged with charting a course on Europe herself. This began to spark her temper. She found it had been less annoying to watch her predecessors dealing with the Europeans, than it was to deal with them herself. Exasperation became her stock in trade. Thirdly, over the next years, beyond her premiership and into her retirement, the pace of the European project would proceed in directions, and with a pace, somewhat to her distaste, even though it was in its essence somewhat Thatcherite. De Gaulle's fears about the attitude Britain might one day take with Europe were amply realised in the shape of Thatcher. Her gathering disquiet became to some extent the trajectory of the Tory Party: a responsorial jingoism would emerge in the wake of the frustration arising out of certain battles.

What were these? Many of them are dry budgetary or constitutional matters. One sometimes raises an eyebrow at the rawness of emotion engendered at the highest levels over things like VAT and rebates. Thatcher was quite capable of being as upset about the plight of a British fisherman as a British fisherman would be. But the main point of contention was the issue – soon to become a perennial one – of payments made by the UK into the EU budget.

Agriculture – as enshrined in the Common Agricultural Policy – had been a central aspect of the European project all along: from the outset, it had been a particular priority for both France and Germany. The goal had been to protect French and German farmers from competition: in time, this had led to overproduction, and the EU was forced to buy up surplus in order to maintain prices. But farming was not so much a priority of the UK: Thatcher felt it was an unfair deal and began to refer at times to getting 'our money' back. As she increasingly began to identify herself with the British state, she began to speak of getting 'my money' back. It was suggested that the UK should give up some of its monopoly on North Sea oil in exchange for a lowering of its net contribution – Thatcher fiercely opposed this, and threatened to withhold VAT payments. Divergent national interests were beginning to trump the European one. Had Robert Schuman been in the room he would have advocated a different approach. In fact, Thatcher's way of going about her business dismayed the most Schuman-like man in the room – Roy Jenkins, who was by now out of government and President of the Commission. Jenkins tried, without much success, to calm her down. For him, Thatcher was not behaving in quite the way one should as a member of a community.

In mitigation, this was a time when the UK was the third poorest of the nations in the EEC, and not far from being the biggest net contributor: Thatcher was fighting on behalf of a country she considered – with some evidence – to be struggling with a stagnant economy. The commitment of peoples to an abstract idea of freedom founders when those peoples start to be poor. Even so, Thatcher might have gone about her business in a more collegiate way. The suspicion remains that Margaret Thatcher did not really like the French: it was as if de Gaulle had met a belated rejoinder and a comparable stubbornness after leaving the scene. At Fontainebleau in 1984, Thatcher won a victory that would attain mythic status on the right, winning the multi-billion pound British rebate. By the early 2000s however, the imbalance had gone the other way, and the

French under Jacques Chirac, now more impoverished than the UK, had begun to wonder why his country, along with the also struggling Italy, had become the chief contributors to the UK rebate. After a marathon negotiation in 2005, Blair gave some of the rebate back, but at the time of the decision to Leave, the UK was still receiving an instant rebate on all EU payments of around £5 billion per year[170].

It seems retrospectively surprising that Thatcher – already riled by the rebate negotiations – signed up in 1986 to the Single European Act. It would lead in time to greater decision-making at the European level, to which Thatcher would grow increasingly opposed. The legislation would be introduced under the Delors Commission: Jacques Delors, a French socialist and future European Commission President, would be a great bugbear for Thatcher and the far right in the years to come. But the reason she did sign the act was that its core intentions were Thatcherite and flowed out of the need for further free trade. It matched up with the sort of Europe Thatcher wanted: a small state Europe. But at the same time, a new harmonisation of EU-wide rules, known as the cooperation procedure, came into force: this gave the European Parliament a chance to have a say in legislation, making it for the first time an entity of real consequence. Qualified majority voting – essentially a weakening of the UK's right to veto legislation – was extended across the whole single market programme. A recent documentary by Nick Robinson for the BBC *Europe: Them or Us* explained that Thatcher simply hadn't read the Act right through – an uncharacteristic mistake[171]. It is as if divisions within Thatcher rippled out to become divisions within her party, and ultimately divisions within the nation. Over time, increasingly provoked by the Delorsian view of Europe, Thatcher ramped up her language, most notably in her 1989 Bruges speech, which is still quoted today with admiration in Eurosceptic circles:

> We have not successfully rolled back the frontiers of the state in Britain, only to see them re-imposed at a European level, with a European super-state exercising a new dominance from Brussels.

Like this the term 'superstate' entered British political parlance. Benn and Jenkins had had a similar-sounding argument – but with the crucial distinction that where Benn had been railing against a free-market Europe, Thatcher was railing against Delorsian federalism.

A changed Europe had created realignment in British politics. Would the arguments of 'Take back control' in 2016 have had quite such validity if something similar had never been said from the lips of a sitting prime minister? Thatcher bequeathed a tone. When Nigel Farage taunted his fellow MEPs after the referendum vote – 'You're not laughing now!' – he was echoing her jingoistic rhetoric. Thatcher's influence was wider still: around this time, a young journalist named Alexander de Pfeffel 'Boris' Johnson began filing pieces from Brussels which established a cartoonish version of the European project. His headlines included: 'Brussels recruits sniffers to ensure that Euro-manure smells the same', 'Threat to British pink sausages' and 'Snails are fish, says EU'[172]. Johnson's fear – too humorous to be deeply held – was one of pan-European sameiness. It was as if Thatcher's comic alter ego had secured a column in the *Daily Telegraph*. When Prime Minister Theresa May stated in 2016 that the next person to find out she was a 'bloody difficult woman' would be Jean-Claude Junker, she was doing a plausible Thatcher impersonation. It is possible that conciliatory rhetoric around the same policies might have yielded a different national mood.

However, if one actually reads Thatcher's Bruges speech, rather than dipping into its most famous excerpt, one finds something which – read with 2016 in mind – seems almost surprising. Thatcher wasn't arguing for an exit from the European Union. Instead she had this to say:

> Let me be quite clear: Britain does not dream of some cosy, isolated existence on the fringes of the European Community. Our destiny is in Europe, as part of the Community.[173]

Lord Acton wrote: 'Power tends to corrupt, and absolute power corrupts absolutely'. By the late 1980s, as her time in office neared its conclusion, this corruption was beginning to be noted in Margaret Thatcher. Her chancellor John Major persuaded her to enter the Exchange Rate Mechanism; she did so only with a show of reluctance – a reluctance, which would be justified by events. But her rhetoric increasingly began to jar. One day in the not-too-distant future Theresa May will leave Downing Street, and Europe shall have been the chief question of her premiership. So it went for Thatcher – her 'No, no, no' uttered first at the 1990s Rome summit to Delors and then at the despatch-box in the House of Commons – was too much for Geoffrey Howe, then Leader of the House of Commons and the longest-serving member of her administration. His resignation was a critique of Thatcher's manner of dealing with the Europeans. Once again we find Churchill invoked:

> I have to say that I find Winston Churchill's perception [a reasonable trade of national sovereignty][174] a good deal more convincing, and more encouraging for the interests of our nation, than the nightmare image sometimes conjured up by my right hon. Friend, who seems sometimes to look out upon a continent that is positively teeming with ill-intentioned people, scheming, in her words, to 'extinguish democracy', to 'dissolve our national identities' and to lead us 'through the back-door into a federal Europe'.[175]

Thatcher would seethe for years to come.

Would the Conservative Party have returned time again to Europe had Mrs Thatcher not been brought down by that very issue? And if the issue had recurred, would it have done so with such emotion?

At any rate, this emotion was now bottled and carried forward into another era – one of economic contraction and rising inequality, where it could easily form part of a protest vote.

FROM MAASTRICHT TO LISBON

By 1992, Thatcher's successor John Major had signed up to the Maastricht Treaty. This created the three pillars of the European Union: European Communities (a renaming of the EEC), Common Foreign and Security Policy (CFSP), and police and judicial cooperation in criminal matters (JHA). It was in other respects a highly ambitious agreement, with political integration to the fore. Maastricht created economic and monetary union – and would lead in time to the Euro. It put in place new Community policies in the spheres of education, culture, co-operation and development, and further increased the powers of the European Parliament: the co-decision procedure came into force, allowing it to approve or reject a legislative proposal, or propose amendments to it. The Council was not legally obliged to follow the European Parliament's suggestions – but it was obliged to listen, and Parliament could veto legislation if its amendments were not accepted. It was an attempt at democratic accountability. But in the UK, with European election turnout in the mid 30 per cent range throughout the early 1990s, and dipping to a low in the mid-20s in 1999 – a figure far below the average European turnout – to give powers to the European Parliament did not feel like giving power to the UK voter. The Belgian voters – with turnout in the 90 per cent range throughout the 1990s and into the present time – no doubt felt differently. Many of those who would rage in 2016 about lack of democratic accountability, presumably had a track record of not exercising their democratic right in the EU context.[176]

In Maastricht, Major claimed 'game, set and match for Britain' after securing an opt-out on the Social Chapter and the single currency. If this was the case, then Britain was a tennis player obliged to keep on entering tournaments. In European politics there are no definitive victories, only temporary accommodations. And in any case, perhaps it wasn't helpful to think of an essentially cooperative project in competitive metaphor: it isn't a turn of phrase that would have occurred to Churchill or Schuman. Life went on. The fiasco over Black Wednesday seemed to confirm the Thatcherite's worst fears about economic integration. In this instance the pound kept falling under the limit set by the Exchange Rate Mechanism – the very system we have just seen Major persuading his predecessor to join. After a massive selling-off of $10 billion worth of pounds by George Soros's Quantum Fund, the Bank of England could not prop up its currency: it was a calamity which cost the Treasury somewhere in the region of £3 billion.

These dramatic events sharpened the polarisation of opinion. Either the ideal Europe was a federal union committed to social improvement of its peoples, or it needed to be jettisoned altogether. A centre ground still existed – as the Blair administration shows – but there was migration to the fringes: UKIP was founded in 1993.

The disaster surrounding the ERM echoes in later arguments surrounding the wisdom of joining the Euro. The UK opted out, but the new money went into circulation on the continent on 1st January 1999. Debate continues into the present day as to the ongoing viability of the single currency. For some economists like Paul Krugman, the European Union is inherently ill-suited to the project of currency union – it is not, to use, the preferred jargon of economists, an OCA – or Optimal Currency Union. For Krugman, the Soros debacle was fortuitous insofar as it took Britain out of the ERM, and made it politically impossible to join a doomed project. In the other camp is Martin Sandbu who in his book *Europe's Orphan*, argues that the Euro is perfectly plausible in theory: it is only that the political will has not been there to forge the right institutions, and to make sensible policy – particularly in the aftermath of the 2008-9 financial crisis. In that instance, the European Central Bank did act as lender of last resort to the banking system, but there was no mechanism in place across member states to engender restructuring. In Sandbu's view, it's not that the Euro won't work per se, it's that it won't work with the system as we currently have it, and especially with the current vogue for austerity policies. Unfortunately, those who recognise the need for different policy-making in the Eurozone tend to disagree on whether further fiscal and political union is required. For Sandbu, the answer is no – the Eurozone will be healthy only if governments can institute smarter policy. Others would argue that closer integration is worth pursuing only if mutualisation of debt can be agreed upon.

Around 2000, the pressure was turned up in a number of ways. First, there was the eagerness of those who believed in the project to accelerate it. Maastricht would be followed by the Treaty of Amsterdam in 1997 which would institute European employment law. The Treaty of Nice (2001) prepared the EU for its 2004 expansion which we have already seen leading to a rise in the net migration numbers in Chapter 15. The Lisbon Treaty created the new positions of the President of the European Council – now held by Donald Tusk – and the High Representative of the Union for Foreign Affairs and Security Policy, currently Federica Mogherini. At Lisbon, a certain Article 50 also came into force – outlining a process nobody expected to happen, by which a country might leave the EU.

In among all this – and exacerbated by episodes like Black Wednesday – was an ever-escalating emotion. Extreme voices on both sides began to dominate the argument: Jean-Marie Le Pen in France and Nigel Farage in Britain began to argue for an end to their countries' involvement in the EU; meanwhile, federal Europe had begun to have an undeniable air of corruption. By 2014, those in favour of Europe would have to endure having the likes of new president of the European Commission Jean-Claude Juncker as their standard-bearer: Juncker had turned Luxembourg into a centre for corporate tax avoidance, proudly courting the investment of Amazon among others[177]. A moderate position – where most people will go, if the political choice before them will permit – was beginning to seem imperfectly represented.

But if the middle position was becoming rarer in some respects it would soon find a champion in Tony Blair.

THE CONSERVATIVES DURING THE BLAIR YEARS

A terrifying possibility now stalks modern British politics, almost unsayable: it is that Tony Blair might have been right from time to time.

Blair's instincts in Europe had been similar to Major's, but he had had a less vexing party to manage. Major had said that Britain would always be at the heart of Europe; Blair sought to maintain this position. Both would sometimes oppose the federalist tendency – Major, in negotiating the Maastricht opt-outs and Blair had sometimes found it cathartic to bait the federalists. Furthermore, he hadn't completely rolled over on the rebate renegotiations, as the right wing press had suggested. But both had sought to keep British involvement in the European project going: Major had signed the Maastricht Treaty and agreed therefore in principle to some version of closer union. Blair's instinct had been to join the Euro, but he had mainly been concerned with wider questions about how the EU should project its power: he felt it was riven with internal debates which were usually to its own detriment. Reading Blair's memoirs, one gets a strong impression of the stress and dullness of dealing with an expanded EU. But he never seriously wavered from a wish to muddle through somehow. In order to deal with the EU, one required patience, and the ability to step back and be philosophical about it: one had to recall Schuman, one had to recall Churchill.

What had happened to the Conservative Party in the meanwhile? It was around this time that Theresa May made her 'nasty party' speech. About the only thing which did identify it was Europe; this made it grow as an issue – harmlessly, when it was in opposition, but with powerful consequences should the party ever return to power. May didn't mention Europe at all in the 'nasty party' speech – but many others were doing so, and some were doing so most of the time. The Conservatives' Europe obsession was evident in the Party's choice of leaders after Major had resigned following Blair's 1997 landslide. Usually this amounted to a simple policy of not opting for Ken Clarke – then, as now, the party's most notable Europhile. William Hague would ultimately settle for the Remain side on the referendum but his initial win owed much to the backing of Thatcher and the supporters of arch-Eurosceptic John

Redwood. This pattern was repeated again in 2001, with Iain Duncan Smith, who really was a Eurosceptic, again defeating Clarke. Duncan Smith was widely considered a poor leader, and would be replaced by the more competent Michael Howard – also a Eurosceptic.

Even Cameron's victory in the 2005 leadership contest had been achieved on the back of saying a good deal of Eurosceptic things. For instance, in the special *Question Time* debate between Cameron and David Davis in November 2005, the future prime minister said: 'I think that we should have a very clear strategic imperative, which is that we need to bring back the powers over social policy and employment policy that are causing so much damage to British business.'[178]

It was impossible even for the moderniser Cameron not to wink continually at the Eurosceptic wing of his party.

As we know, this winking had turned by 2016 to outright concession and the referendum campaign that would oust him.

21 – THE REFERENDUM CAMPAIGN

For all the voluminous coverage in the media, the factual record of recent events is remarkably thin: sometimes in re-
searching a book like this, the best one has to go on is an article in the *Daily Mail*. According to that august tabloid, David
Cameron made the decision to hold the referendum on Britain's membership of the EU at a pizzeria in Chicago's O'Hare
International Airport[179]. The airport in question was named
after Edward O'Hare, who had received a Medal of Honour
in World War II, but for many Remain voters there would
be nothing honourable about Cameron's decision taken over
that pizza, surrounded by bodyguards, while others tweeted
his presence. In the future, President Obama would be among
those – Chancellor George Osborne would be another – who
would ardently attempt to dissuade Cameron from proceeding
with the vote. The UK prime minister would reply to the US
president that it was a 'party management issue'. But it can be
argued that Cameron's job as prime minister was not to lead
the Conservative Party but to lead the nation: to place party
interest over the national interest in the way he did has been
deemed a betrayal of his office.

Cameron's admirers still argue for Cameron's bravery in
giving the British people a say on the matter. They argue that
the issue of Europe, whose sclerotic institutions were eroding
British sovereignty – and even in some quasi-mystical way,
national character – was not one seriously to be avoided: it
was better to get it over and done with. As we have seen, the

European Union had for a long time been caught between the federalists' desire for closer political union, and the wish for a looser arrangement, based principally on a Thatcherite wish to trade. Even so, there are a number of objections to the route Cameron took. As with the Iraq War, the proponents of a misjudgement are forced to argue that their decision is superior to a hypothetical parallel set of events – their argument can never be tested against reality, and can seem a distraction from a chaotic sequence that really did occur. Secondly – and more importantly – if decision-making is to proceed as a series of concessions to noise, then one will end up with the rule of the noisiest. It might be argued that Cameron vacated the centre ground by listening to those types who are always present in any democracy: those who would be better ignored.

On the other hand, one must admit that with Macron ascendant in France, and the reassuring presence (for the time being) of Angela Merkel in Germany, Cameron's legacy doesn't at the moment seem to be an immediate unravelling of the European Union: even so, it must be said that he looks a limited figure, a man who flipped a coin when he might have construed a strategy.

This is not to say that there was no context to the decision to grant the referendum: in politics, there is always context to one's mistakes. To understand the decision, one must rush back in time hurdling in reverse a particular piece of knowledge: Cameron didn't know when he gave his referendum promise that he would win the 2015 General Election outright. In fact, we can look back at his career now and see that the decimation of the Liberal Democrats in that vote – Clegg's party returned only 8 MPs to the House of Commons, down from 57 in 2010 – was the moment when Cameron was finally exposed, to his own detriment, as a Conservative prime minister. It might therefore be said that Cameron is guilty of two superficialities at once: he led the nation into a vote on account of his party interest, while also not expecting to have to go through with it. His thinking was electoral when it should have been moral. According to such a mindset, almost any decision might be made to seem intellectually palatable if only it can be made to seem electorally attractive.

In such a climate, power goes to whoever seizes the megaphone.

THE MAN WHO SEIZED THE MEGAPHONE

Nigel Farage was born in 1964 to Barbara and Guy Farage. Guy Farage was a stockbroker, as Nigel would be; his mother – maiden name Stevens – would cause a minor stir by posing naked in Women's Institute charity calendars into her seventies. Inevitably for someone who has argued the positions he has, it has been noted that the name Farage is ancient Huguenot: Farage is a man of partly French blood arguing for Britishness. Furthermore,

Fig. 19 Nigel Farage.[180]

one of his great-grandparents was German, and benefited from this country's open borders: we owe the existence of Nigel Farage to immigration.

Farage attended Dulwich College, a racially diverse school, where he was made a prefect. This appointment caused alarm in teacher Chloe Deakin for an eye-catching reason: Farage was considered then a fascist and a racist. Deakin wrote to her seniors to complain about the matter:

> Another colleague, who teaches the boy, described his publicly professed racist and neo-fascist views; and he cited a particular incident in which Farage was so offensive to a boy in his set, that he had to be removed from the lesson. This master stated his view that this behaviour was precisely why the boy should not be made a prefect.[181]

The master of Dulwich at the time David Emms continues to argue that Farage never exhibited more than 'cheekiness', but this is not the impression one gets from the following passage of Deakin's letter:

> Yet another colleague described how, at a Combined Cadet Force (CCF) camp organised by the college, Farage and others had marched through a quiet Sussex village very late at night shouting Hitler-youth songs.

It would be unpleasant to try to argue this away: fascism is a line not to be crossed at any age in the name of being a character. Perhaps people do not change as much as they would like to think they do: the Farage who roamed the corridors of Dulwich College feels remarkably similar to the Farage who would eventually emerge on the national stage: insistent, jocular, blurring the lines with a facile humour between what should and should not be said.

Farage was active in the Conservative Party from a young age, but Major's signing of the Maastricht Treaty was too much for him, and he became one of the founding members of UKIP in 1993. By 1999, Farage had made it to the European Parliament: it is one of the features of his career that he finds it easy to do well in these elections when there is a low turnout, but impossible to win a seat in Parliament when more people are taking notice – as his defeat in 2015 in the seat of Thanet South shows. We can note a paradox: Farage's only real power was in an organisation he had dedicated himself to destroying – the European Parliament. But Farage has a thick skin, and has the zealot's option of being able to attribute his setbacks to the presence of ignorant people in the world who do not share his zeal. Even so, Farage is able to point to some victories in the European Parliament. Goethe said that when a man has an idea he sees it in everything. Seeing the shoddiness of the European project in everything, and possessing a naturally abrasive personality, Farage has sometimes been successful in exposing the corruption of some of those high up in the European Union project. He was, for instance, instrumental in bringing to light the case of Jacques Barrot, who arrived as the new EU Commissioner for Tourism and Transport, having not revealed a conviction he had received in France for embezzlement of party funds. Farage revealed it for him – the worst that can be said is that he did so with an immature glee at odds with the high-mindedness of the original project. In the end, in any case, Barrot survived – but Farage had arguably provided a useful service in drawing attention to the whiff of corruption.

More often Farage was simply rude – and worse, rude in the name of a certain plucky Britishness. This was the case even when – indeed, especially when – he claimed not to be. Here he is, for instance, greeting EU President Hermann van Rampuy, in 2010:

> You have the charisma of a damp rag, and the appearance of a low-grade bank clerk. And the question that I want to ask, [...] that we're all going to ask, is 'Who are you?' I'd never heard of you. Nobody in Europe had ever heard of you.[182]

Farage went on to call Rampuy's country, Belgium – the country of Bruegel, René Magritte, and Tintin to name only a few – a 'non-country'. It might also be said that the violation of Belgian neutrality was the circumstance that brought Britain into the First World War – an extravagant gesture if Belgium really were as null as Farage said it was.

But this was the Farage way. He was a man who had found his cause and found a forum in which to promote it. The energy of his rhetoric had reached a kind of critical momentum, and at precisely the moment when there were no comparably memorable voices ranged against him.

He was also beginning to make inroads into the Conservative Party. In fact, the point about Farage in the end is that he could never have prospered alone: indeed, his career until 2016 was largely a story of a man jeering at the margins of the polity. What had changed? It could be argued that Angela Merkel's decision to open up Germany's borders altered the mood of European nations when it came to immigrant peoples; this coincided with a world increasingly hooked on social media platforms which have a way of augmenting anger once it is arrived at, and saying the hitherto unsayable to lift the hysteria up a notch. This might be termed the argument from beneath, and there is no doubt something to it. But at the same time those in high places, within the 2016 Trump campaign, within the Russian government, and in the halls of Facebook – not to mention a welter of far-right figures worldwide from Viktor Orban, to Benjamin Netanyahu and Marine le Pen – were either adding to the radical mood, or in Mark Zuckerberg's case, letting it slide. It would emerge that Arron Banks, one of the biggest donors to the Leave.EU campaign visited the Russian embassy in November 2015: it would also be revealed that Banks, Farage and Alexander Yakovenko – the Russian ambassador – had lunched together in November 2016, three days before Farage was photographed sycophantically thumbs-upping next to Donald Trump in Trump Tower. Matthew d'Ancona picks up the story:

> It also appears that the ambassador offered to help Banks broker a deal involving six goldmines in Siberia. This does not seem, in other words, to be routine schmoozing or glad-handing. It has the whiff of a nexus, suggesting a purpose, or multiple purposes.[183]

And as always when power is established in these times, it cannot help but turn up in one's Facebook feed. It would turn out that throughout the referendum campaign, the soon-to-be-defunct firm Cambridge Analytica had been targeting the Facebook accounts of persuadable voters with the aim to increase the vote in the Leave column. Any sense of illegitimacy about the vote that would accrue from that would also in part accrue to May's eventual premiership. No one would doubt that she had won fair and square by party rules: but her rise to power would always be another aspect of a period of unreality, where one was never quite sure to what extent the electorate had really known its mind.

THE CAMERON PANIC

During the 2010-15 parliament, Cameron experienced two defections from his own ranks to UKIP. One was Douglas Carswell – at the time of the EU referendum the only UKIP MP, and who chose not to stand in the 2017 general election. The other was Mark Reckless, who would subsequently lose his seat in 2015.

Did these defections alarm Cameron unnecessarily? On the one hand, his worries now seem vindicated. In 2016, it would become clear that there were plenty around his Cabinet table – including senior ministers like Michael Gove and Iain Duncan Smith – who were to campaign happily for 'out'. Living with this unease would prove too much for Cameron. But these contrary voices might never have been heard – and certainly not heard to such an extent – had the genie been kept in the bottle: the referendum campaign, intended to clear the air, in fact whipped a reasonably calm sky into thunderstorm. Men like Gove and Duncan Smith – Tory through and through – were never, one now suspects, likely to leave the Conservative Party. If Cameron had a problem then it resided in more independent-thinking backbenchers, like Jacob Rees-Mogg – men without access to the perks of ministerial life – but again one doubts if he would ever have crossed over to the UKIP benches. We shall never know what would have happened if Cameron had faced them down: it is likely that the issue would have been deferred, a mass exodus to UKIP evaded, and that Cameron would have served out his two terms, with his trademark optimistic blandness. Even the eventual referendum campaign appears to show that the fault lines between UKIP and the Conservatives were always likely to hold: the division between the official Vote Leave campaign, and Farage's more quixotic Leave.EU campaign, and the subsequent decline in UKIP support under the lesser leadership of Paul Nuttall, are further indications of an instability in the UKIP project that was probably always there. The French philosopher Montaigne admitted that sometimes, after a period of long vacillation, he made wild decisions just for the pleasure of no longer having a decision hanging over him: there is a suspicion of that here with Cameron. A sudden move in the wrong direction briefly compensated for the anxiety of having made no moves for a long time: the suspicion remains that he might have been better moving decisively and to the good on some other matter, than on moving hastily on this.

But by 2014, UKIP had achieved a plurality of votes in

the 2014 European election – a bad omen, it turned out, for any eventual referendum. Cameron would end up leading a half-hearted army against an army of believers. Of course, in January 2013, Cameron had already offered his in-out referendum, saying:

> Simply asking the British people to carry on accepting a European settlement over which they have had little choice is a path to ensuring that when the question is finally put – and at some stage it will have to be – it is much more likely that the British people will reject the European Union.[184]

Cameron's rationale was therefore that the referendum he was about to give was more winnable than some hypothetical future referendum. This belief looks incongruous now when set against the defeat he was to suffer in this one, but the shock of that defeat is also proof that he wasn't misguided in his fears about the way in which the wind was blowing. Cameron's main mistake was to proceed on an emotive issue with an air of breezy pragmatism: his style of conducing politics never quite matched the enormity of this particular issue.

By May 2013, a draft European referendum bill had been put forward, stating that in the event of a Conservative victory, an EU referendum must take place no later than 31st December 2017. Cameron had already stated that he would campaign 'heart and soul' for membership, but for many he was already caught up in an impossible contradiction: if Cameron was indeed an ardent believer in the European project then why grant the referendum at all? This difficulty, in its infancy in 2013, would mature monstrously during the campaign itself: his every appearance was a visible wrestle with that contradiction. The ambiguity of his position was particularly pronounced when he stood on the steps of Downing Street to review the results of his much-touted pre-referendum negotiation.

> But let me tell you what I believe. I do not love Brussels. I love Britain. And my job – the job of the British Prime Minister – is doing all in my power to protect Britain's interests.[185]

Boris Johnson – hand outstretched for the crown – had the wherewithal to retort that although he did love Brussels, he would be campaigning to leave. It was a small point, but Johnson had already outflanked Cameron. He would campaign in terms of love, whereas Cameron had already committed himself to campaigning for something that he didn't like: in a campaign surrounding highly complex constitutional and legal issues, the emotional framing of the debate would prove decisive. Cameron might instead have borrowed the ardent post-war Churchillian rhetoric which we saw a few chapters ago – the language of peace and international cooperation. To have done so would have been to wrest a meaningful momentum, and to align himself at the same time with the ghost of a revered prime minister. Political campaigns are like symphonies: one must find the right key with which to begin. Cameron hadn't; Johnson had.

You can tell an age by its slurs. The McCarthy era would have been impossible without the accusation 'communist'. In

Shakespeare's time, 'Turk' was an insult – which produces for you the nervous religiosity of the times, and the secret fear of the Islamic Other that permeated Elizabethan society. The events of 2016 have caused the advent of a new barrage of insults – 'neoliberal', 'liberal', 'Remoaner'. To be liberal used to mean that one was tolerant, open-minded about interaction with other cultures. Now it refers to the apathy of privilege, and is suggestive of an unimaginative accommodation with an unjust status quo.

Was there an establishment complacency in the air, of a kind which deserved the surprise result which ensued? Did our governing classes deserve what was coming? In fact, we've already seen it in previous chapters – in the budgets of George Osborne, in the unravelling of New Labour, and in rising inequality from the 1980s until the present time. It is also there in the decline of public discourse, which we glanced off in relation to our heroine in an earlier chapter, in the expenses scandal, in the cheerful failings at Barclays, RBS and Credit Suisse, in a phone-hacking media, and in the legislative failure to move forward with proportional representation.

All these things had given politics and institutional power an ossified look. At its best Brexit can be taken as a pair of electrodes to a corpsed establishment.

But it is hard to avoid the suspicion that all this had too chancy a feel to be finally attributable to the electorate. The knife-edge vote has the feel of spasm, and randomness at work. True, individual foible played out as it did in the true Shakespearean style. A certain complacency had snuck into Cameron. This stemmed partly from recent circumstances. From his narrow 55-45 per cent victory in the 2014 referendum over Scottish independence he appears to have drawn the conclusion that people in the EU referendum would vote, as the Scottish had seemed to do, primarily on economic matters. Cameron may also have missed certain warning signs secreted in his 2015 General Election victory, which had always had a rancid taste to anyone not absolutely pledged to the Tory cause. Many voted Conservative out of a fear of a Miliband-Sturgeon coalition: in some quarters, it was not so much a vote for Cameron, as a vote in favour of an ill-examined English nationalism. The prime minister had been the chance beneficiary of a fickle anger: many who voted for him in 2015 would vote to leave the EU in 2016. Post-referendum, this rage still percolated – this essentially rudderless anger aligning itself to some extent behind Corbyn in the 2017 general election.

In all this, one option had been closed off to Cameron – or rather, he had closed it off for himself. He had missed the chance to keep himself above the fray as Harold Wilson had done in 1975. If he had done so, he might still be prime minister, Theresa May would still be home secretary, and the Cameron administration might be wearily enacting the vote.

THE CAMERON RENEGOTIATION

Cameron's renegotiation formed an important part of his strategy. Intended to illustrate the possibility of reform if only the right UK prime minister (i.e. Cameron) were at the helm, it instead served to illustrate the opposite: the difficulty of navigating the labyrinthine power structures of the European Union would be vividly brought home to the British electorate.

Why did Cameron get less than he hoped for from the negotiations? A few plausible reasons might be adduced. In the first place, few people in Brussels really expected him to lose the referendum vote, and so were ill-disposed from the outset to award concessions. Early in the premiership of Theresa May, reports speculated that some capitals in the European Union were considering giving Britain a seven-year emergency brake on immigration as part of a Brexit deal[186]. Cameron must have read these reports with some irritation: it was the sort of concession that might really have made a difference to him. But there was another problem, which we have already touched upon: the four freedoms of goods, services, people and capital are not, for those who believe in the project, particularly negotiable.

Cameron's ensuing negotiation, if it was deemed insufficient, was not a clinching failure if you happened to feel that relations as they stood with Brussels were not apocalyptically bad. But Cameron had got himself into a position where unless he could get something truly eye-catching, he would hurt his own case. But little eye-catching ever happens in the EU — in one sense, as an instrument of peace, that is inevitable and even desirable. In retrospect, the sluggish and unwieldy nature of the EU meant that the renegotiation was always more likely to feed into the Leave argument, than into his.

But was the negotiation really so bad as all that?

Cameron's gains were a mixture of the cosmetic, the insufficient, and the reasonably substantive. It would not have been a completely wasted exercise had the vote gone the other way.

In the first place, Cameron secured a pledge for Britain never to enter the euro. It was hard to present this as a major coup since for many people this was unthinkable anyhow: even Gordon Brown, a more enthusiastic European than Cameron, had fought to keep us out, and things had declined significantly since then, as we glanced off in Chapter 20. That said, for the committed Europhile, it was not a small concession to acknowledge the existence of another currency besides their own. Cameron also achieved goals on economic governance – securing, for instance, an opt-out on future Eurozone bailouts. This aspect of the agreement was designed to stave off claims by Vote Leave that Britain was caught in a spiral of huge and unpredictable payments. This had been exaggerated by the Brexit camp: by the time of the renegotiation, Britain had only paid out twice: £3.2bn for Ireland in November 2010 (much less than the £7-10 billion feared by the Eurosceptic press) and £4.2 billion for Portugal in May 2011. Any payments in respect of the Greek bailouts were made through the International Monetary Fund – the UK's membership of which few were disputing – and not through the EU[187]. In looking to appease a trumped-up rage, it might be said that Cameron had sanctioned a parallel version of reality – although of course, the difficulty of politics is that numerous subjectivities all jostle on the national scale at once, and must somehow be resolved into national policy. Cameron's negotiation also chalked up a limited win for the financial sector: if British bankers found themselves discriminated against by the Eurozone, it would now be possible for the UK to raise the matter in the Council of Ministers. Although a political recourse for the banking industry, this was obviously only of interest to a small and mistrusted section of the population.[188]

Cameron was also able to secure a commitment in relation to regulation that the Council would look at 'feasible burden reduction targets in key sectors'[189]. This was meant to cater to the oft-heard gripe that European regulation is bad for business. In reality, it was little more than a generalised reiteration of the status quo – a minor victory for the Thatcherite idea of Europe. Besides, those who dislike regulation in business tend to dislike it so much that mere promises are insufficient: for the free marketer like Liam Fox or Andrea Leadsom, only a gigantic sweeping-away will do. Again, for those toiling in poverty, this aspect of the renegotiation would also seem irrelevant: Cameron's economic concessions were not sufficiently eye-catching to swing votes.

The issue of sovereignty would become of crucial importance in the ensuing campaign. The Vote Leave slogan of 'Take Back Control' is that rare thing: a catchy distillation of a constitutional point. How did Cameron fare on that front? He gained a commitment to a British opt-out on 'ever closer union'. Once again, to those who have spotted the perfidy of federalism in their midst, mere assurances like this are not enough. For the Leave side, this was the sort of commitment likely to be reneged upon by Europhiles at some later date, and therefore worth little. Cameron was also able to tout that he had secured a 'red card' for national parliaments on EU legislation. This was progress on the previous 'yellow card' and 'orange card' procedure, since it created the possibility that nation states could club together to demand that legislation be dropped altogether instead of merely demanding its review. But the 55 per cent threshold for the 'red card' was very high, and there were doubts that the Commission would ever table any motion so objectionable for it to be needed.

On immigration – the fateful issue which would cost him in the end – Cameron arguably scored his greatest success. He managed to secure a four-year brake on benefits for migrant workers for a period of seven years. This was intended to answer the claims of Farage and others that the NHS was falling apart at the hands of immigrants – an interpretation which is doubtful as we shall see in Chapter 28. But Cameron had been reduced to seeking policies to pacify a non-specific rage. Political rage is protean: it weaves between facts, content only to grow. Once more we see Cameron responding to a false Eurosceptic narrative, thereby reinforcing it.

Immigration is a good example of another lamentable feature of the renegotiation: its lack of detail. The mechanism was projected to kick in only if a member state could prove that a given migrant had placed 'excessive pressure on the proper functioning of its public services'[190]. But it was not quite clear what 'excessive pressure' meant. For some the negotiation looked suspiciously thin, as if no one ever really intended to act upon it. And while this part of the deal was touted as a win by Cameron, rumours circulated that he had demanded the brake to last not for seven years, but 13.

Cameron's renegotiation ought to have formed an important backdrop to the referendum campaign, but in the weeks that followed it was rarely mentioned: Remainers could only refer to it half-heartedly; Leavers with passing contempt. It had the hallmarks of an exercise too trivial to alter the vast drama of the moment. Cameron had set himself to altering what he had also set himself to defend; when he couldn't substantially alter it, he had to defend it anyway. This fact in itself looked incriminating – he looked like a man loitering about the scene shiftily, when he should have been bestriding it. Just when the European Union needed an advocate, it had found his polished lukewarmth. But then only someone lukewarm to it would ever have granted the referendum in the first place. Like many a fiasco, it was essentially circular.

THE CAMPAIGN ITSELF

As we have seen, the Remain side had hoped to run a campaign according to the blueprint for the Scottish referendum and the 2015 election – namely to focus on the economic risk of altering the status quo. This left the Remain campaign vulnerable to an attack on an issue not revolving around money: the Leave campaign would find an effective one in the shape of immigration.

One keeps returning to the suspicion that Cameron misinterpreted the 2015 General Election result. Here is Rafael Bahr in an article 'How Remain Failed: the Inside Story of a Doomed Campaign':

> Cameron gambled everything on the European referendum because he thought the centre was secure. He and George Osborne believed, as one of their cabinet allies told me: 'It will be about jobs and the economy and it won't even be close.'[191]

Having pulled off the seemingly impossible in 2015, they now expected to be faced with the comparatively straightforward. Optimism about the task ahead was compounded by Cameron's own natural sunniness, which enabled him to think of Gove and Johnson as likely allies until it was too late. It is widely understood today that he was stunned by both Gove and Johnson's decision to campaign against him, with Gove's fickleness particularly hurtful: it is a measure of how quickly events move that Gove in those days was noted for his loyalty. When it came to Johnson, Cameron might have underestimated how much others craved an office he himself had tended to wear casually, as a natural right. The suit of power had always fitted him too snugly, and he underestimated how enviable it looked to those who lacked his serendipity, and who had not worn it.

The difficulty of the job that he had always seemed to enjoy was revealing itself to him suddenly, just as he was about to lose it.

Meanwhile, his opponents had a decisive plan, and several catchy slogans. The words Project Fear cannot help but echo in the mind of anyone who remembers Britain at that time. It was both mantra and taunt. It was a reversal of the old FDR line: 'We have nothing to fear, but fear itself'. That had been a sunny call to a perplexed people in the midst of the Great Depression. This was a cry full of obscure self-pity in a time of comparative prosperity: 'You're trying to make me afraid, but I won't let you.' It assumed an intention on the part of the speaker that could never be proven: the phrase could make simple disagreement escalate suddenly into an outsized accusation. It soon became an obstacle to the Remainers when it came to making their case. Jeering immaturity turned out to have the capacity to be catching: it seemed fun to the Leaver when someone was quoting statistics at them not to quote back an opposing set of statistics, but instead to poke their interlocutor in the eye.

George Osborne, anxious to keep the conversation on the economy, produced an authoritative-looking report estimating how much a potential Leave vote would cost the British economy. In the initial Treasury report, it had been claimed that each household would be £4,300 the poorer in the event of a vote to Leave. This was based on the assumption that the overall economy would shrink by 6 per cent[192]. The precision of the eventual figure left the government open to attack: it was to make an imprecise business like economic prediction seem more precise than it was – and besides, households do not experience uniform destinies which mirror any overall pattern of national GDP. Former Bank of England governor Mervyn King was among those who pounced after the referendum result came in: 'The Treasury is in a difficult position now because it did make forecasts that were exaggerated in terms of at least the certainty and now will have to row back'[193]. In the event of it, Osborne would not have to spend long rowing back his claims because he would be fired by Theresa May.

But before then, he would make other subsidiary claims. One was that a vote to Leave would trigger the necessity for an emergency budget, which he darkly hinted would include further austerity to stave off a recession. He also suggested that a Brexit vote would entail a lowering of house prices: 'there would be a hit to the value of people's homes by at least 10 percent and up to 18 percent'[194]. This appears to have had the opposite effect to what was intended. Quite simply, not that many people own houses – and many are trying to buy them. This was the case even among the privileged in society. Writing in the *Daily Beast* Tina Brown would report back from an aristocrats' lunch of 'lobster and strawberries':

> Brexit has added new gradations to the class divide. Cash-poor country squires now view London, the international city-state that voted overwhelmingly for Remain, as a stew of pushy Poles and women in burqas, an alien place where they can no longer afford to buy their daughter a charming mews flat behind Harrods.[195]

But though these missteps would ultimately be trotted out as reasons for Remain's defeat, the truth was that they were not decisive. The economic argument was very difficult for the Leave camp to win: while the conversation stayed on the economy, the Remain camp was ahead in the polls. Vote Leave was reduced to arguing that in the event of a British exit, there would be an additional £350 million for the NHS – a claim that would be withdrawn quietly, but not sheepishly, by prominent Brexiter Iain Duncan Smith after the referendum.

It was only once the argument moved towards immigration that a shift occurred: it was the turn of the Remain camp to struggle to explain itself. Cameron, concerned to keep his party together, never allowed himself to make a pro-immigration argument – or else was unable to think of one. Instead he hinted that somehow a Britain within the European Union would indeed one day reduce net migration. The concession he had won over migrant benefits grew more insignificant by the day. One by one politicians who had never particularly known the love of the British public, queued up to utter the phrase which had captured the times: 'Take Back Control'. Chris Grayling, Iain Duncan Smith, and Andrea Leadsom for the Conservatives; Gisella Stuart and Kate Hoey for Labour: these people found that after years of shuttling in and out of Westminster unnoticed, they had an audience, one which roared and applauded when they trotted out their sloganeering. And of course there was Nigel Farage, now a perennial fact of British and European politics. His cheek came to seem like pluck; his immaturity, a welcome individuality; arrogance had turned to plausible self-confidence; and his cheerful nihilism now resembled a cavalier abandon.

It was their hour: none could really say how they would take back control, nor even how they would halt immigration. The Australian-style points system which the Leave campaign put forward has been shown to increase the influx of numbers – but this fact, stubborn though it is, was easily trumped by the vigour of the slogan and the catching emotion of the day. Nor could any of them say precisely why immigration is such an evil – since, as we saw in Chapter Fifteen in relation to May's time as home secretary, no such definitive analysis exists. The media this time, in the shape of the Murdoch papers and the *Daily Mail*, was pro-Leave: it was said that Murdoch was irked not to be able to get a meeting at short notice in Brussels, when he could always get one in Downing Street. Meanwhile, the

BBC had pledged itself to neutrality, and the wilder claims of the Leave side, as well as the more tedious knowingness of the Remainers, had to be reported with a straight face. 'The hottest places in Hell,' wrote Dante, 'are reserved for those who in a dispute between friends take no side.'

There was a sense that something gigantic was about to happen.

The Remain camp felt bland – at times it even felt homogeneous. Whereas the Leave camp was a band of strange bedfellows, and perhaps there was a thrilling sense of belonging to something somewhat unusual. True, one could point to some diversity within the pro-EU lobby: there were those pleased with their lives who saw no reason to overturn the status quo; those who didn't want to lose a particular piece of EU funding; and some genuine Europhiles. But there was significant overlap between all these factions. The Brexit camp was a motley crew: millionaires and billionaires who for personal reasons don't like Europe and who cannot see their finances harmed by any political vote on earth; those aristocrats like those referenced in the Tina Brown article who wished for the return of a vaguely nationalistic aristocratic order; those in the business sector who believe in a more deregulated business environment; people with a commitment to an idea of England more Wodehouseian and 1950s-ish, and who now have a champion in Theresa May; those with constitutional concerns about the workings of the EU Parliament; a small portion of genuinely racist people; and finally, and perhaps clinchingly, a large group of the economically disenfranchised, like those football hooligans who, in France for the European Championships, were quoted as chanting 'Fuck off Europe, we're all voting out!'

Against this tide, there was no real answer. Interventions were attempted by Tony Blair, Gordon Brown and John Major – to no avail. The Remain camp tried to get Corbyn and Cameron on the same stage together, but Corbyn refused. It was becoming too late, and then – just like that – it really was too late.

The vote happened. The vote was lost.

THE JO COX MURDER

In among all this increasingly surreal back-and-forthing there was a terrible event. On the 16th June 2016 – a week before referendum polling-day – Jo Cox, the Labour MP for Batley

Fig. 20. A memorial to Jo Cox. Did this change the terms of the debate?[196]

and Spen, left her car on Birstall Street in West Yorkshire. Her intention was to go into the public library to attend a constituency event. A former head of policy for Oxfam GB, Cox had also in her brief time in parliament – she had won the seat in 2015 – been particularly active campaigning on behalf of a greater intake into the UK of Syrian refugees.

She was attacked on her way to the library. Cox received multiple gun and stab wounds from someone shouting 'Britain First', and died at the scene.

The suspect in the case was one Thomas Mair, who has a long history of mental illness, as well as a history of association with far-right groups. He was found guilty of the murder on 23rd November 2016 and sentenced to life imprisonment.

The question before us is whether this murder changed the moral dynamic of the referendum question. Put another way, did the question – 'Should the United Kingdom remain a member of the European Union or leave the European Union?' – change as a result of the Cox murder?

In one sense, clearly the answer is no. The question remains the same in all material respects. Peter Hitchens put the matter strongly in the *Daily Mail*: 'I am repelled and disturbed by the attempt to pretend that this deranged, muttering creep was in any way encouraged or licensed to kill a defenceless, brave young mother, by the campaign to leave the European Union'[197]. The electorate was still being asked a question about what political settlement they would prefer: in spite of the Cox murder, it was still a question about trade, about immigration, and about the long-term viability of the EU. The murder was not to be taken into account. It might even be that the insane are apolitical: a political opinion is an act of committed thought.

However, to live through this murder was to feel something rather different. David Aaronovitch speculated in the *Times* why it was that pro-Brexit people had been quick to dismiss the political language Mair had uttered before committing the murder: 'While they themselves were in no way permissive of the act,' he wrote, 'might they in some way have been permissive of the motive? Or even of the mood?'[198] The murder seemed to elucidate something: it was impossible to imagine anyone committing a comparable murder while crying out: 'Remain'. If, in a binary election, one finds that all extremists must of necessity go uniformly to one camp and not the other, then the referendum question might be said to have undergone a subtle change.

After the vote, figures released by the National Police Chiefs' Council would show that in the week after the vote there was a 58 per cent increase in hate crime. Nor was this a flash in the pan: by the end of July there was a 49 per cent increase relative to the same point in 2015.[199] One already sensed this shift in mood by the time of the Jo Cox killing. To some, the referendum question felt like it had changed to something like: 'Should the United Kingdom remain a member of the European Union or leave the European Union if leaving the European Union also leads to an increase in racist sentiment across the country?' The majority of those who voted to Leave were, of course, as fiercely opposed to random murder as any Remainer. However, they had been able to answer this new question in the affirmative. The Cox murder ramped up the temperature again: it made the vote even more emotional. It also increased the Remainer's despair at the eventual result. Everything kept tending towards gigantic escalation in people's political feelings.

In the end, the Cox murder didn't tip the outcome. Even UKIP stated that it would refuse to contest the Cox seat in a bi-election. However, there was one more postscript. On election night, Farage would say in a UKIP victory delivered in London that the Leave victory had come about 'without a single bullet being fired'.

Farage was accused of poor taste – but then the Cox murder had meant that for some a Leave vote had been not just misguided but in bad taste for at least a week.

THE OUTCOME AT THE POLITICAL LEVEL

17,410,742 voted to leave – a vote share of 51.9 per cent. 16,141,241 voted to remain. The Brexit vote was particularly strong in the North, the Midlands, the South, and in Wales. London, Scotland and Northern Ireland formed significant sections of the 48 per cent who voted to remain. We shall look at the underlying implications of all this in Chapter 27.

If we consider the Carlyle Great Man version of this history, we can see that the vote to Leave was inherently unlikely. Cameron's gamble was probably a good one, except in the event of the remote set of contingencies which did occur. This doesn't make it any less rash, since he was playing at such high stakes.

Even so, he was exceptionally unlucky. In retrospect, everyone had to be behaving unusually and in a very specific way for it to occur – and in fact everyone did behave in that way. At the highest echelon of government, everybody gave an exhibition of their worst selves. It was not enough for Cameron simply to fall victim to a certain cheerful superficiality that had occasionally been noted in him. He had to be superficial and not acting in the national interest. Osborne had sometimes shown himself to be an incompetent author of budgets, but he had usually been able to judge the electorate when he did make a mistake, and manage his party. Here, he was incompetent but failed to play to his usual strengths. On the Labour side of the Remain argument, Jeremy Corbyn had seemed an ineffectual leader if opinion polls were to be believed, but nobody could deny he was a man of convictions. During the referendum, in his remark that he was 'seven, or a seven and a half out of 10' in favour of the EU, and in his refusal to share a platform with Cameron, he showed himself to be lacking both vitality and the courage of his convictions. Corbyn did not deliver his voters, as his New Labour predecessors would have done.

Meanwhile, grandee voices on the Remain side fell on deaf ears. Gordon Brown had been a significant voice in the Scottish referendum, but he could not be expected to have a comparable impact this time around. Blair, the only senior politician who could have made a passionate and articulate argument, was still tarnished by Iraq. John Major was too distant a memory to make a significant difference. Nick Clegg had been too soundly repudiated in the 2015 election to be listened to with real attention so soon afterwards.

This perfect storm continued on the Leave side. Gove's windy intellectualism, which can usually be counted on to alienate those who have to listen to it, was on this occasion capped by the punchy 'Take Back Control' slogan. He also chose this moment, out of all the others he might have chosen, to be disloyal to Cameron. There was more. As Mayor of London, Boris Johnson had pushed a neo-liberal agenda: he chose this moment to become associated with a campaign chiefly identifiable with anti-immigration sentiment. Meanwhile, more radical figures like Nigel Farage, Iain Duncan Smith and Chris Grayling, always extreme in their views, had in the past had the saving grace of unsuccess. This time around, they got the hang of campaigning. They had found a one-off public mood in line with the cherished opinions of a lifetime.

Throughout it all, future prime minister Theresa May was silent. She would not come to Cameron's aid – but neither would she throw her lot in with the Brexit camp. The epic chanciness of it all could only have come about at a time when there was a gap in leadership. It would fall to May eventually to interpret, and perhaps to fix it all. One day perhaps we shall learn what she thought it all meant. For now, it is up to us to ask that question for ourselves.

22 – WHAT DID THE REFERENDUM RESULT MEAN?

There is inherent difficulty in interpreting the result of a referendum. An open-ended question is asked: the emotions of the nation must flood like variegated tributaries into one of two reservoirs. Cameron had embarked on the process in order to 'settle the question for a generation'. But referenda only cause more uncertainty both as to the future direction of the country (see Part V) and as to the interpretation of the state of things.

Cameron had not so much settled the question, as definitively raised it.

We have only one piece of reliable data to wield: on a particular day in June in 2016, about 52 per cent voted to leave the European Union; around 48 per cent didn't. We do not know why each vote was cast, and we have no means of knowing – and even if we could know that, then we would in any case only be finding out about that particular day. Occasionally, a poll by organisations such as YouGov will seek an explanation for the poll such as its August 2016 survey which concluded that 'Leave voters remain apprehensive about the short term future, however, in the main, they do not regret how they voted' and that 'Remain voters are particularly concerned about our national cohesion – perception that the campaign has opened up political and constitutional fault lines'[200] but these are further snapshots – tiny suspicions of reality, which seem to lack the concreteness we would prefer to have before such a gigantic political shift. Indeed, if one were to accept some of the harsher criticisms of the polling industry, the findings may not even reflect reality at all: polling is better suited to analysis of simple voter intention than to analysis of prevailing trends. When it comes to events as complex as the EU referendum, one seeks a scientific explanation in vain. Theresa May, burdened with leadership, has decided against a Hamlet-style panic on this: but it is still worth taking a step back and admitting on her behalf the enormous vexation of this vote, as it may have seemed to her – and as it still seems to many.

Beyond the polls, we are left with shreds of evidence, and usually little better than hunch. It is easy to forget that most of what has been written since the referendum has been anecdotal. We wake each day to an onslaught of speculation, emotive opinion, and barely disguised agenda, all of which is capable of altering retrospectively the actual nature of that time. To see past the complexity of it all to some deeper truth, we need to look at poetry, at art.

THE LARGENESS OF IT ALL

In the ordinary scheme of things, one might wish to become agnostic about the vote, shrug and move on. Many have, in fact, done just that: even in the immediate aftermath of the referendum, there were those who wondered aloud whether some of those who had voted to Remain might put a stop to their keening over social media. This was distinct from the tiresome 'Remoaner' label: it was a point with real humour to it. For instance, Frankie Boyle joked: 'Some people are finally saying they're embarrassed to be British, admittedly because we've left a trading union, rather than the centuries of mass murder, but it's a start.'[201]

As Remainers laughed at this, they were coming into the knowledge that their despair was mockable – and indeed there is a certain type of Remain voter who is now prepared to concede the sclerosis of the European Union, and to admit that the democratic nature of the vote might have some wisdom in it somewhere. The shock of the vote created a certain salutary need for self-analysis: it was a time to revisit one's place in the order of things. But there was a flipside to this. The cries for proportion could also be taken as a wish to reinstate the political apathy which had in a variety of ways had a bearing on the vote: it had been there, depending on your point of view, in the Remainer's wish not to assess the flaws of the EU and to cast a vote for the status quo; or it had been there in the desire of some Leavers to use a referendum over complex economic and constitutional questions to lodge a generalised protest vote. The wish to move past the EU referendum was understandable and at its best pragmatic. But in the end, the referendum shall persist, since we must inhabit its aftermath – this is true both politically and also at the level of the self. As we saw in the last chapter, the character of the nation has changed, whether we like it or not.

On the day of the vote, the sense that a large change was coming made some feel primitive and compelled to seek augury. Across the South of England on the night of the count, thunderstorms rushed down the sky. If you were a Remain voter it was tempting to recall Yeats' poem, 'A Prayer for My Daughter', where the poet stands over the crib of his daughter and hears the 'sea-wind scream upon the tower' and imagines that 'the future years had come/dancing to a frenzied drum'[202]. If you were a Leave voter, the storm seemed a kind of Marseillaise, an exciting upturning of the established order:

> Arise, children of the Fatherland
> The day of glory has arrived
> Against us tyranny's
> Bloody banner is raised... [203]

Of course to those who didn't particularly mind about the vote, it was a storm without any political agenda whatsoever. But the need to politicise the weather resurfaced the next morning, when Nigel Farage, wearing a grin which threatened to slice his face in half, took his victory lap of Westminster, and welcomed the symbolic nature of the sunshine. It was a British thing to observe the weather at such a time, but it was all of a piece with the need to understand the vote and its implications: to claim it as a good ratified by the external world, or to see it as an evil. Beneath all our technological advances, we are still people swept about by circumstance – primitives who require a sign.

In one sense, all this was exaggerated: the EU referendum may not, after all, have been some definitive verdict on our lives. The vote turned up, in the short term, an essentially procedural question about when to trigger Article 50 of the Lisbon Treaty (see Chapter 25), and what terms to seek with the European Union upon doing so. Those questions will be determined by a series of protracted negotiations in a hundred meeting rooms which few of us shall enter. Besides, any Armageddon narrative must answer in the end to the fact of the sun's having risen the next morning. These realisations were in the future: to live through the historical moment was to be bereft of the sense of proportion that would arrive over time. In the epochal headiness of the present, the referendum claimed an importance distinct from what kind of immigration system Britain ought to have, or what sort of trading relationships might be possible with the wider world in the event of a vote to Leave: it was a time of outsized political passion. Like this the referendum accrued its peculiar power.

Indeed, it is not an exaggeration to say that the health of communities – an alleged concern of those who feared the impact of immigration – was obscurely affected by it. We have already noticed the increase in race-related hate crimes that the vote engendered. But there were a thousand smaller stories to do with strain on friendships and the bonds of families: it affected families and friendships, ruined dinners or disturbed cocktail parties, and the vote each person had cast became a known fact about them, a sort of personality trait. There were Remainers who steered clear of Brexiters in the period after the vote; Brexiters who sought out the opportunity to crow, or perhaps didn't feel able to admit to friends how they had voted. There was rift, making up, the need to discuss and review. The country was full of people unable to look one another in the eye – and of people learning to look at one another, and at themselves, in a new light.

The vote was to an unusual extent about personal identity.

Why did emotions rise so high? All national plebiscites are chaotic. But when a General Election comes around, the confusion is mitigated by the fact that however unwarranted the eventual result, it can at least be changed, should we wish, in four or five years' time. We lurch from one result to another, never quite sure why we travel in the direction we do. Though a given result might cause significant sections of the population sadness or even despair, it never quite scrubs away a presiding optimism: with the right will, and enough explaining of our point of view, the result can be different next time around. The experience of living in Britain at the time of the referendum vote was more acute: a generational change had come about in the political settlement – but no one was quite sure how it had happened, whether it was the right thing to have done, or even whether it might be changed. The Brexiters had wished to take back control – but in the aftermath of the vote, one had a sense of having greatly ceded it: the country would now be subject to a thousand contingencies, ranging from the priorities of a new prime minister – Theresa May – whom the nation had not elected, to the wishes of the 27 countries over whom it now had little or no leverage, and to the make-up of a polity whose power balance would be tested and retested in the months to come. It was all irregular, which meant it was either exciting or frightening. The only certain thought was that political life would be different, and perhaps so much so that the texture of life itself had also altered, though in unnameable ways.

The time since has been a process of slow reckoning – under the curious and broken wing of the premiership of Theresa May – with the result. There is still danger in analysing the vote at all. Nevertheless, whenever one returns to the vote, a suspicion keeps arising: this is the sort of contention and rage that can only be sparked by disagreement over immigration. If we don't begin with that issue, then we risk not understanding the vote at all.

WILLIAM SHAKESPEARE V. ENOCH POWELL

If one wished to be provocative, the Remainer's despair might be summed up like this: *After the vote to leave the European Union, Britain had become less like the country of William Shakespeare and more like the country of Enoch Powell*. It goes without saying that a Leave voter would sternly disagree with such a statement: but even so, something like this view might be said to account for the peculiar distress many felt in the referendum's aftermath.

There aren't many samples of Shakespeare's handwriting. He is easy to appropriate partly because of the thin biography, the sense that he was somehow beyond human, an Ariel of unreal gifts, fluttering through London and life, a separate case study. His continuing power is distinct from the politician's temporal claims, and is bound up not in memoranda and legislation but in the lovelier metier of thought and language-music. But human he was, and we have six signatures to prove it – each spelling his surname differently, and never how we spell it. Happily, there is something more: there exists a single speech in a play dating from the early 1590s called *Sir Thomas More*, which is widely attributed to Shakespeare, and the manuscript is likely in his hand. This play, co-authored by Shakespeare with a number of other writers, is a highly selective account of More's life, and revolves around the Ill May Day riots in 1517, when a wave of protests was sparked by the number of immigrants living in the capital, particularly the Flemish of Lombard Street.

The relevant speech comes from Scene Six, the whole of which is reliably attributed to Shakespeare. It is an indication that some things don't change. It doesn't matter if it's 1517, 1590 or 2016, there will always be those who wish there were fewer 'foreigners' around. At the same time, there will also be those who will contest the wisdom of the anti-immigrant position. In the part-Shakespeare play, the anti-immigration view – one could say, the Brexit view – is put forward by John Lincoln, a broker who Holinshed – the source for *More* – recorded as the only man to be executed as the result of the disturbances. Here he is in dialogue with the carpenter Williamson, discussing immigrants:

> Williamson: Trash, trash; they breed sore eyes, and 'tis enough to infect the city with the palsey.

> Lincoln: Nay, it has infected it with the palsey; for these bastards of dung, as you know they grow in dung, have infected us, and it is our infection will make the city shake, which partly comes through the eating of parsnips.[204]

The immigrant is presented here as an infection – an alien unfit for interaction with the superior English. One thinks of Nigel Farage's posters during the 2016 campaign where crowds of Arab refugees were stamped with the phrase: 'Breaking Point'. Lincoln was the Farage of his day.

In *More*, the Remain position is put by Thomas More himself, who arrives on the streets to disperse the crowds. Shakespeare gives him these wonderful lines:

> Grant them removed, and grant that this your noise
> Hath chid down all the majesty of England;
> Imagine that you see the wretched strangers,
> Their babies at their backs and their poor luggage,
> Plodding to th' ports and coasts for transportation,
> And that you sit as kings in your desires,
> Authority quite silenced by your brawl,
> And you in ruff of your opinions clothed;
> What had you got? I'll tell you: you had taught
> How insolence and strong hand should prevail,
> How order should be quelled. And by this pattern
> Not one of you should live an aged man,
> For other ruffians, as their fancies wrought,
> With selfsame hand, self reasons, and self right,
> Would shark on you, and men, like ravenous fishes,
> Would feed on one another.[205]

1590 and 2017 link up in these lines. After the referendum result, Boris Johnson leaving his home in what should have been an atmosphere of secure triumph, was instead assailed by a crowd of reporters and furious Remainers: he wore exactly the look of a man who sat as a king in his desires, but found the throne thornier than expected.

It might be objected that this is a dramatic speech, and that it is unfair to seek to co-opt Shakespeare into a Remain viewpoint. Indeed, one might recall other speeches in Shakespeare of a more Brexity nature – the 'this sceptered isle' speech in *Richard II*, and parts of *Henry V* spring to mind. But this would be a stretch. Shylock in *Merchant of Venice* is a further testament to Shakespeare's imaginative sympathy with other races ('If you prick us, do we not bleed?'). The circumstances of Shakespeare's life are also suggestive: the Mountjoys, with whom he lived on Silver Street in the early 1600s, were Huguenot minorities. The Shakespearean vision, as well as Shakespeare's life, is a celebration of diversity and inclusiveness: it is an internationalist view of England. But whatever view we take of Shakespeare's likely personality, for the despairing Remain voter, it was precisely this Shakespearean view of life – a Britain intimately connected with the variegated nature of humankind – which appeared, rightly or wrongly, to be at stake.

Fig. 21. William Shakespeare.[206]

When articulating the Remainer's view of the Leave argument, it might seem unfair to place a figure as mighty and perennial as Shakespeare opposite a 21st century politician of any stripe – but again, that was all part of the Remainer's despair, that a large set of ideas had been replaced by a petty one. And in any case, the Leave approach *is* difficult to divorce from the figure of Enoch Powell. In his 1968 speech to the General Meeting of the West Midlands Area Conservative Political Centre – which would become known as his Rivers of Blood speech – Powell laid the groundwork for the mood that would sweep the country during the 2016 referendum campaign. In giving voice to anti-immigration sentiment, it became sayable by others.

Early in the speech, Powell relates a chance encounter in his constituency: 'a middle-aged, quite ordinary working man employed in one of our nationalised industries'[207]. The trope reminds one of Craig Brown's spoof of Tony Blair's conference speeches: 'Look, I met this fictional bloke the other day'[208]. Fictional or not, Powell goes on to quote this man as saying:

> I have three children, all of them been through grammar school and two of them married now, with family. I shan't be satisfied till I have seen them all settled overseas. In this country in 15 or 20 years' time the black man will have the whip hand over the white man.

From which he draws the following conclusions:

> I simply do not have the right to shrug my shoulders and think about something else. What he is saying, thousands and hundreds of thousands are saying and thinking – not throughout Great Britain, perhaps, but in the areas that are already undergoing the total transformation to which there is no parallel in a thousand years of English history.

It is possible to object that the speech is bogus in a number of respects. In the first place, one does have the right in a free country to shrug one's shoulders, or to think about other things: we are not compelled to consider the views of all people with equal seriousness in this way, especially if we happen to think they're wrong. Secondly, there was no evidence at all that hundreds of thousands of people were thinking identical thoughts to those of a man Powell claims to have met in the street. The burden of proof is on Powell to make the urgency of his case, not to have it clinched on our behalf by a man in the street.

The speech was criticised in many quarters at the time. But a rhetoric had been bequeathed to those in 2016 who wished to make the Vote Leave argument along anti-immigration lines.

But how does this all look from the other side, from the Brexit camp? Is there a plausible case to be made there that the outraged Remainer might learn from?

Fig 22. Enoch Powell.[209]

The argument here is from the position of reasonable nationalism. It has been argued that the British experience of nationhood, with its parliamentary institutions and legal system evolved over hundreds of years, had given rise to a unique culture. This argument would be more powerful if our institutions weren't steeped in international influence: the very word parliament comes from the French 'parlement', and our legal system is permeated with French terms – 'police', 'sentence', and so forth. Our common law, like our literature, was the product of collision with other influences. But even so the arguments of sovereignty, and individuality of culture are not entirely unShakespearean, in that great poetry – as well as any kind of supreme thought – is always a response to immediate surroundings, and the pith of one's locality.

AFTER THE VOTE

But what did the anti-Powell group in society do after the referendum? They disliked the Leave vote so much that they were inclined to demand another one. This argument would soon be scotched by Theresa May with her 'Brexit means Brexit' mantra – insofar as that phrase could be taken to mean anything, it meant that Britain would indeed be leaving the European Union. But before those epochal words were uttered some 4,143,179 people had signed the following petition:

> We the undersigned call upon HM Government to implement a rule that if the remain or leave vote is less than 60% based on a turnout less than 75% there should be another referendum.[210]

In time, a response came back from the Foreign Office:

> As the Prime Minister [ie Cameron] made clear in his statement to
> the House of Commons on 27 June, the referendum was one of the
> biggest democratic exercises in British history with over 33 million
> people having their say. The Prime Minister and Government have
> been clear that this was a once in a generation vote and, as the Prime
> Minister has said, the decision must be respected. We must now pre-
> pare for the process to exit the EU and the Government is committed
> to ensuring the best possible outcome for the British people in the
> negotiations.

Some claimed that these Remainers were too dismissive of the
democratic exercise they had just taken part in – it was around
this time that the word 'Remoaners' was born. But the position was not without merit. It must be remembered that this
was a period of sudden reversals from the Leave campaign. We
have already glimpsed Iain Duncan Smith cheerfully walking
back that £350 million promise to the NHS, but Boris Johnson
also pivoted in *The Daily Telegraph* in an article entitled 'I cannot stress too much: Britain is part of Europe and always will
be'[211]. Farage meanwhile resigned as leader of UKIP. There was
a general sense of running for the hills. Amid this confusion, it
was galling for certain voters to be called sore losers, since the
campaign had obviously been anomalous in so many respects.
On *Question Time* the satirist Ian Hislop spoke for many:

> After an election or a referendum even if you lose the vote you are
> entitled to go on making the argument. When a government in this

country wins an election, the opposition does not just say, 'Oh that's absolutely right, I've got nothing to say for five years'... The Leave vote has left us with a group of leaders who having lit the fire have all run away saying someone else can clear up the mess. The Prime Minister who put us in the mess has resigned. Everybody is gone. All the people who put their cross down for Leave... seem to be getting a group of people who say: 'We can't stop immigration, we can't get £350 million, and by the way there might be quite a lot of austerity. Sorry – bye!'[212]

Another point might be made in the Remainers' favour. Future historians will not be able to ignore the statistics describing a race-related crime spike in the weeks after the vote. But it will be difficult for them to recreate how it felt to be witness to a story of that kind or to hear second-hand of some race-related clash or other. These came to the Remain voter as worrying fragments of reality – snippets of a country where suddenly the racist enjoyed an obscure validation. Even one's wish to extend sympathy to the opposing side had to have its limits, lest it somehow shade into an accidental endorsement of the far-right agenda.

For many who signed that petition there was precisely this spectre of fascism in mind, and the absolute need to stave it off. By 2018, these worries look overblown – we can see now the extent to which things would settle down, and also that whatever else Britain experienced, it never came close to an individual as unusual as Donald Trump seizing the reins. The very steadiness which makes it so difficult to love Theresa May has at least gone some way to scotching some of the worst predictions made in the vote's immediate aftermath.

THE SELF-SEARCHING OF THE REMAINER

In due course, the vote would settle and many Remain voters were forced into an admission: Londoners in particular had to concede that they didn't know their country as well as they had thought.

There is no capital city in the world that so dominates the country to which it belongs as London does. New York would ultimately have to concede the significance of Chicago and San Francisco. Tokyo cannot quite deny that Osaka exists. For many, London almost *is* the UK – or so plenty had thought. The vote therefore became an experience in coming into knowledge of one's own cliqueiness. To judge by their Facebook and Twitter feeds, many Londoners assumed a landslide for Remain: some, convinced of a cakewalk, even abstained.

By the time the result was announced, the country was full of Londoners asking themselves when they had last been to the midlands. The answer in many cases was that they hadn't. Self-searchingness began to trickle into the literature. When baffled, the human mind reaches for metaphor. One thought, for instance, of walls – Robert Frost's 'Mending-Wall' was a poem much on people's mind then with its marvellous opening line: 'Something there is that doesn't love a wall'. Then in the summer of 2016, Zadie Smith – of *White Teeth* and *On Beauty* fame – published her article 'Fences' in *The New York Review of Books*, and in one swoop, moved the discourse away from journalistic cliché into meaningful terrain. This article, published on 18th August 2016, shows a writer of superior skill and profound compassion chronicling a complex moment. Smith's main thrust is to question just how open-minded about other nationalities the typical Londoner is. Although a hefty 40.1 per cent of Londoners did vote to Leave, Smith's observations challenge Londoners to wonder how much they really know about the immigrant populations which surround and cater to them.

> For many people in London right now the supposedly multicultural and cross-class aspects of their lives are actually represented by their staff – nannies, cleaners – by the people who pour their coffees and drive their cabs, or else the handful of ubiquitous Nigerian princes you meet in the private schools. The painful truth is that fences are being raised everywhere in London. Around school districts, around neighborhoods, around lives.[213]

This analysis is already far richer than anything YouGov can offer us. It admits the fact of immigration but asks us to consider it in conjunction with class – an ever-active fact in English life – and also with a more general tendency towards isolation and non-communication in the modern experience.

To illustrate the point, Smith tells us of a woman, the mother of a boy her daughter has a crush on, who lives in her area of north London. The crush is promising and might lead to a play date. But the play date never happens for a simple reason: the boy comes from a poorer family. Brexit therefore becomes symptomatic of something far more widespread than mere immigration fears: it now has to do with a failure in communities, a failure symbolised by the fences in the article's title. Pre-Brexit Britain was defined by injustices which the affluent chose not to notice, or simply are too removed from to be aware of.

Extreme inequality fractures communities, and after a while the cracks gape so wide the whole edifice comes tumbling down. In this process everybody has been losing for some time, but perhaps no one quite as much as the white working classes who really have nothing, not even the perceived moral elevation that comes with acknowledged trauma or recognized victimhood.

Smith's article asks us to move away from our own emotions into a novelistic sense of empathy for other people – other people, that inconvenient fact of democracy, which sometimes, as with Brexit, really can swerve in to affect your apparently cushioned destiny.

In an age of self-promotion, we might find ourselves less attuned to this approach than we should be. Smith's analysis, in its sophisticated texture and its commitment to the task of trying to understand other people, reminds us that whatever stories we tell ourselves about the world around us should be layered: our suspicions about the lives of others ought to be as imaginative and generous as possible. This is especially a duty during a contentious time. Democracy is things going against you with your say-so: by partaking we imply that we will reconcile ourselves to any result. The unwished-for result might after all be educational – the world's way of telling you that your own opinions aren't definitive. In a democracy, you are provisional until you have heard the views of others. Dante Alighieri, caught up in the internecine world of medieval Italian power struggle, had many days far worse than the 24th June 2016 was for Remainers. He ended up cramming paradise with people who were as angry about Florentine politics as he was.

In Smith's article, we glimpse another possibility: to accommodate the vote into ourselves: to convert it to our advantage.

Smith was not the only one. Meanwhile, John Lanchester in his article 'Brexit Blues' published in the *London Review of Books*, was another writer inclined to reach for understanding:

> To be born in many places in Britain is to suffer an irreversible lifelong defeat – a truncation of opportunity, of education, of access to power, of life expectancy. The people who grow up in these places come from a cultural background which equipped them for reasonably well-paid manual labour, un- and semi- and skilled. Children left school as soon as they could and went to work in the same industries that had employed their parents.[214]

This passage ought to be born in mind when we come to look at Theresa May's brand of One Nation Conservatism in the next chapter. It is difficult to imagine the Theresa May who stood on the steps of Downing Street after her visit to Buckingham Palace not agreeing with Lanchester's passage whole-heartedly. The question will arise in Part V as to whether she is embarking on policies that can seriously be expected to fix it.

Many today, like Smith and Lanchester, are beginning to think in terms of Britain as a whole again. It is felt at every level, in politics, in the arts, and even in high finance. There are, for instance, a few investors – most notably legendary investor Jonathan Ruffer – who have restructured their clients' portfolios to take into account a new outbreak of nationalism within the hearts of human beings; Ruffer has been reported as buying up derivatives linked to the so-called Fear Index, whose value is realised in the event of a major crash to the stock market. In the aftermath of Brexit, one began to look beyond one's locality. Zoe Williams argued that the vote must not be used as a way of stigmatising the North – she pointed out that the South too had voted to Leave[215]. One felt that the vote had created a vacuum and that while bad things might rush in there, good might do so as well. Brexit had, however inadvertently, the character of an intellectual opportunity.

We shall see this manifest itself in lots of ways: in May's emphasis on a northern strategy, in relation to the things she has said in response to the fears of those outside London about immigration, and even in her choice of political hero, the Birmingham politician Joseph Chamberlain.

None of this meant that the vote was the right decision – it might be taken as a mature response to the wrong one.

LITERARY AND ARTISTIC PARALLELS

Over time, people sobered up sufficiently to seek literary parallels. Gradually, the figure of Philip Larkin began to seem significant. This was sparked particularly by Amit Chaudhuri's article in the *Guardian*, 'Why the romance of Brexit bloomed in Philip Larkin's industrial suburbia'. In this article, by an immersion in Larkin's poetry, one begins to see that the idea of England one associates with Brexit – narrow or bracingly patriotic, depending on your point of view – had been percolating in British life for some time in the work of a much-beloved poet. Here is Chaudhuri:

It seems like Larkin had long been preparing his English readership for Brexit. He found his characteristic voice – urbane, colloquial, morose, lyrical, dismissive of lyricism, at once essentially rooted and maladjusted – by his second book, *The Less Deceived*.[216]

Brexit, it might be said, was sanctioned not just by an arguably great prime minister like Thatcher, but by an arguably great poet like Larkin.

The poem of Larkin's that feels most representative of the Leave position, Chaudhuri says, is 'Here', with which Larkin began his 1964 collection *The Whitsun Weddings*. This begins with a description of travelling towards a midlands town:

Swerving east, from rich industrial shadows
And traffic all night north; swerving through fields
Too thin and thistled to be called meadows... [217]

It is an inadequate England – a place of traffic, bereft of green, but perhaps defined by a certain quiet pluckiness: in Larkin the midlands backwaters where he chose to serve out that sentence of deprivation which was the condition he set himself for his poetry, was preferable – obscurely *better* – than anything known to the French or the Italians. In 'Here', the poet's train takes him in the second stanza to the 'surprise of a large town'. It turns out that there is nothing very surprising about a Larkinesque town. We see 'grain-scattered streets' and 'residents from raw estates'. It is not a place to be happy in, but there is no will within the poet to make it better:

Cheap suits, red kitchen-ware, sharp shoes, iced lollies
Electric mixers, toasters, washers, driers –

A cut-price crowd...

The poem has its economics: everything feels home-grown; nothing is imported. It is a localised despair that nevertheless doesn't particularly wish to be disturbed. It is a uniformity which could only derive from a pre-EEC state of affairs – Larkin's England is the same country which Macmillan, Jenkins, and Heath wished to escape.

One indication of the epochal significance of Brexit is that it seems to have placed the poetry that went before into an altered context. It as if the work of Larkin, Amis, and their contemporaries has receded from us overnight – or perhaps it is us who have travelled from them. One question which now occurs when reading Larkin's poetry is whether the sorts of towns Larkin describes escaped from the Larkinesque by being part of the European project. It is estimated that £40 million of EU funding was brought into Hull, although it did vote to Leave. It could be that in Brexit we are observing little more than a cathartic moan from people who are in fact doing well – certainly by historical records, and probably better than they would be doing if it weren't for the very thing they are protesting, the European Union. In Chapter 27, we shall find a similar irony in relation to Wales.

With Larkin, we are never quite sure how much we are witnessing a pose. In 'The Importance of Elsewhere', Larkin relishes the 'salt rebuff' of the Irish tongue 'insisting so on difference'. Never for him the great Europeans, the Dantes and the Goethes and the Tolstoys: he is unSchumanlike in that regard. A non-English writer could never quite be relevant, since the poet's job is to inhabit a specific language. He could be hilarious about this. Here he is writing to Kingsley Amis in July 1946:

> I HATE anybody who does anything UNUSUAL at all, whether it's make a lot of MONEY, or dress in silly CLOTHES or read books of FOREIGN WORDS or know a lot about anything or play a musical instrument... BECAUSE THEY ARE USUALLY SUCH SODDING NASTY PEOPLE THAT I KNOW IT IS 1000-1 THAT THEY ARE SHOWING OFF – *and they don't know it* but *I know it.*[218]

If one listens carefully one can hear an echo of Michael Gove's claim in the referendum that he was 'sick of experts' – there is just that same sense of sticking it to an obscure lot of 'sodding nasty people': it is the fightback of self-pity against an imaginary enemy.

Holding these views, Larkin would have seen no point in reading the Greek tragedies either. And yet the other literary parallel that comes to mind with Brexit is *The Bacchae* by Euripides.

This is a tale of a society gone mad through worship of the god Bacchus. This play – written in 405 BC – begins in Thebes with Dionysus-Bacchus explaining why he has come to the city: he reveals that he has driven the women of Thebes to insanity. These women, full of an obscure religious ecstasy, have gone up to the mountains to observe ritual festivities. The generational nature of the play evokes the 2016 vote: it is made clear that the elderly have rushed off to the hills, in a thrill of madness. Meanwhile, it is young Pentheus who stands for the rational side of human nature, and insists that society remain orderly. He has this specific rebuke to offer Cadmus and Tiresias, his seniors, when they are tempted by the prevailing revelry:

> Sir, I am ashamed to see two men of your age with so little sense of decency. Come, you are my grandfather: throw away your garland, get rid of that thyrsus![219]

In Britain in 2016 there were many young people who felt the same, and wished to tell their father or their grandfather to throw away their garlands. This was the underlying reality — and a chaotic and sometimes painful one — to the bland prose of poll reports like this one by Lord Ashcroft:

> The older the voters, the more likely they were to have voted to leave the EU. Nearly three quarters (73%) of 18 to 24 year-olds voted to remain, falling to under two thirds (62%) among 25-34s. A majority of those aged over 45 voted to leave, rising to 60% of those aged 65 or over.[220]

There was something observably Bacchic about Brexit: it was no doubt for some a thrilling electoral swansong, part-statement of nostalgia and part-shot across the bows of the modern world. But out of these broad divisions, more nuanced cases also emerged: the young person who had been collared by an elderly relative and persuaded by Brexit; or parents who switched their vote after consultation with younger members of their family to the Remain camp. Euripides' great play is suggestive of something that appears to happen once in a while in the sphere of politics: the old become radical, and the young decide on caution. Disruption always affects the young, since they must inhabit its aftermath for a greater period of time.

Brexit, if it can be called a revolution of sorts, is the opposite to the French revolution, or the Communist movements of the 20th century. The elderly had (in general) all the overturning energy; the young (in general) wanted life – and specifically their EU funding – to continue as it was. It was the diametric opposite of the sexual revolution: it was the least sexy of times.

THE WEIRD EPISODE OF ANDREA LEADSOM

In fact, just after the referendum, there was something perceptibly Bacchic about the sight of a group of Andrea Leadsom supporters, including the then Northern Ireland secretary Theresa Villiers marching along Westminster, a band of happy warriors, relishing the fight against Theresa May.

The Leadsom campaign – if its brevity still merits that noun – was both a curious postscript to the referendum, and an odd precursor to the May premiership. Leadsom had come to prominence on the back of her involvement in the BBC Great Debate on 22nd June 2016, the day before the vote. Noting her sudden celebrity, she had run for the leadership as a fresh face, and had briefly benefited from the unravelling of the Gove-Johnson alliance. When in the second ballot Leadsom had defeated Michael Gove, it seemed for a short time that Leadsom might be able to carry forwards the Brexit emotion, and test it on the Conservative Party beyond the parliamentary party. In the event of it, Leadsom would reveal herself a too chaotic and inexperienced character to be plausible as a leader. Questions initially emerged about Leadsom's allegedly deep experience in the business world: this turned out to be less wide-ranging than she had claimed. Next, she gave an ill-advised interview to Rachel Sylvester of *The Times*, where she further illustrated her inexperience, embarking on a surreal riff about motherhood. This is in response to whether she felt like a 'mum in politics':

> Yes. I am sure Theresa will be really sad she doesn't have children so I don't want this to be 'Andrea has children, Theresa hasn't' because I think that would be really horrible, but genuinely I feel that being a mum means you have a very real stake in the future of our country, a tangible stake.[221]

Leadsom tried to claim she hadn't said this; transcripts proved she had. It was possible to note a contradiction in her position: as a Leaver, Leadsom had, in the opinion of many (not least, the young themselves) acted against the interests of the young in a country where that group was overwhelmingly in favour of the UK remaining.

Leadsom at least knew when the game was up. Observing the plight of Jeremy Corbyn's Labour Party, she was anxious not to emulate it in hers. She withdrew from the race:

A nine-week leadership campaign at such a critical moment for our country is highly undesirable.

We need a new Prime Minister in place as soon as possible. Theresa May carried over 60 per cent support in the parliamentary party. She is ideally placed to implement Brexit on the best possible terms.[222]

Like Chuka Umunna on the Labour side in 2015, Leadsom had underestimated the stress of front-line politics.

By the time Leadsom had finished her statement, Theresa May was the prime minister-in-waiting.

23 - THERESA MAY'S DOWNING STREET SPEECH: ONE NATION CONSERVATISM

This book began with a reference to Mervyn Peake's Gormenghast trilogy. In that work, the obscure traditions of the castle, whose origins lie so deep in time as to be impossible to trace, might be the only thing that matters to characters like Flay and Sourdust. But they are wearisome to characters like Lord Sepulchrave who has to spend his life performing them. They are also absurd to the reader who stands outside the novel looking in.

But within that novel there is another class of person: the Bright Carvers, who live outside the confines of the castle, excluded from the workings of power. They are dependent on a deep tradition that they partake in only from afar.

It is a satire that could only have been written by an Englishman – and one might add, an Englishman who had spent his early years in China, and could thus see the workings of our system with a detached gaze. Looked at with Peakean eyes, the process of Theresa May's elevation to power had something of the strangeness of Gormenghast ritual. The elevation of a prime minister always does. At around noon, a group of helicopters begins swirling above a building in the centre of town – a sprawling mass of pinnacled stone that looks as though it was built in the 1300s but was in fact raised with neo-gothic nostalgia in the mid-1800s. As these helicopters swirl, images rush out from them into the homes of millions of people in the nation who pause at what they're doing, and stare at a glass-windowed box in the corner of the rooms of their houses. Meanwhile, apparently knowledgeable people stand outside the building and talk about what is going on inside – they do so without conveying any consequential information.

Meanwhile, a car – in this case, David Cameron's – is leaving Downing Street. To a Martian it would look like some random terraced house in London had all at once become the focus of outsized interest, an interest indistinguishable from a sudden sense of valediction. The car moves through London, and approaches, with something like confident deference, a huge house at the end of the longest and straightest street in the city, while people line up and exhibit an improbable range of emotions from fascination to rage, silent awe and squealing delight. Some of the helicopters follow this car – at some considerable expense – but again no real information is provided, or could have been expected to have been provided.

A few moments later, we get an aerial shot of people milling about a Westminster courtyard: we cannot know their function or their role – we only know their nearness to power, their right to be where we are not. Eventually a middle-aged woman emerges, looking happy and relieved, as if she has been rescued from some captivity within. To the enormous interest of everyone, she also gets into a car. This then performs a slow motion car chase towards the first, as if it had been alerted to some crime within the big house but was somewhat apathetic about it. And yet as soon as the second car arrives, the first is leaving. Who could possibly inhabit such a vast home? Interest will now concentrate upon it: the watching Martian would be surprised to learn that its owner holds almost no executive power at all. Again, knowledgeable-sounding people stand outside and convey no information: there is the same radical juxtaposition between the confidential tone of their reports, and their vacuous content.

A photograph is released showing the woman we saw milling around Westminster curtseying before an elderly lady. The second car re-emerges and the lady walks up to the door of the first house, with a smiley man in tow, and stands before a black door and philosophises triumphantly.

One is anxious not to be flippant. There have been those – one thinks of Edmund Burke – who have considered the British system to be sacred. Of course, if we really did find Theresa May and the Queen ridiculous we would lose a sense of belonging to a national history: this might be more a part of our identity than we are generally aware of. While the notion of the English state as being somehow a gift from God arguably went out with the French revolution, when the origins of all systems based around a reverence for monarchy were definitively questioned, the excitement over any royal wedding shows that few things can plunge us into collective ecstasy so completely as custom: it is our reprieve from the noise of contemporary reality. On such days, one feels surrounded by a profound respect for tradition which might almost open up onto a Burkean mysticism. The accumulation of custom has a certain hold over the imagination. But there is a Gormenghastish strangeness about it all, a sense of ancient ritual impinging on modern lives, and of the cast of characters being committed to follow a procedure whose origins are too deep for them to grasp. All the central figures – Cameron, May, Elizabeth II – are people we think of as powerful, but we can also see how all concerned are themselves in service to tradition and the long-established machinery of power. And what of us, the electorate? We stand outside it, like the community of the Bright Carvers in the Peake novel, as banished subjects, excluded from decision-making. At its best, the referendum vote might be taken as a radical protest against this state of affairs, the cry of the Bright Carvers for the people of Gormenghast to observe their lives. One is a little hesitant about this as a total explanation: 17 million protest votes of this nature would constitute a very sudden explosion of interest in constitutional questions.

It is also possible to consider a certain passage in Virginia Woolf's 1925 novel *Mrs Dalloway*. Mrs Dalloway, a woman of high society, spends the entire novel getting ready for an evening party. But near its beginning, the car of some person of power intrudes upon the lives of the main character. There is a 'violent explosion' outside Mrs Dalloway's window in Bond Street. Everyone stops what they are doing and stares at a car that has drawn up on the pavement. This car belongs, everyone knows instinctively, to a person of power:

> ... mystery had brushed them with her wing; they had heard the voice of authority; the spirit of religion was abroad with her eyes bandaged tight and her lips gaping wide. But nobody knew whose face had been seen. Was it the Prince of Wales's, the Queen's, the Prime Minister's? Whose face was it? Nobody knew.

What are we witnessing when Theresa May passes on her way towards assuming the prime ministership – even if we happen to watch it on our screens? It is something like the seductive power Woolf gives to the observing Londoners in relation to the person in that car:

> But there could be no doubt that greatness was seated within; greatness was passing, hidden, down Bond Street, removed only by a hand's-breadth from ordinary people who might now, for the first and last time, be within speaking distance of the majesty of England, of the enduring symbol of the state which will be known to curious antiquaries, sifting the ruins of time, when London is a grass-grown path and all those hurrying along the pavement this Wednesday morning are but bones with a few wedding rings mixed up in their dust and the gold stoppings of innumerable decayed teeth. The face in the motor car will then be known.[223]

Power again: it is this which makes sense of our Gormenghast democracy. Power, which can create these rituals. Power, which is the glue between the Bright Carvers and the occupants of the Castle. Power, which, like the energy of the world, never lessens in its sum, only mutating to fit the circumstances of the times. Power, which explains David Cameron and Boris Johnson and Michael Gove – the wish to wield it for its own sake, or for the sake of an ideology, or for the good of the world.

Power, which had just arrived in the lap of Theresa May.

MAY'S FIRST SPEECH

One interesting aspect of all this was that May sought in her first speech on the steps of Downing Street to subvert this gap between us and the state – between us and her. It was a speech about power, and what it should be for. In it May argued that government should be used to enfranchise the disenfranchised, and to empower the powerless.

> I know you're working around the clock, I know you're doing your best, and I know that sometimes life can be a struggle. The government I lead will be driven not by the interests of the privileged few, but by yours.

> We will do everything we can to give you more control over your lives. When we take the big calls, we'll think not of the powerful, but you. When we pass new laws, we'll listen not to the mighty but to you. When it comes to taxes, we'll prioritise not the wealthy, but you.[224]

Gormenghast was addressing the Bright Carvers. This speech, more direct than the typical Cameron offering, can be seen in electoral terms: it was in one sense an aggressive move into the ground of the centre-left which had seemingly been vacated (or so went the pre-snap election received wisdom) with good-natured folly by Jeremy Corbyn's Labour Party. Some of her early moves as prime minister – one thinks particularly of grammar schools (see Chapter 29) – would make some feel compelled to wonder whether this first speech was more cosmetic than substantive. And yet her 'nasty party' speech in

2002, together with her work on modern slavery which we saw in Part III, are enough for most to wish to think of her claims to protect the vulnerable in society as sincere. And if she is sincere, then she is espousing something we need to look at: One Nation Conservatism.

Cameron had at various times claimed to espouse this too, so there is a further complexity here: in her speech outside Downing Street, Theresa May was seeking to redefine an idea which had, in theory, been a major part of the outgoing Cameron government.

This first speech of May's is the moment when her government moved from a state of latent potential into actuality.

Words spoken by a prime minister have a different importance to the words of a would-be prime minister: they are now closer to action, and aspire to appropriate a deeper meaning in our lives.

DISRAELI AND ONE NATION CONSERVATISM

The idea of One Nation Conservatism in its original form is indissoluble from one man: Benjamin Disraeli.

In one sense, Disraeli was an unlikely messenger of social reform. Reliably dandyish, and sometimes characterised as a political adventurer, he served two terms as prime minister – one very brief in 1868, which was dominated by questions surrounding the Church of Ireland – and a great reforming administration from 1874-1880. During the second he instigated, along with his Home Secretary Richard Cross some important social reforms including the Artisans' and Labourers'

Dwellings Improvement Act 1875, the Public Health Act 1875, and the Education Act 1876. Most notably the Employers and Workmen Act of 1875 made workers equal before the law, making breach of contract a civil offence and not a criminal one. Another important piece of legislation was the Conspiracy and Protection of Property Act – also passed in 1875 – which gave workers the right to strike. Cross, like Churchill and Jenkins, is another of May's greatest predecessors at the Home Office. Disraeli has some similarities with former US President Barack Obama and with Winston Churchill in that before he was a politician at all, he was a writer – but whereas Obama and Churchill would choose to express themselves in non-fiction, Disraeli wrote novels. In the first instance, as in *Vivian Grey* (1826-7), the future prime minister peddled 'silver fork fiction' – essentially portraits of an aristocratic life Disraeli hadn't seen

for himself. These novels, together with Disraeli's sometimes unpredictable early career under the second Peel administration (1841-6), have caused people to consider Disraeli an opportunist ever since. Questions over his character have their corollary in questions about his philosophical brainchild: do people

Fig. 23 Benjamin Disraeli.[225]

like Disraeli – and indeed David Cameron and Theresa May, who espouse his philosophy – really end up helping the poor or not? Do they even particularly intend to do so?

One argument against claiming the Disraeli position as an insincere one is the long period of time for which he held it. This we know from the novels that followed.

In the 1840s, some decades before his major administration (1868-1874), Disraeli's novels improved dramatically. He outlined his philosophy in two works *Coningsby* (1844) and *Sybil* (1846). *Coningsby* is the better novel, but *Sybil* contains a succinct scene that might be taken as a kind of founding document of One Nation Conservatism. In that second book, the hero, Charles Egremont, the younger brother of Lord Marney, takes it upon himself to investigate the condition of the poor, disguised as a certain Mr Franklin. We can glimpse Disraeli's divided self in his choice of hero: the man who isn't an aristocrat, but did everything he could to become one, must write a novel about the things he really knows – Egremont is investigating a world the author knows better than he would care to admit. A number of visits to the north ensue during which Egremont confronts the reality of industrialization. We see our modern politicians make comparable journeys all the time – leaping on a train from Euston, only they return on the same day. When Theresa May heard that Andrea Leadsom had exited the race, she was on just such a trip to Birmingham. But Egremont's journey is somewhat more profound than any open to the modern Cabinet minister. He meets the radical Walter Gerard, as well as his daughter, the book's eponymous hero.

In the central scene at Marney Abbey, Gerard explains to Egremont the condition of the nation:

> Two nations; between whom there is no intercourse and no sympathy; who are as ignorant of each other's habits, thoughts, and feelings, as if they were dwellers in different zones, or inhabitants of different planets; who are formed by a different breeding, are fed by a different food, are ordered by different manners, and are not governed by the same laws.' 'You speak of – ' said Egremont, hesitantly. ' THE RICH AND THE POOR.'[226]

The rich and the poor. One doesn't need to look very far to see comparisons with the Britain revealed by the vote to leave the European Union. In fact, it is possible to wonder just how effective Disraeli's subsequent One Nation remedy has been if the exact state of affairs which it was meant to correct is still so applicable to society today. True, there are some minor variations. Disraeli could not have foreseen, for instance, the decline of our manufacturing, or the advent of the global economy, developments which have seen wealth migrate south to concentrate itself predominantly in London. But the similarities are striking too. For instance, the poor appear not to have changed their location: it is not entirely a caricature to say that they remain in the midlands and the north, exactly where Egremont found them nearly two hundred years ago. In *Sybil*, one is looking at a state of affairs – and an argument over a state of affairs – that hardly seems to change. If you are born well-off, you shall have to do something foolish to surrender your advantage; but if you are born poor you are, to recall

Lanchester's phrase in the previous chapter, on the receiving end of an 'irreversible defeat'.

On the other hand, this interpretation of British society feels too static really to be true. No doubt there are decades of social mobility housed within the appearance of things which this analysis doesn't quite capture. People really do rise in life, like Thackeray heroines, and people really do fall as well, and experience calamitous loss of status. The analysis is probably too binary to match chaotic reality. On the other hand, if it is an error then it is a remarkably persistent one. It might even be said that Disraeli's description of the condition of society is identical to the diagnosis of another more famous text: Marx and Engels' *Communist Manifesto*, except that where Disraeli speaks of the rich and the poor, Marx refers to the bourgeoisie and the proletariat.

It is only when it comes to how to fix things that the two thinkers, Disraeli and Marx, diverge. At which point, of course, they diverge dramatically. Marx felt that the only solution to the injustice would be for the proletariat to take up arms and overturn the system which is so very much weighted in favour of the rich – the only question is how dramatically, and how violently this shall be done. Here are Marx and Engels – who we last met in Part II in Theresa May's birthplace of Eastbourne – in the *Communist Manifesto*:

> The proletariat will use its political supremacy to wrest, by degree, all capital from the bourgeoisie, to centralise all instruments of production in the hands of the State, *i.e.*, of the proletariat organised as the ruling class; and to increase the total productive forces as rapidly as possible.[227]

Can this wresting be done peacefully? In his *Principles of Communism* (1847), Engels would argue that the peaceable abolition of private property was 'desirable'. For Vladimir Lenin it was such an urgent issue that blood was permitted to be spilt. In 2017, Jeremy Corbyn, with his years of patient but prickly co-operation with parliamentary life, has hoped to bring about a radical alleviation of the poor by peaceable means. But in spite of various disagreements on the left, there is a unity on one point: it is an urgent matter. The emphasis is on the injustice of any individual life having its potential wasted due to bad luck and adverse circumstances of birth. The Disraeli-May position is, of course, different. It is a remedy that is concerned to avoid anything like the Leninist position: in Marxism, the state is meant eventually to fall away, but in One Nation Conservatism, the instruments of the state – the Crown, the Church, the Army and so forth – are not just to remain but to be consistently celebrated. At its best it seeks to safeguard institutions which have been built up for good reason, and with great difficulty; the state is, for people like May, a repository of the best instincts in our collective history. In opposition to this one might say that the cost of this stability is likely to be the very inertia Marx and Engels want to avoid.

So what did Disraeli suggest? In effect, paternalism: the rich ought to become better and kinder, *within the existing system*. Change must come not from the outside agency of revolution, but from within the hearts of the well-off.

Central to the idea of One Nation Toryism is the notion that society is in some sense organic, and slowly morphing into whatever it will become. The best we can do is to put our fingers on the clay while it is still moist and shape it. This might remind us of GK Chesterton's remark about conservatism:

> All conservatism is based upon the idea that if you leave things alone you leave them as they are. But you do not. If you leave a thing alone you leave it to a torrent of change. If you leave a white fence post alone it will soon be a black post. If you particularly want it to be white you must be always painting it again; that is, you must be always having a revolution. Briefly, if you want the old white post you must have a new white post.[228]

For Chesterton, the conservative project is to make sure we retain this white post. Of course, the objection to the Chestertonian position is that it is much too abstract: politics is not about things, but the destinies of people. At least, if it isn't about that, then it is difficult to say what it *is* about. And if we accept this, then we cannot quite accept that politics is ever to be a leisurely matter, a question of keeping unwanted change at bay: power is the moral duty to improve things.

Disraeli sees the prime mover as being the rich – they have wealth and influence. The power to change things amounts to the *duty* to change things. Marx sees the prime mover as being the poor – the disenfranchised do not have much, but they do have a decisive energy of resentment. This is why the idea of the strong man – one thinks of Boxer in Orwell's *Animal Farm* (1945) – plays such a part in Soviet era literature. Lenin came up with what might kindly be called a compromise: a small group of enlightened Marxists must seize the reins and thereby inaugurate the dictatorship of the proletariat. For Disraeli, and many conservatives, this is horribly jarring, like a bone in the body of the state snapping: apart from the shock of violence, it is also an incorrect analysis of the life of nations, lacking that stately sense of development and of story unfolding which is central to the conservative understanding of life. Marxism sees civilization happening according to jolts and jerks – feudalism giving way to the stage of capitalism and capitalism ceding to revolution. For the likes of Disraeli, society is amorphous – it is in flux and barely controllable, and we can only aspire to keep things smooth. For Marx this might be adequate if there were no problem, but since there manifestly *is* a problem, it's not enough. Marxist theory prophesies a world of sudden moves, and dramatic flare-ups of emotion – this is because the frustration of the working class man is more than mere paternalistic reform can cater to.

But what is the One Nation remedy? Disraeli had already put it vividly in the earlier novel *Coningsby*:

> 'Hush!' said Mr. Tadpole. 'The time has gone by for Tory governments; what the country requires is a sound Conservative government.' 'A sound Conservative government,' said Taper, musingly. 'I understand: Tory men and Whig measures.'[229]

There is a strong pragmatic streak in Disraeli's thought which has its roots in electoral reality: once suffrage was expanded in the mid-19th century, the main parties had to think about those who had benefited from the expansion. This remark in the novel found its real world counterpart in the Crossian agenda of the 1870s that we have seen. It should make us a little clearer about what May is seeking to do when she talks, as she did during the very brief campaign which landed her in Downing Street, of putting workers on the boards of companies. It is Disraeli's thought re-embodied in our times: things must be done by the upper classes (company executives, May and her cabinet) for the working classes ('not the wealthy but you'; the 'just about managing'). For Labour there is condescension involved and besides it's not enough: zeal has been replaced with an approach likely to be more incremental. It is sleepy reform – the left-leaning mind detects a sense of unfair drift, and is apt to ask: 'What is politics about after all but the lives of people in the here and now?'

Over time, some Tory prime ministers have been happier than others to invoke One Nation Toryism. Stanley Baldwin managed to do so, as did Neville Chamberlain. The career of Macmillan is further proof that the Conservatives have considerable electoral success whenever they do invoke the rights of workers – or seek an open-minded attitude to minorities, as Cameron did in relation to same-sex marriage. However, here again, one can see the enormity of the career of Margaret Thatcher. It is in Thatcher that we get something very distinct from the Disraeli approach: it is, as we have glimpsed throughout this book, free-market conservatism which would emphasise the freedom of people to help themselves up the food chain. It is quasi-Darwinian and would see attempts of people to help the working poor as an unwarranted impinging on the right of free citizens to do the helping themselves: from this we get Osborneomics. Cameron's notion of a Big Society might be deemed a curious hybrid of Thatcherism and

Disraeli-ism. On the one hand it is One Nation-like in its wish for charitable works to go ahead; on the other, it is arguably Thatcher-like in that the idea was propounded alongside Cameron's voiced wish for a 'leaner, more efficient state'[230].

Where does May stand on this spectrum? We have only hints. On the one hand she talks of placing workers on the board – an idea we shall look at in our chapter on the economy (Chapter 26), and has signified that she is unhappy about executive pay. She has also indicated that she wishes to push ahead with an industrial strategy that at least sounds more comprehensive than George Osborne's Northern Powerhouse. On the other, she is on record as having voted for a range of Thatcherite things over the years.

As of 2018, we don't yet know – and perhaps she doesn't. Besides, with her majority lost in the 2017 snap election, she is now in less of a position to signify what she'd like to do with power, having so much less of it.

JOSEPH CHAMBERLAIN: THERESA MAY'S HERO?

You can tell a person by their heroes. May – characterised as cold, or as the Tricksy Belle of Marsham Street by Eric Pickles – does not always come across as passionate. One cannot imagine her having political idols in the same way that Obama obviously idolises Abraham Lincoln and Martin Luther King. But nevertheless, one of May's closest advisors Nick Timothy is that kind of person and even having departed as a scapegoat for the 2017 general election performance, he certainly has clout with May. Timothy also has a stand-out hero: the

Birmingham politician Joseph Chamberlain – or Radical Joe, as he is sometimes known.

The influence of Chamberlain within May's administration was immediate in that speech on Downing Street. In fact, it came right at the beginning:

> Because not everybody knows this, but the full title of my party is the Conservative and Unionist Party, and that word 'unionist' is very important to me.
>
> It means we believe in the Union: the precious, precious bond between England, Scotland, Wales and Northern Ireland. But it means something else that is just as important; it means we believe in a union not just between the nations of the United Kingdom but between all of our citizens, every one of us, whoever we are and wherever we're from.[231]

Fig 24. Joseph Chamberlain.[232]

It was Chamberlain who gave May's party the 'Unionist' moniker. But Chamberlain is an unlikely figure for May to espouse on the face of it, as he was never a Conservative: he crossed the floor to join the Salisbury administration, after having been a radical Liberal under the Liberal Unionist banner, and a dedicated opponent of Home Rule for the Irish. The Conservative party thus still bears his imprint. It is interesting to note how radical his record is: as Birmingham mayor, Chamberlain had been a fierce champion of the working classes. He was a man unmatched in his zeal, except perhaps by the young Winston Churchill. After a period in business – Chamberlain came from a successful family of shoemakers – he became mayor of Birmingham. Conscious of the conditions in which his own workers had to toil, he promised that Birmingham would be 'parked, paved, assized, marketed, gas & watered and improved'[233]. We can glimpse in this sentence something of the energy of the man: it is a list which its writer does not want to end, and will cede easily to some other list of what needs to be done. Under his aegis, Birmingham was improved – and to an amazing extent. Chamberlain revolutionised the city's water works, creating the Birmingham Corporation Water Department. He also embarked on a programme of slum clearance, opened libraries, swimming pools and schools. He was a national figure before he took his programme onto the national stage.

Take it onto the national stage he did. He was returned unopposed to the Birmingham constituency in 1876. As irrepressible a presence in parliament as he had been in the mayoralty, he would soon play an important role in both the Salisbury and Balfour administrations. Nick Timothy picks up the story:

With his help, the Salisbury and Balfour Governments of the 1890s and 1900s extended democracy to the county councils, provided free education, encouraged home ownership, restricted immigration, and introduced new rights for workers. If Chamberlain had had his way, an old-age pension system would have been added to the list, but even without it, the Unionists' social policies were substantial, and they were down to him.[234]

There are three aspects of Chamberlain's career which seem particularly apt in the post-Brexit landscape, and which must make him seem a suitable fit for our times for Theresa May.

First is that he was a politician who is associated with Birmingham, i.e. somewhere other than London. We have already seen how news of her certain accession found its way to Theresa May while she was in that city. More generally, in an era where London has proven itself to have different leanings and affinities to the rest of the country it is an apt emphasis: in order to govern for the country as a whole May would need to redirect her party's appeal into those areas. One important decision she had to make here was the HS2 project undertaken by George Osborne and, though derided as a vanity project by some, meant to be a way of linking London and Birmingham more quickly. (She would go on to state that she remained 'absolutely committed'[235] to the project). Another question was what sort of industrial strategy she wished to pursue. Secondly, throughout the career of Joseph Chamberlain there is an admirable urgency about the plight of the poor. With Brexit in mind, we can see that to the extent that the vote was an attempt to give vent to a sense of economic disenfranchisement, this was a necessary pivot. If Disraeli's version of One Nation Conservatism can produce only sleepy reform, then something of the Chamberlain urgency – or what Timothy calls 'unambiguous mission'[236] – might have seemed salutary. Thirdly, Chamberlain also advocated protectionist policies: again we can see that to the extent that the referendum vote might be seen a rebuke for free trade and the global pact of neo-liberalism then it must also have seemed to May a wise recalibration. (One potential sticking point here was the presence of arch free traders like Liam Fox in key positions in her Cabinet). However, all this also met the objection that the referendum was based around such an open-ended question, that it was impossible to know whether these things would meet with the approval of the 52 per cent, or the 48 per cent, because throughout the first period of her premiership one wasn't quite sure how emotions had settled in the referendum's aftermath. And although we will never be able to say with any real certainty why everyone voted as they did, it was to clear up this lingering confusion that May called the 2017 general election, the result of which with gentle comedy, bestowed on her another perplexing outcome.

So May began her administration with a One Nation Conservatism speech. Afterwards as she waved at the photographers, questions could not help but rise to mind. Was this really a new era in Conservative politics or a mere footnote to the Cameron years?

24 – THE FORMATION OF A GOVERNMENT

As Theresa May made her speech evoking the ghosts of Chamberlain and Disraeli, the Cameron administration receded rapidly into the past. Power, once it is surrendered, flutters away, like a scrunched-up newspaper in the wind. May went inside, was introduced to the nuclear codes, and set to work.

There is a logic of politesse about these opening hours of a premiership: the Queen had asked her to form a government, and May set about doing so. But beneath the charade of question and answer, and appearances maintained, something much more visceral was taking place: power was newly wielded – and it was being lost.

The creation of a government is a prime minister's first duty. Power must be constituted: it must flow into certain channels, as a stay against chance, and as a fulfilment of whatever priorities the new leader has. A reshuffle or government formation is therefore a window into a new leader's approach: it is the conductor's first waves of the baton. There are few prime ministers who haven't from time to time been thought of as having 'botched' a reshuffle. The formation of the first Cabinet is especially important. As T.S. Eliot wrote, 'In my beginning is my end'[237]. It is a triumphant moment in which, paradoxically, seeds of failure are sown. In early photos of Thatcher's administration, Geoffrey Howe seems to lurk, a time bomb of to-be-tested loyalty. And from the moment Blair permitted Brown the chancellorship, the dysfunctional nature of his premiership had been cast in stone.

And Theresa May? She disappeared inside 10 Downing Street, fulfilled in the achievement of a lifelong ambition. Although it might not have been in evidence at the time – and though no one then knew the circumstances of her failing – observers would one day come to feel that there were numerous hidden reasons for her not to be smiling. One reason was the largeness of the task in hand: the referendum vote had revealed both a divided party and a divided nation; it also opened up onto a dizzying range of seemingly insoluble policy problems which we shall look at in Part V. A possible explanation for Cameron's defeat had been that he had been focused during the campaign on reuniting his party *after* victory rather than concentrating on winning the vote to begin with. He had not fought when the fight had been on: like some placid general, he had offered clemency amid battle. The task Cameron had expected to be conducting now fell to May: having begun the process of uniting the country in her speech outside Downing Street, May now had to disappear inside and, sharpish, become the sort of person her party might unite behind.

Reshuffles are complex: there are too many elements in play, and too much fallible humanity at issue, for any set of appointments to seem wholly successful. Just as the feelings of the nation about a whole range of issues cannot be satisfactorily encapsulated in a single cross on a ballot paper, so the vote cannot be reflected in the new look of a government: this must, of necessity, consist in cosmetic alterations to a series of ministries, alongside perhaps the creation of some new ones, or the destruction of others. It is worth emphasising that these institutions are unlikely to answer to any profound need of change in the electorate – they are buildings which most people never visit, or particularly mind about: elections are one arrangement of remoteness from the people swapped for another. But nor are they likely to change all that much interiorly: the tremendous continuity of the civil service serves as a buffer to shock innovations, and much of a prime minister's early period of rule – the struggle is especially vivid in the memoirs of Tony Blair – is spent in figuring out how to circumvent or accelerate the machinery of government to one's advantage. The challenge of politics is precisely to manage a series of structures remote from people's lives while continuing to appeal to those people. A reshuffle is the first reminder to the electorate that most things won't change, and indeed can't really be expected to change: it turns out that the Foreign Office will after all not relocate to your village and continually check in on your opinions about what to do next. Any expectation of freshness quickly cedes to the eternal Gormenghastery of British public life. The civil service was there before the referendum; it will be there after it. Government will continue as an inexorable thing, separate from your life – marbled and impressive perhaps, but also aloof and centralised, and essentially inscrutable. Reshuffles are the moment when we have this reconfirmed for us, to the prime minister's quiet disadvantage.

If that were all a reshuffle consisted of, then they would be far simpler than they are. May was also in the position of needing to manage the egos of all Cameron's cabinet ministers – some of whom, as we shall see, would soon become former cabinet ministers. There were also the expectations of certain MPs who assumed they would be in line for promotion.

But above all this, and most important – and not always satisfactorily considered by her predecessor, as we have seen – was the national interest. For May, all these matters were complicated by the enormity of the referendum vote since all the usual complexity of a reshuffle would be seen through a post-referendum filter. Each minister would be not just a minister, but a Remainer or a Leaver: it would be a reshuffle conducted with the predominant bifurcation of the day in mind. Furthermore, the national interest was no longer quite such an abstract idea as it usually is to prime ministers: it too had to be understood through the prism of the referendum.

This first reshuffle was therefore not just a formation of a government but a live interpretation of the referendum result.

THE OUSTER OF GEORGE OSBORNE

As Theresa May walked into 10 Downing Street, removal men lurked outside. Cameron was already on his way to stay at a friend's in Holland Park. He would be photographed the following day outside a café in Notting Hill, sipping coffee – a regular civilian. Every new prime minister must contend with images of their predecessor's political mortality like this, precisely at the moment of their greatest strength.

But there was another symbol of political mortality waiting next-door to hear May's verdict upon his tenure: this was the chancellor George Osborne, and he would in fact be joining Cameron for that coffee in Notting Hill the following morning. There had been some speculation that Osborne – much too tainted now to continue as chancellor – might manage a sideways move into the Foreign Office. But this was wishful thinking and failed to take into account how much things had changed.

Within the first hour of the May premiership, he had been fired. Though she could not then know that she was firing the future editor of the *Evening Standard*, the departure of Osborne showed May's preparedness to make dangerous enemies: the difficulty of being prime minister is that one cannot, and should not, be at any one time a cause of unanimous happiness. What did the decision to remove Osborne say about May? Michael Portillo would later state on the BBC's *This Week* that the removal of Osborne could be seen as a policy of getting rid of anyone 'too clever by half'[238]. Had she judged her man well? By 2018, Osborne still feels a reasonably unthreatening figure, despite his sometimes needling stewardship of the *Standard*: he had perhaps long been neutralised both by a series of shambolic budgets, and by his front-and-centre and figures-quoting involvement in the referendum campaign. Osborne was already an emblem of an era that had fast receded: he was also, of course, a chief reason for the unravelling of that era. It was probably a simple wager on May's part: for Osborne to rebel now would be premature. For a while there was sinister talk of Osborne 'fuming on the backbenches'. There were other rumours that he was, in fact, relieved no longer to be the nation's bogeyman and bearer of austerity: this was the man who had been booed at the 2012 Olympics, and was perhaps tired of that side of public life.

Like this, a man once-powerful sneaks off the stage, never to be powerful again in quite the same way: prior to assuming stewardship of the *Evening Standard*, he took on a well-paid job for fund manager Black Rock, and after indicating his desire to stay on in the Commons to fight for his Northern Power-house agenda, left his Tatton constituency in April 2017, albeit while suggesting that he would one day return. It might be that the likes of Osborne – born to privilege, and the expecta-tion of power – wear power lightly while they have it, and are not overly depressed to lose it: they have always somewhere in their bones felt powerful in any case. Their lives have been an alignment with power, a continued knowledge of it: fifty years spent attaining influence and wielding it cannot slough off entirely because of the inconvenient fact of having techni-cally been deprived of it.

May's replacement for Osborne was Philip Hammond, a sort of ally of May's, although reports would surface over time of a certain strain in their relationship particularly after his shambolic first budget in 2017. Hammond was also of the class of '97. Under Cameron he had been foreign secretary, during which time his main achievement was to marshal UK involvement in the nuclear deal with Iran, although he also secured an authorisation from parliament for military action against ISIS in Syria. He fits the recent mould of the straight man chancellor – Darling, Major, Brown and Lamont were all in their ways, and at different times, safe-looking men – suits who are expected to background themselves on every day ex-cept Budget day.

Hammond's voting record is, like May's, a record of loy-alty. As a creature of the Cameron government, he has voted continually for reduction in central government funding of local government; he has also tended to vote against paying higher benefits to those unable to work, and to those with disabilities[239]. However, it looked like a safe appointment precisely in the position of government where most voters like to see a safe appointment. The issues he faced on the economy shall be dealt with in Chapter 26.

AMBER RUDD, MAY'S SUCCESSOR AS HOME SECRETARY

Another element in any contemporary reshuffle is the balance between men and women in Cabinet. Prior to the reshuffle, the new prime minister was expected to have more women in her Cabinet than in any preceding administration, but in the end one minor surprise was that slightly fewer women than might have been expected rose to the top of government.

Even so, it would have been unthinkable for May not to have another woman in one of the top four jobs in government and in the shape of Amber Rudd at the Home Office this is what she did. One did not particularly envy Rudd the job of serving under a fairly formidable person like May in a job which May herself knows backwards, although once the *Daily Mail* had outed her as a direct descendant of Charles II, the readers of that estimable journal knew that she had the right blood for it. Rudd made her name as Secretary of State for Energy and Climate Change – an area we shall look at in Chapter 30 – and was also married at one time to the late critic AA Gill. She had been more visible as a Remain campaigner than either May or Hammond, and even made a notable contribution in the BBC's last televised debate, delivering an obviously pre-prepared line with some élan: 'Boris, well he's the life and soul of the party, but he's not the man you want driving you home at the end of the evening.'[240]

Rudd was in the position of needing to deliver on the issue of immigration in the wake of the referendum: an issue that was just about possible for May to hide from. Rudd would not be so lucky – particularly after the manifesto in the 2017 general election repeated the Cameron government's pledge to lower it significantly. She had minor success in November 2017, when the official figures showed a drop to 230,000 down 106,000 for the year ending June 2017[241]. To succeed in her brief, she would therefore need to be among those in the Cabinet pushing for limits to EU migration in any Brexit negotiations – and yet as a Remainer, she had been espousing not long before, with more passion than May had ever done, keeping the single market status quo with the EU, together with an unaltered approach to free movement of peoples. May had indicated areas of possibility in reducing migration – particularly in relation to labour migrants arriving without a specific job. The May administration saw an opportunity to reduce student migration, with Nick Timothy having suggested that only the top Russell Group universities – the 24 perceived to have the best teaching and research facilities – should be able to admit foreign students.

An early clash with the French over the asylum system showed the complexity of Rudd's position. Some on the right in France such as Nicolas Sarkozy – soon to undergo the traditional corruption investigation of a French ex-president – saw the Brexit vote as a chance to alter aspects of the UK-France arrangement they didn't like, chief among them the Le Touquet agreement which allows UK border officials to turn away migrants at Calais. Rudd retorted that this was a non-starter, but it showed how, going forwards, the UK government would have to play to two galleries at once: the European interest upon whose cooperation progress depends; and the heterogeneous and unpredictable UK electorate, which it would ultimately answer to. Meanwhile, Rudd sought to discourage a more open policy between the UK and Australia in a post-Brexit world; she also suggested that companies should have to declare which foreign nationals they are employing. These proposals have been widely condemned by business leaders, who don't much like Whitehall interfering with their operations. These are the typical desperate measures of the embattled home secretary in the age where immigration ought to be lower in the opinion of many, but when there appear to be real difficulties in the implementation of secure borders.

Other matters would land on Rudd's desk – equivalents to matters like the Stephen Lawrence murder and the Hillsborough inquiry that we saw in May's in-tray in Part III. The first was whether to hold an inquiry into the treatment by South Yorkshire police of striking miners at Orgreave in 1984-5. To order another inquiry would potentially have further undermined the morale of the police, but in the wake of the findings over Hillsborough, which provided an important elucidation of events for victims' families, the moral case to proceed appeared a strong one. Rudd chose not to. She also continued to face the ongoing headache of the Independent Inquiry into Child Sexual Abuse, which aimed to look at widespread sexual abuse. Early in her tenure, Rudd vowed to continue the inquiry after the resignation of Justice Lowell Goddard, but she could not afford any mistakes in relation to new appointee Professor Alexis Jay, since Goddard was the third resignation in a sensitive and expensive inquiry which had come to feel ill-fated.

On the legislation front, Rudd would need to continue May's fight against modern slavery, and would also be charged with bringing forward legislation on extremism, a hangover from Cameron's last Queen's speech before the referendum. This would aim to give a range of new powers to ban extremist organisations, close premises which are used to spread extremism, and prevent the spread of hate speech online – all of which would need to be done without alienating the peaceable majority of the Muslim community.

DIVIDING UP THE FOREIGN OFFICE

The most eye-catching of all Theresa May's moves in the reshuffle was her restructuring of the Foreign Office.

The Foreign Office was already arguably a diminishing force in British politics before May formed her first administration, and it is certainly far weaker now. The loss of influence of the Foreign Office is partly attributable to the vanity of prime ministers who have of late wished to be hands-on in forging their own place on the international stage: they have gone to where the glamour is. To various extents, and for different reasons, Thatcher, Blair and Cameron were all their own foreign secretaries. But the referendum result threw up such unimaginable complexities that May deemed it unfit for purpose. She elected to carve it in three, with its responsibilities now spread across three spheres of influence: a Department for International Trade under Liam Fox, a Department for Exiting the European Union under David Davis, and a reduced Foreign Office under Boris Johnson.

The claim of the Leave camp had been that a post-Brexit UK would be free to trade with far-flung jurisdictions – no more the regulated trade with the EU, but a new dawn of free trade with the likes of India, Australia, and, under President Donald Trump, a bilateral agreement with the US. The chief advocate of that view, Dr. Liam Fox – who had also been a brief but quixotic leadership candidate against May in the post-referendum leadership election – was rewarded for his fervour with a ministerial role in this new department. Fox is a curious character, always sunnily running for the leadership and always sunnily losing. He did so in 2016, probably with little more than the intention of restoring himself to prominence. That much he managed. Fox's credibility had been called into question in 2011 when he had resigned his position as defence secretary amid the emergence of the fact that he had lobbied Tory donors to pay his best man Adam Werrity £157,000 to accompany him around the world as a self-styled advisor when in fact Werrity had had no such official role. There is a certain shamelessness about Fox. Men like him know that maintaining the appearance of having done nothing wrong for long enough can eventually be made to look like blamelessness. And thus he came smirking up Downing Street, not necessarily an edifying sight for the Remain voter – but for the Leave side, a coup of sorts: a dash of free trade in a country which had only a few weeks beforehand, seemed to ask, however obliquely, for the advent of a new Britishness.

There were other things for Leave to cheer. The Department for Exiting the European Union came into being, a nod to the enormity of the task ahead. In charge of this new entity would be David Davis, a Eurosceptic with a reputation for free-thinking, and even restlessness. Davis had been defeated for the leadership by Cameron in 2005, but served for three years as his shadow home secretary. Even in that role, which requires, as we have seen, an unshowmanlike doggedness, Davis displayed instability, resigning on 12th June 2008 as shadow home secretary in order to recontest his own seat in a bi-election: his plan was to draw attention to the issue of the erosion of civil liberties in the wake of the July bombings in 2005. In making this quixotic move, he also announced another motivation: he said he had grown bored. He seems to have been unfazed about any inconvenience his yielding to boredom caused to Cameron; Cameron, in turn, let him drift to the backbenches. Looking at the appointment of Davis to the May administration, one wondered even then if he might not one day dramatically flame out again, although one had to admit that one factor against his doing so was that he was so ideologically committed to leaving the European Union. It would remain to be seen whether Davis had mellowed into a compliant late-middle period: it was also unclear precisely how his department would interact with the prime minister's office, and the foreign office during the negotiation – indeed just after the vote, it didn't have a postal address. Eventually offices were found at 9 Downing Street. Anyhow, from his office next-door to the prime minister, Davis would need to handle one of the paradoxes of the Brexit position: namely, that those who had railed against the bureaucracy of the European Union were now left with a bureaucratic task many times greater than implementing EU directives.

But the big surprise was, of course, the identity of the foreign secretary himself – the man we looked at briefly in Part I of this book. Having been stabbed in the back by Gove, Johnson had worn the look of a man confirmed for evermore in the position of a well-paid journalist and jobbing MP. He had looked vaguely seedy – an emblem of miscalculation. Having hogged the limelight for months, he was suddenly shockingly irrelevant. Now here he was again – the man who had campaigned for Leave in the expectation of securing increased influence in a Cameron cabinet after a Remain victory, suddenly the foreign secretary in a new administration committed to exiting the EU.

To a large extent, it was this new look to the Foreign Office that gave the impression that the May government had moved to the right of the Cameron administration. It suggested a Eurosceptic zeal that hadn't before been found at the top of government. That was perhaps a legitimate reflection of the result of the referendum. But it was also around this time that there was increased usage of the term 'Brexiteers' to describe those who had argued for leaving the European Union.

It was a swashbuckling, expansive, and vaguely thrilling term – thus were Iain Duncan Smith or Chris Grayling turned by a linguistic quirk of journalists into characters in an Alexandre Dumas novel.

STRATEGIES BEHIND THE FOREIGN OFFICE SPLIT

These appointments represented Theresa May's spin on the referendum result. It was an act of free interpretation – a reading of what had happened. Another prime minister in the same position might have done something quite different.

Why did May choose to divide up the Foreign Office in this way? In the first place, May was under pressure to appoint a well-known figure from the Leave campaign to one of the top four positions in government. Her other options were therefore limited – Michael Gove as chancellor perhaps, or a top appointment for Andrea Leadsom. In choosing Johnson, she was picking the lesser of three evils: Gove she would rebuke for disloyalty; Leadsom had shown herself in her own campaign to be manifestly unready for top level politics. Johnson had other things in his favour: while he had reached accommodations with a campaign not noted for its truthfulness, he had at least been the most moderate voice on the Leave side. Before that, he had been a clownish but plausibly centrist mayor.

Why the Foreign Office? Might someone with his history of making offensive remarks about foreigners not have been better sent to the Treasury or the Home Office? Here, Johnson's experience as mayor in working across the world with other cities was likely decisive. In any case, the appointment did not represent a complete endorsement of Johnson: she had put her main Brexiter in the weakest of the three possible departments, and then made that department weaker still. Johnson would preside over a much-diminished entity. Another interpretation was that May, a quasi-Remainer, had simply asked those who did believe in the decision to leave the EU to carry out the job themselves. Johnson would taste the effects of his comedy; Fox and Davis would feel the sting of their own zeal. It has also been seen as a self-protective strategy: should it prove impossible to get everything Britain wanted from its negotiations with the European Union, then May would plausibly be able to say that it wasn't her fault: it was an insurance policy, designed to protect her should she need.

It would not always pan out well; there would be squabbling. The question would immediately emerge as to who was really running the Brexit negotiations – the department set up specifically to do so, or the Foreign Office which, with its embassies across the world, had traditionally handled such matters. In August 2016, while May was on holiday in Switzerland, a letter written by Dr Fox was leaked in which the new International Trade Secretary was seen to be arguing that foreign trade should be siphoned off entirely from the Foreign Office. One could see his point: it wasn't precisely clear what his department was doing at all, if not that. However, Johnson had not achieved his boyhood dream of a fiefdom in government only to surrender it immediately. He rebutted it, giving the electorate the impression that Fox's department is one with no real remit.

In the short term, the division of the foreign office at least created an appearance of unity. But was that immediate gain worth it? For some observers, May had repeated Cameron's mistake of putting party above the national interest. The *Economist* described the decision as 'dismal' before going on to say:

> It [the reshuffle] treats the FCO, a giant national asset, as a tool of domestic political management and thus suggests a drastic downgrade of Britain's ambitions on the world stage.[242]

This was particularly alarming as it suggested she hadn't learned the lessons of her predecessor. Cameron, as we have seen, had failed in the end to pursue the national interest: May's cabinet might be said to repeat this error – and precisely at the point in time when one might most expect her to have learned from it.

HIRINGS AND FIRINGS

But there were also signs of a certain admirable firmness.

First there was Stephen Crabbe, the Work and Pensions Secretary, who had had a brief stab at the leadership after the referendum, coming in second-last ahead of Liam Fox. His ambitions had evaporated when flirtatious extramarital texts had surfaced. May initially said Crabbe could keep his job if he wanted, but asked if she could expect any further revelations. Crabbe joined Osborne on the backbenches. This story hints at a possible strength of May's: namely, if you were working for her, you might be frightened not to let her down. It would be up to Crabbe's successor Damian Green to deal with the possible shortfall that would arise in pensions, if growth continued to be slow. Green would also be slated to handle the ongoing debacle over the introduction of universal credit, beset for years now by IT delays.

In a similar vein, Michael Gove was summoned to Parliament and informed by the prime minister that colleagues had 'concerns about his loyalty'. She added that he might want to go away and prove his loyalty on the backbenches. Gove, a man whose famous courtesy has now been elaborately offset for all time by a reputation for treachery, politely replied: 'Thank you very much, Prime Minister' and left. [243]

A few other positions need to be commented upon. Leaver Chris Grayling was rewarded for running May's leadership campaign with the Transport portfolio, and would need to decide whether to proceed with a new runway at Heathrow. He would also handle the HS2 project, and in time add to the difficulty of this author's commute by failing to prevent the disastrous rewrite to timetables which came into force to unanimous misery in May 2018. Grammar school-educated Justine Greening took over at Education from Nicky Morgan – we shall see in Chapter 29 that her grammar school education was a likely contributing factor to her landing the job. Jeremy Hunt, the widely disliked health minister, was curiously reported to have been fired. This caused jubilation among junior doctors with whom Hunt had been in a bitter dispute over working hours and pay. But this jubilation was reversed when it was announced he would remain in post after all. Jon Whittingdale, the Culture Secretary was also fired, and announced to journalists that he was off to get drunk. It would be up to his successor Karen Bradley to finish off the negotiations over the BBC charter.

There were some other notable female appointments. Liz Truss became the first woman to hold the position of Justice Secretary and Lord Chancellor; Lord Falconer, a previous occupant, still scarred like much of the legal profession by Grayling's tenure under Cameron, worried that Truss had no legal experience. It would be up to Truss to decide what to do in respect of the UK's relationship with the European Court of Human Rights in Strasbourg – as we have seen, not an entity beloved by May. By 21ˢᵗ August 2016, she had already abandoned Michael Gove's projected introduction of problem-solving courts on the grounds of their being too 'soft on crime'[244] – another move to the right. She had also stated she would place extremists in separate prison units. Meanwhile, she had hardly endeared herself to the legal profession at large – many lawyers would report a disturbing remoteness, and even lack of understanding of the law, in their dealings with Truss.

Andrea Leadsom, though she had not been deemed suitable for one of the four major posts, was appointed Secretary of State for the Environment – and, to the dismay of many, the Department of Climate Change was abolished. This was seen as another move to the right. Leadsom is on record as saying that she would favour no regulation for business whatsoever; she would now head a department where the question of sensible regulation would have its share in determining the future of the planet. The government's response to the abolition of the Department of Climate Change was to say that its work had been subsumed into a new Department for Business, Energy and Industrial Strategy. It might also be said in defence of this move that Nick Hurd – son of Douglas – seemed a sound choice as climate change minister. George Monbiot – not an easy man to please on this – called him 'an adult among her [May's] pet buffoons'[245]. Finally, Priti Patel, a prominent Leaver, headed up the Department for International Development, where she immediately made herself unpopular for suggesting that the international development budget was too generous. She also claimed that much of it was being wasted and stolen: when challenged to say how much during an appearance before the Commons committee, she was unable to give a figure[246]. Nor was leaving the EU projected to be a straightforward matter for her: in 2010, the UK contribution amounted to some 15 per cent of EU development budgets, and it would be necessary to strike a deal here, as in other areas.[247]

THE VERDICT ON THE RESHUFFLE

Over time, it would also be noted that a more austere form of government was emerging: by mid-August May had introduced a cap on pay for special advisors. No more than £72,000 could be paid without her say-so. This measure, intended to curb the perceived excesses of the Cameron years, would have been more impressive if it had stretched to her then chief advisors Nick Timothy and Fiona Hill, but this was not the case.

It might also be said that in a time of crisis, May had missed the opportunity to form a more imaginative Cabinet. She had stood on the steps of Downing Street sounding like a centre-left prime minister – and for many this was a smart move. But the impression persists that she might have made her appointments better reflective of the confused condition of the nation. May stood as prime minister at a time of great crisis. Difficult negotiations lay ahead, and aside from Brexit, there was a host of other issues – climate change, international terrorism, inequality, and an underfunded NHS – in urgent need of resolution. It might have been an opportune moment to have assembled a national government. Perhaps a New Labour MP might have been made a Minister for Social Justice. The likeable Caroline Lucas MP, now the joint leader in the Green Party, would have been an excellent choice as Minister for Climate Change. Perhaps the much-diminished Liberal Democrats could also have accepted a seat at the table. May's government would have then reflected far better the divided mood of the nation; it would have suited the extremity of her predicament as a new prime minister. Instead the Cabinet she assembled – clever in some respects – lacked the breadth and vision the moment required. What resulted was a reminder of May's partisan nature: it was a government of 'my party'.

But the decisions had been made, and these were the people she had chosen to work with.

In the next section we shall look at the work she had to do, and how she began to go about it.

PART FIVE

THE MAY INHERITANCE

25 – ARTICLE 50 AND ALL THAT

What then were the problems faced by Theresa May, freshly installed as prime minister? Like all prime ministers, she was met not only with the great complexity of contemporary reality, but with what William Gladstone – of all her predecessors perhaps the most energetic at mastering the complexity of government – called 'the immense multiplication of details on public business'.

Gladstone was referring to Robert Peel's private complaint about the accumulation of ministerial duties – Peel found it, for instance, onerous to correspond with the Queen. I suspect Peel would have been aghast at the expectations of his counterparts today: not only does Prime Minister's Questions sit in the calendar as a possible source of distracting gaffe, but television – which May plainly has little relish for – must be continually appeased.

The eminence of the office, with all its possible levers and manoeuvres, opens up onto possibilities too great to compute: the main elements of government must be comprehended, given direction to, and continually presided over, while keeping in mind how all the individual parts interrelate – how, for instance, the price of sugar might affect the public health, or how the strength of the economy impact on the funds available to tackle, say, an embarrassing education system. The office requires a sympathetic sense of the multiplicity of human pursuits. Its essence is difficulty: the diversity of the nation's interests must be caught within a set of policies unlikely to work optimally for all, or even for many. One's constituency is the

entire nation – that is, 65 million people with differing personalities, instincts, interests and alignments: the prime minister
is meant to reconcile the irreconcilable. The role implies the
need for a sophisticated and politically-attuned legal and economic understanding alongside a capacity to articulate detail:
to turn the finicky nature of administration into poetry.

If the complexity of the office were to end there it might
be a blessing. But it is also a running test of judgement – a
trial of one's knowledge of human nature. One must decide
which matters to tackle, which to delay on, and which to leave
alone. The prime minister must take into account the *vertical*
complexity of each issue. When one turns definitively to pursue a problem, one must be careful that there is not a hidden
intractability to it, or secret pockets of vehement resistance to
one's solution. May would not always be successful in deciding where to direct her energies: one thinks of the enormous
amount of time she would devote, for instance, to articulating
her social care policy, only for it to be abandoned. Some would
also wonder how well she understood the likely clinchingness
of the Irish border question (see Chapter 27): at times on that
issue, she would act as though reality could be altered by her
own optimistic assessments.

Nor is any political issue *static*. In selecting six problems in
these following chapters, I have made a concession to simplici-
ty on behalf of the reader (and the writer) which reality doesn't
make for prime ministers. There is a range of issues from culture and housing, to transport and international development,
which I have not had room to include in this section; Theresa May has not had the luxury of being able to exclude them
from her administration.

Even those which I have included can only be snapshotted here – and then only snapshotted at a blur. Indeed, each major problem May faced when she took office in the summer of 2016 might be said to have a particular relationship with time. The questions of whether and when to trigger Article 50 of the Lisbon Treaty would set the clock in motion; besides, the question itself had pressures attached to it and May could not delay forever. Meanwhile, the economy (Chapter 26) was continually altering as stock markets fluctuated, as jobs figures and ONS reports trickled in, and as the Bank of England rendered its predictions. The issue of the devolved nations (Chapter 27) was in continual shift as those countries' respective leaders sought to shape their own careers and peoples, and as those efforts were reported on with the media's self-delighted hysteria. Meanwhile, a bad winter – as in fact would happen in early 2018 – might easily give new urgency to the perennial crisis in NHS funding, and re-alert the public to the inadequacy of the nation's ageist social care arrangements (Chapter 28). Education (Chapter 29) is perhaps the least dramatic – or perhaps least inclined to melodrama – of the problems May faced, but it should be at the top of any prime minister's concerns since an uneducated country cannot be expected to succeed. Finally, climate change (Chapter 30) is a matter which most scientists, and a large majority of the public, consider to be of utmost importance: the consensus is that the effects of rising temperatures must be imminently reversed to prevent a catastrophe for our grandchildren, and – terrible thought – even for our children.

Across every area of life, there was no time to lose.

Unfortunately, May's difficulties didn't end there. The prime minister's agenda could only be tackled with the human material at the prime minister's disposal, as we saw in Chapter 24, and within a framework of slow-moving democracy: Gladstone's 'details on the public business' again. Indeed, one imagines that the parliamentary framework must be a significant comfort to politicians in general, and to prime ministers in particular. It is a machine intended to stave off the chaos of life, and at least gives a starting-point for tackling problems: a venue for a speech, a place to instigate legislation. Even so, one sometimes feels as though the highest office is possessed of less tangible influence than one tends to think when set against how much there is to accomplish: wise prime ministers have shrugged their shoulders at these limits, knowing that it can lead to the dictator's ancient complaint: that all this would be solved immediately, if we were to do away with finicky democracy and replace it with the rule of some strongman.

It must be wondered how many leaders, faced with such a difficult task, have simply preferred not to look too closely at their predicament, and chosen instead to muddle through: indeed, reality being complex as it is, and human capacity being limited in numerous respects, there must always be some degree of trusting to luck in all leadership. But perhaps all this is to emphasise only the burdens: each person around the Cabinet table, and especially the prime minister, has the great ego boost of being important to protect them from self-doubt, in addition to the physical comforts of power, somewhat at odds with the tribulations of the public which they have pledged to remove. And the law, which the prime minister is in a unique position to change, really is a powerful tool: a just alteration to it – as with May's splendid efforts regarding the Modern Slavery Act – can ripple out from Westminster to improve the lives of strangers: the possibility of this forms too little, one suspects, of the adrenalin attached to the job, but it would be cynical to imagine that someone like Theresa May is in Downing Street solely for the food, or to be near the Turners in the White Drawing Room.

Even so, one could forgive the incoming prime minister a holiday before she took on a task of such magnitude as Brexit. In August 2016, Theresa May took her annual walking holiday with her husband in Switzerland. It was a moment of deserved escape for the new prime minister: she traded the backbiting and white noise of Westminster for the open spaces of the mountains. Of course, government is never prepared to leave any prime minister alone: power rushed out of Westminster and up the Swiss mountains to disturb her peace. The Foreign Office squabbles between Fox and Johnson reached her ears, and a statement was released – perhaps dictated beside some great rock – saying that she was 'unimpressed'[248]. It has been obscurely decided that we need proof of our prime ministers on holiday, and so there was an awkward photo op. It is hard to imagine that the holiday didn't have some foreboding in it: by 2018, with EU negotiations proceeding at a limp pace, it would look as though she had had no time for a holiday at all. As she walked those hills, all that she had really told the nation was that 'Brexit means Brexit'. It had been up to Ken Clarke in the House of Commons during David Cameron's last PMQs to flag the difficulty: 'no two people can agree on what Brexit means'[249]. This would hold true throughout 2017 and into 2018.

May appeared caught up in the sort of unfathomable complexity where to make any public moves was potentially to make things more complex again, simply by moving the pieces around. A kinder interpretation of her slow approach might be that she was memorising the pieces on the board before altering them.

THE DILEMMA OVER ARTICLE 50

It can be almost salutary after having speculated about the ins and outs of the human drama in Westminster to be faced with the raw letter of European law. It is to travel away from one's usual means of accessing information – the media – into the weather of the actual problem.

Over the holiday, May knew that the success of her administration would depend upon when and whether to trigger Article 50 of the 2007 Lisbon Treaty. It would be a matter of timing. In the summer of 2016, May was caught between the so-called 'hard Brexit' lobby who longed for an immediate trigger, and the 'soft' Brexit camp who urged caution. There were incentives to take her time: delay would have brought her the chance to reflect, and deepen her preparations. But the hard Brexit camp deemed the UK to be in such a strong position that a considered approach would be tantamount to time-wasting: this urgency housed a fear that the vote would be reneged on by a shadowy establishment who, after all, had campaigned almost uniformly to Remain. Even so, an atmosphere of fools rushing in would pertain to the early stages of the negotiation: the Brexit Secretary David Davis would frequently find himself accused of ill-thought out strategy. In his dealings with his counterpart Michel Barnier, the EU's Chief Negotiator, he would at times exhibit a smirking blitheness which made observers doubt whether he comprehended the scale of his mission.

Article 50 joins UN resolution 1441 among the small number of segments of international law that have acquired celebrity. At first it might seem surprising – it is this clause which has provided them with an exit, after all – that Brexiters hold the Article in disdain. This is because it stacks the odds against any country wishing to leave: it sets a two-year deadline that can be extended only unanimously, thus making it likely that any country seeking to exit the European Union will have to do so in a detrimental hurry. The Article 50 decision was one of Cameron's principal bequests to May: in the lead-up to the referendum Cameron was adamant that he would trigger Article 50 immediately should he lose the vote. His decision to resign was a distraction from the fact that he didn't – this surely *was* in the national interest, and might even count as an act of opportune statesmanship, but it left May with an unenviable in-tray. For a while May hinted that all would be well without saying how or why. But by autumn, the 'hard' Brexit camp had won. At the October Conservative Party conference, the prime minister had announced that she would trigger article 50 by March 2017. On March 29th 2017, she made good on that promise.

THE ARTICLE ITSELF

The relevant sections of Article 50 read in unabashed legalese:

1. Any Member State may decide to withdraw from the Union in accordance with its own constitutional requirements.

2. A Member State which decides to withdraw shall notify the European Council of its intention. In the light of the guidelines provided by the European Council, the Union shall negotiate and conclude an agreement with that State, setting out the arrangements for its withdrawal, taking account of the **framework for its future relationship with the Union**. That agreement shall be negotiated in **accordance with Article 218 (3) of the Treaty on the Functioning of the European Union**. It shall be concluded on behalf of the Union by the Council, acting by a qualified majority, after obtaining the consent of the European Parliament.

3. The Treaties shall cease to apply to the State in question from the date of entry into force of the withdrawal agreement or, failing that, two years after the notification referred to in paragraph 2, unless the European Council, in agreement with the Member State concerned, unanimously decides to extend this period.

4. For the purposes of paragraphs 2 and 3, the member of the European Council or of the Council representing the withdrawing Member State shall not participate in the discussions of the European Council or Council or in decisions concerning it.

A qualified majority shall be defined in accordance with Article 238(3) (b) of the Treaty on the Functioning of the European Union. [my emboldening][250]

Article 50 invites us into the arcane processes of the European Union: the language is undeniably drab, in tones of conference room beige and grey, and for a Brexiter particularly, bereft of the hearty medieval notes of English common law. The argument runs that we are adrift in a labyrinthine machinery, one which lacks the individual vitality which nations can bring to their statutes. A brief acquaintance with any volume of Halsbury's laws will probably cure us of this romantic view: besides, this is word as function, and never intended to be poetic.

Even so, there is the suspicion that it is all *intentionally* impregnable. A European treaty can never be understood in isolation. Instead mysterious 'guidelines' from the Council hover at its edges, adding another layer of confusion for any country anxious to leave. In the Council, a qualified majority means 55 per cent of member states, representing 65 per cent of the EU population[251]. This needs to be agreed with Parliament, about a third of which is Eurosceptic, in order to achieve consent: this is considered a high bar with a simple majority vote required. The word 'framework', in the first section placed in bold, also has potential significance. If Barnier – nudged perhaps by the Macrons and Merkels of this world – had been minded to be generous, this provision gave him authority to authorise wide-ranging talks about possible trade relations between the UK and the EU alongside negotiations about the terms of departure: the plane-hopping urgency surrounding the December 2017 Phase One Agreement was an attempt to have made sufficient progress to move onto these. But the statute is also stark and seems to engender loneliness in the departing nation: there is no statutory obligation for the European leadership to promote a benevolent course of action, although Leavers rightly argue that any petty vindictiveness would run counter to common business sense. This faith of the Brexiter presents an interesting contradiction: the Europeans, so perfidious while we were in the EU will become immediately easier to deal with once they contemplate our awesome departure. Another irony is evident: the talks shall not be witnessed by those who voted for it, or even by those who led the campaign to exit. Among the central figures of the Leave campaign, only Johnson stood a chance of being in the room. Those who considered Brussels undemocratic and had sought to 'take back control' would have the hidden nature of the 2017-19 negotiations to contend with.

There is a further complexity about Article 50, befitting the complex structures of the EU. That reference to Article 218 (3) – the second section I have placed in bold – refers to the fact that the process shall be negotiated by the European Commission following a mandate from EU ministers and concluded by EU governments 'acting by a qualified majority, after obtaining the consent of the European Parliament.' The Commission was to act as negotiator but the Council of Ministers, EU governments, and the EU Parliament would at various points all have their input. Any one of these could throw matters off course; all would have to be taken into account. Too many contingencies were at work: a groundswell of disapproval in the European Parliament could affect things as much as the European President Jean-Claude Junker, or any of the 27 remaining heads of government. Leaders would be able to demand alterations to areas of policy in exchange for agreement to the deal itself – or even to a single aspect of it. This might include anything from Spain's wishing to revisit the question of Gibraltar's sovereignty, to Denmark's longstanding desire for mutual fishing access[252].

Any hypothetical disagreement would then need to boomerang back to May and her negotiating team. She would then need to manage the emotions of both her own divided party (and, eventually the DUP as we shall see in Part VI) – not to mention, respond to the mood of the nation. All this would need to be done while also attending to the welter of matters which run-of-the-mill governments face: these have usually been sufficient to keep past prime ministers busy. From the European side, there would be no immediate unanimity on how to treat the United Kingdom as it made its exit: punitive and conciliatory voices would form a dissonant music. To add another layer of complexity, many countries would face elections during the negotiation period, so it wouldn't be clear what kind of national governments May would be negotiating with: in 2017, for instance, an expected mainstay of the EU scene, Angela Merkel struggled to form a convincing coalition after the rise of the far right in Germany, lessening her becalming influence upon negotiations. Meanwhile, by 2018, an ugly far right coalition had come to power in Italy.

Mark Sedwill, permanent secretary to the Home Office and a former senior diplomat, was among those who voiced concern:

There will have to be significant changes to free movement in whatever arrangement we reach, so the question then becomes how much
access to the single market our European partners are going to give.[253]

But here the term 'European partners' was fluid: May would
be dependent on continued European goodwill during a period of political fluctuation. Again, it was a curious end to a
campaign that promised to take back control.

WHAT KIND OF AGREEMENT WOULD MAY SEEK?

Free trade agreements would be a mantra of the May administration in the coming years. But a straightforward free trade
agreement with the EU was not desirable. The preferred option was a more complex 'mixed agreement': but in opting for
this, her predicament attained new complexity.

A mixed agreement involving provisions relating to things
like services, transport and investment protection, would require ratification not just by the European Parliament, but also
from national parliaments. Such an agreement could be blown
off course by a groundswell of national feeling in any member
state. Not only this but when May took over the reins of power no consensus existed as to what constituted a mixed agreement. For instance, in an article like 'The Impact of Brexit on
the EU's International Agreements' by Guillaume Van der Loo
and Steven Blockmans, we appear to be witnessing a widespread unpreparedness:

... However, the situation becomes paradoxical when one considers, first, that in terms of competence delimitation, it is difficult in mixed agreements to draw up a catalogue; and second, that the other contracting parties might want to seize the opportunity to revise the terms of the agreement if the UK decided to withdraw its own signature.[254]

The UK had voted to remove itself from a set of agreements that many had an incentive to alter. Brexit would not only be about the UK leaving the European Union. It would also create a moment of unprecedented fluidity in the European project; it was a chance for those who were staying to reshape Europe into something more palatable to them.

Due to these difficulties, May had great incentive to seek a simple deal. A swift wrench, while desirable for obvious reasons, would be difficult politically since both May, and large sections of the British people arguably viewed trade as less important than immigration – or so it seemed to May. The resolution of this matter would have to form part of wider discussions. On his Facebook page, Robert Peston shared the following scoop:

I am reliably told that Brexit, for May (and therefore for us), equals:

1. discretionary control over immigration policy;
2. discretionary control over law-making;
3. no compulsory contributions to the EU budget.

Why those three pillars of our new relationship with the EU? 'It's what the people voted for', a senior government member tells me – with a certainty that suggests it would be pointless to raise doubts.[255]

By December 2017, the Phase One Agreement had shown May much more willing to capitulate than Peston's confidante thought. It would later be difficult to recall how much the notion that she wouldn't budge under any circumstances had been part of the mythology of her first months as prime minister.

May was in a bind: either she would upset those who wanted significantly less immigration, or she would alienate those who would continue to need access to the single market. Access to that market of course meant simultaneous acceptance of free movement of peoples. It looked a stark choice: either self-limit one's access to the single market and risk the health of the economy, or keep access to that market, and risk a public backlash over immigration. Before Article 50 was triggered, Ian Birrell was among those concerned by the scale of the task facing the fledgling administration:

> Already Eurosceptic zealots are pressing May to trigger article 50, which starts the formal two-year exit process. One expert in Zurich laughed when I suggested a country with an economy as complex as Britain could sort out a new trade deal with Europe in this time. It took the Swiss 17 years to negotiate one insurance agreement; there has still been no deal on joining the open market for financial services, one reason their banks set up offices in the City of London.[256]

Greenland provided another example of a less than speedy exit: that country, which has the population of Croydon, and whose government mainly needed to construct an agreement around the fishing industry, took three years to leave the EEC in 1984, which was itself far less complex than the EU of 2016.

May had often called the referendum result unambiguous, but it was also unambiguously marginal. There were numerous temptations for it to be abandoned.

THE FINANCIAL AND LEGAL IMPLICATIONS OF ARTICLE 50

In the first months of her premiership, whenever there was any serious talk of May triggering Article 50 there was panic in financial markets and a consequent drop in the pound. For example, on 19th August 2016 Bloomberg reported that May was 'sympathetic' to the case for starting divorce in April 2017 'at the latest'. This did indeed turn out to be her position, but it triggered a big sell-off of sterling. Neil Wilson, markets analyst at ETX Capital, was glum:

Big sell-off in sterling this afternoon amid rumours the UK wants to invoke Article 50 in the first half of 2017... That means invoking Article 50 by April, putting paid to speculation that the UK would have several years to prepare to leave the EU. The less time the UK has to get things in order, the greater the market fears the fallout.[257]

For a while after the April 2017 hint, May seemed to strike a more cautious note – and the economy rewarded her by performing better than Remainers had expected. Even so, at the autumn party conference when May reiterated her early 2017 position, sterling panicked again. The pound would remain well beneath its long-term average into 2018, with each panic ceding to a kind of stable gloom. Within the major banks one could find both bearish sentiment (Deutsche, HSBC) and bullishness (Barclays): it was an image of uncertainty.

There remained the possibility that many in May's government – and perhaps May herself – were blasé about the task ahead. David Allen Green explained in the *Evening Standard*:

> Millions of pounds of funding for agriculture, regional development and scientific research comes from the EU. Almost every policy area you can think of, from medicines to television, has a EU component and many UK public bodies depend daily on EU institutions providing information.

> Each policy area needs to be examined so the Government will put appropriate measures in place. All this will have to be done on top of what the Government will be doing anyway running the country, in a period of budget cuts and spending freezes, and with a civil service that is 20 per cent smaller than in 2010.[258]

Not only did May have a considerable problem, but she had a considerable problem for which she wasn't satisfactorily staffed.

The situation was also illustrative of certain tensions between the law, which moves slowly and needs to be changed thoughtfully, and business, which detests uncertainty, and hankers after swift action. The European Communities Act 1972 (ECA) would now be repealed on the back of a Great Repeal Bill: this was eventually brought forward in 2017. In one respect, this was a relatively simple matter of ending the UK's constitutional relationship with the EU. But there was also the vast amount of legislation which parliament had passed during the 40 years of its membership in order to comply with EU law: the House of Commons library was not exaggerating when it called the exercise: 'one of the largest legislative projects ever undertaken in the UK'[259]. EU directives and regulations would also need to be reconsidered. In some cases – where, for instance, the implementation of regulation had in the past been overseen by EU regulatory bodies – they would need to be rewritten. There was also doubt as to whether judges would continue to have reference to the judgements of the European Court of Justice – for the period during which all this legislation was unpicked they likely would, and probably would do beyond.[260]

It was the sort of vexed situation where to still be in position in seven or eight years' time would have suggested great skill, or luck on May's part. This was before she made her life so much harder by calling the 2017 snap election.

Of course, the intricacy of all this, made some ask another question – some in hope, others with pre-emptive annoyance: 'Would it actually happen?'

THE ATTEMPT TO BLOCK BREXIT

The consequences of departure seemed sufficiently steep for some to enter a period of defiance – or childish denial, depending on your point of view. This approach would still be ongoing among the Liberal Democrats – and in the mind of Tony Blair into 2018. Furthermore, a dramatic moment would occur in December 2017: resigning his position as chairman of the National Infrastructure Commission, Lord Adonis would say in his resignation letter to May: 'If Brexit happens, taking us back into Europe will become the mission of our children's generation, who will marvel at your acts of destruction'.

This attitude would sometimes be presented as pie-in-the-sky, but as the Irish border question dragged on through 2018, and as the House of Lords amendments on the Withdrawal Bill were met with concessions by the government, it could appear that the wishes of the Leavers would never be accomplished both because the task itself was too difficult, and because too few people high-up really wanted it.

Besides, in the flux of life, no question is ever definitely settled: there remained possible brakes on the process. The first was a legal challenge, which became known as *R (on the application of Miller and Dos Santos) v Secretary of State for Exiting the European Union* which was brought by Gina Miller, the dynamic and soon-to-be-famous co-founder of wealth management firm SCM Direct, along with other plaintiffs, who argued that her and her husband's business would be materially affected by a British exit. The case was a vehicle to argue that Article 50 could only be triggered by Parliament – a body which at the time of the case was 73 per cent in favour of Remain – and not at the wish of the Prime Minister. It was litigation of great constitutional importance. At the centre of it was an interpretation of what the 2015 Referendum Act had meant. Had the referendum been purely advisory, effectively handing the government a prerogative power to enact the result, or had it merely been a sort of elaborate questionnaire, for parliament to do with what it would? It amused some that if the case were to go against the Brexiters then their only right of appeal would be to the European Court of Justice. In the event of it, it did go against the government, with the judgement reading:

> Bearing in mind this unique history and the constitutional principle of Parliamentary sovereignty, it seems most improbable that those two parties had the intention or expectation that ministers, constitutionally the junior partner in that exercise, could subsequently remove the graft without formal appropriate sanction from the constitutionally senior partner in that exercise, Parliament.

But this dramatic trial had an undramatic sequel. In the end, the government put forward a bill, and it passed without any amendments. Gina Miller would later express her annoyance: 'I thought, 'What is the point of you?' Everyone is talking about democracy and sovereignty but no one is willing to act on it.'[261]

Another route seemed ripe with possibilities for the Remainers: there was the hope that the House of Lords – which like the House of Commons is broadly in favour of remaining – might delay matters. Baroness Wheatcroft, the former editor-in-chief of the *Wall Street Journal Europe* and the *Sunday Telegraph* had expressed optimism, stating that the House of Lords might delay legislation:

> And I would hope, while we delayed things, that there would be sufficient movement in the EU to justify putting it to the electorate, either through a General Election or a second referendum.[262]

At the time, this seemed somewhat quixotic: one never knew quite what this 'sufficient movement' would have entailed, especially as the European Union wasn't particularly known for swift movement on anything. Wheatcroft would get her General Election, although not quite in the way she supposed; but by 2018, the Lords had sent the EU Withdrawal Bill back to the House of Commons with suggested amendments, and the government was forced into making concessions: it proved that it is not quite the toothless chamber of caricature. The Remain camp would continue to have the House of Lords on their side – for some, a rare bastion of good sense, for others an unelected frustration. It would be of particular relevance when it could articulate concerns which chimed with a sufficient number of potential Tory rebels in the other chamber.

THE TRIGGER PULLED

For May, it was a case of damned if you do and damned if you don't.

She could construe the vote as a direct mandate, and enact the wishes of a slim majority of the country. Or she could note the closeness of the vote, and proceed cautiously. This second option, though it would have suited her forensic temperament in many respects, had the downside of looking like vacillation: it would not have been palatable to her, having witnessed the far right's power over Cameron, to discover their ire in the event of a delay to the Article 50 trigger. To pause might in any case have engendered only limited gratitude from the left.

Whereas to proceed might win her a genuine following on the right.

This decision taken, all that remained was the timing. We have touched on the common sense temptations of waiting: a too-quick trigger of Article 50 might create a period of concerning risk, whereby critical trade, security and environmental laws would not be clarified by 2019. Critical aspects of life, like the European arrest warrant, data sharing and climate change laws might still be unclear on the eve of a likely General Election, to her own detriment. May hadn't at this time decided on calling the 2017 General Election: the possibility of facing the electorate in 2020 would still have been in her calculations. In fact, one calculation in pursuing that vote may have been that in facing the electorate in 2022, she might have time to rescue matters if a deal had fallen through.

After a longish honeymoon period where May's habitual indecision was permitted by the public to be seen as icy calm, she opted for an early trigger before – as we shall see in the next part – seeking that ill-advised mandate from the country. In so doing, she had set the country definitively on the course of leaving the European Union: from that point on, talk of a second referendum would have to contend with the sense of momentum which was caused by the Article 50 time limit. In the end, it was a Remainer, May, who signed off Brexit. She had been empowered by a referendum called by another Remainer, Cameron. Indeed, throughout the entire 2016-18 period, in either Cameron's or May's cabinets, only one occupant of one of the four great offices of state has agreed with the course of action Britain has taken: Boris Johnson, and even he had made Remain-ish noises from time to time. It was an overturning of the establishment by the establishment itself: or rather an insurgency sanctioned by incompetence in the highest places.

Another matter needs to be noted. Before the vast complexity of leaving the European Union, May had announced something whose ambition appears to have been overlooked: she had said that she didn't want the next years to be defined by Brexit. This was realistic in one sense: Brexit was not the only thing she would face. In another sense, it showed notable ambition which, if made good upon, had the potential to launch her into the ranks of the great prime ministers.

But it also might be interpreted as a hubristic wish: as we shall see, the UK's departure from the European Union was the unleashing of chance into every area of life.

26 – THE ECONOMY

The Remain script in the event of Brexit was sometimes characterised as quasi-apocalyptic. Everybody knows how the Bank of England, the IMF and the Cameron government feared things would go. In the event of a vote to Leave, foreign investment would be immediately pulled, leading to a contraction across sectors – especially in manufacturing and construction – which would in turn generate a precipitous loss of confidence, further worsening the economic outlook, in a gyre of unpleasant news. We would be plunged with foolish immediacy into a dangerous new world. A sharp drop in consumer spending would ensue. The High Street would become a place of caution and quiet – shoppers would approach tills, consider Britain's departure from the European Union, and then turn for the street with sad shakes of their heads. Meanwhile, shareholders would look on aghast at falling stock prices. The government would be forced to take to the streets to peddle UK bonds in desperation for more revenues. Once again, we would see the curious and slightly comic Black Wednesday-style footage of traders despairing before data-busy computers, their heads in their hands, like footballers who've missed penalties. The so-called DIY recession would hit.

To the pleasure of the Brexiter, who could claim vindication – and to the relief of those Remainers who disliked the idea of a recession even if it seemed to prove them wrong on the referendum – it didn't turn out like that. Throughout the summer and early autumn after the vote, the economy was, superficially at least, well-behaved. In fact, it might more truthfully be said that the post-Brexit economy mirrored the political limbo that the country found itself in after Cameron's resignation, and as May made her first grapplings with the job. It was all unreal – an image of a sleepwalking economy, and a country in shock. Once departure from the EU became reality, the worst-case scenario predictions from before the referendum began to look odd when set against this sluggish limbo: Cameron's team never expected its worst fears to be tested because it expected to win. The pace of macroeconomic life had not been sped up by the decision to leave. Instead, it seemed almost to have been slowed down, while investors paused to consider the ramifications of the referendum.

Perhaps the constant nature of the campaign, together with the shock of the result, engendered a wish to think about other things: the world of culture suddenly opened up as a possible source of relief: that summer, for instance, saw the Rio Olympics, with its pleasing dissimilarities to British politics. In the absence of any immediate structural change to the country's relationship with Europe, people reverted to previous consumer behaviour. The sky had not fallen in.

NOTES ON A LOWER POUND

For a few weeks as the Brexit vote settled, the political developments amassed. The electorate had been protagonists only briefly as they had cast their ballots; politics returned to being a spectator's sport.

Straight after the vote George Osborne announced that he

would rush through an emergency cut to the corporation tax from 20 to 15 per cent. This didn't happen: corporation tax would remain at 20 per cent. But May had taken note: the 2017 conservative manifesto would include a commitment to cut that tax to 17 per cent. Osborne was like a man trying to finish his sentence while being forcibly escorted from a bar. It was both a defiant parting shot and, from a man who would soon edit the *Evening Standard*, an opening salvo in a new career: Osborne would not go gently into the good night of retirement. Osborne was sending a message to international business that Britain remained a place to trade with: only future budgets would tell whether these were the dying throes of neoliberalism, or a sign of its continuation. The early signs were that his successor as chancellor Philip Hammond would do some slight tweaking – for instance, he abandoned Osborne's stringent deficit targets – but his winter budget in 2017 was quietly dull, and his 2018 speech primarily notable for its gloomy growth predictions.

At any rate, Osborne – power ebbing from him – had no political capital with which to embark on his emergency budget: there would, after all, be no sharp raising of income and inheritance taxes and no punitive cuts to the NHS budget. Previous dark talk of a £30 billion black hole in the public finances evaporated. Osborne was unrepentant about the language he had used during the campaign, but he was offering an altogether different emphasis now:

> I don't resile from any of the concerns I expressed during the campaign, but I fully accept the result of the referendum and will do everything I can to make it work for Britain.

> It is inevitable, after Thursday's vote, that Britain's economy is going
> to have to adjust to the new situation we find ourselves in.[263]

In the same statement, he also touted the Bank of England's 'robust contingency plans' which he said were calming financial markets. After the referendum, Osborne shelved his plan, much touted for many years, to run a budget surplus by the end of the parliament. Reading back these transcripts, one wonders whether Osborne expected to be kept in position. As we know, everything was tending towards his firing.

What was the economic story after the vote? For one thing, the post-Brexit pound would be, in spite of occasional rallies, worth less than it was: it experienced a sharp dip from its pre-Brexit life of 1.4 against the Euro, to a value of 1.16 against the same in late August and 1.12 by year's end. This devaluation constituted a 31-year low; by 2018, a weaker pound had become the norm, and it still stood at 1.14 in June of that year. There is debate, however, as to what this means. A lower pound is cheering to Brexiters, who discern in it not some harsh verdict on overall economic performance, but the possibility of a correction to the nation's current account deficit. The UK has, in fact, run a persistent current account deficit over the last thirty years, meaning it imports more than it exports. For instance, in the first quarter of 2016, its deficit was £32.6 billion or 6.9 per cent of GDP – up from the average across 2015 of 5.2 per cent of GDP. By the second quarter of 2017, the deficit was £22.3 billion, and 4.4 per cent of GDP; by the fourth quarter it was £18.4 billion: 4.1 per cent of GDP[264]. A high current account deficit can in some cases be caused by an overvaluation in currency. The typical Brexiter – Liam Fox is the most prominent example – thinks Britain is one such case, and that loss of value to the pound shall create a rosy dawn for free trade, on the back of higher exports.

One objection to this is that devaluations are usually helpful only at a time of high interest rates and high unemployment, whereas Britain in the aftermath of the referendum had to endure the opposite state of affairs of low interest rates – for nearly a decade at 0.25 per cent, though they did rise incrementally to 0.5 per cent in November 2017 with rumours of future rises – and unemployment at record lows. Paul Johnson of the Institute for Fiscal Studies, observing this state of affairs, argued that an economy with a lower pound would 'result in an immediate hit to our standard of living.'[265] Another objection to the Liam Fox position is that the absence of a current account deficit has not always been good for those economies that have managed to achieve it – stagnation in Japan is the oft-cited example. Finally, a current account deficit is much less of a worry in an economy that can depreciate its currency. By keeping the pound, the UK can do this, rendering comparisons between the UK economy and struggling Eurozone economies invalid. Any cheer to be had about a lower pound, and the subsequent decrease in the current account deficit, needs to be reasonably muted.

A lower pound is not good in other ways – it has, for instance, not been good for sterling investors. Less importantly, but of widespread interest to a nation of enthusiastic holidayers, a falling pound makes journeying abroad more expensive. There were, for instance, unhappy scenes at Luton and Stansted airports in August 2016, when travellers were unable to get even a single euro for their pound. In 2017, those taking a European holiday would find that their break was around 22 per cent more expensive[266].

RESTRUCTURING THE UK ECONOMY (OR PERHAPS NOT)

But for Liam Fox and David Davis – and perhaps for Theresa May – these are short-term shocks and wholly endurable, for the sake of what is really required: a complete restructuring of the UK economy.

For the Leaver, a reduction in the current account deficit might potentially buffer the UK economy from the burden of high interest payments should the finance industry – so-called 'hot money' – dry up. This also speaks to the nostalgic wish for the UK to once again 'make things'. At its best, this raises the laudable prospect that the UK should make itself more useful to the world. Even so, there were those who reckoned that leaving the European Union was not the way to enact such goals, and others who pointed out that to intentionally wound the UK financial services sector was to propagate a dangerous fantasy: in 2017, the financial services sector contributed £119 billion to the UK economy, 6.5 per cent of total economic output[267]. It could be argued that all the UK had done by proceeding with EU departure was to weaken investor expectations: those who make things – or want to make things – should, after all, still be eager to attract investment, provided it is investment of the right kind.

One person who particularly feels investment has too often been of the wrong kind is Prime Minister Theresa May, who in her sole policy speech during her 2016 leadership campaign, drew attention to a problem she and her advisers feel passionately about.

> As we saw when Cadbury's – that great Birmingham company – was bought by Kraft, or when AstraZeneca was almost sold to Pfizer, transient shareholders – who are mostly companies investing other people's money – are not the only people with an interest when firms are sold or close. Workers have a stake, local communities have a stake, and often the whole country has a stake.[268]

It was an instance of May channelling Joseph Chamberlain. Her words recalled not just the Chamberlain who championed workers – and we might note the reference to Birmingham workers – but the Chamberlain who advocated tariff reform, and a more protectionist economy for the British Empire. In a world where Amazon is altering the high street, and where international private equity firms too often tie up the companies they buy in unmanageable debt – the oft-cited example is Maplin – May's complaint was a timely one.[269]

But there is now some doubt as to whether May is really so opposed to foreign investment as the above passage would suggest. Early in her premiership a situation came along to test her Chamberlain credentials. This was the projected £23.4 billion takeover of ARM – the UK's sole world-leading hi-tech electronic company – by SoftBank, the third largest public company in Japan. This was the kind of deal that May had dedicated herself to opposing in her Birmingham speech. The importance of ARM was not in doubt: it designs chips with low electric power consumption, which makes them ideal for handheld devices such as iPhones and Game Boys. The firm employed 3,000 people, and was of particular importance to the environs of Cambridge, where its headquarters are located.

But May and Philip Hammond in their statement regarding the transaction – which was finalised on 5th September 2016 – fell in line with neoliberal orthodoxy, stating that the sale had turned a 'great British company into a global phenomenon'[270]. It could have easily been a statement from the Osborne Treasury.

The decision could not have been palatable to the likes of Fox and Davis. One might add that the current account deficit is caused by precisely this world of cross-border mergers and acquisitions, and is for many the cause of the decline of British manufacturing, contributing to that unhealthy financial services-driven economy, where money is arguably too weightless an affair – unconcerned to build communities but instead rushing to create a boost to the FTSE 100, which itself tends to benefit a relatively small number of canny higher net worth individuals. The argument runs that at the same time that Britain ceased to make things it reshaped its priorities towards financial services, cross-border insurance and law – in short, everything that facilitates the flow of international money, and glues together the patchwork global economy. For Napoleon, Britain was a nation of shopkeepers; it has become a nation of corporate lawyers. But in this instance, as in the case of Chinese and French investment into Hinkley Point (see Chapter 30), May showed herself submitting, however reluctantly, to the status quo.

In doing so, she was accepting powerful realities, and could do little more than have Chancellor Philip Hammond talk in platitudinous terms of a 'reset' to the UK economy. The shape of things would remain largely as it had been – for instance, the share prices of FTSE 100 companies have not only held, but have gone up since the vote, and would reach a high of 7,687.77 at the end of 2017. This is not surprising since these companies make most of their money abroad: a falling pound is good for them. The FTSE 250, a slightly better indicator of the UK economy, took the brunt of the initial losses, falling rapidly but would later recover. Such is the world of international money: resilient if you vote to stay in the European Union and resilient if you vote to leave it.

THE GOOD NEWS AND THE INDIFFERENT

If one was inclined to take the falling pound as good news, there was further reason for cheer.

To observe the economy in late 2016 was still to feel that one had entered a parallel reality where the referendum hadn't happened. When consumer data arrived in late August 2016, it showed that the shop tills had been happily trilling for much of the summer. Some attributed this to the sunshine; others wondered whether an Olympics feelgood factor had been at work. The reality was likely more hard-headed than this: with the pound having fallen, tourists had discovered that they could afford to come the UK, and had embarked on a round of carefree spending while in the country. By September 2016, the Office for National Statistics had issued its assessment of the post-referendum economy. It was a portrait of moderate good health. A 1.4 per cent jump in retail sales in July was followed by a 0.2 per cent decrease in August – but this second figure was still up by 6.2 per cent from August 2015.[271] Meanwhile, in prices generally, in house prices, and in unemployment data, things were all normal (although the effects of Osborne's stamp duty hikes were still being felt in the prime central London market throughout 2018). True, construction was flat in July – but not to any alarming extent. The dip in manufacturing output – by 0.9 per cent in July – was also within acceptable margins.

That report was, of course, an image of the economy Cameron and Osborne had bequeathed, and not a description of anything May and Hammond had since been able to create. It concluded on a note of anti-climax:

> The post-referendum picture is still emerging and will continue to do so over the coming months, quarters and years. Information so far generally covers short-term indicators with other important information not yet available.[272]

There were further reasons for caution. Businesses tend not to make big decisions over the summer. The great unknown in the UK economy remained the extent of the impact – if any – which Brexit might yet have on investment and on services. It was possible to fear that weak investment would in time drive up inflation, and that consumer spending would decline. By the end of the first quarter of 2017, there were already signs of such a scenario unfolding. The temptation for Chancellor Philip Hammond to embark on stimulus policies, such as government infrastructure spending, proved too great and he splurged in the 2016 Autumn Statement, and in the 2017 budget. At the beginning of 2017, there were signs of slowdown as inflation began to feed into consumer behaviour: but by March 2018 inflation had dipped again to 2.5 per cent, though wages remained for many depressingly stagnant. The country was limping along.

Everything depended on whatever spin one was prepared to put on the data. As early as July 2016, construction was experiencing a dip, albeit within known margins. The value of construction contracts for July dropped by 20 per cent to £1.5bn; some sought to link that to Brexit. Likewise, in commercial development, in the aftermath of the vote, M&G Investments, which runs a £4.4bn property fund, and Aviva Investors, whose fund has assets worth £1.8bn, barred withdrawals.[273] This was alarming. But there was positive reaction from both the construction and commercial development industries to Hammond's first 2017 budget, drowned out at the time by the U-turn over the unwise raise of National Insurance for the self-employed.

In the majority of cases, investors were waiting to see how negotiations between the UK and the EU would proceed. Investment is often referred to by commentators as a monolithic thing which shall either enter or exit the economy all at once. The health of the British economy over the next decade would not be decided by one broad perception, but by thousands of individual decisions. Post-Brexit investors observed the falling pound and considered their options. Would it make them feel discretionary about London investment, but correspondingly rather bullish about buying property up in Manchester? There would be a good deal of pent-up investment throughout the negotiating process. The question was whether over time a consensus would emerge in favour of Britain as a sensible place to invest. Paul Krugman explained:

> Either we see financial business exiting London, and it becomes clear that a weak pound is here to stay, or the charms of Paris and Frankfurt turn out to be overstated, and London goes back to what it was. Either way, the pent-up investment spending that was put on hold should come back. This doesn't just mean that the hit to growth is temporary: there should also be a bounce-back, a period of above-normal growth as the delayed investment kicks in.[274]

True, some banks began relocation operations: Goldman Sachs to Frankfurt, JP Morgan and Barclays to Dublin, and HSBC to Paris. But in all cases, these were modest moves, and the banks as always were tight-lipped about their real intentions. Rented office space somewhere isn't always an indicator of a shift in global power. There would be no sudden disaster nor immediate triumph. Dublin's housing crisis was too acute to host vast numbers of bankers; Frankfurt lacked London's cultural life; and Emmanuel Macron's attempts to shake up France by reducing the corporate tax burden were causing him marked unpopularity. Society is flexible and amorphous: at any one time, millions of people might make decisions tending one way or another. Or they might prefer not to make a decision at all. Over time these decisions accumulate into reality. And then reality is chopped up and packaged as history. But the status quo always has the whip hand because change takes human will, time and money and these are not always in the offing.

TOWARDS AN EQUITABLE ECONOMY

Is it true to say that the Cameron-Osborne economy was inequitable?

Attempts were made on several fronts towards a fair economy – the country the pair sought to create never quite matched the harshest caricature of their time in office. The policy of the National Living Wage, for instance, was a tweak of one of Blair's earliest achievements – the National Minimum Wage Act 1998. It aimed to increase the minimum wage to at least £9 an hour by 2020: there would be talk during the 2017 general election campaign of Red Theresa, but there was a Red George from time to time too. Any time the minimum wage is raised it always causes objections from some large companies that it will impinge on their profits and therefore cause them to raise prices: in this instance, Lidl said that it would pay its staff the new wage, which was seen as a victory for the Chancellor[275]. Osborne's Northern Powerhouse strategy also sought to 'transform Northern growth, rebalance the country's economy and establish the North as a global powerhouse'[276], according to the document which accompanied its launch.

But for his critics, Osborne sought to do this with too much Chinese investment, and with too much emphasis on much derided vanity projects such as High Speed Three: 'I don't want to commute to bloody Leeds. I want to be able to get into bloody Manchester,' as a woman in the suburbs of Manchester told the BBC[277]. Theresa May was referencing the Northern Powerhouse strategy during her Birmingham policy speech when she expressed her preference for 'a plan to help not one or even two of our great regional cities but every single one of them'. Perhaps it was a question of style: Osborne never quite managed to seem the friend of the poor. So obviously a member of the metropolitan 'elite', and a highly strategic politician, there was the perception that he could only ever pose as their champion. It had often been stated by Osborne that if those in the financial services sector were ever hit by higher taxes they would immediately leave the UK. There is the suspicion that if this is so, what is needed is not a further reduction in the corporation tax, but a more paternalistic, and perhaps less petulant, class of the rich. But nor should one underestimate the stress that many medium-sized businesses face in dealing with compliance and regulation which take up time which should be given over to transactional work, or to family life.

May was better suited to making the case for a more responsible corporate culture than Osborne had been. In the first place, May emphasised a commitment to a fuller industrial strategy, and to a culture of more responsible investment. She also announced her intention to enact major reforms of corporate governance. This was intended to include curbs on executive pay – as Liberal Democrat Vince Cable tried but failed to do during the Coalition. Interestingly, her 2017 election manifesto would be silent on this point. May also stated her preference to enact something like the recommendations of the Bullock report of 1977, and give workers seats on company boards, as well as the right to take leave for a year from a job in order to care for a sick relative – an idea perhaps inspired by her mother's battle with MS which we saw in an earlier chapter. This would be another backwards leapfrog, as it were, over the Thatcher administration: but with inequality high, and the referendum result opening the lid on a general resentment about the gulf between privileged and poor, it felt an opportune time to broach this particular issue. May also suggested that she would clamp down on accountants who assist clients in crafting tax avoidance schemes[278].

As with the range of things May's government wished to do, her reforming instincts would remain subject to the process of leaving the European Union. We can see in her decision to let the ARM transaction go ahead that her instinct to protect British communities vied with the fear that if she did so too much, investment would indeed be withdrawn at a critical point, and that she would be left with a gap in the public finances not unlike the '£30 billion black hole' that Osborne is now mocked for having predicted.

In this area, perhaps more than any other, May was subject to forces outside her control. 'Hard times,' was Benjamin Disraeli's verdict on his 1880 general election defeat, and though it was a charitable verdict on an administration which had arguably fallen short in the sphere of foreign policy, any prime minister can find themselves buffeted by unexpected storms. It needs to be said about the early years of the May administration that it took place within a nearly surreal bull market of some eight years standing, where for many the stock markets seemed dangerously overvalued. True, unemployment remained at record lows for the time being, but it remained to be seen, once the levy broke, what the reaction would be from business owners. 'Either we've rewritten the rules of economics and all you need for economic growth is a printing press, or there's a reckoning and we're going to run out of steam,' said Paul Abberley, CEO of Charles Stanley, adding: 'Intellectually you have to assume it's the latter.'[279]

Global indebtedness – measured at $164 trillion in 2016 when May took office[280] – combined with a surreally climbing FTSE to worry business leaders: the ascent in stock markets seemed to many not to be satisfactorily underpinned by capital investment, but instead – in Abberley's words again – to be 'a bit accounting-based'. By 2018, banks were beginning to increase allocations to hedge funds in some portfolios – a typical move when a bear market is deemed to be upcoming. Meanwhile, the rise of bitcoin and other cryptocurrencies – not to mention the blockchain infrastructure that sits under it – seemed to promise a true global economy without the need for intermediaries such as capital market lawyers and clearing houses: it is true that government would have a role to play in that brave new world, both in introducing regulation and taxation to that space, and in redirecting human potential following the job losses that inevitably arise from seismic shift, but even so it all seemed to be happening quickly – and often with a marked libertarian streak.

These developments were occurring across the nation, and the world, and without any recourse to the opinion of the occupant of 10 Downing Street.

27 – THE OTHER UNION

Just beneath the headlines of 'Britain Votes to Leave', there was a related headline which was of great importance in its own right: 'Britain votes to Leave but Scotland votes to stay'.

Scotland in fact voted to stay by a larger margin even than London, trumping its 59.9 per cent share for Remain with 62 per cent. The entirety of Scotland in all its mulls and bens, and in its urban areas, is more Europhilic than the fully metropolitan London. At first glance, and when one bears in mind the 2015 General Election where Scottish Nationalist MPs were returned in 56 out of 59 seats, the vote appears counterintuitive. We have almost come to think of Scotland as a country crying out for independence. But its mood in the 2016 referendum does indicate a wish to belong: Scotland wants to eschew one union and embrace another.

These contradictions can be resolved to some extent. In the first place, Scotland is not crying out for independence from the United Kingdom – or at least not necessarily, and certainly wasn't crying loud enough for it in 2014. The dramatic gains for the Scottish National Party in the 2015 General Election have tended to obscure the plebiscite that preceded it. In that referendum, the No side won, with 2,001,926 (55.3 per cent) voting against independence and 1,617,989 (44.7 per cent) voting in favour. There is no persuasive evidence that Scotland would now vote to leave the UK in a second post-Brexit referendum. Indeed, there is evidence to the contrary in the shape of a YouGov poll published on 30th July 2016 which showed that by 53-47 per cent, Scotland still favours remaining part of the UK[281]. Across the landscape of her inheritance from David Cameron, this almost qualified as a stable fact for Theresa May.

There are common denominators in the 2014 and 2016 votes: for instance, Edinburgh's population of 378,012 voted 61.10 per cent against Scottish independence, and 74.4 per cent against leaving the European Union: by that reckoning, Brussels is nearly 15 per cent more popular than Westminster. Meanwhile Glasgow, with its higher poverty, voted 53.49 per cent in favour of Scottish independence – but it was 66.6 per cent Remain when it came to the EU[282]. In each case, about 10 per cent of the electorate seems to rush over from the anti-UK column into the pro-EU column. It is objected by the Scottish Nationalists that the world has moved on since that 2014 result. But those on the other side of the argument are able to point to another development: in the May 2016 Scottish elections, the SNP in fact lost ground, and the Conservatives made gains under their likeable leader Ruth Davidson. This result – together with a general referendum fatigue – looked likely to stave off a groundswell of calls for another vote over Scottish independence when May took office. This suspicion would also be backed up by the Conservatives' minor gains in Scotland in the 2017 General Election.

Even so, the insistence of Scottish nationalism, and the possibility that it might yet flare up again, would remain another possible headache for May – particularly so long as the impressive Nicola Sturgeon headed up the Scottish Nationalists. This isn't to say there aren't difficulties with the SNP position. Some point to the contradiction of railing against the power of the Bank of England over their lives, while also being happy to accept the role of the European Central Bank. Against this, Alex Salmond – Nicola Sturgeon's predecessor as leader – used to argue that an independent Scotland would gain a seat on the Council of Ministers, and over time enjoy not just a Commissioner but an increased number of MEPs. For Eurosceptics, this is a strange fantasy, more fitted to the pre-Maastricht world, where a country like Scotland would have been capable of greater clout. By 1995, the academic Peter Lynch was lamenting a lack of 'political and intellectual' leadership at the top of Salmond's party: 'Put simply, the SNP has not given much thought to the European Union since Maastricht.'[283]

For some it seemed as though the SNP had been drifting through life without thinking all that much about European membership, but vaguely considering it a good idea. But it might equally be considered sensible for a country that wishes to start out on its own to have close economic ties with as many countries as possible.

BLOCKING BREXIT FROM NORTH OF THE BORDER

A one-issue party is usually predictable, and often flat-footed, in that all external phenomena must go through that particular filter. Sturgeon is a nimble and intelligent politician married to an inflexible position: she argued that the EU referendum result constituted an argument in favour of Scottish independence. She would feel the same if meteors rained down on Aberdeen.

In fact, she did more than argue this position. She even made the claim that Scotland could block Brexit, thus joining the House of Lords, Gina Miller, the Supreme Court and the Liberal Democrats as being among those who aspire to do so. This is Sturgeon explaining her approach on *Sunday Politics Scotland* to host Gordon Brewer on 26th June 2016:

> If the Scottish parliament is judging this on the basis of what's right for Scotland, then the option of saying we're not going to vote for something that's against Scotland's interests, that's got to be on the table. You're not going to vote for something that is not in Scotland's interests.

Pressed as to how this would make the Leave portion of England feel, Sturgeon became briefly a hero for Remainers:

> I can, but it's perhaps similar to the fury of many people in Scotland right now as we face the prospect of being taken out of the EU against their will. I didn't create these situations. I'm trying to navigate the best way forward through them.[284]

It was a time when Sturgeon had the field to herself. This occurred during that brief period – before May's accession, and with Cameron ineffectually languishing in Downing Street – when Sturgeon looked to be the Remainer's last best hope. This thrill was brief. Soon constitutional lawyers introduced doubts as to whether Sturgeon had the legal and constitutional power to be much more than a headline-grabbing irritant to the prime minister. Ruth Davidson wondered aloud whether Sturgeon had misunderstood her powers. Adam Tomkins, a leading constitutional law expert and newly-elected Conservative MSP, agreed:

> Holyrood has no power to block Brexit. It is not clear that a legislative consent motion would be triggered by Brexit, but withholding consent is not the same as having the power to block. The Scottish parliament does not hold the legal power to block [the UK exiting the EU].[285]

In short, the Holyrood parliament would be able to refuse its consent to any devolution settlement that might be incorporated into the Brexit process – but this was not the same, as Sturgeon had thought, as having a veto. Even so, it was yet another thing for Theresa May to think about.

Meanwhile Sturgeon endured a frosty reception in Europe. In late June, she secured a meeting with Jean-Claude Juncker and with Martin Schulz, president of the European Parliament – but she was denied a meeting with Donald Tusk, the president of the European Council. High-ranking German officials also refused to meet with her on a separate basis, calling it an internal issue: it was a reminder of the persistent fact of the United Kingdom.[286] Sometimes one wonders whether it is even desirable for an independent Scotland to take its seat on the Council. Simon Jenkins is among those unimpressed by the prospect:

> This is a recipe for Greek-style disaster. Scotland might enjoy the spurt of investment and growth that tends to greet new states, as in Slovakia

or partly autonomous Catalonia. But the most likely sequence is brief euphoria followed by budgetary crisis, retrenchment and austerity. The emergence into the sunnier uplands of small-is-beautiful independence would be slow and painful.[287]

Again there is the sense that the Scottish Nationalists are more knotted over Europe than they know. One particularly notes Sturgeon's willingness to be a part of a Eurozone pledged to precisely the kind of austerity which she routinely railed against, with striking success, during the 2015 General Election.

On the other hand, there is always contradiction to be found in membership of the European Union – things one doesn't like but has to endure.

Sturgeon, like most pro-Europeans, presumably thinks the benefits outweigh the drawbacks.

A VISIT TO SCOTLAND

Shortly after Sturgeon returned from this sobering trip, Theresa May was installed in Downing Street, pledged to the antithesis of the Sturgeon position – not only a Scotland still part of the United Kingdom, but also a United Kingdom no longer part of Europe.

On 16th July 2016, as Euan Malcolm put it in the *Scotsman*, 'things took a turn for the serious'[288] when May made her first visit as prime minister to see Sturgeon in Bute House. Would a second referendum on Scottish independence need to be called? Each woman had weaknesses in their argument. Of the two, May's hand appeared the stronger: she could argue against further upheaval, and point to the 2014 results, as well as the 2016 Scottish elections. Even so, neither was May in a straightforward position: saddled with Brexit, she must have realised how precarious the union may come to seem to many Scots who voted Remain – and even to those who voted Leave – if she would prove unable to reach a satisfactory deal with the EU.

Meanwhile, Sturgeon's weakness was the same as it had been in 2014: doubts over the economic viability of an independent Scotland. It was not completely clear also whether the likely instability over a potential trigger to Article 50 would help or hinder her. On the one hand it might strengthen the case for a new settlement for Scotland; on the other, it might make people more cautious, and not wish for another round of change. Meanwhile, at Bute House, the usual platitudes, at odds with the profound national emotions roiling under the surface, were spoken with the eternal decorousness of professional politicians. Here is May, speaking aloud, while saying nothing:

> I'm willing to listen to options and I've been very clear with the first minister today that I want the Scottish government to be fully engaged in our discussion. I have already said that I won't be triggering Article 50 until I think that we have a UK approach and objectives for negotiations – I think it is important that we establish that before we trigger Article 50.[289]

In the event, she would trigger the Article anyhow without any evidence of the conversion of Sturgeon to her cause. Meanwhile it was left to Scottish Secretary David Mundell to clarify matters and describe a more probable reality:

> Theresa May doesn't agree with Scotland being an independent country, I don't agree and two million people in Scotland who voted in our own referendum don't agree with that. So... we're not going to be in agreement with the idea that there should be another independence referendum.[290]

May's strategy would be to dig in her heels and refuse. In doing so, she would at least fend off further confusion. But her doing so would be somewhat dependent on getting a good deal with the EU. Even if May could manage to produce a deal that suited Liam Fox and David Davis, it was hard to imagine it suiting Sturgeon. There was one thing in her favour: when Cameron granted the Scottish referendum, it was in response to the SNP surges in the Scottish parliament elections in 2011. But in 2015 Sturgeon was at the crest of her popularity: the 2017 dip in the SNP's electoral performance could now be adduced as evidence of diminished interest in a referendum. In that respect, if in no other, the 2017 General Election result would prove helpful to May.

But even if all these political problems could be addressed, May still faced a complex administrative task in matching the devolution settlement to post-Brexit reality. The European Convention of Human Rights and EU law are both incorporated into Scottish law: for instance, section 29(2)(d) of the

Scotland Act 1998 (SA) provides that Acts of the Scottish Parliament that are incompatible with EU law or with ECHR
rights are 'not law'[291]. This meant that all relevant devolution
legislation would need repeal: this would require a Legislative
Consent Motion under the Sewel Convention. Put simply, it
was not an area Westminster is really meant to vote on without
the consent of the devolved legislature – which, under Sturgeon, was not likely to be especially forthcoming. This predicament might look dry and procedural, but it was the sort of
thing that could easily spiral. A vivid example of this would
occur on June 13th 2018 when SNP MPs would walk out of an
instalment of PMQs in protest at the lack of debate and Westminster 'power grab' in the EU Withdrawal Bill.

It might be seen as a catastrophic mistake of Cameron's not
to construct legislation that took into account an eventuality
like this among the devolved nations: for instance, some lament
the lack of a threshold requirement for each of the devolution
jurisdictions for the vote to Leave to have been valid. So that
although May's position in relation to Scotland felt solider
than in other areas, that was in itself more a measure of her
general difficulty than any noteworthy straightforwardness regarding this particular matter: at any other time, even with
the SNP loss of seats in the 2017 general election, the Scotland
situation would be enough to keep most prime ministers up at
night. But for May, given all her other difficulties, it had to be
relatively low on her list of worries.

NORTHERN IRELAND: A PERENNIAL PROBLEM

The result was similar in Northern Ireland. In the lead-up to the EU referendum Tony Blair and Sir John Major took a trip to Magee College in Northern Ireland. By this time, Brexit was increasingly beginning to seem a possibility. Blair's post-Iraq toxicity was still such that even he had come to acknowledge that he needed to be carefully deployed – but it was felt that on this particular issue the principal architects of peace in Northern Ireland might be shown side by side advocating continued membership in the EU to some advantage.

What did they say? Looking stricken, Blair stated that it would be 'profoundly foolish to risk [...] foundations of stability'. Major, who seems more plausibly a sage with each passing year, said: 'The unity of the United Kingdom itself is on the ballot paper in two weeks' time'[292]. This language might look dramatic. But the Remain argument was that in the event of a vote to Leave, the status of the Irish border would change from a porous one, where people are currently free to come and go as they please, to an external frontier between the EU and the UK, and all the possible causes for mutual suspicion that can arise from customs checks and frontier controls. As Jonathan Powell, who had been Blair's chief negotiator in Northern Ireland from 1997-2007, and thus more than a little qualified to pontificate on the matter, would later write in the *Financial Times*: 'The problem with the Northern Ireland border is not how long it takes a lorry to cross, but the issue of identity. Putting in infrastructure at the border and closing off small roads to stop smuggling will reopen the question of identity settled in the Good Friday Agreement.'[293] This was, in part, a rebuke to Boris Johnson who was secretly recorded in June 2018 as saying the stickiness of the border question was an example of the tail wagging the dog: indeed, into 2018 there were signs that the Brexiters couldn't quite bring themselves to believe in the importance of the matter.

But then this underestimation of the question's magnitude was evident before the referendum too. The then Northern Ireland Secretary, Theresa Villiers, a prominent Brexiter, retorted to Blair and Major after their visit to Magee College:

> It's perfectly possible to maintain that free movement with Irish citizens. After all we give them privileges in the UK which we accord to no other EU citizens, like the right to vote in our elections.

Villiers also argued that there would be no need for frontier controls. In the event of it, Northern Ireland agreed with Blair and Major – 55.8 per cent voted to remain in the EU, but as everyone knows, it's the world of the Theresas – May and Villiers – which the Irish people are left to inhabit. Even so, over time May accepted the importance of not violating the Good Friday Agreement: this admission, added to the EU's refusal to countenance either a 'maximum facilitation' arrangement or 'a customs partnership', together with the DUP's refusal to accept any border checks in the Irish Sea, by 2018 was threatening to derail the possibility of any meaningful Brexit: 'The only reason there isn't more noise is that the Brexiters do not realise it yet,' wrote Powell.

All this was in the future. As May took office, the short-term economic news was good, with Northern Ireland ben efiting from the ramifications of a plunging pound. But once again there was a sense that these were early days and that the long-term outlook was likely to be more sobering. In March 2016, Raoul Ruparel of Open Europe conducted a detailed analysis in an article called 'How might the effect of Brexit on Ireland and Northern Ireland be managed?', in which he had raised concerns May would now need to address:

> We found that leaving the EU could either lead to a permanent gain of 1.6% to UK GDP by 2030, in a 'best case' scenario, or a 2.2% loss to GDP, in a 'worst case' scenario. The more realistic range of outcomes is likely to be between -1% and +1%. As one of the UK's closest trading partners the impact on Ireland could also be substantial. In a worst case scenario Ireland could see a permanent loss of 3.1% to GDP in 2030. Even in the best case scenario the loss would still total 1.1% GDP.[294]

A best-case scenario of a 1.1 per cent contraction cannot be called promising. Furthermore, the Irish were unlikely to re-tain the same influence that they had achieved in recent years in the EU without the UK in it: with the UK departing, it would no longer be able to command the 35 per cent share of the vote alongside Germany, the Netherlands and Sweden which traditionally prefers a free trade approach to economic matters. In the days before Emmanuel Macron burst on the scene with his rather alarming self-confidence, it was feared that post-Brexit France had the upper hand, which might lead to a more protectionist – and less outward-looking – Europe-an Union.[295] These fears were arguably mitigated by Macron's 2017 presidential win, but the election didn't change the fact that France has historically been the most federalist nation in Europe. Furthermore, Macron – nuanced politician though he is – had historically argued for unThatcherite things like harmonisation of corporate taxes and minimum wages.

Of course, it was theoretically an opportunity for a city like Dublin – English-speaking, and with a similar geographical location to London – to mop up hypothetical job losses in the financial services sector if the City of London were to lose its passporting rights, as May eventually accepted it would. But this was likely to overestimate the City's resilience, and to underestimate the scale of Dublin's housing crisis, which means it isn't yet a fit host for legions of banking staff: unfortunately estimates that between 20,000 to 40,000 new units needed to be built were being met with a mere 10,000 new units on the ground. 'They [the City of London] are the most intelligent people in the world, they've got to find a way round it,'[296] as Ciaran Hancock, business editor of the *Irish Times* said.

Of course, the Ireland Development Authority would continue to talk up Dublin's chances, and some banks did purchase office space in Dublin and Cork, alongside the big tech firms like LinkedIn and Facebook, but the excitement wasn't enough to mitigate the more tangible worry that 16 per cent of Ireland's manufactured goods and 19 per cent of its services go to the UK. The stark fact remained that future tariffs on these would be costly for the Irish economy.

THE IRISH BORDER

So what would happen to the border? This was another consideration which May would need to negotiate: in fact, guarantees on that matter would end up being conditional on proceeding with trade talks. Since the advent of the Good Friday Agreement, it had been possible for the Irish to move back and forth throughout the UK, and for those with UK passports to do the same in Ireland. Those driving north from Dublin to Belfast, and across the border, note little more than the absence of translations on the signage. As so often in this period, immigration was at the centre of the right's concern: the Leave campaign wished to reinstate stringent checks as a way of preventing EU nationals coming in 'through the back door'. Without securing some change to the current arrangement, May appeared to run the risk of failing to deliver on what she had come to regard as her core task: the reduction of immigration.

As so often with Brexit, the questions proliferated dizzyingly. If May wanted to reform the status quo, what would the new visa requirements be? Would there be customs duties? What administrative costs would be attached? How would she administer them?

It didn't end there. In the preamble to the British-Irish agreement of 2014, it was explicitly stated that relations between the two countries were founded on their respective membership of the European Union, and that the countries wished:

> ... to develop still further the unique relationship between their peoples and the close co-operation between their countries as friendly neighbours and as partners in the European Union.[297]

This would obviously no longer be the case, if Britain was to leave Europe. There was also the possibility that there would be less cooperation between the countries on terrorism and crime: until the EU referendum, these matters had been handled under the European Arrest Warrant, and so continued information-sharing would be dependent on how May proceeded on that front.

Worryingly, there were already signs of political tension. The Northern Ireland's Deputy First Minister Martin McGuinness – who would die shortly after in March 2017 – called for a border poll on a united Ireland after the UK had voted to leave the EU. In addition, as a result of the vote, Northern Ireland would no longer receive so-called 'peace money' to fund projects aimed at supporting the region's peace process. It was impossible to see this as good news.

May initially hedged her bets. During the referendum campaign she had said that it was 'inconceivable' that border arrangements would not be required in the event of Brexit. But by the time she had visited Belfast during her premiership she had changed her tune:

> Nobody wants to return to the borders of the past. What we do want to do is to find a way through this that is going to work and deliver a practical solution for everybody - as part of the work that we are doing to ensure that we make a success of the United Kingdom leaving the European Union - and that we come out of this with a deal which is in the best interests of the whole of the United Kingdom.[298]

Again, May resorts to platitudes; again words are spoken that upon analysis have little or no meaning. It is another measure of the complexity of the situation that nothing of substance on these important matters would be said for over a year. In the event of course, there would be an additional complexity levelled at the Irish question: May's snap election would snooker her into leading a government dependent on the support of the pro-union DUP, which though Eurosceptic also opposed any kind of hard border.

No one solution could possibly be expected to meet with agreement from everyone – and coming to a solution on this was critical in terms of moving on to apparently more important matters. As a result, it would attain an importance which the Leave camp began to consider outsized. Boris Johnson's frustration was palpable in remarks made to a Thatcherite campaign group in 2018, and leaked to *BuzzFeed* in June 2018:

> It's so small and there are so few firms that actually use that border regularly, it's just beyond belief that we're allowing the tail to wag the dog in this way. We're allowing the whole of our agenda to be dictated by this folly.

Johnson' answer was the technology-based solution called 'maximum facilitation' – or max fac for short:

> Concentrate on maximum facilitation... That's what we want. Solve the technical problem. We can easily find a solution that allows us to have trade that is frictionless as possible... with our continental friends and partners while still being able to do free trade deals. It's not beyond the wit of man.[299]

And yet it was arguably beyond the scope of the public purse. In the *Guardian*, Richard Reed, the co-founder of Innocent Drinks, was arch when considering the HMRC's chief executive's view that 'max fac' would cost British businesses between £17 billion and £20 billion a year: 'To put that into a context even Boris Johnson would understand,' he wrote, that's a cost of around £350m a week. I don't remember seeing that on the side of any big red buses.'[300]

So while the Remainers – and crucially, the EU – doubted the feasibility of that, the Remainers' idea of a 'customs partnership' was also far from optimal especially when set against the fact that the existing relationship was plainly desirable in lots of respects. This was an essentially hybrid solution whereby the UK would remain in the customs union – anathema to Brexiters, of course – while being able to independently trade with other countries outside the bloc: it was predictably dismissed by EU negotiators as 'magical thinking'. It raised the spectre of further bureaucracy – which the project to Leave had apparently been embarked upon to remove – since companies would need to track goods to their final destinations and then invoice the HMRC in order to claim back the difference between UK and EU tariffs. Taking back control was seeming like a fiddly business indeed.

All in all, no one option met with everybody's agreement: there were simply too many interested parties with differing views. Faced with this difficulty, May would need to become adept at finding language to put off the problem in the hope that it would somehow be resolved incrementally, and the answer reveal itself over time. Meanwhile the Brexiters couldn't wholly be acquitted of ignoring the depth of the historical problem in Ireland, and by association, the enormity of the Good Friday Agreement: to risk jeopardising it was one thing, but to do so in a blasé fashion was worse still. Around 250 years beforehand, the great statesman Edmund Burke had said: 'Whether you regard it offensively, or defensively, Ireland is known in France. Communications have been opened, and more will be opened. Ireland will be a strong dyke to keep out Jacobinism, or a broken back to let it in.'[301] And the subsequent career of a gigantic figure like William Gladstone was dominated by his mission to pacify Ireland. It was another instance of the thin nature of Johnson's classical learning: to have read Tacitus is not necessarily to have understood him. History is to a large extent the study of the difficulty of peace: to act as if this isn't so is a dubious trait of a foreign secretary.

WALES: THE SELF-INFLICTED WOUND

The case of Wales was different to the results in Scotland and Northern Ireland, and therefore presented challenges of another kind. Wales voted to leave the EU – with 854,572 (52.5 per cent) adopting the Brexit position. There was a particularly high turnout among Welsh Labour voters.

This was a surprising result because Wales had traditionally been among the big beneficiaries of UK membership of the EU. Lord Hain, a former Secretary of State for Wales, was among the first to express his shock in that shocked time:

What leave voters will find is that they will be pleased in the short-term but in the long-term, the consequences are very serious. Those that voted leave are the ones that benefit most from EU funding.[302]

Hain's view was backed up by the facts. Wales enjoyed an annual net benefit of £245 million from the EU.[303] Doubts now surfaced about the Welsh government's planned (and unpopular with environmental groups) M4 relief road and the South Wales Metro project, which aims to electrify some valleys lines in the south. Both had been intended to proceed with European funds: by mid-2018 neither had gone ahead, although in respect of the latter economy secretary Ken Skates had assured the public that 'nothing has been cancelled'[304] . Also under threat was the £218 million that Welsh farmers received in direct payments under the Common Agricultural Policy. During the referendum talks, Leavers had said that this money would be replaced but it wasn't immediately clear where the replacement funds would come from. All May said initially – as with Scotland and Northern Ireland – was that she wanted Wales 'involved' in talks.

But perhaps we shouldn't feel too surprised by this vote: there is the perception that Wales – the great country of the Mabinogion poet, Dylan Thomas and Roy Jenkins, after all – continually slips to the back of the minds of Westminster politicians. Perhaps it was apposite then that during the 2017 General Election, when May went to launch her Welsh manifesto with its plans for a prosperity fund to replace EU aid after Brexit, she nevertheless ended up spending most of her time U-turning on her policy for social care – in England.

28 – HEALTH

The previous three chapters might be said to comprise May's immediate priorities but as we have observed, there are many other duties that form part of the job of prime minister: being prime minister in a time of great confusion did not absolve May of them. Besides, the new leader had already stated that she intended to be more than just the prime minister who handled Brexit. One measure of the difficulty of the May administration was that while a great task loomed in the shape of Brexit, there were plenty of other crises that would have hit her without it. Some had an intractable feel – Islamic terrorism and the war in Syria seemed like they could expect no definitive resolution even if May's premiership happened to be a very long one. Others required urgent action: we shall look at questions pertaining to climate change in this section. Some – and the one we are about to discuss is a prime example – were partly the result of the very tight fiscal policies of the Coalition.

Put simply, over the years leading up to the referendum, as the cost of the nation's healthcare has risen, a mere 'ring-fencing' by the Coalition of NHS spending had come to seem inadequate. There were repeated fears that the NHS was 'breaking at the seams' and needed May's immediate attention.

THE NHS AND BREXIT

First, the evergreen problem of Brexit.

On the face of it, there was less to worry about on this score since healthcare had never been an area of specific EU competence: the NHS – and other countries feel the same way about their healthcare systems – is too distinctive to submit to the rule-making of Brussels. However, this doesn't mean that leaving the European Union would have no bearing upon the future of British healthcare. In fact, the two things – the NHS and leaving the EU – were already bound up together, even before the vote to Leave, by the specific promises made during the campaign. Some of this could be surreal. On 21st March 2016, the *Daily Telegraph* published the views of UKIP's health spokesperson, Louise Bours MEP, under the headline 'Britain's NHS can't survive staying in the EU'[305]. Bours' argument was that the coming campaign would provide the electorate with the chance to choose between the NHS or the EU, 'because we can't have both'. A philosopher might call this an example of a 'false dilemma'. But Bours had set a tone that would be picked up by the more respectable wing of the Brexit camp. The £350 million figure – the money that would allegedly be available per week to put into the NHS in a post-EU Britain – was placed on the side of Boris Johnson's battle bus. As we saw in Chapter 21, it was a figure that entered the public imagination in a way which no figure put forward by the Treasury did.

The state of the NHS would therefore be another barometer of the success of Brexit; its improved condition was promised by the Leave campaign precisely in the event of the result which did transpire.

What were the actual consequences for the NHS of the referendum result? It was another opportunity to consider how woven into the fabric of national life membership of the European Union had become. The NHS – no matter what imagery of ring-fencing the Coalition attached to it – had never been some island within national life, a haven of state-sponsored care: it was an interconnected aspect of modern Britain. Like everything else, it would have to answer to Brexit since it was profoundly affected by both the country's immigration policies and by the overall performance of the economy. May would need not only to handle Article 50 negotiations cannily enough not to cause a slowdown in the economy: she would also need to find an agreement which satisfied the views of the Brexit camp on immigration, while also continuing to staff the NHS. The problem again had an insoluble look: by June 2018, faced with a creaking healthcare system, the government had accepted the need to soften the immigration rules for non-EU nurses and doctors – a relaxation which May had apparently spent most of her career seeking to avoid, or at the very least fudge. It was left to Andrew Foster, chief executive of the Wrightington, Wigan and Leigh NHS hospital trust, to articulate the mood of absurdity:

> It's absolutely barmy that one branch of government is trying to increase the capacity of the NHS and another branch is stopping it from doing so.[306]

The pressure would be in part economic. The falling pound was not an auspicious start to such a difficult balancing act: if a prolonged decline in sterling were to have the effect most experts predicted, leading over time to an increase in the cost of living, such developments would also hit drug prices – not to mention other goods and services which the NHS needs to purchase. This was, or so one would have thought, another incentive for May to seek a deal with the EU retaining access to the single market. Further, a deal chiefly structured around the imposition of immigration controls would be unlikely to help an organisation whose chief problem besides lack of cash was its being woefully understaffed. The National Audit Office states that in 2014, the NHS experienced a shortfall of 5.9 per cent – a figure which translates to around 50,000 full-time staff: this had led to alarming shortages in nurses, midwives and home visits.[307]

One way to fix this was devastatingly simple: to give the NHS more money. This was tried by the Blair administration, and though it did lead to a dubious increase in middle managers, found to be successful in many respects. But most agree that the money must be combined with the recruitment of foreign doctors, nurses and other health professionals. A relatively small number of these came from the EU – around 4.6 per cent of the total NHS workforce, and 6 per cent of GPs[308], but even so it would be astonishing indeed had May failed to guarantee their right to work in the UK: the numbers might have seemed small in percentage terms, but there was persuasive evidence that this unsung 55,000 had been instrumental in keeping the system together. This is not to mention the 80,000 in the adult social care sector who do likewise[309]. It was therefore deemed unfortunate that May initially refused to guarantee the status of EU nationals working in the UK, claiming instead the right to use them as a bargaining chip in future negotiations. It is true that Jeremy Hunt – the bane of every junior doctor – had occasionally sought to reassure existing workers of their continued importance. But the words of a prime minister carry more weight than those of a health secretary: it was another example of an unkind moment.[310]

The UK debate continued to be driven by the noisiest: Farage had been vocal on the effect of EU migration on the NHS. Demagogues must take their stand precisely where there is least data available, and whip up fear from there. Farage had always stated that EU migration was responsible for the travails of the health service. It therefore needs to be stated baldly that we have no reliable data on immigrants' usage of the NHS. All else is provisional analysis – and interpretation of that provisional analysis. It must also be said that the evidence as we have it – slender though it is – points towards the advantages of an integrated system. For instance, a survey by Nuffield conducted by Steventon and Bardsley in 2011, emphasised the youth of most EU migrants, and the attendant fact that many do not need care, and are therefore unlikely to burden hospitals[311]. Meanwhile, research conducted by the London School of Hygiene and Tropical Medicine and York University found that the UK is a net exporter of patients[312]. Professor Tamara Harvey also points to figures from 18 hospitals, which show that 25 per cent of their private income came from medical tourists, but that they only constituted 7 per cent of patients. The NHS appears to be making a handy profit out of this much-derided 'medical tourism'.

There are further worries: UK pensioners living abroad, for instance, faced the possibility that the outcome of eventual negotiations would not guarantee their treatment. Nor was the health service likely to be spared the complex legal tasks ahead. For instance, the EU working time directive – which provides that workers cannot work more than 48 hours a week – though undoubtedly a well-meaning piece of legislation intended to protect workers from overwork, caused problems for the training of doctors across a variety of specialisms: the UK government was one of the few governments to allow doctors to opt out. Post-Brexit most NHS employee contracts would need redrafting – a vast and unnecessary administrative exercise, some argued, when the priority should be the provision of care. There was also the question of whether Britain would continue its involvement with the European Medicines Agency, which had its headquarters in London. This agency aims to protect the health of all EU citizens, and there were doubts as to whether the UK would wish to continue involvement within its framework. Not to do so would have effects on the pharmaceuticals industry: companies could potentially find it harder to sell drugs into the EU from the UK, and vice versa. The EMA was also set to introduce new harmonisation of drug trial rules in 2018: a moment of hope for those with cancer or those like May's mother who suffer from conditions like multiple sclerosis which are near to major breakthroughs: would Britain benefit from these developments, or be left behind?

In the end the idea that the location of the EMA could ever form part of the Brexit negotiations turned out to be pure fantasy, and indeed after the vote which transferred the agency to Amsterdam (at the same time it was decided that the European

Banking Authority should move from Canary Wharf to Paris),
Michel Barnier would mock Theresa May:

> Brexit means Brexit. The same people who argue for setting the UK
> free also argue that the UK should remain in some EU agencies. But
> freedom implies responsibility for building new UK administrative
> capacity.[313]

Barnier added, triumphantly, that the remaining 27 countries
would continue to work together, deepening knowledge and
ties. It is difficult to view this as a positive moment in the history of British medicine.

THE DEBATE OVER PRIVATISATION

May was also entering a longstanding, but increasingly heated
debate about privatisation in the NHS. In order to understand
the extent of the contention, one must understand the historic
moment in which the health service had been born. The logic
of universal healthcare was best stated by Aneurin Bevan, the
health minister responsible for introducing the NHS, in his
1952 testament 'In Place of Fear':

> The field in which the claims of individual commercialism come into
> most immediate conflict with reputable notions of social values is that
> of health.[314]

It was an urgent point in history: those who did come home
from the Second World War wished to have a country worth

returning to: why risk their lives for a country which didn't look out for their welfare? The war against Hitler had at least engendered a meaningful sense of solidarity among the survivors. True, there were those complaining at the time that a financial opportunity had been missed, but until the Thatcher years the NHS remained remarkably free from intervention by the private sector. But by the end of Margaret Thatcher's time in office, Oliver Letwin was arguing in *Privatising the World* (1988) that the NHS should henceforth be run as a business. Letwin's eventual centrality to the Cameron government was an expression of a strong Thatcherite bent in that administration.

By 1990, an internal market had been introduced to the NHS as a result of the controversial NHS and Community Care Act. The NHS recalls on its website that hospitals would now 'manage their own budgets and buy healthcare from hospitals and other health organisations'[315]. It is that 'other health organisations' – redolent almost of afterthought – that was central to those reforms and which has been particularly contentious: it altered the character of the NHS, admitting private providers into the system. The change, unwarranted as it seemed to some, was also highly expensive to administer: it would be estimated at about £10 billion annually within a couple of decades[316]. This state of affairs was not reversed by the Blair government: an element of competition remained, which for many undermined the original intention of the NHS, and distanced the New Labour administrations from the true values of the left. But years of government funding under Blair meant that the NHS in 2010 experienced record levels of patient satisfaction. Meanwhile Foundation Trusts were introduced. This was an Orwellian term: really they were quasi-independent businesses – another aspect of the internal market.

The trouble is that it has been noted that private providers can have a tendency to cancel operations. As Dr Louise Irvine, of the National Health Action Party, would tell the BBC in 2015:

> The problem is that private companies cherry-pick what they want to do. They naturally do the easy stuff, leaving the NHS with the more complicated elements that are more expensive. That can cause real problems.[317]

After the Coalition came to power, nobody seems to have been prepared for the enormity of Andrew Lansley's 2012 Health and Social Care Bill. It was the largest reorganisation in the NHS's history. The Coalition claimed that 'they will never privatise the NHS'[318]: they were helped to some extent in this by the difficulty of defining privatisation. Their principal argument was that so long as the system remained free at the point of use, talk of privatisation was inaccurate. But the bill contained a range of provisions which pointed in the opposite direction. Here is Raymond Tallis in a fine article for the *Times Literary Supplement*:

> All contracts had to be opened up to 'any qualified provider' (so that Lockheed, makers of Hellfire missiles, could seriously bid for end-of-life care in Staffordshire). All parts of the NHS would become Foundation Trusts, and they could earn up to 50 per cent of their income

from private patients. Crucially, the Secretary of State for Health was no longer responsible for providing, only for 'promoting', comprehensive health care.[319]

In actual fact 'any qualified provider' was a mere rewrite of an earlier phrasing introduced under New Labour 'any willing provider' and described an identical procedure. But there is little doubt that the NHS was drifting away from its original purpose: the profit-making motive had replaced – or, at least, begun to threaten – the care motive. However, most people accept that in some instances – one example is gamma knife radiosurgery – it isn't financially viable for the NHS to own the machines required to do the operations, but viable for them to send patients to the private sector for those procedures to be carried out. In many cases the face of private capital is not so sharkish as some people's worst fears. The main worry, as always, was money: Blair, and his most radical health secretary Alan Milburn, hadn't minded a more flexible set of structures so long as the funding had been there.

Likewise, there is the suspicion that patients don't mind the underlying structures so long as they get the care they need.

Under the Coalition, when less money had been available, people began to mind again: it could be argued that a debate about funding keeps becoming a debate about the means of delivering care.

Even these domestic-seeming issues could not be unravelled from the EU referendum. Many – though by no means all – who had argued most fervently for remaining in the EU were also likely to be those who worried about increased privatisation in the NHS. But the EU, in its pursuit of the Transatlantic Trade and Investment Partnership with the Obama administration in the US – in that innocent time before the advent of Donald Trump – had been looking to bind itself to an agreement which would, in the opinion of the *New Statesman*, 'open the floodgates for private healthcare providers that have made dizzying levels of profits from healthcare in the United States'[320]. Against this it should be said that nothing in EU law – or in TTIP – encourages privatisation of national healthcare systems. Even so, some had legitimate concerns about the impact of EU competition and procurement rules on the NHS.

In theory, the country had withdrawn itself from an arrangement that might well end up advancing the goal of the international privatisation of healthcare. This would be more encouraging to those worried about the future of the NHS, if those who remained in charge of the UK government weren't also seemingly committed to that same project.

MAY'S FIRST FORAYS INTO HEALTH

It has long been accepted that the primary duty of a government is to look after its citizens. For any administration but May's, the situation in the NHS would be top of the agenda – as it was for instance for Blair in 1997. But for May, it would sometimes seem a footnote to the Brexit question.

Sometimes, while people were looking at Brexit, May did some radical things. Chief among these was the scrapping of the government NHS bursary. This generous but necessary provision would be replaced with loans from 2017, thus saving the government an estimated £800 million. But these payments were given to nurses, midwives and therapists, and were intended to make the exceptionally demanding training such people undergo – and which taxpayers expect them to have undergone – financially viable. These courses typically involve some 4,600 hours of training: to work on top of that can mean that somehow one has to work a 70-hour week. It is further objected by those dismayed by the scrapping of the bursary that the government has money enough for the £200 billion Trident nuclear warheads – which don't seem to work as one might like something costing that amount to work – but not for this. The government may have made a mistake in picking again on the young – a petition of 160,000 signatures would protest the measures, and it is difficult to say to what extent their anger contributed to May's own poor showing in the 2017 election. Like this, a government consumes itself in bad policy. Time is taken to draw up a bad policy, time is taken in defending it, and then very often time is taken up in having to withdraw it as quietly as possible, and then come up with a better one.

May had also made some curious moves on social care (her election U-turn is described in the next section), and childhood obesity – a problem Cameron had planned to tackle, but which May would water down. Here is the Treasury's description of the problem:

> The UK has one of the highest obesity rates among developed countries, and it's getting worse. By 2050, over 35% of boys and 20% of girls aged 6 to 10 are expected to be obese. The estimated obesity-related cost to the NHS is over £6bn.[321]

Quite apart from the public health implications here, there is again the question of the grim state of the NHS's finances. Here, May was unpersuaded by the case to continue with the Cameron measures which would have entailed restrictions on the sale and marketing of unhealthy foods: under May, all that would go ahead would be a small tax on sugary drinks. Since the problem overwhelmingly affects working class families – the 'just about managing' of her Downing Street speech – this was deemed a disappointment. It was another example of the small state Conservative in her triumphing over the One Nation Conservative.

The debate over health has a similarly rigid feel to the debate over schools: those on the left such as Owen Smith sound as though they want it to be 100 per cent publicly-funded which would place great strain on care; Jeremy Hunt has been quoted as calling the NHS a 'a sixty-year mistake'[322] no longer relevant to the twenty-first century, although since becoming health secretary he has tended to take a more nuanced position (or perhaps to keep his real opinions to himself). There have been imaginative attempts to adduce solutions to the problem: one such is a tax specifically intended for the nation's health budgets. This notion, known as a hypothecated tax, put forward by former minister and part-time doctor Dan Poulter, is intended to address the funding problems directly. There is the possibility of its introduction through a raise in national insurance. Such a policy would have the advantage of guaranteeing the NHS a constant flow of income independent of the fluctuations of the individual economic moment: advocates argue it would mark an end to the 'boom and bust' funding which has beset it in its brief history. The King's Fund has also argued that an NHS watchdog modelled on the Office of Budget Responsibility should be introduced.

But if these are potentially imaginative solutions to an entrenched problem – the hypothecated tax was backed by Tim Farron's Liberal Democrats in the 2017 General Election – then the new prime minister's start on education was enough to make one doubt whether it is the kind of suggestion that will appeal to her.

29 – EDUCATION

As we have seen, during the referendum campaign, Michael Gove had announced that he was 'sick of experts'. It was a surprising thing for any politician to say, but particularly astonishing for a man once in charge of the country's education policy: it is difficult to say what education is, if it is not the handing on of expertise from one person to another. Gove would later say that he had been misquoted, and that he had been particularly thinking about the (admittedly somewhat discredited) profession of economists, but the point was that Gove – albeit among the more intellectual politicians – had struck an anti-intellectual note that seemed to capture the emotive nature of the times.

However, Gove's side won the referendum, and so this anti-intellectualism – shot through with a certain knee-jerk pride-at-being-British – would be carried forward to a nation that still needed to construct an education policy.

How would the victory of the armies of less expertise alter that system, and the lives of those who had dedicated themselves to increasing the nation's store of knowledge?

THE UNIVERSITY SYSTEM

There were fears that leaving the European Union would be particularly deleterious at the higher education level. The art historian Kenneth Clark once remarked that the great movements in history – the medieval church, 20th century science

– are essentially international. If you are highly interested in something you usually don't care about the nationality of those who share your passion. The Brexit vote seems to say that we do care – suddenly and rather a lot – about people's nationality: it is partly this which gave the Vote to Leave its anti-intellectual character.

One thing we have already learned is that the UK cannot expect people of other nationalities not to notice when it experiences an internal spasm of nationalistic sentiment. People do notice – and especially in today's interconnected world, they react. For instance, it is no surprise to find that by mid-2016 there were already instances of UK researchers asked to step down from EU research projects. Ian Sample wrote:

> In one case, an EU project officer recommended that a lead investigator drop all UK partners from a consortium because Britain's share of funding could not be guaranteed. The note implied that if UK organisations remained on the project, which is due to start in January 2017, the contract signing would be delayed until Britain had agreed a fresh deal with Europe.[323]

There was the possibility that the EU project officer in question was acting in panic. That was certainly the impression that May and the Chancellor Philip Hammond would seek to create: the Treasury went on to confirm that scientists and universities would have their former EU funding matched by a post-Brexit Treasury. Similar guarantees were made in respect of infrastructure projects and agriculture: this money would have to come from somewhere, and at a time when the government could hardly expect high tax receipts in the aftermath of triggering Article 50. These guarantees did not necessarily change the frustration: funding that was there before had now been lost – and arguably for no good reason.

But the enormity of Brexit provoked larger questions: had Britain become a less interesting place to study? Had it become a less welcoming place to be? Such questions would later come to look melodramatic. Cambridge is still the university of Newton and Empson; Oxford retains its greatness too. But the fact remained: £1 billion in funding would need to be made up: someone somewhere – whether government, bank, university or taxpayer – would come up against the fact that money that should have been there, would not now be forthcoming. Theresa May's alma mater Oxford, for instance, received more research income than any European university, with about 40 per cent coming from the EU. Lord Patten, the university's chancellor, explained:

> Our research income will of course fall significantly after we have left the EU unless a Brexit government guarantees to cover the shortfall.[324]

Would the university system decline? Or would it by clever management and restructuring of its funding arrangements not decline at all? Either way, it was hard to see how British universities had become better as a result of the vote.

The question of student visas also arose. During her tenure at the Home Office, May had made attempts to reduce the number of student immigrants coming in. It was part of her wider fight to bring net migration down into the tens of thousands: rules were introduced to stop 'abuses' of student visas, making it harder for education providers to sponsor international students. Students would no longer enter the UK to pursue 'Mickey Mouse' degrees. This raised the question as to what constitutes a Mickey Mouse degree: one can certainly imagine the person who thought that, say, Aquinas studies were Mickey Mouse in 1284, or that the study of evolution might have been deemed frivolous in the 1870s: humankind prospers precisely by open-mindedness about avenues of enquiry. May – and her successor Amber Rudd – would retort with the estimate that one in five foreign students overstay their visas and continue to live in Britain long after their courses have finished. But to another bent of mind, this is a compliment to the nation – an endorsement made by bright young things about the desirability of this island, and its ongoing importance in the world's story.

But the UK-Europe relationship is always a two-way thing: if the British student were to look at these domestic prospects and wonder whether it might not be better to head abroad, the vote had already begun to make that difficult also. For instance, Maastricht University in the Netherlands stated in 2016 that if Britain leaves, its tuition fees 'might' rise, from the current rate of £1,600 to between £6,300 and £8,360.[325] Although this announcement was couched in the language of welcome to international students, some wondered about the wisdom of it: the aim may have been to create a spike in short-term applicants but it gave the place a stringent reputation.

It might be that in some cases, knowledge can have a free character that can favour the autodidact. A Brexiter might plausibly argue that no amount of EU funding can give you Milton: only a reading of *Paradise Lost* can do that. However, in a host of areas like science and research, such arguments tend to underestimate the importance of partaking in an international structure of cooperation. The UK universities wrote the following in an open letter to the media:

> While no-one is suggesting that UK universities could not survive outside the EU, leaving would mean cutting ourselves off from unique support and established networks and would undermine the UK's position as a global leader in science, arts and innovation.[326]

This raised the stakes. If the UK had become less likely to find a cure for cancer, or slower to improve our description of nature as a result of the Brexit vote, then it had done a very baffling thing. Professor Sir Robert Lechler, President of the Academy of Medical Sciences, was among those who expressed concern about the future of science and research in the UK – particularly in relation to archaeology, classics and IT, the subjects into which the highest proportions of EU funding had historically gone. Stephen Moss –a professor of biomedical research at University College London – further explained:

> Scientific research is unusual in that it is both highly collaborative and highly competitive. Imagine running a marathon in which your desire to win is matched by a compulsion to help your fellow runners. In science, being a good collaborator while retaining a competitive edge means being able to recruit the most talented people regardless of nationality.[327]

It remained to be seen what sort of emphasis May would place on this during her negotiations, although May did strike some as less inclined towards the sciences than some of her predecessors. One thinks particularly of Margaret Thatcher's pride in her chemistry background, and Blair and Brown's respect for the climate change consensus among scientists. Whatever attitude May opted for, it was likely that departing the European Union would lead to a real terms reduction in budgets for projects. Who could say which projects which might have been funded, would now not go ahead? Would there be potentially rewarding courses which, to use the words of Nick Hillman, director of the Higher Education Policy Institute, would 'no longer be viable'[328] as a result of the new status quo?

Was it too melodramatic to wonder which advances this generation might be denied as a result of a narrow win in a chaotic referendum?

GRAMMAR SHOOLS, FREE SCHOOLS, ACADEMIES

Seeing, as she must have done, the great complexity of her overall predicament, one might have expected a sort of minimalist strategy from May in the first instance. In some respects, this is what the electorate got with the repeated mantra, less illuminating each time it was uttered, of 'Brexit means Brexit', and bland assurances to everybody that they would have their EU funding restored. We would, to use the prime minister's oft-repeated phrase, 'make a success of it'.

One could forgive her this: the scale of the task must have needed assessment before it was commented upon.

What seemed less forgivable was the way in which she emerged from this period of quiet, only to embark on an immediate revisit of the eternal grammar schools question. The signs had been there for a while – as we have seen, they were there in her maiden speech. But there had been recent signals too. In the early part of 2016, May had supported a project by a local council in her Maidenhead constituency to open a satellite to an existing grammar school. When May stood up at the British Academy in London and said the following, there were no surprises:

> For too long we have tolerated a system that contains an arbitrary rule preventing selective schools from being established – sacrificing children's potential because of dogma and ideology. The truth is that we already have selection in our school system – and it's selection by house price, selection by wealth. That is simply unfair.[329]

We have already seen the arguments for and against grammar schools in Chapter 11: to have them again in 2016 was to feel that we were going around in circles. During Prime Minister's Questions on 14th September 2016, Jeremy Corbyn out-foxed May, asking her to name experts who supported her position. When she was unable to do so he quoted back Cameron's opposition to her. Soon after the policy was put forward, Cameron announced that he would be leaving parliament altogether – something he had previously said he wouldn't do. Some suspected that the grammar schools reversal hadn't helped. If the matter had been brought to a vote with him still in the chamber, a considerable distraction would have ensued: for instance, he had once labelled the debate surrounding them 'pointless'.

In the same speech, May also indicated that she favours a further expansion of free schools. This wasn't new either: she had previously advocated police and crime commissioners opening up alternative provision free schools. This is May speaking at the Policy Exchange in February 2016:

> Future PCCs should bring together the two great reforms of the last Parliament – police reform and school reform – to work with and possibly set up alternative provision free schools to support troubled children and prevent them from falling into a life of crime.[330]

In the shape of her joint chief of staff Nick Timothy, May had a bona fide expert on education. Timothy took unpaid leave from his role as director of the New Schools Network – an organisation dedicated to giving advice to those who intend to set up free schools – in order to join the May administration. May's policy might be termed the Big Society 2.0. On one side of the argument are those parents who feel happy to be able to tailor the schools they want for their children, free from local authority control – very often this will mean faith schools of some description. On the other are those who suspect that the scheme is open to abuse, and worry, for instance, about the prevalence of retrograde faith-based teaching.

Other ideas were in the works. The 2017 election manifesto would outline May's plans to fight for fairer funding under reforms to the national funding formula – a plan first mooted under Cameron to help direct funds more satisfactorily towards impoverished areas. The intention was to remove funding from the hands of local authorities and place it in the hands of central government: it is a further reminder that what Tories find unpalatable is not so much government *per se*, but local government – the faceless arm of bureaucracy that destroys the free workings of a community. This was opposed by the Labour Party, which argued that spending per pupil would now likely be inadequate for the next parliament. For Labour, Conservative talk of fairness was a smokescreen for cuts, and with good reason: the Institute for Fiscal Studies projects a fall of school spending per pupil by some 8 per cent. The poet and teacher Phil Brown is among those who are blunt about the Tory plans:

> In pure financial terms, the choice between major parties is a very simple one. The Labour party will spend more money per pupil on education than the Conservatives – any obfuscation of this is numerical sleight of hand.[331]

Others have noted that beyond May's grammar schools proposals – which because of their divisive nature were always likely to create headlines – there were other more interesting proposals. For instance, she suggested in her British Academy speech an amendment to future access agreements, so that universities might be required to sponsor schools in return for higher tuition fees. This policy dates back to the Blair administration: the idea was originally put forward by Lord Adonis – the Minister for Schools from 2005-2008 – and was best articulated in his 2012 book *Education, Education, Education*. Adonis' work draws attention to the importance of an active state within the academies programme – he is also an advocate of retaining the right to use central and local government in order to improve failing schools – or close failed schools. Adonis also advocates 'vetting the bona fides of academy sponsors so that only those with good credentials and credibility are allowed to run state-funded schools'[332]. Would May, the believer in small government, have the same will as Adonis to make the system work?

May also argued that faith-based Catholic schools are more effective than faith schools set up by other groups – Muslim, Hindu, Sikh and Jew. May appeared to be recalling her own education as she said that Catholic schools are:

> ... more ethnically diverse than other faith schools, more likely to be located in deprived communities, more likely to be rated Good or Outstanding by Ofsted, and there is growing demand for them.[333]

Finally, May stated that she wished to see private schools do more to earn their charitable tax breaks – such as set up state-sponsored schools and also fund places to more children from poorer backgrounds. George Eaton was among those impressed: 'With a majority of just 12, and the epic task of delivering Brexit, the Prime Minister may yet find that she has overreached. But May has shown that she is not content merely to hold power – but to use it.'[334]

Given that she touched on these things, it must have been frustrating to have found all the headlines centring on the grammar schools section of her proposals. But then as a front-line politician for many years, one wonders why she hadn't predicted this. May sometimes expends political capital by not thinking things through properly.

30 – CLIMATE CHANGE

'Mad dogs and Englishmen go out in the midday sun'. When historians come back to look at 2016 they might recall this truth of Noël Coward's: it may by then be seen as one of the maddest on record, but it is on track certainly as one of the hottest. At times this author has wondered whether there might not be some correlation between the two. The Spanish, the Italians have been equable in the heat: the UK, unused to it, was driven by the anomalous temperatures to create this unusual referendum.

Caught up in the confusion and noise of the present, it is difficult to look at the referendum as history will, because we cannot understand its ramifications regarding what will come to seem the chief problem of our times. If the severest effects of climate change can be averted, it will likely come to seem a mere quirk of our democratic history. But if it becomes another reason why the problem wasn't tackled, it shall be seen as a folly on a greater scale than present suspicion can voice. If this second holds true – which one hopes not – then it will be little consolation to have pointed out that it was known at the time. We have already seen Amber Rudd operating as the then new home secretary. Her previous position in the Cameron administration had been as Secretary of State for Energy and Climate Change. Charged with articulating the Remain position, she was hardly less pessimistic after the Brexit result than she had been before it. Here she is reviewing the results to the Business and Climate summit in London:

> While I think the UK's role in dealing with a warming planet may
> have been made harder by the decision last Thursday, our commit-
> ment to dealing with it has not gone away... However we choose to
> leave the EU, let me be clear: we remain committed to dealing with
> climate change.[335]

Rudd went on to highlight the possibility of higher energy
bills for British people in the event that Britain were to leave
the single energy market; her particular worry here was the
impact of Russia which, she said, might find it easier to hike
prices on a post-Brexit UK. For some, the stakes had been
higher all along than the financial implications. The sole Green
Party MP Caroline Lucas had been among those who had also
campaigned to Remain, publishing an article called: 'If we're
to win the climate struggle, we must remain in Europe'[336].
Lucas particularly noted that European solidarity was instrumental in rescuing the otherwise disastrous 2009 conference
at Copenhagen since it made it harder for countries in Asia to
renege. George Monbiot, one of the most vocal and informed
advocates for meaningful climate change policy today, also let
it be known he would vote to Remain.

But in taking this position, Monbiot also stated that there
were many things about the European Union he didn't like:
like Jeremy Corbyn he was seven and a half out of ten in favour. After the vote, he would begin to think in terms of the
opportunities for climate change advocates of the new reality.
The European Union is such a vast organism that we are not
quite in the realm of the clear-cut. This makes one inclined to
ask the question:

IS THE EUROPEAN UNION GOOD FOR CLIMATE CHANGE?

In making this assessment, one comes up immediately against the peculiar nature of the problem.

On the one hand, nobody is in doubt about the international nature of climate change. When we try to imagine the worst-case scenario, we can only conceive of it as a sudden realisation of our smallness before the hard facts of rising oceans and rising temperatures – it would be an experience of nationality falling away before the revelation of a humanity held in common, and all but squandered. Given this fact, belonging to something like the European Union might have been both fitting and helpful: to partake in international forums would have been to share in technical and scientific knowledge, perhaps in an atmosphere of hastening progress. It might be added that many of the regulations instigated by the European Union have been sensible. Under this analysis, the EU has been seen as a helpful buffer to the possible recalcitrance of Conservative governments, with their natural small government distaste for the regulatory framework required to solve the problem.

However, not all that the EU has done on climate change has met with unanimous approval, as we shall see.

What was Cameron's record like on climate change? His most important move – indeed perhaps his most important act as prime minister – was to sign Britain up as a signatory to the landmark Paris agreement with 196 other countries within the so-called United Nations Framework Convention on Climate Change. This agreement seeks, in its own words, to 'keep the increase in the global average temperature to well below 2 °C above pre-industrial levels and to pursue efforts to limit the temperature increase to 1.5 °C above pre-industrial levels'[337]. This treaty needed to be ratified by 55 countries that produce 55 per cent of emissions to enter into force. The process of ratification for EU states – which together make up 12 per cent of emissions – took place on 5th October 2016, shortly after May had become prime minister, and went into force on 4th November. It was an instance of Europe speaking together on an important issue. But if it was a chorus, it wasn't joined into by the UK. Instead, it was more of a round, with the UK joining a verse later: its instruments of ratification were deposited on 18th November 2016, and came into force on 18th December. Here is Theresa May in her maiden speech, delivered on 20th September 2016, to the United Nations:

> In a demonstration of our commitment to the agreement reached in Paris, the UK will start its domestic procedures to enable ratification of the Paris agreement and complete these before the end of the year.[338]

When May sets herself a deadline – as with the triggering of Article 50 – she tends to make sure she meets it: this is in contrast to former President Barack Obama who made a habit of crossing his own red lines.

There were more decisions for May to make in relation to the UK relationship with the EU with regard to climate change policy. As part of the EU, the UK had been the second largest player in the EU emissions trading system – the largest cap-and-trade system in the world. On the morning after the referendum vote, carbon prices tumbled 15 per cent against fears that a post-Brexit UK would leave the system. This market was reformed in tandem with the implementation of the Paris Treaty, with agreement reached between member states in February 2017. But that reform – known as the ETS Phase IV reform – would not now be led by a Brit: Conservative MEP Ian Duncan announced in the wake of the vote that he would be resigning his position. This was deemed by many a sad moment for British involvement in international climate change efforts. Eventually, Claire Parry, the energy minister, would confirm that Britain would remain subject to the EU's emissions rules until at least 2020 – albeit with a much reduced influence.

This was not all. As in other areas, May's government would need to review environmental legislation and decide what would apply in a post-departure UK, and what would not: again May had been presented with the chance to remake much of the legislative landscape in her own image. Friends of the Earth were among the organisations who lamented the potential loss of the nature directives, pointing out that many beautiful spots in the UK, including Cannock Chase, Flamborough Head, Dartmoor and Snowdonia have been protected by the EU. Its website states that 'before the Directives, we were losing 15 per cent of our protected sites a year. Now it's down to 1 per cent.'[339] One hoped that May – the outdoorsy holiday walker –would wish to keep those in place, but it was by no means certain she would.

Even George Monbiot, no-one's idea of a thoughtless Europhile, had this to say about the directives:

Though the EU's directives are compromised and under threat, they are a lot better than nothing. Without them we can kiss goodbye to the protection of our wildlife, our health, our conditions of employment and, one day perhaps, our fundamental rights. Without a formal constitution, with our antiquated voting arrangements and a corrupt and corrupting party funding system, nothing here is safe.[340]

Monbiot had also railed against certain initiatives of the EU, such as the rule stating that only bare land is eligible for the majority of farm subsidies, which he argues is bad for wildlife. Another bugbear is the EU's encouragement of biodiesel as a replacement for transport fuel: Monbiot argues that this policy has been injurious to rainforests in Indonesia[341]. Neither do many environmental campaigners like the corporatist face of the EU which is intent on negotiating trade deals such as TTIP and the Trade in Services Agreement, whose priority is said to be the creation of business for multinational corporations and not environmental standards. But then the same people are equally concerned about an environmental 'race to the bottom' when May goes in pursuit of her trade deals.

After Britain's departure, climate change progress would be dictated by the quirks of each individual government. If history is anything to go by, this is likely to have mixed results. True, the UK government has sometimes shown itself a world leader in climate change – it was certainly so under Blair and Brown. The 2008 UK Climate Change Act, a notable achievement of the Brown era, requires the UK to work to achieve an 80 per cent reduction in carbon dioxide emissions from 1990 levels by 2050. But although this narrative of UK science leadership more or less held under the Coalition, it was already unravelling by the time Cameron left office, particularly as there was always some doubt about Osborne's commitment to tackle the problem. Here he is in the lead-up to the 2013 Conservative Party conference:

> I want to provide for the country the cheapest energy possible, consistent with having it reliable, in other words as a steady supply, and consistent with us playing our part in an international effort to tackle climate change.

> But I don't want us to be the only people out there in front of the rest of the world. I certainly think we shouldn't be further ahead of our partners in Europe.[342]

Next to the average opinion of a Republican presidential candidate in the US, this is immensely reasonable. But next to the scale of the problem, it is inadequate and the vote to Leave seems to leave fewer safeguards in place against the Osbornes of the future. While May, Hammond and the new business secretary Greg Clark all talked of tackling the problem, they had all been implicated in the mixed Cameron-Osborne legacy. By 2015, Osborne had begun to limit financial support for renewable energy projects and had also rejected stronger binding targets for renewable energy generation and energy efficiency.

To the extent that the hard right of the Conservative Party was now in the ascendancy, there was worry about the will to move forwards. 'While not all Eurosceptics are climate sceptics, few climate sceptics are not also Eurosceptics,' as environmental analysis group E3G wrote in a private briefing note.[343] And here is Nigel Farage in proud-and-ignorant default mode: 'I haven't got a clue whether climate change is being driven by carbon-dioxide emissions.'[344] Theresa May is not Nigel Farage – as was shown by a thoughtful article 'It's Britain's duty to help nations hit by climate change', published in the *Guardian* in December 2017. Even so, to the extent that the Farages of this world now had a voice, this didn't bode well if one were urgently concerned about the problem.

MAY'S CLIMATE IN-TRAY

As usual, May had a surreally steep task ahead. In addition to all these general considerations, there were a number of particulars needing her attention. In the first place, the second Cameron government had sometimes been recalcitrant under Liz Truss – the then Secretary of State for Environment, Food and Rural Affairs – in the implementation of European limits on air pollution. If May sought to loosen regulations on air, what would be the health cost of potential pollution? The same applied if she sought a settlement whereby the Water Framework Directive didn't apply to UK businesses.

Secondly, Britain was in compliance with the Habitats and Birds Directives: so far it has done so in spite of cries from some that the cost of doing so was high. In an instance like this, would the electorate be faced with May the walker, who holidays in the Swiss Alps, or would it instead find May the liberal conservative, who instinctively dislikes Europe, and knotty regulation? May was tight-lipped on these issues too.

Despite these worries there were factors likely to guard against a dramatic slide in environmental standards. The UK continued to be a signatory to numerous international treaty obligations under the Kyoto Protocol on carbon emission reductions. It also had commitments under the OSPAR Convention on marine pollution, and the Bern Convention: Brexit could not alter these. It was also hoped that there would be many voices – from columnists, campaigners, and NGOs – to protest any backsliding. As in other areas, there was a lot to be said for the status quo ante. For instance, in order for the UK to meet its obligations under the Paris Treaty, any replacement trading scheme would need to be linked to the EU ETS.[345] The essence of Brexit is often a renegotiation about doing away with a perfectly acceptable state of affairs, in order to arrive back at something resembling what was there previously. One wishes the nation's energies could be devoted to producing solutions to the underlying (and urgent) problem rather than to some interminable fiddling around the periphery: on climate change, one wishes that if the UK had to leave the EU, it had done so sooner. Its timing could hardly be worse from the only perspective that really matters – the planetary one.

More broadly, there was the question of how green May wished to make the domestic economy. In the first instance, the extent of money available for low carbon energy subsidies for the years beyond 2020 would be eagerly watched by environmental campaigners in the 2017 budget: alas, an 800 per cent tax increase on solar panels was announced, as well as – though it was squirrelled away in the budget document and not mentioned in Hammond's speech – the scrapping of the levy control framework without any replacement.

May had also mooted a possible change to the way in which proceeds from fracking are shared so that some 10 per cent would go straight to residents affected by the process, and not to councils. This was an attempt to make good on her promises in her first Downing Street speech to look out for the disenfranchised, but it was also an expression of her usual distrust in local government[346]. It is also inadequate to those who deem it necessary for there to be no fracking at all: it is a fairness measure where a climate-oriented measure is needed. It was also a barometer of the busyness of May's administration that her government was at this time also in consultation over a third runway at Heathrow: the Airports Commission had reported in 2015 that the runway should go ahead. This decision, which would be big for most governments, was among May's smaller undertakings. But again there were fears that the desire to 'make a success of Brexit' might mean that environmental concerns were outweighed again by economic ones in the transport sphere too.

THE HINKLEY DEBACLE

Hinkley Point (Fig. 25) is located at the mouth of the River Severn and the Bristol Channel.

It currently boasts two nuclear power stations. One is the now defunct Hinkley Point A, which closed in April 1999 following safety worries. Hinkley Point B meanwhile, with its two advanced gas-cooled reactors, is projected to be decommissioned in 2023. In 2013, David Cameron announced along-side the Chinese premier President Xi, that EDF Energy – the mainly state-owned French company which also runs Hinkley Point B – had reached an agreement with China General Nuclear Power Corporation (CGN) for a new nuclear power plant at Hinkley Point – called Hinkley Point C. It was George Osborne's brainchild, and reflected his desire – which might almost be said to have been an obsession – to 'formally connect' the London and Shanghai stock exchanges.

The argument was that the investment would lead to job creation, while also forming part of the UK's energy mix. This was not all: Hinkley was intended as the first in a triptych of new power stations all funded in part with Chinese money: the others were projected to be at Sizewell in Sussex and Brad-well in Essex.

Hinkley wasn't even predominantly a Chinese venture: state-owned CGN would pay £6 billion of the £18 billion cost,

Fig. 25 Hinkley Point[347]

but EDF energy was projected to have a majority holding. In spite of that, the headlines focused on Chinese involvement, because of that country's record on human rights and also because of perceived threats to security. These last were twofold: in the first place, there were worries in the industry about the safety of Chinese construction. In the second – and we know for sure that these worries reached the ears of Theresa May – fears abounded regarding Chinese intentions in embarking on the project.

We know these concerns reached May, because they were vocally held by her joint chief of staff Nick Timothy.

Timothy viewed Hinkley Point as a direct threat to national security. His article on Conservative Home entitled 'The Government is selling our national security to China' outlines his case. In the first place, Timothy worried about the human rights implications of accepting Chinese investment: he would make a sharp distinction between good and bad investment, with Chinese money counting among the latter. Timothy noted that the Americans have more stringent attitudes towards Chinese investment, and favours that approach. But Timothy's main concern is that the venture would prove a front for a brazen round of Chinese espionage. He observed that the Chinese National Nuclear Corporation's website states that its *raison d'être* is to increase the value of state assets and to build the national defence. The board of the corporation are also high-ranking communists. The May camp also had similar doubts about Huawei's investment in the telecommunications sector. Vince Cable, who served as Business Secretary during the Coalition, reports the following:

Fairly early on in the coalition, she wanted to introduce a more stringent test of foreign investment, based on the American model of screening out projects that threaten national security... Secondly, my recollection was that when approval was sought for Hinkley, she raised objections on grounds of national security issues and China.[348]

After becoming prime minister, May initially put the deal on hold saying that she wanted to look at all its 'component parts'[349]. This was reported as a humiliation for EDF Energy, who were taken by surprise, the glasses of champagne withdrawn in dismay from their lips. This delay – coming at a time when the future of British business was far from assured – needed to be explained. May sent a hand-written letter through her Asia minister to the Chinese premier Xi explaining that the UK 'looks forward to strengthening cooperation with China on trade and business and on global issues'[350]. One wonders how reassured the premier was. Justin Bowden, the GMB union's national secretary for energy described the decision as 'bewildering and bonkers.'[351] It seemed to some that there would now be a 7 per cent gap in the electricity grid, and 25,000 fewer jobs than there might have been on account of arguably paranoid fears.

But for many, the eventual decision to proceed – one wonders what Timothy thought of it – was another sign that Brexit might prove very difficult. The momentum of the world of international money had won again, as it had done in the case of the sale of ARM. There were grounds to lament the decision: nuclear waste continues to be a fear, and the safety concerns both in relation to national security and in relation to the standard of Chinese construction, have not gone away just because May approved the decision. The prime minister could plausibly argue that these opening decisions had too much momentum behind them for her to block them, and that future decision-making, where she could start from scratch, might lead to more imaginative policy when it came to Chinese investment.

But the fact remained: May had again rubber-stamped the decisions of her predecessor, and had done little more than let it be known she was not happy about it. May sometimes has a way of making power look an awful lot like powerlessness — but then that is the case often with prime ministers. In fact, it is a *leitmotif* of this book.

THE SCALE OF THE INHERITANCE

To look at the problem of climate change is to realise the peripheral nature of a thing like Brexit. I have written often in these last chapters of the scale of the challenge that May faced, but it is also possible to step back and see that in another sense, she primarily faced the problem I have just been outlining here. She came to the premiership at a critical juncture: the same will be true of all leaders who rise to power over the next decade. She was the beneficiary of the statesmanship of Barack Obama and others in that she had before her an international framework that could begin to tackle the problem. But May would also need to elaborate an energy policy that matched the science community's estimation of the gravity of the situation.

History might almost be said to have been building all along towards the question of climate change, and the ultimate viability of the human project. The world's wars, its fluctuations and ascendancies, may come to seem strangely provincial: inward-looking spasms which for all their bloodiness may come to look quaint when set against the existential crisis we now encounter. History has been an interweaving of local legends and vendettas: now, in the shape of the environmental crisis, we encounter a grander tale – a sort of master narrative. It is this which renders the excitable talk of post-Brexit trade deals worrying: the irrelevant language of nationalism is angled at a world which needs to grow out of that kind of thinking. The catching nature of the referendum period, and its time-consuming complexity, are diametrically opposed to our species' interests. The suspicion remains that the finest trade deals Liam Fox can sign, while they might give short-term gains to the few who would benefit, would nevertheless not answer the core problem. Not only does Brexit absolutely fail to address our predicament – it creates a new one, Brexit itself, which is distracting, possibly futile, and definitely secondary to the vast rethink we really need to conduct. We have discovered that the world can die due to a misplaced priority on a meeting's agenda paper.

Theresa May became prime minister at a time when the sustainability of human civilisation was in doubt. In that sense, she was not overambitious when she stated that she had more to do than Brexit: she was stating the obvious. And perhaps it was this sense of how much needed to be done, that nudged her during the early part of 2017 towards a disastrous decision:

to go to the country and ask for the kind of majority to which might be attached the authority to solve the numerous problems alluded to in this section.

PART SIX

2017 AND BEYOND

31 – THE SNAP ELECTION AND THE ACCIDENT OF POLITICS

Britain had no time to dwell on the Easter weekend.

Tuesday morning broke, and soon the typical website-goer in the United Kingdom began to receive unusual intimations: an announcement was due from outside the door of Downing Street. It was then that the question of the day – 'Why?' – began drifting through Westminster and, via the Twitter account of Laura Kuenssberg, out into the wider country. Was Theresa May, a known type II diabetes sufferer and 60 years old, about to resign? Had the nation somehow gone to war again? Or would there be a surprise election? On the last point, there were persuasive reasons to think not. There had, for instance, been numerous previous denials from the prime minister herself, most notably in September 2016 on *The Andrew Marr Show*:

> I'm not going to be calling a snap election. I've been very clear that I think we need that period of time, that stability, to be able to deal with the issues that the country is facing and have that election in 2020.[352]

May's office had also released a statement a few weeks before the Easter weekend stating that the prime minister would not be calling a vote, with a Downing Street source quoted as saying 'it's not something she plans or wishes to do'[353].

To reinstate the theatrical in politics one must simply surprise journalists. These remembered denials began to feel hollow on 18th April 2017, as the media – huddled in their insectoid camera-scrum outside Downing Street – noticed that the prime ministerial crest was not displayed on the lectern. This was a sign that what would ensue pertained to party and not government business.

And then, wrong-footing everyone again, May walked out of No. 10 Downing Street 15 minutes earlier than expected. She looked, as always, like someone on her way to somewhere else. The cameras twitched; the microphones jostled. May was brisk:

> I have just chaired a meeting of the cabinet, where we agreed that the government should call a general election, to be held on the eighth of June. I want to explain the reasons for that decision, what will happen next and the choice facing the British people when you come to vote in this election.

Like this, May stood before the country – a woman neither particularly known nor extravagantly loved – and sought to ratify the accident of her rise to power, and that strange day with which we began when Gove and not Johnson had ended up running for the office she now held. She was preparing to gamble it all again.

What ensued outside 10 Downing Street was business-like, which is to say it was the opposite of poetry. May's public addresses remained reminiscent of someone pausing in the street to tell you the time. As usual, it was impossible not to lament the poetry deficit. As May detailed her approach to Europe, there would be no rallying cry: the nation was instead asked to partake in the logic of her premiership so far. The referendum result. The necessity of honouring it. The failure of the Westminster parties, including her own, to be as cooperative as she might have wished. The words amassed with the mercilessness of someone who has seized a microphone at a wedding. Except that here a demand was made on listeners: to accommodate her decision to hold this election into their own lives, and vote – and perhaps vote for her.

She didn't give the appearance of knowing that she was exposing herself to the whims of chaos.

UNDERSTANDING CONTEMPORARY REALITY

In the case of the referendum, no two votes were the same: each had had their complex personal history. Beneath the surface – under the 52-48 figure – one could infer the presence of informed and misinformed voters, instances of clear thinking and the presence of incoherent emotion. Cool-headedness and rage, apathy and passion, realism and idealism: all these things percolated, but unnameably. The referendum was a witch's brew, where one cannot guess at the ingredients. 'How now, you secret, black, and midnight hags? What is 't you do?' asks Macbeth in Act IV, Scene I. 'A deed without a name,' the witches reply[354]. If the vote to leave the European Union and the 2017 General Election that would follow each occurred within an information-rich age, then it is remarkable how little we know about the meaning behind them.

This might open up onto a discussion about history. Medieval historians are used to the idea that when there is very little information to hand, history becomes a primarily creative exercise in extrapolation: in some ways this book has been forced to track that method. By way of illustration, it has been suggested that the practice of medieval history is best understood as an upside-down triangle (Fig. 26). In this example, the point upon which the triangle stands, represents your scant source material: the external facts about the world you can be reasonably sure of – birth and death dates, statutes, a few written scraps, architectural hints, stray personal artefacts. In medieval history, it is this slender point which one must work out from. The historian's task is one of inference outwards, along the first two sides of the triangle, from the thin facts, towards whatever

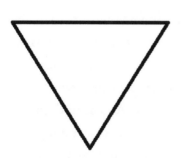

history you have the gumption to write: it is both a creative and a deductive art.

Fig 26. This triangle might represent medieval history: one must extrapolate outwards from a slender base of information.

The task for the historian of contemporary events might instead be likened to a triangle the right way up (Fig. 27). Here, the base line of the triangle represents the great range of your possible source material. If one is studying Nazi Germany, for instance, instant access is granted to vast reams of footage, survivor testimony, newspaper articles, *Mein Kampf, The Diary of Anne Frank, If This is a Man* and the rest of the memoir literature, thousands of speeches and reportage on those speeches, as well as what memoranda you can find about the processes of Hitler's government. The contemporary historian's task is different: it is a process of selection in order to create an emphasis – the historian must laser along the two right-way-up sides of the triangle, into whatever is to be said. One must pinpoint.

Fig 27. This triangle might represent the practise of modern history: one must infer from a wide base of information.

Interestingly, contemporary history – where there are so many facts agreed upon – turns out to be a mix of the two: the facts are often just as contentious as they are in medieval history, but there is the same impression of voluminousness which one gets when studying the twentieth century. And as with modern history, the predilections of the historian keep coming between the historian and the task in hand. One's own taste in truth – the insistent fact, in other words, of one's self – proves in the end to be interventionist.

One's day to day life during the referendum felt much more like that second triangle. Each voter had a slew of available information: we rolled from cycle to cycle, bewildered not by a dearth of news but by too much of it. To understand completely the life of the nation would entail an unthinkable toil through billions of tweets and Facebook posts, memes and

YouTube sensations. We are bamboozled by up-to-the-minute footage, and real time reportage on that footage: no sooner has something happened than we are already being informed of its meaning, and these interpretations themselves cause shifts in the dialogue, and sometimes swift responses at the policy level (which themselves need to be discussed in real time). It is a constant increase in information – as if the base line of that second triangle were continually widening, until it might almost resemble infinity. We have invented methods of communication which hold up the mirror faithfully to a chaos which previous generations, turning their newspapers sedately, were better positioned to ignore.

So that while the experience of living through major events should in theory look like the second triangle, in actual fact it can feel rather more like the first: this proved to be especially so during the era of Cambridge Analytica when one realised just how wide reality is, and how various voter experience was at the Internet level.

Epic confusion is the ground note of reportage about our reality. It is as if both triangles have collapsed. But then things as they really are never look like a sign. They look like life.

Theresa May came to us within this anxious world – a seemingly steady presence in a country on permanent red alert. She announced that she was confident she had the clout and seriousness – or to paraphrase her own election slogan, the strength and stability – to navigate this exceptionally difficult terrain. Unfortunately, she had overestimated herself.

THE CAMPAIGN ITSELF

May's repeated use of the slogan 'strong and stable' might be accounted her first mistake. In fact, it spoke to a deeper flaw in her as a politician which we have glanced off often in this book. Her lack of rhetorical gift can sometimes seem not so much a personality trait as a sign of an unnuanced leader – or even an arrogant one. Long exposure to the workings of power seem to have created an expectation of power's continuation without her having to do very much more than articulate her minimum intentions.

Almost unnoticed – indeed, when she had seemed at the height of her power – hubris had snuck in. As the nation watched her repeat the 'strong and stable' slogan through the first weeks of the election, its frustration perceptibly increased and soon transfigured itself into mockery. John Crace dubbed the prime minister the Maybot; the label stuck. The British public began to plot a surprising result.

The UK electorate does not readily forgive authoritarians – or it would at least like its demagogues to be charismatic. May seemed to anticipate a victory without having to do much. In her refusal to debate with the other party leaders, and in her frequently vague policies, one had the impression of a leader accidentally taunting voters. It was the sort of tin ear one normally associates with prime ministers in their later years – Thatcher in 1990, Blair in 2006. In May, it evidenced itself far sooner than expected: those years as home secretary and her long-established nearness to the epicentre of power had taken their toll on her judgement. In the event of it, Amber Rudd, a few days after the death of her father, stood in for May at the leaders' debate when the prime minister refused to show up: the poignancy of Rudd's situation was not enough to make viewers forget that the democratic moment, which May had after all summoned into being, hadn't found the prime minister in especially democratic mood.

All this might have been overlooked by the electorate had it not been for the debacle over the release of the Conservative manifesto, in particular its proposals on the social care crisis. Labour had pledged to lay the foundations for a National Care Service, although it wasn't clear whether this was to be funded out of wealth taxes, an employer care contribution or a new social care levy. The Liberal Democrats meanwhile suggested a 1p rise in all rates of income tax to create additional revenue to fix the problem, with a view to moving eventually towards the hypothecated tax we mentioned in Chapter 28. In seeking to add her own solution, May must be credited with approaching a problem that her predecessor's administration had failed to tackle. She was certainly wading into a treacherous area of policy: the incumbent at the time David Mowat was the ninth social care minister in 15 years. However, one must also add that the May administration had been snookered into considering the matter because the scale of the problem had become unignorable: as of November 2016, around half a million old people received no care whatsoever, and according to a report by Leonard Cheshire Disability '48% of disabled adults who say they need social care do not receive any support at all'[355]. May – and Nick Timothy – proposed that funding for reform would be met out of the cost of that most sacrosanct thing to the English, and especially to the Tory-voting English – their homes. David Brindle observed a flaw in the prime minister's approach:

When May's team was drafting the manifesto, it must have seemed a good soundbite to guarantee that everyone in England could be sure of passing on £100,000 to their children, whatever care costs were incurred. If a minority would be hit by having to spend against the value of their homes to pay for homecare, not just for residential care as at present, that could be spun as a tough but stateswomanlike choice.[356]

In attempting to enlarge her constituency, May had shown herself cavalier about her own, whose support she had presumed. This was also the moment when one came to see the thinness of her gambit to turn Labour seats blue with a few slogans about the JAMs. Perhaps the same gamble played out in 2020, backed by concrete policy achievements (her revised Northern Powerhouse strategy, for instance), and the familiarity of having been a visible champion of the poor for years, might have been more successful.

It was another sign of the difficulty of moving the Conservative party into the Joseph Chamberlain, or One Nation, state of mind. The Thatcherite conception of life proved resilient, and May soon came under great pressure. To own a home is arguably the key project in the life of many British people; and to inherit one is often the hope of young people who, particularly post-Lehman, don't earn enough ever to own one otherwise. As she had done on the Go Home vans, and as she had also done on the rise to national insurance for the self-employed in the 2017 budget, May pivoted immediately and announced that there would be an 'absolute limit' to what people would be expected to pay before the £100,000 floor was left. Effectively she had introduced a second cap to make people feel better about the first, leaving a trail of confusion in her wake.

Even then, she might have been able to retain some face if she hadn't at the same time announced that 'nothing had changed' even though it now seemed that it had. An admission of having listened to concerns and altered course would have sufficed. In any case, the policy remained in doubt. What, after all, was this 'absolute limit' that people would now pay? The prime minister refused to say. Her confusion undermined her 'strong and stable' message, and she lacked the agility to create a new narrative, or the sense of humour to laugh it off. Self-deprecation is a technique somehow not open to May, as it has been to others – one thinks of Blair, Reagan, and even George W. Bush.

The misery of the ensuing terror attacks in Manchester and London Bridge didn't seriously alter the narrative in a terror-weary nation. There was something unforgivable about May's handling of that election: arrogance on its own might have been overlooked as the strength she sought to project; a simple misstep on policy could have been navigated in the usual way; blandness of utterance might have served to suggest a woman of imminent deeds; aloofness from the debates might have been seen as her being above the fray. But all these flaws, coming one after the other and taken together, amounted to an unforgettable toxicity. May had come up against the unpredictability of the electorate, and had been unable to tame it by any show of character or genius.

Power was ceding to chance by way of hubris. It is an ancient narrative: most leaders will ultimately fall short of taming the heterogeneity of reality to their own wishes. But few fail so swiftly as May did – but then few seek to test their power right away.

ON CHAOS AND POLITICS

As polling day arrived, May was still expected to win at least a 50 seats majority in spite of these numerous slips. Instead, the returns were far worse than all but a few outlying polls had suggested. May fell short of a majority, squandering the reasonably benign position bequeathed to her by Cameron. London was lost. The north, with deep ties to Labour, had not rethought its allegiance because of May's stated intentions to consider them. Thanks to the likeability of the leader of the Scottish Conservatives Ruth Davidson, the party had made gains in Scotland, with 12 additional seats, but this was a slim consolation against the real story: under the apparently unelectable Jeremy Corbyn, Labour had gained 30 seats, partly due to a significant increase in the youth vote. A secure but slim mandate had been replaced by the inability to govern alone.

One could discern pattern within the strangeness of it all. As in the referendum, there was protest. But May hadn't reckoned on the anger of a legion of young people frustrated by a gerontocratic referendum result percolating in the electorate: the anger seen in 2015 and 2016 had simply mutated again. The post-election reshuffle felt like a variation on her first. This time around, Gove came in having defended May during the campaign with a series of articles in the *Times*; Andrea Leadsom was moved to Leader of the House of Commons. Meanwhile, the question of Ireland and the nature of its post-Brexit border had been a secreted worry in the Brexit vote: it would come decisively to the fore now. The only way May could form a government was by striking a confidence and supply agreement with Arlene Foster's Democratic Unionist Party. With an obscure complementarity, Scotland retreated as an issue, and the future of the United Kingdom seemed assured for the time being.

All this made one think not of triangles – of easy lines of information to be sifted and sorted – but of complex patterns, modulation, and elaborate development. Faced with the tapestried complexity of it all, one instead feels one should consider the Mandelbrot diagram (Fig. 28). This image, full of strange

Fig. 28. The Mandelbrot set.[357]

beauty, was named after Benoit Mandelbrot (1924-2010) – one of the pioneering figures of Chaos Theory.

Mandelbrot's image, with its generating centre emitting a hypnotic weave, is full of a mystery too rich for metaphor, unless we simply cheat and say it reminds us somehow, obscurely, of life itself. It is at odds with other mathematical images in this respect. For instance, Isaac Newton had posited an essentially linear reality. In Newton's laws of thermodynamics, bodies move like billiard balls in a given direction, unless some contrary force acts upon them. But Newton's world of direct momentum, and Euclidean predictability doesn't match the hearts of human beings and the strange processes of politics. When we consider Einstein's theories, our minds struggle to compute light's secret characteristics – its bendiness, its duality, and its close-knit relation to time. Finally, in quantum theory, reality is secretly counterintuitive and magnificently strange: this weird world of action at a distance – where the arrangement is too fragile for an observer even to make their observations without disturbing their own ability to measure – seems to have little in common with the efforts of human beings to build a just world. It feels tucked away, and insufficiently macro.

But within twentieth century mathematics, a branch of enquiry arose devoted to the description of the movement of dynamic systems – things like the flow of water in a pipe, or the swinging of a pendulum in a clock. Mandelbrot spent his career attempting to explain that a similar pattern was underpinning all processes within the natural world – in nature, in human activity, and by implication, in democratic politics.

This was fundamentally unNewtonian, unEinsteinian, un-Bohrian. In Mandelbrot, atoms are not predictable as they are in Newton, they do not bend as they do in Einstein, they do not jitter as they do in Bohr – they join up, and become implicated in systems, which in turn develop and surprise us. In fact they exhibit sufficient flux to become new systems: it is the mathematics of mysterious development. And again, Mandelbrot's description of life, in fact, feels rather a lot like life itself. As he famously wrote:

> Clouds are not spheres, mountains are not cones, coastlines are not circles, and bark is not smooth, nor does lightning travel in a straight line.[358]

One might add that history isn't told in triangles. Furthermore, it could be said that democratic exercises are not vote-counts – they are natural processes as blurred and interiorly intricate as any other natural process; they partake in the overall strangeness of things. In time, Mandelbrot was able to find a new geometry – which he termed 'fractal geomtery' – to describe the way in which apparently simple phenomena derive from chaotic fractal processes. James Gleick explains: 'Clouds, mountains, coastlines, bark and lightning are all jagged and discontinuous, but self-similar when viewed at different scales, thus concealing order within their irregularity. They are shapes that branch or fold in upon themselves recursively.'[359] It is that self-similiarity which I wish to touch upon now.

Figure 29 shows a diagrammatic representation of a Julia set – a fractal process within what is called the complex plane.

This is a geometric representation of the complex numbers established by the real axis and the perpendicular imaginary axis – that concept is of use to mathematicians, and indeed the whole concept of imaginary numbers was a particular frustration for Lewis Carroll. For us, it is enough to know that Mandelbrot has taken a series of mathematical coordinates and hoisted them, via a computer, into the realm of the visual. In other words, Figure 29 is – or aspires to be – a portrait of something really going on throughout nature. Mandelbrot would measure these processes in the human sphere – his first paper was about the fractal nature of cotton prices. Human beings, from you and me, to Theresa May, are subject, says the chaos theorist, to these fractal processes. This should not be too surprising: we are naturally occurring facts. Even so, a strange beauty is shown to be at work: these images might suggest a mind – or an electorate – in receipt of information, subtly churning it – subject to, and partaking in, the obscure

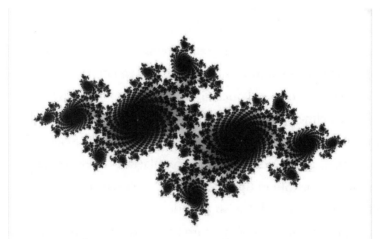

Fig. 29 A Julia set.[360]

434

flux of the world. They are stately, silent, strange – analogous also perhaps to the Disraeli idea of the state which we encountered in Chapter 22.

If nature were shackled to some Newtonian plan, it would lack the right means for development. But if it were too chaotic, and liable always to be veering off into no pattern, things would fail to cohere.

Sometimes in this book we have witnessed something like the unifying patterns of Chaos Theory unfolding in the political sphere: we saw them in the unlikely events which led to the ascendancy of Theresa May; in the strange growth over time of the European Union; in the drift of the state, as Disraeli saw it; in the weird, almost ghostly, complexity of May's to do list; and then again in the subtle mutations of the 2017 General Election result.

THE MORAL ASPECT

We have moved from a choppy understanding of reality, to something more holistic – even symphonic. It is a pattern which is alleged to be coursing through nature, and even within the behaviour of human beings.

But it should be said that Chaos Theory is open to certain objections.

In the first place it is subject to the critique that Karl Popper levelled against science in his 1934 work *The Logic of Scientific Discovery*. Put simply, scientists are often wrong; and can any theory really encapsulate reality? Popper wrote: 'no matter how many instances of white swans we may have observed, this does not justify the conclusion that *all* swans are white'[361]. The history of science shows rather a lot of instances where white swans turned out not to be white. Newton, Einstein, Bohr and Mandelbrot all describe quite different worlds. At its worst, Popper's work seems to display a slight contempt for what has really been achieved in science. But it might also lead us in the direction of a still deeper mysticism, while also reminding us that moral philosophy must still have its place within a full 21st century understanding of life.

Reinhold Niebuhr – one of the foremost Protestant philosophers of the 20th century – considered the world a predominantly moral predicament: it is divided between the children of light, who are usually well-meaning but continually fall short, and the children of darkness, who are responsible for the world's portion of tyranny. Niebhur describes this conflict:

> Since the survival impulse in nature is transmuted into two different and contradictory spiritualized forms, which we may briefly designate as the will-to-live-truly and the will-to-power, man is at variance with himself.[362]

The question arises as to whether a figure like Theresa May belongs to the former, whether she has 'the will-to-live-truly', or to the latter, whether she has the 'will-to-power'. This book shows her, like most people, divided. To use Niebuhr's phrase, she is 'at variance with herself'.

Most of us, in our day-to-day assessments of Theresa May, do use moral language – when we call her the Maybot we are pointing to a deficiency in her, a lack of courage and moral imagination. Those who call her a second Thatcher (an epithet much more commonly deployed before the 2017 general election than after), are pointing to a contrary interpretation: that her toughness, or strength of character really amounts to a moral boon for the country. But whichever view we take, I doubt many would seriously argue that the moral nature of the prime minister is of no consequence whatsoever. To admit this is to concede her potential importance as an agent of causation within the prevailing structures of nature – whether we deem them to be Newtonian, Bohrian, or Mandelbrotian or perhaps answerable to some other better description.

Once this moral dimension is (re)admitted into our understanding of politics, questions arise. Is the moral aspect of things overlaid onto nature and the Chaos Theory depiction of reality? Or are the physical and the moral world working in tandem?

Here is an exchange in Tom Stoppard's Chaos Theory-inspired play *Arcadia*:

Chloe: The universe is deterministic all right, just like Newton said, I mean it's trying to be, but the only thing going wrong is people fancying people who aren't supposed to be in that part of the plan.

Valentine: Ah. The attraction that Newton left out.

This reminds us of the difficulty of squaring our descriptions of nature with the human realm of power struggle, system creation, electioneering, and ideological endeavour in which we have watched May at toil. The suspicion remains that only a powerful personality can tame Mandelbrotian nature: it takes great courage, supreme words, exceptional moral insight, and a profound capacity for articulating the truth, to reach across the divide between the self and external nature, and really reach the hearts of others, sufficient to tilt them with any degree of reliability in the direction one wishes them to go.

Throughout this book we have used Winston Churchill, for all his faults, as an example of another way of doing politics. Towards the end of this book we shall look at W.E Gladstone as another example – and perhaps a better – of Carlyle's Great Man.

But Britain under the hubris of Theresa May came to seem almost an image of nature: it felt like a government unguided by any knowledgeable hand, a place rudderless and adrift within complexity.

By June 2017, it was as if her rote slogans and absenteeism on the campaign trail had ceded the terrain of leadership, and nature had rushed in.

THE ECONOMICS OF PLACE

But to admit the importance of the self of prime ministers is not perhaps to admit very much. It is merely to observe that human beings, endowed with consciousness, press forward with their own uniqueness. Politics is an aspect of our self-consciousness: it shows us reaching for some ideal lodged within us of a perfect society.

But what would Utopia look like? And has Theresa May,

in her short and largely hubristic tenure of the prime minister-ship, made any particular contribution to it?

In Niebuhr's view, the ultimate goal of human society is towards a viable world community. For Niebuhr, all religions have a germ of universalistic philosophy within them, which must logically lead humankind towards a state of organisation that would transcend the individual narratives of nations. This tendency found ratification in the 20th century with the advent of the great supra-national structures: the UN, NATO, WTO, and the EU. In our own time, it has been furthered by techni-cal advances in a range of areas from aeronautics, computers, and in the creation of blockchain technology.

Niebuhr's was not a new dream: it was, for instance, im-plied by Goethe in his concept of Weltliteratur – a literature which observed no borders. As Goethe told Eckerman towards the end of his life:

> I am more and more convinced that poetry is the universal possession of mankind, revealing itself everywhere and at all times in hundreds and hundreds of men... I therefore like to look about me in foreign nations, and advise everyone to do the same. National literature is now a rather unmeaning term; the epoch of world literature is at hand, and everyone must strive to hasten its approach.[363]

The career of Theresa May is perhaps best understood as a re-vanchist exercise against this tendency. Watching May call the 2017 election, it was possible to remember another speech de-livered at the 2016 Conservative Party Conference, when May had strayed into the genuinely revealing:

> But today, too many people in positions of power behave as though they have more in common with international elites than with the people down the road, the people they employ, the people they pass in the street. If you believe you're a citizen of the world, you're a citizen of nowhere. You don't understand what the very word 'citizenship' means.

This phrase 'citizen of nowhere' has been widely claimed as a stern rebuke to Remainers. But the phrase in its right context is not a taunt to those who still think it would have been preferable to remain in the European Union, so much as an exhibition of Anglican teacherliness: it was a moment of finger-wagging by May the communitarian. One might wonder whether the reinstallation of a sense of community is what was primarily at stake in the election from May's perspective – perhaps it is even the prime mover of her career. She wants us all to be citizens of a country populated with people more akin to Theresa May.

Theresa May, in her pandering to the right wing of the party and the nationalistic sentiments she has been known to utter, might be considered as especially unhelpful in the crucial Niebhurian project of internationalisation. May's career appears by these standards undeniably provincial and retrograde – a spanner in the international works. Even so, I doubt whether Niebuhr would have been particularly surprised by her career. Here he is in *The Children of Light and the Children of Darkness* (1944):

Pure idealists underestimate the perennial power of particular and parochial loyalties, operating as a counter force against the achievement of a wider community. But the realists are usually so impressed by the power of these perennial forces that they fail to recognize the novel and unique elements in a revolutionary world situation.[364]

May can certainly be accused of failing to be suitably excited about the possibilities of a new world community: her talk of cats and the Human Rights Act, her obvious queasiness about foreign investment, and her belief in a perhaps narrow idea of England certainly do not suggest a champion of a diverse global order.

But Niebuhr is also clear that national sentiment – or 'particular and parochial loyalties' – cannot be rubbed away all at once, and indeed it would not be desirable for the sake of the variety of life for us to do so. The 2008-9 crisis appears to suggest that the international structures we currently have don't answer sufficiently to the needs of local communities: belonging to these also constitutes a significant part of what it means to be human. An international trade deal does not give rise to fêtes, and there appears to be a part of human beings that isn't opposed to fêtes. Certainly, any verdict on the career of May must hinge on how seriously we take these 'parochial loyalties'. If we do think of Englishness as a thing whose diminution or dilution ought to be fought, then we might have some sympathy towards her agenda. But if we feel that the project of universality trumps any such considerations, then we are liable to judge her premiership harshly.

None of this is to say that the Brexit vote represented an outburst of protectionist sentiment among 52 per cent of the population. As we saw in Chapter 21, it was a vivid reminder of the unpredictability and selfhood of one's fellow citizens: it was as if millions of people suddenly announced that they existed, whether they knew about politics or not. Here is Zadie Smith in her 'Fences' article:

> Doing something, anything, was in some inchoate way the aim: the notable feature of neoliberalism is that it feels like you can do nothing to change it, but this vote offered up the rare prize of causing a chaotic rupture in a system that more usually steamrolls all in its path.

Seen in this light, the referendum on EU membership appears to represent a battle between the quiddity of the self, and the claims to the universal validity of the scientific method, with which the Remain campaign had hoped to carry the day. Perhaps it would have done so if its science had been better. But this remains David Cameron's best pitch to history: he was the man who gave the disenfranchised – Theresa May's 'just about managing' class – the chance to remind the political classes of their predicament.

One tolerant interpretation of May's premiership therefore is that it is an attempt to restore communities back to life. May interpreted the Brexit vote as a cry for localism – for texture and nuance in our communities. It might have been one in the eye for the politicians, but it was also a rebuke to our architects. The referendum vote could even be seen as a moment in the history of aesthetics: people were expressing their repugnance with the uniform globalised look of our high streets today. To be alienated in place is always after a fashion to be alienated from history – and politics. Brexit can have come as no surprise to the psycho-geographer. To the extent that May sought to address this process of homogenization, she deserves credit. But the way in which she did so – by pandering to prejudice and a bogus nationalism – earned her a rebuke in the 2017 General Election that many felt to be justified.

As the election results came in, it became clear that May had no mandate after all for a so-called soft Brexit. She gambled everything for no decent reason, and lost damaging her own reputation and the nation. Perhaps the most startling statistic of the General Election 2017 was this: as the results came in, people realised that the dizzyingly complex EU negotiations were due to start in 11 days' time.

Fig. 30 Grenfell Tower, June 2017.[365]

GRENFELL TOWER

Grenfell Tower stands in West London in the most affluent neighbourhood in the United Kingdom. It looms above the Westway and the wedding-cake Georgian architecture as another dubious answer to the London housing crisis, rearing up as if height were a thing to be striven for, for its own sake. Perhaps an alien visitor would consider it an emblem of power, but really it was a reminder of the scale of poverty in an unequal society. It was an essentially tautological architecture: an imposing reminder of impoverishment. Before it became a symbol of the Age of Brexit, it was a symbol of West London: it meant inequality before it meant death; it was ugliness and misery, before it was calamity; and it was poverty before it flamed in the skies as a possible rebuke to Theresa May and all her works.

The lead-up to the fire that would define the period just after May's disastrous election would be picked over exhaustively. David Cameron had announced in 2012 that he intended to 'take a lot of fear out of the health and safety monster and make sure that businesses feel they can get on, they can plan, they can invest, they can grow without feeling they are going to be strangled by red tape and health and safety regulation.'[367] It was a business-centric agenda, but it seems to have created a somewhat blasé attitude regarding the dignity of those not building these tower-blocks but living in them. It was also based around a conflation: a building regulation is not a health and safety regulation – the first is of absolute importance to safety; the second may indeed lead to minor absurdities. Reading back his public utterances, one is never quite sure if Cameron knew which one he was referring to: we have glimpsed similar fudges in this book over the deficit-debt question, and also in regard to encryption. Cameron had a willingness to pontificate on questions he hadn't yet understood. There are signs that the inhabitants of Grenfell – many of whom had protested that their only route of escape in the event of fire was down a single staircase – paid a heavy penalty for the Conservative attitude to regulation. Of course, it was going too far to say – as did Shadow Chancellor John McDonnell – that the government had been guilty of 'social murder'. But a culture of negligence had been permitted to prosper.

The fire started on 14th June 2017: it would later be discovered that it had been caused by a broken fridge. It began just after midnight and soon had spread rapidly, helped by inadequate cladding, a component of which was supplied by Arconic, which would shortly be subject to legal action from shareholders. Scenes of horror ensued: a baby was thrown from a window, and thankfully saved; some people on the top floors, who would never escape, were seen waving spectrally from the upper floors; and there was also the story of the woman who overran her bath, thus saving herself. The next morning, a helicopter panicked and skirled above the building's blackened frame, helpless to turn the clock back and undo the tragedy.

May – already damaged by her botched snap election – visited the scene the following day. She didn't meet any of the 71 victims' loved ones or other survivors but instead sought a closed meeting with the Civil Contingencies Secretariat, the department of the British Cabinet Office responsible for emergency planning. This prompted comparisons with George W.

Bush's lackadaisical response to Hurricane Katrina in his second term as president. Even a natural ally like former Shadow Chancellor Michael Portillo argued that she 'should have been there with the residents'[368]. Again it seemed that May's long period in government was beginning to create a certain tin-earedness about the emotional needs of the times: this was a nation exhausted by terror attacks and inequality, who couldn't now – as they had tended to do before the election – excuse the prime minister's natural reticence. There was a sense of late period Thatcher or Blair, where suddenly a popularity which had been hollow all along was dramatically surrendered – and vulnerability rushed in to fill the vacuum where admiration had been. A tired country needed leadership, and in this case it was supplied by Buckingham Palace, whose advisors had more wisdom, releasing a statement noting the 'very sombre national mood'[369]. This seemed more meaningful than May's later announcement of a £5 million fund for victims of the fire, which had the look of a concession to unpopular froideur.

In time the poets and the musicians would react. Local resident Damon Albarn, the polymathic musician, would describe the area around Grenfell in evocative terms for BBC Radio Four's *The World This Weekend*:

It's always been one of those roads, where at one end you can hear the birds sing at dusk and at the other kids hang outside the takeaway on their way to the football pitches under the Westway. It's the kind of place that brought me to West London in the first place nearly 30 years ago, a place where there is real community, always evolving, always multi-cultural at its heart, a place that even before the Windrush generation had been a destination for new Londoners.

Albarn proceeded to lambast the government ('No more division. No more scare tactics. Just honest practical caring governance'). Perhaps if May had heard this address she would have been particularly hurt by that last taunt: wasn't that precisely what she had promised on the steps of Downing Street, when she had appeared to go over the heads of the Tory Party, and speak directly to the 'just about managing'?

Of course, it was possible to take the May-bashing too far. The prime minister was at times lambasted almost as if she herself had invented fire and insufficiently safe cladding as part of some malevolent scheme to destroy people unlikely ever to vote Conservative. In reality, anyone who has grown up in a Tory constituency will have met Theresa Mays: kindly in themselves, but austere in their modes of expression. They might lack the expansive charitable spirit of a Barack Obama or a Jo Cox, but it is because they have developed otherwise – towards pragmatism perhaps, or else in the direction of an inarticulate pity. Prime ministers eventually collide with their faults: but in that hot June in 2017, May was colliding far sooner than she or anyone expected, and her flaws in any case were multiplying before our eyes. Now looking like she might be the shortest serving prime minister since Bonar Law, events kept contriving to make her seem inadequate.

It was possible also to think of it as a watershed moment – a chance for a society to emerge with viable policies to match May's Just About Managing rhetoric. The poet and novelist Ben Okri published a long poem in the *Financial Times*:

Those who were living now are dead

Those who were breathing are from the living earth fled.

If you want to see how the poor die, come see Grenfell Tower.

See the tower, and let a world-changing dream flower.[370]

It may have been clumsy as poetry but it expressed a valid wish.

This author went down to Grenfell on the morning after the fire. Walking north from Holland Park, the helicopters could be seen rushing in and out of the trees. It was an unusually hot day. Eventually, turning west onto Walmer Road, was the famous husk – no longer televised; resolutely real. It had not quite seemed plausible on the Internet that morning: here it was. And here on Walmer Road were the real responders – the Red Cross vans, and the milling police; the kind face kept alternating with the distraught look, the one attempting to cancel out the other. At the local church, I was told that clean underwear and clothes suitable for work were at a particular premium: these people, sometimes characterised as lazy scroungers by the right wing press, obviously intended to return to their jobs – the normality of a day's tasks were for many the most viable approach to the trauma of the day.

People circled the tower doubtfully, staggered by the dumb fact of it – the hundreds of narratives altered or ended by these same flames still licking up above. One sensed the danger of making an emblem of it: what entails suffering ought never to be reduced to the ease of symbols. That would be to outrage the actual tale, and the diverse memory of those who found themselves caught up in such a claustrophobia of panic as their last experience of life. Even so, the image of a burning tower has its undeniable resonance: it was the rushing in of nature to confound human creation. It suggested bad government.

HER STRANGE SUSTAINING

Unexpectedly, Theresa May did remain in power through 2017. The General Election results were not in their essence any less catastrophic than Cameron's 2010 performance – indeed in terms of her share of the vote they were better. But Clegg and Cameron had had their rose garden moment back then, and had managed to create a plausible theatre. The Liberal Democrat leader had been plainly delighted to have his party in power at all. Meanwhile, Cameron – after 13 years when the one-time natural party of government had been regularly rebuked at the polls – though he had been unable to beat the unpopular Gordon Brown outright, had at least achieved his personal ambition of becoming prime minister. Their enthusiasm had been sufficiently infectious for the country to accept the Coalition with a portion, however small, of the protagonists' optimism.

By contrast, May's arrangement with the Democratic Unionist Party had no such joyousness attached to it. This was partly due to disappointed expectations, of course. But also, it felt like a short-term sticking-plaster: it was a mere confidence and supply arrangement, without any binding coalition agreement of the kind which had kept the 2010-15 government intact. Nor was the British public admitted this time to the rose garden: there would be no smiles, no vivid moment of coming together. The British electorate quite rightly views an absence of theatre with suspicion – as essentially undemocratic. Instead, this government would be cobbled together within unlovely closed meeting-rooms. The eventual agreement was signed not by the leaders, May and Arlene Foster, but by Tory chief whip Gavin Williamson and the DUP's Sir Jeffrey Donaldson. That was taken as a sign of May's weakness in some quarters: a new agreement wouldn't need to be stitched together if May were to quit during the parliament. May was now in that awkward position where all her actions were widely interpreted to her own disadvantage. She was able to form a government – but only on the back of having been comprehensively rejected by the people that government would serve.

It was a cataclysm for May: her sense of her own rectitude, and of her opponent's folly, had been acute, and endorsed by everyone in her circle. It showed a lack of imagination at the heart of her administration. May draws all her wisdom from 'my party': she had struggled to find a language to fit the fierce dynamics of the modern world. And yet, bereft as she was, her consolation prize was still the prime ministership: one suspects that the fact of power, however nominal, was something which she deemed worth continuing for. She would wake up in the morning for as long as possible as prime minister, and not have to look at the phrase 'shortest-serving' in front of her name for the rest of her life if she could help it.

Meanwhile, reality would shuffle again. Northern Ireland received its expected boon of significantly increased funding – around £1 billion, as well as relaxed funding rules in relation to a previous £500 million previously committed. It was possible to take a dim view of this: during the campaign the Tories had regularly mocked Labour's 'magic money tree', arguing that Corbyn's socialist policies were not properly costed. Now, with a craven abracadabra, this not insignificant amount of money had been found by May in order that she might remain in power. Meanwhile, John Major stated that a minority government would have been more ethical since it could preserve the UK government's impartiality, deemed an essential part of the landmark Good Friday agreement. Major told the BBC's *World at One*:

> I am concerned about the deal, I am wary about it... People shouldn't regard it [peace] as a given. It isn't certain, it is under stress. It is fragile. And although I don't expect it suddenly to collapse – because there is a broad consensus that wishes it to continue – I think we have to take care with it, and take care that everything we do does not exaggerate the underlying differences that still are there in the Northern Ireland community.[371]

The arrangement also ensured that May's opinion would be sought on any issue arising out of Northern Ireland: one such was the vote on 25th May 2018 to repeal the Eighth Amendment of that country's constitution, effectively overturning its strict abortion laws. This would become a vivid example of May's hampered situation. The DUP could not be expected to be happy about a result which they would regard as sanctioning the murder of, to use Arlene Foster's word, 'the unborn'. But May's ranks in her own party are full of those inclined to emphasise the importance of women having access to safe and legal procedures. What would rankle in this instance would be May's characteristic tentativeness: by that point, she would need the DUP's votes for the EU Withdrawal Bill that June. In her public utterances she gave every appearance of wishing the situation would go away, at least for the time being.

But perhaps one must be sympathetic here: abortion cuts to the very heart of life – it is a sacred issue and the one where one can least predict which side an individual will come down on. For that reason – as May would frequently point out – it is usually a free vote when it comes before the House of Commons. Even so, as May submitted to the DUP deal, she was inevitably binding herself to various high-wire acts in the future: these would be undertaken on a more or less hourly basis for however long she could retain sufficient equilibrium to remain in office.

What followed was an unhappy Queen's Speech from a prime minister who had once pledged to alter the very nature of her party and the meaning of modern conservatism. Her promises to review the pensions triple lock had to be jetti- soned, as were her promises to review the fuel allowance. The ghost of Joseph Chamberlain had retreated from the chamber: in the end there simply hadn't been the votes for a revised con- servatism, or at least not as it had been presented by May in the 2017 campaign. Some of what May was unable to do was to the good: her plan to scrap free school meals for five to sev- en year olds would likely have been unpopular. Her pledge to reopen the foxhunting debate may also have cost her political capital, and over an issue which animates only an infinitesimal percentage of the population: in putting it forward in the first place and in shelving it after the vote, it showed May again as the archetypal practitioner of politics as concession to noise. Perhaps most importantly to May herself, her plan for further grammar schools, so exhaustively outlined and fought for, were now once again unfeasible. Seeking to wrong-foot her enemies, May had confounded herself.

Unless she was able dramatically to recover, May would forever be attached to the idea of hubris, the leader who reached for more when she already had most of what she needed. It could also be said that she had surrendered the opportunity to be a transformational prime minister out of a desire to be an extremely long-serving one.

May would proceed now, she said, 'with humility'. But her weakness would now be a chief fact in the EU negotiations: suddenly the departure bill owed by the UK to the European Union – which the EU was tentatively reckoning at €55-75bn (£48-66bn) – looked distinctly like it would need to be paid. The necessity for some kind of interim deal once the Article 50 negotiating period expired in 2019 now seemed all too obvious: no amount of jingoistic rhetoric could alter the stubborn fact of time. May's ideal of an English judiciary blissfully absolved from the rulings of the European Court of Justice was also less likely: any transition deal would surely involve some measure of continued belonging to the single market which would in turn mean that a range of industries – from aviation to financial services – would fall under that court's sway. May's vision of a Brexit primarily committed to lowering immigration had also come under fire; so too had any fantasy about a hard border in Ireland. Her Chancellor Philip Hammond –

who she would likely have removed had she won – took to *The Andrew Marr Show* to call for a business-friendly withdrawal from the EU.

By June 2017, May was left only with power – a power difficult to divorce from personal failure and a certain loneliness. Power which lacks the vitality of a true and imaginative moral energy – the kind that we associate with our greatest leaders – must ultimately be too weak to assert itself. At such a point, all cedes to chance: if the swirl of natural forces we glimpsed in the Mandelbrot diagram are not mastered, they shall cheerfully do the mastering themselves. By 2017, May was bereft of her closest advisors, unloved by swathes of the electorate and at the behest of forces set to sweep her wherever they chose.

But then, like a force unguessed-at in a science experiment, the unexpected happened: May began to exhibit a strange resilience. Bad news came upon bad news, without any good news to provide relief. Her disastrous coughed-through, mocked-at 2017 conference speech ceded to resignation after resignation, as Priti Patel, Michael Fallon and Damian Green were all forced to resign. But counterintuitively, May kept getting up in the morning. By the end of 2017, she was still in office and with a reasonable amount of progress on the negotiations to her credit. After the Phase One Agreement between Britain and the EU was reached, one realised that for all the sensation of the referendum vote and its dramatic aftermath, reality is stubbornly incremental. The world is always muddling through somehow, sustaining us through apparent chaos. Amid our little arguments, the buoyancy of actuality keeps intervening. Human ingenuity was not cancelled by the decision to leave the European Union. We have been taught that crisis is a human invention. At any moment in Britain during these last noisy years it has been possible to look out the window, at the bird hopping in the hedges, or the baby in the pram, and suspect that the folly of politics has a precise counterbalance in the glory and strangeness of life: in fact, I have argued in this chapter that it is underpinned by it.

POSTSCRIPT
FROM SKRIPAL TO CHEQUERS

Throughout this book I have sought to compare the imaginative politician with the forensic. Winston Churchill has frequently served as an example of the former; May, naturally, has been our example of the latter. May hasn't come out well from that comparison – oratorical flair cannot compete with administrative capacity (not that Churchill was lacking in the latter, nor that May can definitely be said to possess it all the time).

But sometimes during the writing of this book I have felt another figure rear up: the formidable figure of William Gladstone. This is a politician whom May really might have emulated. She could never have addressed the House with the poetry of 'We shall fight them on the beaches': but she might have been a moral force in a confused world, as Gladstone was. Indeed, until the calling of the disastrous 2017 snap election, it wasn't impossible to imagine that she might have been true to the promise which we observed in the first part of this book: Theresa May might have been a moral counterpoint to the absurdities of Johnson, the hyperactive volubility of Michael Gove, or the slick blandness of Osborne and Cameron – just as the nation had once needed Gladstone to balance out the marvellous gumption of Benjamin Disraeli. She really might have amazed the world as Gladstone did with a superior work ethic, and mastery of detail. That was her chance in history:

but by the middle of 2018 this didn't seem to have happened. And her falling short was illustrated in varying degrees by two major events.

In the first instance, there was the discovery on 4th March 2018 of the poisoning of Soviet double agent Sergei Skripal and his daughter in a park in Salisbury. The scene is eerie to contemplate: a father and daughter found languishing together on a park bench in the open light in one of Britain's sleepy cathedral cities. Amid Zizzis and other chain restaurants, it always seemed an unlikely venue for seismic global events – but then, geopolitics must unfold somewhere.

May moved methodically: after launching an investigation, she announced on 12th March 2018 that the poisoning had been caused by a Russian-developed Novichok agent, considered to be the most powerful ever developed. Days later, steadily logical, she declared Russia responsible and expelled 23 Russian diplomats. At the centre of it all was, of course, the power-addled mind of Vladimir Putin, alongside whom May is an appealingly sensible figure. Putin has long since nominated himself as grandmaster in a bloody and unnecessary international chess match. If it were not for the allure of power – his shares in oil companies and his numerous dachas – Putin would amount to little: he is the sort of man who, consequential on earth, cannot be expected to amount to much in eternity.

The Skripals would prove unexpectedly hardy and survive: the agent hadn't been administered in sufficiently deadly amounts. Their attempted murder showed May in a good light: she was horrified, and expressed that horror – though not as theatrically as Blair would have done, nor with quite the true and resounding rage one might have expected from a Gladstone, or even a deeply religious prime minister like Gordon Brown. Even so, one began to wonder whether all the embarrassment of the snap election might somehow cede to a certain popularity, and that she might have a 'Falklands moment'. May successfully managed to orchestrate a chorus of disapproval – with even Donald Trump's wildly unpredictable America among those condemning a Russian regime which its president had often threatened to admire. When Yurial Skripal recovered, she was quoted as saying: 'No one speaks for me.' It was a marvellous assertion of dignity and autonomy before the outrages perpetrated by governments, and the manic attentions of the press.

But May didn't have time to ride any political momentum arising from this. Soon, with an inevitability to which she must have grown wearily accustomed, another scandal broke, and May again lost control of the narrative. The Windrush scandal – named after HMT *Empire Windrush* which brought a group of 492 migrants to the port of Tilbury on 22 June 1948 – began with a series of interviews in the *Guardian*. It was revealed that Caribbean nationals including Paulette Wilson, who had lived in the UK for more than half a century and Anthony Bryan, who hadn't been to Jamaica since the age of eight, had faced the threat of deportation under May's government. It was a miserable story: this was the generation so memorably photographed by Charlie Phillips in all the beauty of their assimilation, and who had made real contributions to national life. One of those who had faced dire treatment was Renford McIntyre –a former NHS driver who arrived in the UK in 1968. To the natural shock was added the sinister fact of the policy's secretive nature. The Windrush generation had thought to find a home – and having found one, had been roundly told it wasn't home after all. In the letter to the Hebrews – a book which Theresa May is meant to have read, and whose creed she professes to live by – we read that we must be hospitable since we might be entertaining angels unawares.

What was the cause of this harsh treatment? It was traceable to the outset of the Cameron administration: the great Tory bugbear of immigration targets, which we saw May grapple with in an earlier chapter. Once the miserable interviews were published in the *Guardian*, the government floundered – embarrassed to have a policy which they had privately advocated publicly exposed. The home secretary Amber Rudd initially apologised and announced like many a home secretary about to resign that she would stay on as the only imaginable person to fix the mess. She claimed that there had been no culture of Windrush targets within 2 Marsham Street. This was a prelude to democracy's friend, the leaked letter: this showed Rudd writing to the prime minister, professing 'the aim of increasing the number of enforced removals by more than 10% over the next few years'[372]. From that moment, her resignation was a needed catharsis. She would return to the back benches to think on her 346-vote majority in her constituency of Hastings and Rye. Her tweeted apology would secure 792 inscrutable 'likes' on Twitter:

> I wasn't aware of specific removal targets. I accept I should have been and I'm sorry that I wasn't.[373]

Rudd's departure, which May privately fought against, showed the prime minister again helpless before the complexity of events. As a former home secretary, and as a prime minister with a particular interest in immigration, it seemed scarcely credible that she would have been ignorant of this state of affairs. Again, one was forced to wonder whether May was properly reading her correspondence. A nastiness had seeped once more into policy-making: somehow, in the crucial lead-up to council elections, she had managed to give the impression that she sees anyone with a whiff of foreignness about them as a statistic to be driven down in the name of some abstract and more British happiness.

MAY AND THE GOD QUESTION

Philip Magnus, William Gladstone's great biographer, begins his book with this salvo:

> The vast majority of mankind have believed, however imperfectly, throughout the ages that the whole of human life is in service to God.

May had often said things which chime with this. Yet we find throughout May's career very little of the Gladstonian conscience – or at least, May had never successfully dramatised, let alone enacted, whatever theology she possessed, nor wrestled publicly with the moral plane as Gladstone always did: she had not felt able to elaborate upon the relationship between politics and religion, and had failed to make of her premiership anything vivid. Of course, she inhabited a different age – one where, as Alistair Campbell put it, 'we don't do God'. But it is part of the opportunity of being prime minister to transform the mood of the times. In fact, good prime ministers always do.

This made May particularly struggle against a cruel and essentially absurd figure like President Donald Trump. Faced with obvious venality, she seemed able to do little more than protest friendship. When in June 2018, Trump managed to create a typically eccentric G7 meeting, advocating the return of Russia to that group after a period during which he had imposed an unwarranted and hostile 25 per cent tariff on steel and 10 per cent on aluminium imports from the EU, Canada and Mexico, May said: 'We work closely with President Trump, and the UK has a very good relationship with the United States.'[374] The first part of that statement could not be entirely true, since it was difficult to point to one instance – whether it be on the Paris climate accord, or the Iran nuclear agreement – when one could see evidence of meaningful cooperation. And yet it was difficult to imagine what else May could have said: it was part of the sheer scale of May's bad luck that she wasn't even blessed, as every one of May's predecessors stretching back to at least Winston Churchill had been, with a ready ally in the person of the President of the United States.

Even so, it is remarkable how few examples there are in May's career – with the exception of the Modern Slavery Act – of a conscience bursting through to create a new debate, or to claim for herself an already existing situation. Instead her political life seems to consist of a series of almost neutral manoeuvures. Her predicament can sometimes appear more interesting than she is; and her career is more noteworthy for what it lacks than for what it contains. We saw in our opening chapters how May came to power appearing to possess certain promising traits: we have seen her holding hands with her father in the vicarage where she grew up, and end up holding hands with Donald Trump at the White House. In demeanour, she seems to be a Christian prime minister in the Gladstone mould; but if this is so then she seems remarkably mobile when it comes to morality. How deeply held are her convictions? It is possible to know everything that Gladstone thought about the bread and wine – and much too much about what he made of Homer – but one can never be sure what May thinks about what she holds dear. She is not religious in the discursive sense. Gladstone was an Old Testament prophet; May not a prophet at all, and never aspiring to be one. By 2018, she seemed unable to imagine a plausible paradise on earth. In this sense, she seemed an old-style Hobbesian conservative, primarily espoused to the fending off of some chaos that might arise were she not residing in 10 Downing Street.

It could be said that political eras can be divided between those defined by a clash of personalities and those where the predominant note is a war of fundamental principle. When principle is at stake – as in the European Union question – we tend to have less time for silliness: we saw in our opening chapters how May might well have been a natural fit for the times. But people crave imagination in politics to a greater extent than one might have supposed: there is a widespread longing for courage, dynamic debate, and poetry. We go to politics not just for our problems to be solved but for good theatre. In any case, as we saw in our chapters on policy, there remains the suspicion that complicated problems are solved not just by taking one side against another, but by allying oneself to a welling-up of the collective soul. Profound feeling is the only synthesis: it is this which frees the slaves, or brings about the lasting shifts. The human heart is the true power on earth: it is this which a leader must wield in order to change the world.

As the May administration went by, and particularly in the middle of 2018, an unlikely figure began dominating the news with increasing frequency: he seemed to possess some of the qualities that May lacked; and he was able to do this while seeming to be a harmless parody of the English aristocracy. This was Jacob Rees-Mogg: for a while it was impossible to ignore this eccentric son of the *Times* journalist William Rees-Mogg. Staunchly pro-Brexit, and opposed to any encroachment of EU law on British national life, he at least spoke with a conviction which had been missing while the electorate had been watching the Goves and the Johnsons slug it out to no known purpose. He seemed to belong to something. Referred to as the Honourable Member for the 17th century with a kind of bemused fondness by his fellow parliamentarians, Rees-Mogg brought to British politics a deep respect for parliamentary process, together with a belief in the uniqueness of national tradition, and a lofty, if slightly staid, religious sensibility. His distaste for Europe had some of the Johnsonian comedy, but none of its opportunism; he seemed to have wit without superficiality, and all his beliefs stemmed plausibly from a commitment to the Catholic faith. His words seemed to have some other origin than any of his contemporaries: eccentric as many of his solutions were – his opposition to gay marriage was particularly unpopular – they at least seemed to derive from principle.

The idea of Rees-Mogg as prime minister was for many an absurd step too far even in a surrealist age: but his ubiquity – and the fact that people were even considering someone so seemingly at odds with the liberal gains of the post-war period – was another reminder that if people do not find leadership in the prime minister of the day, they shall seek it elsewhere: more than anything Rees-Mogg represented an appetite. The need for someone other than May was starting to look very real. It wasn't clear whether Rees-Mogg even coveted the prime ministership – but May had created in the electorate the urge to dream of someone other than her as leader.

And what had happened to those other rivals we met in Part I of this book, those with whom she had once seemed so closely associated? David Cameron would pop up occasionally, and always unrepentantly – a man seemingly comfortable with his decision to grant the referendum. George Osborne continued his somewhat spiteful tenure of the *Evening Standard*, where he rarely missed an opportunity to cast the day's news as yet another defeat for the woman who had sacked him from the Treasury. His behaviour was however perhaps slightly less objectionable than that of Boris Johnson who handled his time in the Foreign Office in a way reminiscent of Gordon Brown's resentful occupancy of the chancellorship during the Blair years: beneath Johnson's blithe charm was a man who deemed the sliced-in-three Foreign Office too small a playground for a man of his classical education. In June 2018 Johnson was leaked expressing frustration at a gathering of 20 Tories at the Institute of Directors in London: he even went so far as to imply that Donald Trump, for whom he expressed increasing admiration, would make a better fist of Brexit than

May.

And Gove? He had played the wisest hand: he hadn't had to spend much time on the back benches and had been rewarded with the post of Secretary of State for Environment in the aftermath of the 2017 general election debacle. His tenure there has been typically hyperactive and seen him introduce bans on microbeads and fuel combustion vehicles. Even so, this was not a new unambitious Gove: in June 2018, he delivered another remorselessly long speech to the Policy Exchange about the need to restructure the global economy and lessen the power of 'crony capitalists'. It sounded — and indeed perhaps was — a bid for the chancellorship, an office he continued to covet. It is, of course, in Gove's nature to roam far from his brief: there is something irrepressible about him. His ambition is always tethered to intellectual curiosity; Johnson's intellectualisms appear in service to his. May had sometimes been helped by seeming to lack intellectual reach: as we saw, during the strange summer of 2016 when she won the prize, and where we began this book, it had made her act with plausible straightforwardness while her boy rivals had seen fit to turn useless somersaults.

At times, May had seemed to vacate the prime minister's chair even while remaining leader: she was the Banquo prime minister, although a ghost at her *own* feast. The examples of her powerlessness kept accruing. In May 2018, she was stunned to find that, with Sajid Javid having replaced Rudd on her crucial Brexit sub-committee, that she had no majority to pursue her plan of a customs partnership with the EU. By June 2018, she was still a sort of gilded go-between, trying to placate David Davis on the timeframe for the Northern Ireland border issue to be resolved, while also making regular winks to the

Remain camp that somehow all would be well with British trade. She wasn't in a position to say either way – not only, one suspected, because she now lacked the power to do so, but because she has never convincingly known her mind, and not just on this. Even in the lead-up to the successful passage of the EU Withdrawal Bill on June 20th 2018 May again had to find compromises between Dominic Grieve's 'rebel faction' – although there was little rebellious about the upright Grieve – and the Brexiters who didn't want Parliament to have any 'meaningful vote' in the event that there would be no deal in EU negotiations. In this instance, a compromise was made but one was reminded of Zeno's arrow paradox, where the distance between origin and destination of travel is endlessly halved and then halved again, never to reach its target. As Tom Stoppard has George Moore say in *Jumpers*:

> It was precisely this notion of infinite series which in the sixth century BC led the Greek philosopher Zeno to conclude that since an arrow shot towards a target first had to cover half the distance, and then half the remainder, and then half the remainder after that, and so on *ad infinitum,* the result was, as I will now demonstrate, that though an arrow is always approaching its target, it never quite gets there, and Saint Sebastian died of fright.[375]

Of course, the joke is that arrows really do reach their targets. In Britain in the post-Brexit period the suspicion was that events were really moving towards a showdown that couldn't be delayed forever. Would the May administration be able to stave off the moment of real disagreement *ad infinitum* with a series of legislative fudges, and the arrow never reach Saint

Sebastian? Or would there be a real point of reckoning and the arrow strike home?

But again, this is to think in lines, as Newton did, when life itself is more like the Mandelbrot sets we saw before. What would happen to Theresa May's premiership seemed to owe so little to her: few prime ministers have risen so high to fall so quickly. To watch her lead the country was to watch a leaf in a chaotic storm – she was, as Gladstone said in another context, 'entirely dependent upon the weather.' Gladstone had written to his wife Catherine in 1845:

> Ireland, Ireland! That cloud in the west! That coming storm! That minister of God's retribution upon cruel, inveterate, and but half-atoned injustice! Ireland forces upon us those great social and great religious questions – God grant that we may have courage to look them in the face, and to work through them.[376]

In 2018, that cloud seemed that it might again come from Ireland or that it might come from Brussels or Westminster, but by the summer of 2018, even with the EU Withdrawal Bill secured, there was that same need of courage and the urgent presence of those 'great... questions'. The question was whether May would find some courage within herself to face them, or whether she would drift, a mere aspect of the pattern.

THE RESIGNATIONS OF DAVIS AND JOHNSON

Then, with seeming suddenness, Theresa May did find that courage, and summoned her ministers to Chequers in Buckinghamshire with a view to thrashing out a deal. A set of photographs by Joel Rouse exists which commemorates this decision. They also show the extent to which power in Britain is related to history – and perhaps to nostalgia. Theresa May's Cabinet is depicted from above in groupings of influence and alliance. Gathered under venerable portraiture in a superbly high-ceilinged room suggestive of a National Trust property, we glimpse the essential looseness of government, its bedraggled talkative nature. In the first image, where a cylinder of sun pours through a skylight, the only person absent is the prime minister. Even so, this image of circling and seated ministers is intended to convey her power: without her, we are meant to feel, they are disparate, like pupils chatting before the headmistress enters.

It is perhaps noteworthy that Boris Johnson and David Davis are shown to be ostentatiously tieless – the lax attire of incipient rebellion. One also notes Philip Hammond seated under a portrait of Charles II in animated dialogue with Chris Grayling – a Chancellor of the Exchequer ready for any challenge, talking to a Transport Secretary who has repeatedly shown himself underprepared. But once again, the principle thing to note is our utter distance from proceedings – we shall likely never stand in that room, never know these people who are carving the destinies of our lives, and our children's lives.

According to ITV news this little party segued into a banquet lunch consisting of…

BBQ chicken thighs, a 'wheat-beets-squash' salad and feta, a Chequers estate new potato salad, estate-grown mixed leaves with summer tomato salad and pomegranate dressing[377].

All of which sounds very healthy, although not quite the Pol Roger-dominated feast of which Churchill might have approved. One imagines a working lunch, the mind divided between fork and paper – 120 pages, in fact, of the so-called Chequers proposal, intended to put all debate to rest, and have unity reign in the Conservative party and the country at large. It was theatre, yes – but intended to be a play with substance.

When May finally made her move she seems to have hoped that the drama of the occasion might somehow act as cover for the difficulty of her position. In the event of it, all the optimism stemming from the ensuing 'agreement' would be lost extremely rapidly. Indeed it would be surrendered over the weekend. But it is worth remembering what was attempted. The political historian Peter Hennessey has been among those to lament that, particularly in the Blair years, the notion of collective rule by the Cabinet has been displaced by sofa government and the whim of the prime minister. After the afternoon's talks, May explained that she had hitherto in her premiership encouraged latitude in her ministers to state their individual views on Brexit, but that things had now moved onto a definitive new phase. In her own triumphant words: 'Agreement on this proposal marks the point where that is no longer the case and collective responsibility is now fully restored'[378]. The broad intention was surely a benign one; it is to be lamented that it would prove illusory. On the other hand, she had shown less appetite for collective rule when she had been more powerful; shackled to the DUP, and surrounded by in-fighting, Cabinet responsibility had become a necessity.

What was the proposal? It posited something along the lines of the relationship which Norway has with the EU: in that country, annual payments are met (and met easily thanks to the country's gargantuan sovereign wealth fund) in exchange for membership of the single market. The country therefore accepts a wide scope of EU rules over which it has no influence. It toils, in Brexiter parlance, in the miserable condition of a 'rule-taker'. It had been an arduous business for May to arrive at this position. After so much build-up, it was always liable to disappoint: the same suggestion, arrived at in 2016, would have met with mockery from people always likely to mock it, but at that point it would not have been suggested by a weak prime minister but a strong one. Besides, what resulted at Chequers was by no means comprehensive: for instance, services – an area which covers around 80 per cent of the UK economy – merited only a cursory mention: its text fondly and blurrily imagined a UK which would retain 'regulatory flexibility' and accept less EU market access. Meanwhile, the facilitated customs arrangement remained confusing to many, and unfeasible to those who understood it. As so often in the May government, the detail was absent because its presence would have flared up emotions: these blanks indicated a government in denial.

There were signs that May guessed the weakness of her position. Certainly, she was anxious to leave nothing to chance: ministers were asked to leave their phones at the door, and a sense of momentousness was aroused in the media. Laura Kuenssberg, the BBC's eyes and ears at these occasions, wrote on her blog: 'Often the hype about a political event is in inverse proportion to the drama of what actually comes to pass. Maybe not this time'.[379] She turned out to be right about this – and in ways she couldn't have foreseen. But what the carefully choreographed day did was to illustrate the limits of theatre in politics when disagreement is so fundamental, and passion surrounding it so intense. Another photograph was released of Theresa May standing before colleagues articulating her plans: Penny Mordaunt, the International Development Secretary, has her arms sceptically folded; David Davis, not known for being good on the detail, frowns at a binder. But May looks confident and assertive – finally conducting the orchestra.

It was all intended to show her absolutely in charge. And indeed for 24 hours or so, she did seem more powerful than at any time since the election. The image of Norway briefly dominated the discourse – that oil-rich and entrepreneurial nation of four million people seemed suddenly a state of affairs which might seriously be emulated by Britain. Perhaps the Brexit boys had been shown a more plausible reality than theirs, and must accordingly fall in line.

But May had misjudged the extent of the opposition. In retrospect, she never could have expected the uncompromising suddenly to find compromise palatable. Over the weekend and into the following week, news came through – hoisted on websites, secreted in phone updates – of the resignations of first David Davis and then of Boris Johnson. These resignations, though lumped together as part of the same narrative, were really conducted for very different reasons. The former was a genuine protest from a man who has never been able to imagine a reality composed of greys. It would have been impossible for him to argue in Brussels a position he couldn't begin to stomach; his successor Dominic Raab would be left to do so instead. Davis had perhaps always been working at cross purposes with May. May had all along been a pragmatist; Davis, an ideologue. May had sought to fudge her true priorities, and had encouraged Davis in a stringent view of reality. The prime minister found in the end that confiscating her Brexit secretary's phone had done little to alter a difference of opinion so wide as to be unbridgeable.

Meanwhile, Johnson's was the exit of a man whose principle consideration was – as it was at the beginning of this book – to appropriate the course of action most likely to lead to his becoming prime minister. Johnson had moved to the right since the Cameron premiership. He had mistaken the approbation he had received from certain quarters as evidence of a more general vindication: many politicians have a tin ear for applause. But this slight hardening of opinion appeared small when set against the vast continuum of his ambition which would always be the chief fact about him.

In the end, the fanfare surrounding the resignations died down reasonably swiftly. Perhaps ministers, dulled by the possession of power, forget how calamitous its loss can be: they think of resignation not as a drop but as a chess move sideways. In that process, they forget that they are losing all the paraphernalia of power by which further moves might be made. Certainly, Johnson would look like a man surprised at his predicament as he was photographed emerging from the foreign office on the day of his resignation. Ambition is always confusing since reality is so complex that it never knows how to attain its object; whereas principle is contained within and suggests a roadmap easily to hand. On the day of his resignation, Johnson was another image of chaos in that chaotic time. By September 2018 he was reduced to writing in the *Daily Telegraph* that the Chequers agreement 'means disaster' for the UK, although Amber Rudd, now a loyal backbencher, was among those to lament the lack of a concrete counter-proposal. But Johnson remained a plausible prime minister in waiting − along with many others − as the leaves began to turn, if one could only overlook the clown contender's marital challenges. Meanwhile, with Michel Barnier refusing to countenance any departure by the UK from the four freedoms, the dreaded words 'no deal' entered the public discourse with greater frequency.

This was how the government looked as it went into the 2018 conference season: uncertain and adrift, lacking sufficient muscularity within itself to reach for truth. It was as if the world had become too opaque, and too likely to inspire contrasting passions, to be properly discussed anymore. The administration of Theresa May had become a blinkered person, prophesying sunshine, while on its brow feeling the first drops of storm.

Then, on September 17th, a sunny day for most of the UK, May appeared on BBC *Panorama*, warning that it was 'her Chequers deal or no deal at all'. Meanwhile, Boris Johnson wrote in the *Daily Telegraph* that attempts to resolve the issue so far were a 'constitutional abomination' and even reached for one of his biggest claims yet, comparing May's efforts to find compromise to 1066. Reported the same day, a BBC survey suggested that most now thought Brexit would have a negative impact; the IMF chimed in that a no-deal Brexit would 'entail costs'. A 'no deal' scenario began to look genuinely likely; there were those in the UK, admittedly of the more easily perturbed frame of mind, already thinking of stockpiling food. And that wasn't all. The Irish border issue was still unsolved, and the European Union – in spite of Michel Barnier's wish to 'de-dramatise the question' – remained a formidable negotiating partner. Throughout it all, like a buffeted cliff, May remained impassive – as we have seen her do throughout this book – determined not to be known, it seemed, whatever the political weather.

ENDNOTES

1 M. Peake, *Titus Groan*, Vintage Books, 1998, p. 98.

2 J. Updike, *Buchanan Dying*, Act II.

3 J. Updike, *Rabbit Redux*, Alfred A. Knopf, 1971, p. 67.

4 C. Marlowe, *Tamburlaine the Great*, Act IV, Scene III.

5 Theresa May launch statement, 30th June 2016.

6 Ibid.

7 This file is licensed under the Creative Commons Attribution-Share Alike 4.0 International license. Author: GingerJesusFMIRL.

8 Suetonius, *Twelve Caesars*. Book II.

9 This image is licensed under the Creative Commons Attribution-Share Alike 3.0 Unported license. Author: Yair Haklai.

10 This image is a work of an employee of the Executive Office of the President of the United States, taken or made as part of that person's official duties. As a work of the U.S. federal government, the image is in the public domain. Author: Pete Souza.

11 Home Office, Creative Commons License.

12 This image is appropriately licensed under Creative Commons License 2.0.

13 This file is licensed under the Creative Commons Attribution 3.0 Unported license. Author: Andrew Burdett.

14 This file is licensed under the Creative Commons Attribution 2.0 Generic license. Author: ukhomeoffice.

15 Theresa May launch statement, 30th June 2016.

16 Ibid.

17 D. Millward, 'Why should I do the hard –?' David Cameron 'told aides he would rather quit than do all the work for his successor', published in *The Telegraph*, 25th June 2016.

18 H. Cole, 'Theresa May: a big beast in kitten heels', published in *The Spectator*, 25th November 2014.

19 This file is licensed under the Creative Commons Attribution 2.0 Generic license. Author: Policy Exchange.

20 Quoted in J. Ellison, 'No small talk, more shoes' published in *The Financial Times*, July 13th 2016.

21 Quoted in K. Rawlinson, 'Michael Gove has 'emotional need to gossip', claims former Boris aide, published in *The Guardian*, 4th July 2016.

22 'Trojan Horse 'plot' schools timeline', published on BBC News, 16th July 2015.

23 'May and Gove in row over extremism in schools', published on BBC News, 4th June 2014.

24 A. Travis, 'Theresa May v Michael Gove: personality clash with a long history', published on *The Guardian*, 2nd July 216.

25 This file is licensed under the Creative Commons Attribution 2.0 Generic license. Author: Think London.

26 B. Johnson, 'If Blair's so good at running the Congo, let him stay there', published in *The Telegraph*, 10th January 2002.

27 Boris Johnson: I will not be the next Tory leader, published in *The Spectator*, 30th June 2016.

28 J. Cowley, 'The May Doctrine', published in *The New Statesman*, 8th February 2017.

29 Transcript of *The Andrew Marr Show*, 4th September 2016.

30 This comes from is an interview published in the *New York Herald*, European Edition, in 1915, when Churchill was the first lord of the Admiralty. It was republished by *The International Herald Tribune* to commemorate the 50th anniversary of Churchill's death on January 24th 2015.

31 This file is licensed under the Creative Commons Attribution-Share Alike 2.0 Generic license. Attribution: Oast House Archive

32 P. Larkin, *Collected Poems*.

33 C. Brown, Break out the Spam, Mabel, we've done it!', published in the *Mail Online*, 28th June 2016.

34 From domestic servants to Prime Minister: The rise and rise of Theresa May's family fortunes, published on findmypast.com, 11th July 2016.

35 Theresa May announcement speech, 30th June 2016.

36 This interview is, somewhat amazingly in a long career, arguably the best source about May and can be listened to in full here: http://www.bbc.co.uk/programmes/b04pr6q9/segments.

37 The words to this hymn were sung by Isaac Watts, and were published originally in 1707.

38 These words are a translation by Edward Caswall of Thomas Aquinas's 13th century words.

39 I have taken my information regarding this sad episode from: J. Atkinson, 'I was in crash that killed PM's Dad', published in *The Sun*, 17th July 2016.

40 R. Mendick, 'Theresa May: the highest achiever of all in the starry, Oxford University geography class of '74', published in *The Telegraph*, 16th July 2016.

41 This file is licensed under the Creative Commons Attribution-Share Alike 3.0 Unported license. Author: iFaqeer.

42 A. Pearson, 'Theresa May interview: 'I probably was Goody Two Shoes at school' published in *The Telegraph*, 21st December 2012.

43 This file is licensed under the Creative Commons Attribution-Share Alike 3.0 Unported license. Author: Sigerson.

44 P. Wright, 'Theresa May's 'Wimbledon set' usurps David Cameron's 'Notting Hill posh boys'', published in *The International Business Times*, 20th July 2016.

45 Hansard, Volume 613, 20th July 2016.

46 D. Laws, *Coalition The Inside Story of the Conservative-Liberal Democrat Coalition* , Biteback Publishing, 2016, p. 251.

47 Tony Blair in the House of Commons, 6th July 1983.

48 David Cameron in the House of Commons, 28th June 2001.

49 S. Coughlan, 'Education, education, education,' published on BBC News, 14th May 2007.

50 I am indebted here to D. Gillard, 'Axes to Grind: the first five years of Blair's academies' published www.educationengland.org.uk in April 2007.

51 Theresa May in the House of Commons, June 2nd 1997.

52 Theresa May speech at the Conservative Party Conference, October 2002.

53 Ibid.

54 Y. Cooper, 'Theresa May helped to divide Britain. She won't heal it', published in *The Guardian*, 7th July 2016.

55 MPs expenses: the 12 worst claims, published in *The Mirror*, 5th February 2010.

56 D. Summers and A. Topping, 'MPs' expenses: the good, the bad and the ugly' published in *The Guardian*, May 11th 2009.

57 P. Krugman, 'Does Greece need more austerity?', published in *The New York Times*, 19th June, 2015.

58 T. Lee and Z. Beauchamph, 'Brexit: 9 questions you were too embarrassed to ask', published in *Vox*, June 25th 2016.

59 Theresa May announcement speech.

60 M. Gilbert, *Churchill: A life*, Two Volume Set, Folio Society, Volume 1, p. 253.

61 Ibid, p. 243.

62 This work is in the public domain in its country of origin and other countries and areas where the copyright term is the author's life plus 70 years or less.

63 This file is licensed under the Creative Commons Attribution-Share Alike 3.0 Unported license. Source: Dutch National Archives, The Hague, Fotocollectie Algemeen Nederlands Persbureau (ANeFo), 1945-1989, Nummer toegang 2.24.01.05 Bestanddeelnummer 929-0833

64 L. Muchowiecka, 'The end of multiculturalism? Immigration and Integration in Germany and the Uniteed Kingdom', published in *Inquiries Journal*, Vol 5., No. 6, 2013.

65 A. Johnson, 'Don't know your debts from your deficits? You're not alone', published in *The Independent*, 26th August 2012.

66 G. Osborne, speech to the Conservative Party conference, 3rd October 2011.

67 P. Krugman, 'Debt is good for the economy', published in *The New York Times*, 21st August 2015.

68 Ibid.

69 May's first prime ministers' questions, Hansard, 20 July 2016, Volume 613.

70 'Police 'must do more' despite cuts - home secretary', published on BBC News, 29th June 2010.

71 'J. Boxell, May on collision course with police', published in *The Financial Times*, June 29th 2010.

72 Home office announcement, 'Crime down by more than 10% under coalition government', 23rd January 2014.

73 Ibid.

74 D. Barrett, 'Violent crime jumps 27 per cent in new figures released by the Office for National Statistics' published *in The Telegrap*h, 22nd January 2016.

75 Home office announcement, 'Crime down by more than 10% under coalition government', 23rd January 2014.

76 'Effective communication with government is key for moving policing forward' published by the Police Federation, 22nd January 2016.

77 Home Office, Policing in the 21st Century: Reconnecting police and the people, presented to Parliament by the Secretary of State for the Home Department by Command of Her Majesty July 2010.

78 A. Travis, 'Scrap police and crime commissioners, say former Labour home secretaries' published in *The Guardian*, 13th February 2014.

79 A. Travis, 'Government critics fear low turnout in police commissioner elections', published in *The Guardian*, 3rd May 2016.

80 T.Blair, *A Journey*, 2010, Random House, p. 633.

81 This remit can be found at: www.nationalcrimeagency.gov.uk/about-us/what-we-do.

82 Transcript from *The Andrew Marr Show*, 6th October 2013.

83 S. Jenkins, 'A British FBI has got no chance against London's very own KGB', published in *The Guardian*, May 10th 2012.

84 R. Evans and V. Dodd, 'Stephen Lawrence case: Theresa May orders inquiry into police spies', published in *The Guardian*, March 6th 2014.

85 Statement from the new Prime Minister Theresa May, 13th July 2016.

86 Final Report of Inquiry by Lord Justice Taylor into the Hillsborough Stadium Disaster; Text submitted to the Home Secretary 19 January 1989, p. 50.

87 T. May, Speech to the Police Federation, 2016.

88 V. Dodd, 'UK police forces 'still abusing stop-and-search powers', published in *The Guardian*, 11th February 2016.

89 'A defining moment for Theresa May and the police', published in *The Telegraph*, 23rd May 2014.

90 Z. Williams, 'Go home or face arrest.' By whom – the minister?' published in *The Guardian*, 27th July 2013.

91 Ibid.

92 J. Legge, 'Vince Cable: 'Go home' poster campaign aimed at illegal immigrants is 'stupid and offensive', published in *The Independent*, 28th July 2013.

93 Blair, *A Journey*, p. 205.

94 Dustmann, C. and Casanova, M. and Fertig, M. and Preston, I. and Schmidt, C.M. (2003) The impact of EU enlargement on migration flows. (Home Office Online Report 25/03). Research Development and Statistics Directorate, Home Office: London, UK.

95 N. Watt and P. Wintour, 'How immigration came to haunt Labour: the inside story' published in *The Guardian*, 24th March 2015.

96 MIGRATION: AN ECONOMIC AND SOCIAL ANALYSIS [OCTOBER 2000] A joint research study by the Home Office Economics and Resource Analysis Unit and the Cabinet Office Performance and Innovation Unit.

97 'At-a-glance: Conservative manifesto', published on BBC News, 13 April 2010.

98 Net migration statistics for year ending March 016, published by Migration Watch UK.

99 'Theresa May: I won't resign over UK Border Agency row,' published on BBC News, 8th November 2011.

100 'UK Border Agency told to relax passport checks – full documents' published in *The Guardian*, 7th November 2011.

101 Home Office Identity and Passport Service, Annual Report and Accounts 2012-13.

102 M. Hillier, 'The passport fiasco was easily avoided – so why the delays, Theresa May?' published in *The Guardian*, 13th June 2014.

103 S. Hilton, 'We can cut immigration levels by making every Briton employable' published in *The Telegraph*, 18th September 2016.

104 T. May, A Beacon of Hope, delivered to the Conservative Party conference, 6th October 2015.

105 Home Office, Impacts of migration on UK native employment: An analytical review of the evidence (Ciaran Devlin and Olivia Bolt, Department for Business, Innovation and Skills Dhiren Patel, David Harding and Ishtiaq Hussain, Home Office), published in March 2014.

106 J.Kirkup, 'Theresa May's immigration speech is dangerous and factually wrong', published in *The Telegraph*, 6th October 2015.

107 Tennyson, 'Dark House', from *In Memoriam*.

108 *G. McKinnon v. Government of the USA Secretary of State for the Home Department*, [2007] EWHC 762 (Admin) Case No: CO/5897/2006.

109 House of Commons Home Affairs Committee, *The US-UK Extradition Treaty Twentieth Report of Session* 2010–12.

110 The US-UK extradition treaty: twentieth report of session 2010-12, Volume 1, p. 6.

111 A. Johnson, 'Theresa May took the easy way out over Gary McKinnon', published in *The Telegraph*, 18th October 2012.

112 'Gary McKinnon extradition to US blocked by Theresa May', published on *BBC News*, 16th October 2012.

113 Ibid.

114 W. Hague, 'Meticulous, steely, and loyal to her friends: Theresa May is the perfect person to lead us out of the EU', published in *The Telegraph*, 11th July 2016.

115 R. Creswell and B. Haykel, 'Battle Lines: Want to understand the jihadis? Read their poetry', published in The New Yorker, June 8th and 15th, 2015.

116 Ibid.

117 This file is licensed under the Creative Commons Attribution 2.0 Generic license. Author: UK Home Office.

118 M. Vermuelen, 'UK House of Lords rules that Abu Qatada can be deported with diplomatic assurances to Jordan', published on *legallift.com*, 18th February, 2009.

119 B. Johnson, 'On top of everything else, Abu Qatada costs us a small fortune' published in *The Telegraph*, 13th February 2012.

120 Theresa May's 2011 conference speech, delivered 4th October 2011.

121 G. Heffer, 'Tory MP: Remaining in EU will see Brussels handed control of our criminal courts' published in *The Express*, May 17th 2016

122 Quoted in G. Heffer, 'Tory MP: Remaining in EU will see Brussels handed control of our criminal courts', published in *The Express*, May 17th 2016.

123 J. Blanchard, 'Theresa May breaks pledge to hold vote on European Arrest Warrant' published in The Mirror, 11th November 2014.

124 This work is in the public domain in its country of origin and other countries and areas where the copyright term is the author's life plus 100 years or less.

125 Home Office policy paper, Modern slavery strategy, published on 29th November 2014.

126 This is from the entry in relation to the UK on www.globalslaveryindex.org.

127 National Crime Agency, *National Referral Mechanism Statistics – End of Year Summary 2014*, (National Crime Agency, January 2015), p. 2

128 Hansard, 4 Nov 2014 : Column 789.

129 Ibid.

130 S. Connolly, 'Theresa May has 'failed' victims of child slavery and 'should be ashamed', published in *The Mirror*, 31st July 2016.

131 'Theresa May pledges £33m boost for fight against slavery in Britain' published in The Guardian, 31st July 2016.

132 Hansard, 4 Nov 2014 : Column 789.

133 www.globalslaveryindex.org.

134 Ibid.

135 Establishing Britain as a world leader in the fight against modern slavery Report of the Modern Slavery Bill Evidence Review Baroness Butler-Sloss, Frank Field MP (Chair) and Sir John Randall MP.

136 Theresa May pledges £33m boost for fight against slavery in Britain' published in The Guardian, 31st July 2016.

137 Ibid.

138 2017 UK Annual Report on Modern Slavery, p. 4

139 Hansard, 4 Nov 2014 : Column 789.

140 S. Connolly, 'Theresa May announces new crackdown on modern slavery' published in *The Independent*, 30th July 2016.

141 This file is licensed under the Creative Commons Attribution 2.0 Generic license. Photographer: GCHQ/Crown Copyright

142 D. Laws, *Coalition*, p.251.

143 Ibid.

144 *Liberty and Security in a Changing World*, Report and Recommendations of The President's Review Group on Intelligence and Communications Technologies, 12 December 2013.

145 Remarks by PM David Cameron, quoted in J. Ball, 'Cameron wants to ban encryption – he can say goodbye to digital Britain', published in *The Guardian*, 13th January 2015.

146 Transcript of *The Andrew Marr Show*, 1st November 2015.

147 K. Bamber, 'Why we need real judicial sign-off in the Investigatory Powers Bill', published on www.liberty-human-rights.org.uk, 9th December 2015.

148 Oral statement to Parliament, Home Secretary: Publication of draft Investigatory Powers Bill, 4th November 2015.

149 G. Eaton, 'Labour demands stronger safeguards in Investigatory Powers Bill', published in *The New Statesman*, 8th November 2015.

150 'Question of the fortnight: will the Snoopers' Charter turn UK into a police state?', published in *Computer UK*, 22nd June 2016.

151 Oral statement to Parliament, Home Secretary: Publication of draft Investigatory Powers Bill, 4th November 2015.

152 Remarks by Prime Minister David Cameron, 20th February 2016.

153 PM speech on the UK's strength and security in the EU: 9 May 2016.

154 T. Ross, 'Boris Johnson: The EU wants a superstate, just as Hitler did', published in *The Telegraph*, 15th May 2016.

155 Jo Cox MP dead after shooting attack, published on BBC News, published on 16th June 2016.

156 Mr Winston Churchill speaking in Zurich 19th September 1946.

157 Churchill letter to Turkish President Ismet İnönü in 1943.

158 This file is licensed under the Creative Commons Attribution-Share Alike 3.0 Germany license.Flag of Germany.svg. Attribution: Bundesarchiv, Bild 183-19000-2453 / CC-BY-SA 3.0.

159 Text of the Treaty of London, 1949.

160 Robert Schuman, speaking in Strasbourg, 16 May 1949.

161 Factsheet on the European Commission published on europa.eu.

162 Treaty establishing the European Economic Community, EEC Treaty.

163 Edward Heath, *The Course of My Life* (Hodder and Stoughton, 1998), p. 214.

Opening statement at the United Kingdom application to join the EEC in Paris, 10 October 1961.

164 C. Moore, 'Ted Heath failed as both a man and a politician, published in *The Telegraph*, 20th June 2010.

165 Quoted in M. Cockerel, EU referendum... lessons from 1975, 23rd February 2016.

166 *Against the Tide. Diaries 1973-1976* (London: Hutchinson, 1989), pp. 346-347.

167 Quoted in M. Cockerel, EU referendum... lessons from 1975, 23rd February 2016.

168 David Cameron's speech to the 2006 Conservative Party conference in Bournemouth.

169 Quoted in C. Moore, *Margaret Thatcher: The Authorized Biography, Volume One: Not For Turning*, Penguin, 2014 (2nd. Ed) p. 306.

170 'The UK's membership fee' published on fullfact.org, 25th February 2016.

171 This documentary can still be viewed in full on BBC iPlayer at time of writing.

172 M. Fletcher, 'Boris Johnson peddled absurd EU myths – and our disgraceful press followed his lead', published in *The New Statesman*, 1st July 2016.

173 R. Roberts, 'How one man changed how British politicians felt about Europe – forever', published in *The New Statesman*, 29th February 2016.

174 Howe quotes Churchill as saying; 'It is also possible and not less agreeable to regard this sacrifice or merger of national sovereignty as the gradual assumption by all the nations concerned of that larger sovereignty which can alone protect their diverse and distinctive customs and characteristics and their national traditions.'

175 Geoffrey Howe resignation speech in House of Commons, 13th November 1990.

176 My figures for this paragraph are taken from: http://www.ukpolitical.info/european-parliament-election-turnout.htm.

177 S. Bowers, 'Jean-Claude Juncker can't shake off Luxembourg's tax controversy', published in *The Guardian*, 14th December 2014.

178 Question Time, 8th July 2016.

179 C. Michallon, 'Is this the tacky airport restaurant where Brexit began over a cheap pizza slice? Fateful decision to hold vote was 'reached in Chicago O'Hare pizzeria' while David Cameron waited for flight' published in *The Daily Mail*, 25th June 2016.

180 This file is licensed under the Creative Commons Attribution-Share Alike 3.0 Unported license. Source: Diliff.

181 M. Crick, 'Nigel Farage schooldays letter reveals concerns over racism' published on channel4.com, 19th September 2013.

182 Remarks of Nigel Farage to European Parliament, 25th February 2010.

183 M. D'Ancona, 'The 'bad boys of Brexit' have some big questions to answer', published in *The Guardian*, 10th June, 2018.

184 Quoted in 'David Cameron pledges EU referendum if Conservatives win next election', published on www.rte.ie, January 24th 2013.

185 PM statement following European Council meeting: 19 February 2016.

186 T. Helm, 'Brexit: EU considers migration 'emergency brake' for UK for up to seven years' published in *The Observer*, 24th July 2016.

187 'Reality Check: Will the UK pay for future euro bailouts?' published on BBC News, 5th June 2016.

188 S. Booth, 'What did the UK achieve in its EU renegotiation?' published on openeurope.org.uk, 21st February 2016.

189 Draft European Council Directive on Competitiveness, published on politico.eu.

190 P. Foster, 'EU deal: What David Cameron asked for... and what he actually got', published in *The Telegraph*, 14th June 2016.

191 R. Bahr, 'How Remain failed: the inside story of a doomed campaign' published in *The Guardian*, 5th July 2016.

192 HM Treasury Analysis: the long-term economic impact of EU membership and the alternatives, April 2016.

193 Quoted in P. Inman, 'Mervyn King: Treasury's exaggerated Brexit claims backfired' published in *The Guardian*, 27th June 2016.

194 T. Brown, 'Beware Boris Johnson: The Power of the Cunning Clown,' published in *The Daily Beast*, 27th June 2016.

195 Ibid.

196 This file is licensed under the Creative Commons Attribution-Share Alike 4.0 International license. Author: Philafrenzy.

197 P. Hitchens, 'I want Jo's killer to hang. The Left want to use him for propaganda', published in the *Daily Mail*, 26th November, 216.

198 D. Aaronovitch, 'Dog whistle politics can be a deadly game,' published in *The Times*, November 24th 2016.

199 C. Mortimer, 'Brexit caused lasting rise in hate crime, new figures show', published in *The Independent*, published Thursday 8th September 2016.

200 J. Latter, 'Post-Brexit focus groups: No regret from Leavers', published on *yougov. co.uk*, August 11th 2016.

201 F. Boyle, 'Theresa May has vowed to unite Britain – my guess is against the poor', published in *The Guardian*, 12th July 2016.

202 W.B. Yeats, 'Prayer for My Daughter'.

203 The Marsellaise. The song was written in 1792 by Claude Joseph Rouget de Lisle in Strasbourg.

204 W. Shakespeare, *The Oxford Shakespeare, The Complete Works*, (2ⁿᵈ ed. Edited by J. Jowett, W. Montgomery, G. Taylor, and S. Wells'. Thomas More, Scene 6, p. 821.

205 Ibid.

206 This work is in the public domain in its country of origin and other countries and areas where the copyright term is the author's life plus 100 years or less.

207 E. Powell, 20 April 1968 address to the General Meeting of the West Midlands Area Conservative Political Centre

208 C. Brown, 'Tony Blair: A Conference Speech' published originally on *The Daily Mail*, republished on *parodies.org*.

209 This file is licensed under the Creative Commons Attribution-Share Alike 3.0 Unported license. Author: Allan Warr.

210 Petition: EU Referendum Rules triggering a 2nd EU Referendum. The petition was eventually debated on 5ᵗʰ September 2016.

211 B. Johnson, 'I cannot stress too much that Britain is part of Europe – and always will be', published in *The Telegraph*, 26ᵗʰ June 2016.

212 Ian Hislop, remarks on *Question Time,* 8ᵗʰ July 2016.

213 Z. Smith, 'Fences: A Brexit Diary', published in *The New York Review of Books*, 18ᵗʰ August 2016.

214 J. Lanchester, 'Brexit Blues', first published in *The London Review of Books*, 28ᵗʰ July

215 Z. Williams, 'Think the north and the poor caused Brexit? Think again' published in *The Guardian*, 7ᵗʰ August 2016.

216 A, Chaudhuri, Why the romance of Brexit bloomed in Philip Larkin's industrial suburbia', published in *The Guardian*, 8ᵗʰ August 2016.

217 Larkin, *Whitsun Weddings*, 1964.

218 Letter from Philip Larkin to Kingsley Amis, July 1946.

219.Euripides, *The Bacchae and Other Plays*, trans. P. Vellacott, Penguin Classics (1953), p.189.

220 'How the United Kingdom voted and why', published on lordashcroftpolls.com, June 2016.

221 R. Sylvester, 'I'm sure Theresa will be really sad that she doesn't have children', published in The Times, July 9ᵗʰ 2016.

222 T. Sculthorpe and M. Dathan, 'New Tory leader Theresa May vows to make a 'better Britain' as she prepares to move into Downing Street on WEDNESDAY after Andrea Leadsom quits the race for No 10,' published in *The Daily Mail*, 12ᵗʰ July 2016.

223 V. Woolf, *Mrs Dalloway*, Penguin Classics, (2000) p. 9.

224 Statement from the new Prime Minister Theresa May, 13ᵗʰ July 2016.

225 This work is in the public domain in its country of origin and other countries and areas where the copyright term is the author's life plus 70 years or less. Author: Cornelius Jabez Hughes, British (1819 - 1884, London, England London, England)

226 B. Disraeli, *Sybil*, first published in 1845, Oxford World Classics, p. 88.

227 K. Marx and F. Engels, *The Communist Manifesto*, 1848.

228 G.K Chesterton, *Orthodoxy*, CreateSpace Independent Publishing Platform, (2015) p. 9

229 B. Disraeli, *Coningsby*, 1844, p. 123.

230 N. Watt, 'David Cameron makes leaner state a permanent goal' published in *The Guardian*, 12ᵗʰ November 2013.

231 Statement from the new Prime Minister Theresa May, 13ᵗʰ July 2016.

232 This work is from the George Grantham Bain collection at the Library of Congress. According to the library, there are no known copyright restrictions on the use of this work. Bain News Service, publisher.

233 Quoted in D. Dilks, *Neville Chamberlain, Vol I: Pioneering and reform 1869-1929*. Cambridge University Press, p. 15

234 N. Timothy, 'Our Joe. It is time for the Conservative Party to remember its historical debt to Radical Joe Chamberlain', published on *Conservative Home*, December 24ᵗʰ 2012.

235 'Theresa May remains 'absolutely committed' to HS2 rail link', published in *The Guardian*, 29ᵗʰ April 2017.

236 Ibid.

237 T.S Eliot, 'East Coker' from *Four Quartets* (1943).

238 *This Week*, 14ᵗʰ July 2016.

239 From Philip Hammond's entry on www.theyworkforyou.com.

240 BBC Great Debate, 22ⁿᵈ June 2016.

241 Migration Statistics Quarterly Report, November 2017-12-30.

242 'In the Map Room with Theresa May', published in *The Economist*, 23ʳᵈ July 2016.

243 Quoted in T. Ross, ''Theresa May's Night of the Long Knives' published in *The Telegraph*, 16ᵗʰ July 2016.

244 J. Doward, 'Liz Truss abandons Gove's plan for problem-solving courts', published in *The Guardian*, 21ˢᵗ August 2016.

245 G. Monbiot, 'The climate crisis is already here – but no one's telling us' published in *The Guardian*, 3rd August 2016.

246 B. Quinn, 'UK development minister challenged over 'wasted aid' claim' published in *The Guardian*, 14th September 2016.

247 EU Development Assistance - International Development Committee – Sixteenth Report. The published report was ordered by the House of Commons to be printed 17 April 2012.

248 Quoted in A. Hawken, 'Bitter Cabinet feud between Boris and Fox as trade secretary tells Theresa May to break up the Foreign Office', published in *The Daily Mail*, 14th August 2016.

249 Last prime ministers' questions of David Cameron, 13th July 2016.

250 Article 50 of the Lisbon Treaty.

251 This comes from a fact sheet on http://www.consilium.europa.eu/.

252 J. Freedland, 'Whether leavers like it or not, Europe has a say on how Brexit will happen', published in *The Guardian*, 10th August 2016.

253 P. Wintour, 'UK officials seek draft agreements with EU before triggering article 50', published in *The Guardian*, 22nd July 2016.

254 Guillaume Van der Loo and Steven Blockmans, The Impact of Brexit on the EU's International Agreements, published on CEPS, Friday, 15 July 2016.

255 Robert Peston Facebook post, 16th August 2016.

256 I. Birrell, 'Theresa May's Swiss holiday will show her just how bad Brexit could be', published in *The Guardian*, 15th August 2016.

257 'Sterling down as Article 50 speculation resurfaces', published in *The Financial Times*, 19th August 2016.

258 D. Allen Green, 'Brexit means Brexit – but in reality it's a long time away', published in *The Evening Standard*, 8th August 2016.

259 'Legislating for Brexit: the Great Repeal Bill,' House of Commons Library, published 2nd May 2017.

260 I have been reliant here on Brexit - UK and EU legal framework published by Norton Rose Fulbright, June 2016.

261 R. Shrimsley, 'I sacrificed my safety. MPs walked away,' published in the *Financial Times*, 8the April 2016

262 'House of Lords could delay Brexit, peer claims', published on BBC News, 1st August 2016.

263 G. Osborne's post-Brexit statement, published on politicshome.com on 27th June 2016.

264 These figures come from the Office of National Statistics.

265 This is taken from www.economicshelp.org 'Problems of a current account deficit'.

266 P. Collinson and R. Jones, 'The post-Brexit pound – how sterling's fall affects you and the UK economy', published in *The Guardian*, 19th August 2016.

267 Figure taken from a parliamentary briefing: 'Financial services: contribution to the UK economy' published by the House of Commons Library, April 25th 2018

268 T. May, 'We can make Britain a country that works for everyone,' delivered in Birmingham to launch her national campaign on 11th July 2016.

269 For a description of some of the pitfalls of private equity see C. Jackson, 'Is Private Equity such a Sure Thing?' published on Spears online, 16th March 2018.

270 R. Peston, Facebook post, 18th July 2016.

271 Office for National Statistics, Retail sales in Great Britain: Aug 2016.

272 Office for National Statistics, Assessment of the UK post-referendum economy: September 2016.

273 L. Elliott, 'What cost Brexit? Soon we'll know', published in *The Guardian*, 14th August 2016.

274 P. Krugman, 'Still confused about Brexit macroeconomics?', published in *The New York Times*, 12th July 2016.

275 'Lidl to pay recommended living wage' published on BBC News, 18th September 2015.

276 The Northern Powerhouse: One Agenda, One Economy, One North A report on the Northern Transport Strategy, March 2015.

277 R. Harrabin, 'Five issues that will shape the Northern Powerhouse', published on BBC News, 22nd February 2016.

278 H. Fearn, 'Finally Theresa May has done what David Cameron never had the stomach for – cracking down on tax avoidance' published on The Independent, 17th August 2016.

279 C. Jackson, 'Interview with Paul Abberley,' published in *Spear's* magazine, Issue 61, Jan/Feb 2018.

280 This figure comes from the IMF's April Fiscal Monitor.

281 Poll published on *yougov.co.uk* on 30th July 2016.

282 Referendum results on BBC News.

283 D. Torrance, 'Just why is the SNP so Europhile?' published on Think Scotland, undated.

284 L. Brooks, 'Nicola Sturgeon: Scottish parliament could block Brexit' published in *The Guardian*, 26th June 2016.

285 Ibid.

286 S. Johnson, Nicola Sturgeon snubbed by EU member states including Germany', published in *The Telegraph*, 29th June 2016.

287 S. Jenkins, 'Stop lecturing the Scots. They want freedom, not wealth', published in *The Guardian*, 26th November 2013.

288 E. Malcolm, 'May meeting leaves Sturgeon short of options', published in *The Scotsman*, 16th July 2016.

289 'May says won't trigger Article 50 until have UK-wide approach' published on *Reuters* 15th July 2016.

290 'Brexit: PM is 'willing to listen to options' on Scotland', published on BBC News, 15th July 2016.

291 S. Douglas-Scott, 'British withdrawal from the EU: an existential threat to the United Kingdom?' published by http://www.centreonconstitutionalchange.ac.uk/.

292 Quoted in 'Major and Blair say an EU exit could split the UK' in BBC News, 9th June 2016.

293 J. Powell, 'The Irish border question heralds the end of Brexit', published in the *Financial Times*, 11TH June 2018.

294 R. Ruparel, 'How would Brexit impact Ireland?', published on openeurope.org. uk, 15th April 2015.

295 'How would Brexit impact Ireland?' published on irishforeurope.org.

296 Remarks made to the author in an interview in November 2017.

297 F. Connolly, 'Brexit: Should we stay or should we go?' published on New Law Journal on 16 June 2016.

298 Quoted in 'Theresa May on NI post-Brexit: 'No-one wants return to borders of the past' published on BBC News, 2th July 2016.

299 Johnson's remarks were reported in 'Explosive Leaked Recording Reveals Boris Johnson's Private Views About Britain's Foreign Policy' by Alex Spence published in BuzzFeed on 7th June 2018.

300 R. Reed, 'Max-fac' is an idiotic idea that will bankrupt British businesses' published in the *Guardian*, 24th May 2018.

301 Quoted in P. Magnus, *Edmund Burke*, p. 276, John Murray, 1939.

302 'EU referendum: Welsh voters back Brexit' published on BBC News, 24th June 2016.

303 R. Wyn Jones, 'Why did Wales shoot itself in the foot in this referendum?' published in *The Guardian*, 27th June 2016.

304 Quoted in 'South Wales Metro upgrade 'ruled out' for some valley lines, published on bbcnews.co.uk on 7th March 2018.

305 L. Bours, 'Britain's NHS can't survive staying in the European Union', published in *The Telegraph*, 21st March 2016.

306 Quoted in 'Immigration rules for non-EU doctors and nurses 'softened'', published on Skynew.com, 14th June 2018.

307 National Audit Office, 'Managing the supply of NHS clinical staff in England' published on 5th February 2016.

308 List of Registered Medical Practitioners – statistics published on the website of the General Medical Council.

309 Health and Social Care Information Centre 2015; Skills for Care 2016

310 I have been helped in writing this passage and by H. McKenna, 'Five big issues for health and social care after the Brexit vote', published on *The King's Fund*, 30th June 2016.

311 Steventon A, Bardsley M., 'Use of secondary care in England by international immigrants.' J Health Serv Res Policy. 2011 Apr;16(2):90-4.

312 J. Hanefeld, D. Horsfall, N.Lunt, Richard Smith, 'Medical Tourism: A Cost or Benefit to the NHS?' first published on http://dx.doi.org/10.1371/journal.pone.0070406, on October 24th 2013.

313 Remarks by Michel Barnier at the Centre for European Reform, 20th November 2017.

314 A. Bevan, *In Place of Fear A Free Health Service*, 1952, Kessinger Publishing (2010), Chapter 6.

315 This is taken from the 'History' tab on the NHS website.

316 R. Tallis, 'End of the NHS?', published in *The Times Literary Supplement*, 7th September 2016.

317 N. Triggle, 'NHS privatisation: Why the fuss?', published on BBC News, 20th February 2015.

318 Question: Will 'Any Qualified Provider' lead to privatisation of the NHS, with private companies cherry picking the easiest cases and services?, from *The National Archives*, published 30th March 2011.

319 R. Tallis, 'End of the NHS?', published in *The Times Literary Supplement*, 7th September 2016.

320 B. Cooper, 'How the EU is making NHS privatisation permanent', published in *The New Statesman*, 2nd December 2013.

321 Quoted in J. Ashley, 'Theresa May's climbdown on obesity is her first big mistake,' published in *The Guardian*, 19th August 2016.

322 Quoted in Jeremy Hunt is controversial appointment as health secretary, published in the *Daily Telegraph*, 4ᵗʰ September 2012.

323 I. Sample, 'UK scientists dropped from EU projects because of post-Brexit funding fears', published in *The Guardian*, 12ᵗʰ July 2016.

324 Ibid.

325 H. Jones, 'What does Brexit mean for students? We answer your FAQs', published in *The Guardian*, 12ᵗʰ July 2016.

326 'What does the Brexit mean for education?' published on www.eliteeducationgroup.co.uk, undated.

327 S. Moss, 'My laboratory would fall apart if Britain left the EU', published in *The Guardian*, 28ᵗʰ August 2015.

328 H. Jones, 'What does Brexit mean for students? We answer your FAQs', published in *The Guardian*, 12ᵗʰ July 2016.

329 H. Stewart and P. Walker, 'Theresa May to end ban on new grammar schools', published in *The Guardian*, 9ᵗʰ September 2016.

330 'Theresa May urges police commissioners to open free schools for 'troubled children', published in Schools Week Reporter, February 4ᵗʰ 2016.

331 From Brown's essay in *Tactical Reading, A Snappy Guide to the Snap Election*, Eyewear, 2016. p. 106

332 A. Adonis, 'Three lessons for Mr Gove,' published in *The Spectator*, June 2016.

333 G. Eaton, 'Theresa May's education revolution means more than just new grammar schools', published in *The New Statesman*, 9ᵗʰ September 2016.

334 Ibid.

335 'Brexit makes it harder to tackle climate change,' published in *The Telegraph*, June 29ᵗʰ 2016.

336 C. Lucas and J. Aston, 'If we're to win the climate struggle, we must remain in Europe,' published *in The Guardian*, 12ᵗʰ June 2016.

337 Text of 2015 Paris Agreement between 197 countries on climate change within the United Nations Framework Convention on Climate Change.

338 T. May, remarks to the United Nations, on 20ᵗʰ September 2016.

339 S. Lowe, 'What has the EU done for nature?', published on *Friends of the Earth*, 7ᵗʰ February 2016.

340 G. Monbiot, 'I'm starting to hate the EU. But I will vote to stay in,' published in *The Guardian*, 10ᵗʰ February 2016.

341 G. Monbiot, 'These Brexiters will grind our environment into the dust', published in *The Guardian*, 20 July 2016.

342 'I don't want UK to be at forefront of tackling climate change, says Osborne', published in *The Guardian*, 28th September 2013.

343 S. Stefanini, '5 ways Brexit will transform energy and climate', published on *politico. eu*, 24th June 2016.

344 Quoted in E. King, 'Nigel Farage on climate change in his own words', published on climatechangenews.com, 11th March 2011.

345 I am grateful here for the assistance of this Clifford Chance briefing note: 'Brexit - What will happen to Environmental & Climate Change Law?', published on the firm's website in April 2016.

346 'Households could get fracking payments under government plans', published on BBC News, 7th August 2016.

347 This image was taken from the Geograph project collection. See this photograph's page on the Geograph website for the photographer's contact details. The copyright on this image is owned by Richard Baker and is licensed for reuse under the Creative Commons Attribution-ShareAlike 2.0 license.

348 T. Ross, 'Hinkley Point nuclear deal: Theresa May demanded national security checks on Chinese investors, says Vince Cable', published in *The Telegraph*, 30th July 2016.

349 R. Mason and T. Macalister, 'Theresa May could face Hinkley Point C nuclear row at G20 meeting with Xi Jinping', published in *The Guardian*, 3rd September 2016.

350 A. Asthana, 'Theresa May reassures Xi Jinping over UK-China relations' published in *The Guardian*, 16th August 2016.

351 'Hinkley Point nuclear plant delay 'bonkers' says union', published in BBC News, 29th July 2016.

352 Quoted in 'A flashback to all the times Theresa May said a snap election was a terrible idea because it would cause 'instability'', published in *The New Statesman*, April 2017.

353 M. Weaver, 'The many times Theresa May ruled out a general election', published in *The Guardian*, Tuesday 18th April 2017.

354 W. Shakespeare, *Macbeth*, Act IV, Scene 1.

355 Published on ComRes.com, 2nd November 2016.

356 D. Brindle, Theresa May's U-turn is a chance to rethink social care, published in *The Guardian*, 23rd May 2017.

357 Steffen Rehm has released this image worldwide into the public domain.

358 J. Gleick, 'Fractal Vision', published in the *New York Times* on 26th December 2016.

359 Ibid.

360 This work has been released into the public domain by its author, Eequor. This applies worldwide.

361 K. Popper, *The Logic of Scientific Discovery*, first translated into English in 1959.

362 R. Niebuhr, 'The Children of Light and the Children of Darkness', published in *Major Works on Religion and Politics*, published by Library of America, 2015, p. 451

363 Eckerman, *Conversations with Goethe*, epr. North Point Press, 1994. p. 132

364 R. Niebuhr, 'The Children of Light and the Children of Darkness', published in *Major Works on Religion and Politics*, published by Library of America, 2015, p. 451

365 This file is licensed under the Creative Commons Attribution 4.0 International license. Author: Natalie Oxford

367 N. Watt, 'David Cameron pledges to tackle 'health and safety monster' published in *The Guardian*

368 Quoted in PM criticised for failing to meet Grenfell Tower fire survivors, published on Skynews.com, Friday 16th June, 2017.

369 Quoted in London Fire: Queen reflects on 'sombre national mood' published on bbc.oc.uk, 17th June 2017.

370 B. Okri, 'Grenfell Tower, June, 2017', published in the *Financial Times,* 23rd June 2017

371 Remarks of John Major reported in 'John Major warns deal with DUP could threaten 'fragile' Northern Ireland peace process', published in the *Evening Standard*, 13th June 2017.

372 Quoted in N. Hopkins 'Amber Rudd letter to PM reveals 'ambitious but deliverable' removals target,' published in the *Guardian*, 29th April 2018.

373 Quoted in, 'Home Secretary Rudd resists calls to quit, apologises for immigration policy error' published on reuters.com, 27th April 2018.

374 May's remarks at the G7 press conference in Quebec, 10th June 2018.

375 T. Stoppard, *Jumpers*, 1972, Act 2, published by Faber.

376 William Gladstone letter to Catherine Gladstone (12 October 1845), quoted in John Morley, *The Life of Wiliam Ewart Gladstone: Volume I* (London: Macmillan, 1903), p. 383.

377 Quoted in 'Inside the Chequers talks', published on itv.com, 6th July 2018

378 Quoted in G. Parker and J. Pickard, 'Theresa May restores cabinet collective responsibility' published in the Financial Times, July 7th 2018.

379 L .Kuennsberg, 'A dramatic day in store at Chequers', published on the BBC 6th July 2018.

ACKNOWLEDGEMENTS

A book like this could only have been written by a writer confident that he has the backing of his publisher. My thanks therefore go to Dr. Todd Swift who has leant his extraordinary editorial energies and boundless passion for books to a work which other publishers would have avoided. I am always mindful with Todd that any time he takes in editing me is time stolen from his composing the contemporary poetry I really want to read. I thank him for his friendship and for his guidance with the text these past years: let it be registered here in writing that I owe him an excellent lunch.

Nor would this book have been possible without the many kindnesses and stylistic touches of Edwin Smet, who has now designed three books of mine. This one asked more of him than just skill; it also asked for patience, and grace under pressure. Edwin is the sort of man who goes beyond the call of duty for you and then refuses to tell you what his favourite drink is, thus denying you the possibility of sending him a crate. But he has my email if he is ever thirsty.

At times, this book pushed us all to the limit. To take current events and turn them into something fixed, but which still has the movement of life in it, is to enter into a daily war with the news cycle which I would not recommend. Everything that happens to your subject must be wrested from that day's headlines and made to fit the whole. The only way to do that is to make sure you have a structure both plastic and firm – a thing with both roominess and parameters. I have said many times during the composition of these pages that my next book will be about someone safely dead. But I will admit that there is an addiction at work, and that I sometimes catch myself jotting down notes for Volume II.

This is a book about chance and power. But everything comes down in the end in politics to individual happiness, which can in itself be reduced to that other large noun – love. I will finish then by saying to my wife Jade, and to my son Beau, that their love is what pushed this book over the line. I have always been a little alarmed by that remark by José Martí – always quoted with approval by Christopher Hitchens – that every man should be ashamed to die until he has written a book, planted a tree, and had a son. There seems no reason why one shouldn't substitute the word 'son' for 'daughter' or 'book' for 'opera'. Here quotability is tied to patriarchy – and even to the invidious and absurd assumption that somehow one isn't a success if one hasn't had children.

But it's also open to another criticism – namely that we box-tick life's successes with solitary air punches. For instance, I now find that, with my wife's purchase of a magnolia tree for our garden this year, I have jumped, though never particularly intending to, through Martí's hoops. Except I didn't jump through any of them alone. This summer we lowered our tree into the lawn's corner together.

C.J.
London, September 17th 2018

SQUINT
BOOKS

OUR OTHER TITLES IN THE SQUINT SERIES

Squint Books focus on the 21st Century Digital Age, from Pop Culture to Politics, Art to Science, with an emphasis on Key Figures

BARACK OBAMA – INVISIBLE MAN

DONALD TRUMP – THE RHETORIC

DRAWBRIDGE BRITAIN – LOVE AND HOSTILITY IN UK IMMIGRATION
        FROM WINDRUSH TO THE PRESENT

JEREMY CORBYN – ACCIDENTAL HERO

MAGNETIC NORTH – JUSTIN TRUDEAU

LANA DEL REY – HER LIFE IN 94 SONGS

ROGER FEDERER – PORTRAIT OF AN ARTIST

TACTICAL READING: A SNAPPY GUIDE TO THE SNAP
        GENERAL ELECTION 2017

THE EVOLUTION OF HILLARY RODHAM CLINTON

THE FRAGILE DEMOCRACY

THE VIRTUOUS CYBORG

WWW.EYEWEARPUBLISHING.COM